Theodicy

Theodicy

Special Issue Editor

Jill Graper Hernandez

MDPI • Basel • Beijing • Wuhan • Barcelona • Belgrade

Special Issue Editor
Jill Graper Hernandez
University of Texas
USA

Editorial Office
MDPI
St. Alban-Anlage 66
Basel, Switzerland

This is a reprint of articles from the Special Issue published online in the open access journal *Religions* (ISSN 2077-1444) from 2017 to 2018 (available at: https://www.mdpi.com/journal/religions/special_issues/Theodicy).

For citation purposes, cite each article independently as indicated on the article page online and as indicated below:

LastName, A.A.; LastName, B.B.; LastName, C.C. Article Title. *Journal Name* **Year**, *Article Number*, Page Range.

ISBN 978-3-03897-228-0 (Pbk)
ISBN 978-3-03897-229-7 (PDF)

Cover image courtesy of pixabay.com user Lars Nissen.

Contents

About the Special Issue Editor

Jill Graper Hernandez is Professor of Philosophy at the University of Texas at San Antonio. She is the author of "Early Modern Women and the Problem of Evil: Atrocity & Theodicy" (Routledge 2016) and "Gabriel Marcel's Ethics of Hope: Evil, God & Virtue" (Bloomsbury 2013).

Editorial

Introduction of Special Issue "Theodicy"

Jill Graper Hernandez

Department of Philosophy and Classics, University of Texas, One UTSA Circle, San Antonio, TX 78249, USA;
jill.hernandez@utsa.edu

Received: 6 September 2018; Accepted: 7 September 2018; Published: 12 September 2018

For a topic that many have thought long-solved, theodicy in the 21st-century has thus far produced novel approaches, uncovered new dilemmas, juxtaposed itself with other philosophical and religious fields, listened to new voices, and has even been done through uncommon methodologies. Though never removed from the logical problem, theodicy at least in the near future will generate unique arguments related to the phenomenology of lived suffering, modal claims across worlds, the possibility of ameliorative analysis, narrative theodicy, and standpoint difficulties in generating theodical discourse. This special issue is dedicated to extending the platform for clear and interesting perspectives on new dimensions of theodicy, or in reclaiming perspectives on the topic that have been largely ignored in philosophy of religion.

Rather than coming to a consensus about the nature, scope, and future of theodicy, the authors in this volume create new avenues for exploring an age-old problem: is the existence of God consistent or compatible with the presence of suffering in the world?

The anthology is organized thematically. The papers in the first grouping all could be headlined under, "New Dimensions in Narrative Theodicy", because they either rely upon narratives for theodical engagement or critically engaged into whether narratives can be used for a theodical purpose. Sue Whatley provides a meta-theodical piece that marries Flannery O'Connor's complication of good and evil to the theology of Pierre Teilhard de Chardin's concept of "unification" to argue that despair need not be the ultimate phenomenological experience of suffering. Jill Hernandez draws upon the narrative work of Margaret Cavendish to argue that Cavendish—despite her unorthodox theology—provides a unique advancement about how to eradicate moral evil while preserving free will. Mark Scott prefers to take up the problem of suffering at home, and focuses on hope as a theodical tool, embedded in the work of contemporary American novelist Marilynne Robinson. Poetry, rather than novels, is the means by which A.K. Anderson introduces his concept of "enestological theodicy", the view that that the presence of God is experienced in the midst of suffering through the deeds of humanity.

The second segment of essays focuses on "New Dimensions in Worlds and Value", and shifts to multiverse theodicy and the types of worlds God could or should instantiate, if such a being existed. Michael Almeida argues against several leading multiverse theodicians on the basis that they unnecessarily restrict the creation of multiverses to those that meet some threshold of goodness. Klaas Kraay is one such interlocutor of Almeida's, and he replies that Almeida's theistic modal realism is not that different from his view, but instead pivots upon whether the lack of universes that surpass a goodness threshold is a "bug" (as Almeida suggests) or a desirable feature of a theistic ontology (as forwarded by Kraay). Marshall Naylor's paper contends that, regardless of the content of any particular world, there are no worlds that are better overall than any other world, regardless of whether God prevents evil for the betterment of any particular world. Atle Ottesen Søvik argues for a rich version of indeterminism, to justify his view that the only way to account for to explain token goods as well as goods in an eschaton is to distinguish between unique type and token values. Joshua Thurow articulates a "mystical body theodicy", in which God could allow evils in part to contribute to facilitate the shared value of human unity.

The third theme of the special issue raises "New Challenges in Theodicy", and each paper presents heretofore unexplored obstacles to theodicy, or cast the problem of evil in a unique way. Sari Kivistö and Sami Pihlström contend that theodicies fail morally because in their quest to objectively problematize the problem of evil and justify extreme harm, they fail to recognize others, and their suffering. Anthony Pinn goes even further, and argues for a conception of "theological absurdity", or an existential angst that comes from realizing that theodical projects can neither create answers to the problem of socially-induced suffering, nor make philosophical progress in doing so. Theology is not ill-equipped to tackle theodicy, Joseph Rogers suggests, but needs better tools to do so, such as the "indecent theology" of Marcella Althaus-Reid, which offers a queer lens through which to view suffering, the sufferer, and God. Eric Wiland challenges the problem of evil as a problem for theodicy—if "good" and "evil" are "attributive adjectives", then God is never defective for failing to prevent suffering since he is not a member of any kind that has standards of goodness internal to him.

Whereas the third theme focuses on challenges for the project of theodicy itself, those in the fourth evaluate the prospects for theodicy into the future, both as an academic project and phenomenological problem. Nasrin Rouzati engages with historical Islamic theology to show, first, that the problem of evil in Islam is not a problem, but divine providence, and second, that the efficacy for theodicy is that God's plan is inextricable with human spiritual experiences in the world. Jennifer Geddes takes up Levinas's claim that theodicy has ended but argues that we can never prescribe the end of theodicy for a sufferer, who always is entitled to work through the violence of her suffering however she chooses, even through the imposition of theodicy. Scott Williams extends Marilyn Adams's "horrendous evil" theodicy to a subspecies of horrendous-difference disability to demonstrates that time-bias, if rejected, can show that all persons (despite ability) can participate in horrendous evils—evils which can be defeated by God. Finally, Amber Griffioen requires theodicy, in order to remain efficacious, to shift its perspective onto those who suffer, with the result that theodicy becomes a process of therapeutic imaginings of God, which can help the sufferer and her community through struggle.

Throughout the text, the authors push their readers to consider the question of theodicy anew. The promise for academics, students, and lay people who are interested in the problem of suffering and evil is that discourse on theodicy has opened up new avenues of thought, and new paths for discovery.

Funding: This research received no external funding.

Conflicts of Interest: The author declares no conflict of interest.

Essay

The Thin Blue Line of Theodicy: Flannery O'Connor, Teilhard de Chardin, and Competitions between Good/Good and Evil/Evil

Sue Whatley

English, Stephen F. Austin University, Nacogdoches, TX 75962-3007, USA; swhatley@sfasu.edu;
Tel.: +1-936-468-2031

Received: 17 January 2018; Accepted: 23 March 2018; Published: 24 April 2018

Abstract: This essay explores the concept of theodicy in Flannery O'Connor's works of fiction. O'Connor's fiction complicates the subjects of good and evil, moving the reader through what seem to be competitions not only between good and evil, but also between actions of good and actions of evil. Characters align themselves with one force, then another, in a constantly fluctuating system, and there is no traditional pattern of Christian warfare that we would expect orthodox Catholic writing to produce. Sometimes, evil brings about the resolution of the narratives, and sometimes actions of good fail to redeem. It is only through the theology of Pierre Teilhard de Chardin that we may have a full understanding of O'Connor's Christian vision. For O'Connor, Teilhard's system of a dynamic eternity, which is in the process of unification, gives a greater understanding of our human reality, as it is a world where evil is used at the service of the Divine. It serves her fictional goal as well, as it allows her to rescue violence and evil from its power for despair.

Keywords: Flannery O'Connor; Teilhard de Chardin; good and evil; theodicy; Christian vision

---

"What has given the South her identity are those beliefs and qualities which she absorbed from Scriptures and from her own history of defeat and violation: a distrust of the abstract, a sense of human dependence on the grace of God, and a knowledge that evil is not simply a problem to be solved but a mystery to be endured". (O'Connor 2009)

In the Augustinian sense—that "evil" is the absence of good—we can accept that God is not a creator of evil. The most persistent problem of good and evil—especially that of a domestic sort—lies not in the question of whether good and evil exist, or even in the question of how to resolve the Divine Paradox, but in the actual *naming* of what is good, and what is evil. The adage "beauty is in the eye of the beholder" might ring true for "good" as well, for every generation brings forth recognition, reversal and intention in the process of identifying destructive forces and ultimate evil. Author Flannery O'Connor, an orthodox Catholic, bore witness to the phenomena, and she on more than one occasion indicated that through God's allowance of the existence of "an evil," one may become more than his/her original conception. We are "blessed in our deprivations" (*The Habit of Being*, pp. 168–69). It is with some hesitation that I conflate the terms "deprivation" and "evil," though I will maintain that, in much of O'Connor's fiction, the two are—if not indistinguishable—at least easily associated. Some of these deprivations are man-made, while others exist as random natural phenomena. Regardless of the source, a multitude of deprivations and evil actions unify O'Connor's narratives; they vie for narrative control, and they lead to the only moments in the fiction we might label as "resolution." Oddly enough, the actions which we might call "good"—or at least those which seem to be moving the characters toward it—also seem to be competing with each other in much the same manner.

That critics find O'Connor's notions of good and evil confusing is an understatement. Today, she is noted as one of the greatest spiritual writers of the Twentieth Century, and the literary quality of her work has allowed a kind of bridge between literary purists and seekers of theological fiction. Even so, many of her readers fail to discern any Christian design in her work, and some even celebrate the absence of that traditional structure. Others, however, armed with O'Connor's own theological explanations come to the fiction with a sense of expectation, and despite O'Connor's statements about using exaggeration in order to have the "blind see" and the "deaf hear," the actual identification of good and evil has proven to be a rich source of debate in the critical work that has ensued. John Hawkes, a fellow novelist and early critic of O'Connor's work, claimed that "O'Connor uses the voice of the devil to destroy man's belief that he [himself] is rational" (Gentry 1986, p. 143). Others concur that the narrator is a sadistic or devilish figure (Clair Katz Kahane and Josephine Hendin, among others) and O'Connor herself did not disagree (Gentry 1986, p. 143). How, then, does a Christian novelist avoid inferior, didactic writing while attempting to make clear a spiritual path? O'Connor's rich fictional world allows entrance to an extension of reality—what she called a "reality of distance"—and it underscores the difficulty of assigning simple labels to complex actions of good and evil.

In all but the rarest works of Divine Comedy, the battle between good and evil is central to the impetus of each character's actions, and that same current determines the eventual unity of the story. In some sense, O'Connor's fiction is no different. Readers are likely aware of the actions and forces which seem to push toward outcomes that we might consider good or evil. The challenge lies in identifying where those forces of good and evil manifest themselves. If evil brings forth suffering, and deprivation is one cause that leads to suffering, then the eradication of the cause of that deprivation must be the goal of Christian and humanist. It is difficult to conceive of a deprivation as anything other than "not good," but deprivations fall into a hierarchy. Deprived of food, man may turn to theft in order to survive or bring about the survival of his/her children. This state of existence draws sympathy from most humans, as they recognize human suffering. A mother might even be compelled to personal depravity in order to provide shelter for her children. Modern story tellers explore the dilemma ad nauseum, especially in film and television; stories that push the boundaries of good and evil flood every venue—the drug addict mother who sells drugs, not to score another fix but to hire the best (worst?) attorney whose connections with the judge may keep her from losing her children. The crime syndicate leader's tortured childhood at the hands of his father has led him to become the toughest person in his borough. The hierarchy grows, and where the line is to be drawn between frailty and maliciousness is indeed a problem of philosophical proportions. In our attempt to discern an individual's motivation, we might possibly find ourselves understanding and "forgiving" an action of depraved indifference, though many might certainly categorize it as evil. Inversely, we might forego our ability to sympathize with the actions of a character whose mistaken judgment leads to the deaths of hundreds of people, and to his own eternal misery and guilt.

The concept of good and evil, then, is always subject to parameters, to those examples that are "surely good" and "surely evil." From there, we move to judge or at least relegate actions and people to the category of good and bad, edifying or evil. When characters are created then, on that very fine line, and the readers' or critics' judgments do indeed co-create the script, they are forced to decide whose actions then are those to follow, and whose actions clearly depart from the new sensibility the reader must have after engaging the text.

My early arguments against popular feminist dismissal of O'Connor's contributions sought to redeem her maternal characters from the general perception that they are, at best, socially broken and impotent, or, at worst, catalysts of agony and torture for their children. Instead of seeing them as agents of human misery, *evil* it might be labeled, I have urged that we see them as "equally flawed"—in a violent world, where humanism and Divine Grace are hidden from view. In addition, while I still maintain my claim that O'Connor's matriarchal characters are no more destructive/evil than their children or peers in her fiction, it may be time to consider just how difficult the dichotomy, when any one character is charged with "good behavior" and another with "bad behavior." In engaging fiction, as with engaging life, when we seek to separate God from man, good from evil, the task becomes more complex with every consideration. As our compassion grows, it is easy enough to conclude that all characters, all people, are flawed; the result of this kind of reasoning is human understanding. We come to understand human frailty and identify our own negative actions as such. The danger, however, is that we may become complacent in our estimation of our own flaws, satisfied to some extent that we are no longer facing a "greater judgment" than others, that we are just as likely to be redeemed as they. Our own desire to rid ourselves of actions that lead to others' misery is often mitigated by our growing sense of our participation in human frailty.

It would be easy to fall into this trap when reading O'Connor's work, given the sheer amount of violence depicted. Make no mistake, O'Connor's fiction is not a defense of human frailty, nor does she invite the kind of sentiment that would allow for it. She is not a "humanist" in the sense of defending man's frailty and warns against the mindset of the "average Catholic reader":

> By separating nature and grace as much as possible, he [the average Catholic] has reduced his conception of the supernatural . . . He forgets that sentimentality is excess, a distortion of sentiment usually in the direction of an overemphasis on innocence, and that innocence, whenever it is overemphasized in the ordinary human condition tends by some natural law to become its opposite. (*Mystery and Manners*, hereafter *MM*: O'Connor 1962, pp. 147–48)

With O'Connor, we are not merely viewing a simplistic system of identifying good and evil, but, instead, witnessing competitions between "good" actions. Likewise, we are viewing competing actions of evil. O'Connor's vision seems to insist that whether through our own evil, fallibility, or good, we are somehow brought face to face with God, and thereby prove his existence on a personal level. God, then, uses the existence of evil, just as he uses the existence of good, in order to bring about spiritual awakening. If the struggle between good and evil characterizes the literature of several thousands of years, then O'Connor pierces the simplicity of those categories by depicting the struggle between layers of "good" and the additional struggle between layers of "evils." O'Connor's stories clearly reveal an evolutionary process in the competitions between the forces of good, evil, and good/evil.

In her most anthologized story, "A Good Man is Hard to Find," O'Connor's serial killer, referred to as "the Misfit," leads the Grandmother to a place of "goodness," a place where she meets God for the first time. Oddly, he does so by the use of violence, and the horrendous atrocity of killing her family, and, while violence is usually associated with evil and it would be difficult to label the mass murder of a family (including young children and a baby) as anything else, in this story, as with many of her works, violence becomes "strangely capable of returning [her] characters to reality and preparing them to accept their moment of grace" ("On Her Own Work," *MM*, p. 112). The grandmother's true self is questionable as well, though she carries herself in a manner that emanates kindness and respect. She lies when it is convenient, and she manipulates her son. These actions, coupled with her inability to think before she speaks, lead to her family's deaths and her own. In a hierarchy of sin/evil, readers are hard pressed to see a discernible difference between the grandmother and the Misfit. The simultaneous actions of evil on the part of the Grandmother and the Misfit lead them both to a place of discovery, what Teilhard de Chardin calls the "omega point"—where a person meets God and must decide whether to accept Grace or not. The grandmother's declared recognition of the Misfit as a serial killer, leads to her family's ultimate demise. When she attempts to rectify her mistake and save her own life by calling him "good," the Misfit thanks the grandmother. Later, when she twice more repeats the claim, he first claims that he is not "good," then later reverses again: "'I never was a bad boy that I remember of...but somewhere's along the line, I done something wrong'" (*Flannery O'Connor: The Complete Stories*, hereafter *CS*: O'Connor 1987, p. 130). At a certain point, the Grandmother recognizes the benefit of pleading the cause of Christian redemption and asks the Misfit to pray; the Misfit places his cards on the table: if he had been "there"—with Jesus as he performed the miracle of raising someone from death—he "'would of known and I wouldn't be like I am now'" (*CS*, p. 132). The Misfit believes the argument is over, but in the one moment the Grandmother opens herself to true human compassion, calling him "'one of my babies,'" (*CS*, p. 132) his notions of pleasure (to go about doing meanness) are shattered. His final line assures the reader that neither goodness nor evil bring any kind of victory or pleasure. He has been brought to a moment of confrontation, and he is "there"—face to face with God, in the form of a stubborn, selfish old woman, whose contribution of "good" is in the fraction of a second before death: "'Shut up, Bobby Lee...It's no real pleasure in life'" (*CS*, p. 133).

It appears the questionable nature of labeling "good" and "evil" was a concern for O'Connor throughout most of her writing life. In one of her early stories, "The Turkey," a young boy "tries on" his habit of evil, just as he tries on his habits of "good." Ruller, lost in his rich fantasy world, is pulled into a spiritual reality when he discovers an injured turkey, one which he might be able to capture and take home. He envisions his parents delighted as he enters the front door, "screaming, 'Look at Ruller with that wild turkey! Ruller! Where did you get that wild turkey?'" (*CS*, p. 43). Ruller's belief that his parents "might like to have him catch them one" reveals his position in the family dynamics (*CS*, p. 43): his older brother Hane has apparently been acting out, defying not only family expectations but societal ones as well. The expectation that Hane may end up in the "penitentiary" has caused so much disharmony, that Ruller's initial desire is to please his parents.

Ruller's altruism is short-lived, however, and soon we see that the goal of pleasing others has a self-interested flip-side. He wants to please his parents because he is in competition with his brother. As the chase of the turkey continues, Ruller surmises that his parents will begin to discuss him, instead of Hane, in their late night conversations. Soon Ruller has torn his clothes and begins to worry about the trouble he might get in, and the turkey begins to become a necessity, rather than a boon. However, the turkey seems to evade him, and, when it appears he will not be caught, Ruller thinks that "somebody had "played a dirty trick on him" (*CS*, p. 45). The disappointment and apprehension he experiences morphs his intention for "good" into defiance and blasphemy. Ruller begins vocalizing slang words, progressing to curses which incorporate the name of God, and he is delighted with himself, laughing and giggling with every subsequent vulgarity. He mentally plans his own spiritual demise, inventing elaborate scenarios about lies and thefts he could engage. Ruller is not a child who mimics others, lacking a sense of good and evil. He knows he shouldn't be angry with God for "sticking things in your face and making you chase them all afternoon for nothing... But that was the way he felt" (*CS*, p. 48).

But the story does not end with Ruller's slipping toward evil. The turkey dies of exhaustion, a sign that Ruller sees it as a sign that "God had stopped him before it was too late" (*CS*, p. 49). In addition, Ruller is appreciative; he contemplates what God wants him to do, the "good" actions that can transform society—bequeathing money to the town poor, and "found[ing] a place for boys to stay who were going bad" (*CS*, p. 51) or "a home for tenants children" (*CS*, p. 51). Ruller's estimation of himself grows exponentially, as he prides himself in his resistance to the temptation of evil. He feels so "chosen" by the Divine that he asks God send him a "beggar" so that he may donate the only money he has on him—a dime. Both the reader who is looking for a story depicting the conquest of good over evil and Ruller himself are thwarted, as the story has yet another reversal. The country boys who seem to be the inspiration of Ruller's magnimanity follow and soon overtake Ruller and the turkey he carries, stealing it before Ruller has an opportunity to even realize what is happening. There the story ends. The reader is left to assume that Ruller's pride will be checked, that his eventual understanding of God will grow deeper than the simple notions he has developed while chasing and capturing the turkey. Neither Ruller's good behaviors nor his evil ones bring the ultimate spiritual victory—but instead the spiritual world is illuminated by its competitions between "good" actions and intentions, and the similar competitions between evil actions.

All of these competitions provide Ruller's experience of revelation and growth. He has no model of good to follow, and it is only in the experience of both that he finds the path of spiritual discovery. In addition, we as readers have just as much difficulty locating the forces of good and evil. Is it God who provides the turkey and evil which snatches it? Or evil which provides and God who takes away? O'Connor gives closure to the story and the murky business of defining "evil" and "good" with her final line of the story: Ruller is "certain that Something Awful was tearing behind him with its arms rigid and its fingers ready to clutch" (*CS*, p. 53). If this spirit is, indeed, the spirit of God, working to move Ruller on a spiritual path, why then does the narrator label it "Something Awful"? The play on terms "awful" and "awe-ful" further underscores the difficulty of identifying the forces of good and evil. Our question about the force that determines Ruller's outcome is yet to be answered. Only Ruller's future, his actions and decisions that spring from this encounter with the turkey, will serve to prove whether the force was a good or evil one.

In some of O'Connor's stories, it is difficult to see any victory other than one evil over another. The stories "A View of the Woods" and "The Comforts of Home" both offer protagonists who compel little sympathy, and there seems to be no moment of grace or redemption. Critic A. R Coulthard considers "A View of the Woods" one of O'Connor's least effective stories, and notes that O'Connor herself was frustrated in her work on the piece. Coulthard calls the story O'Connor's "worst piece of fiction." She goes on to address the failure of the author to offer characterization that elicits sympathy or respect (Coulthard 1987). Mr. Fortune and his son-in-law Mr. Pitts vie for control of his granddaughter, Mary. When she chooses neither her grandfather nor her father for guidance or resolution, even the sympathy that would normally be afforded a child disappears. Her murder of her grandfather further cements the verdict: none of the characters clearly approach Grace within the confines of the story. In "The Comforts of Home," Thomas's mother seems sympathetic, compassionate, but falls prey to Star Drake's (Sarah Ham) manipulations. What begins as an effort on his mother's part to help the "unfortunate" ends in Thomas's mother's accidental death, and his arrest, based on Star's arrangement of fake evidence and lies. Thomas's inability to allow his mother's more compassionate nature to rule him sets him up for the accidental violence which takes his mother's life. While she is alive, Thomas is pulled between his mother's kind nature and the memory of his powerful father, who has died years before. When his mother dies, he is left with only his father's physical power, explosiveness and penchant for violent action.

In other stories, the competitions between actions of good and actions of evil seem more evident. "The Displaced Person" offers a litany of good and evil traits within all characters, but none seem to gain ultimate control over the characters' actions. Mr. Shortley's attempt to take advantage of any female in charge, smoke in the dairy, and tout his white privilege over the black workers on the farm undermine any sense of goodness he might claim as a defense for the injustice he receives in being replaced by new workers on the farm. Even Mrs. Shortley's "extreme" and visionary faith, a kind of faith that O'Connor seems to approve of, is centered in the notions of social hierarchy and racism. Mrs. McIntyre's story begins with her being urged towards compassion for the displaced family, and her action of hiring Mr. Guizac and providing for his family seems a movement in the direction of "good." However, Mrs. McIntyre's intentions for bringing in the displaced family are no purer than Mr. Shortley's desire for undeserved advancement. She intends to modernize and use to her advantage the desperation of a family who is at the mercy of strangers. During subsequent visits with the priest, she seems to move further away from theological enlightenment or human compassion, and she rages against the priest's guidance: "'As far as I'm concerned, Christ was just another DP [displaced person]'" (*CS*, p. 229). She pits Mr. Guizac, Mr. Shortley, and the two black farm hands, Astor and Sulk, against each other, offering up her financial worries and the threat of dismissal to push competition and more productivity. And when Mr. Guizac arranges the marriage of his "white" cousin to Sulk, her adherence to the racial status quo of the South leads her to not only to threaten to put the Guizacs off the farm, but also to collude with Mr. Shortley and Astor in inaction when the tractor threatens to run over Mr. Guizac. The actions of good and evil are constantly mutating in O'Connor's stories, and none seems to produce clear, discernible power over characters who would seem to be moving on the trajectory toward Grace.

It is with O'Connor's connections to Teilhard de Chardin that we may see her Christian narrative intent, and understand how competitions between good actions and competitions between evil ones all lead to Divine order and unity. O'Connor takes her cue from Teilhard and his three basic laws governing the structure of reality. Teilhard's dilemma as a scientist is that he wanted to investigate those matters which the Church saw as threatening—evolutionary theory included—and his theories would of course have to account for ways to rename or reclaim science as divinely inspired—or at least contained. Teilhard's three basic laws—the law of conservation of energy, the law of entropy, and the law of complexity seek to explain the dynamic system in which the natural world and the spiritual world move simultaneously toward clear unification. The law of conservation of energy and the law of entropy suppose the finite system of creation and the way in which systems of nature maintain balance and flow. The law of complexity stems from the first two laws but pushes understanding of the natural world to account for man's place in the system. Teilhard claims that all things bear some degree of consciousness, but that man by design holds "the highest degree of consciousness." Within these concepts, all matter has the potential and an obligation to become more complex; through this "complexification," existence is given the power to change, and the unified world becomes greater than the sum of its parts (McCarty 1976, pp. 40–42).

In their book, *Teilhard's Seven Stages of Suffering: A Spiritual Path for Transformation* Louis Savery and Patricia Berne examine Teilhard's notions about how God transforms evil. Teilhard offered guiding principles: God is capable of making good come out of evil; everything is capable of being transformed into good; the transformation may not be completed instantly; spiritual practice may be capable of redirecting unwanted feeling and restoring energy; those practices would include a dialogue with unwelcome feelings, forgiveness, spiritual will making, and prayers of thankfulness during times of suffering as well as prayers to the Holy Spirit for patience (Savery and Berne 2015, "Stage 4: Patience").

Teilhard's understanding of human frailty, deprivation, and evil is that all these will be made to serve Divine Good. We would rightly call this evolutionary theodicy, as time and revelation together will ultimately reveal the Divine use of those matters. Though she does not use the terms evolutionary theodicy or Divine convergence, O'Connor understood the radical nature of the concept and its ability to encompass evil and direct it toward good. O'Connor's notions of the dramatic movement from evil toward good can be seen in her explanation of her character the Misfit from "A Good Man is Hard to Find": "I don't want to equate the Misfit with the devil. I prefer to think that, however unlikely this may seem, the old lady's gesture, like a mustard seed, will grow to be a great crow-filled tree in the Misfit's heart, and will be enough of a pain to him there to turn him into the prophet he was meant to become" (*MM*, pp. 112–13). She also understood the concepts surrounding convergence as an answer to the failures of the Church to satisfactorily explain and alleviate human suffering. She once replied to her friend Betty Hester that the church could not be explained simply by Freudian theories or Carl Jung's meta-theory of archetype: "The things that you think she [the true church, not "vapid" Catholicism] will be added to will be added to her [emphasis mine]" (*The Habit of Being*, hereafter, *HB*: O'Connor 1979, p. 99).

In a letter to friend Rosalyn Barnes, O'Connor indicated that Teilhard's laws governed not only the title but the substance of her story and beyond: "I have also written and sold to *New World Writing* a story called "Everything That Rises Must Converge", which is a physical proposition that I found in Pere Teilhard, and am applying to a certain situation in the Southern states and indeed in all the world" (*HB*, p. 438). It is also within this system that we find O'Connor's inability (perhaps refusal) to make absolute the elements of evil and the elements of good. In her story, "Everything that Rises Must Converge" the refusal to delineate between good and evil is even more apparent. If we follow a traditional engagement of the story, sorting out which character is protagonist and which is antagonist, we may find ourselves, as many of my students, offering Julian up as a kind of protagonist: he is angry at his mother, and he carries a righteous indignation over her belief that white people are "superior." He recognizes the flawed social order, and appears to push toward equity for black citizens, who clearly can afford the same clothing and practices as their white counterparts.

However, this reading would be erroneous, and it would certainly not bring us any closer to an understanding of God, or an awareness of his existence in the world as the purveyor of good, because to see the story that way is to invite self-satisfaction. Julian is the target of the epiphany, and before he gets there, O'Connor takes us through his failures: he maintains a lack of affection and respect for a woman who has sacrificed and supported him, even after the time when most parents would expect self-sufficiency. Julian, ironically, practices a kind of hierarchy of person, much deeper and much more subtle than his mother. He only wants to sit with "educated" blacks, and not in an effort to share intellectual experience. He simply wants to irk his mother. When his plan to humiliate her over the black doppelgänger fails, he cannot be satisfied with his mother's self-correction. Instead, he sets out to "show her." He belittles her, he talks to her as an infant, and reveals his willingness to conscript people of another race and objectify them in order to teach his mother a lesson: he contemplates his mother "desperately ill and his being able to secure only a negro doctor" (*CS*, p. 414). He ultimately reveals his own sordid bias and racial distortion when he chooses to sit with "some of the better types" of black people on the bus (*CS*, p. 414) and mentally laments his own loss of social privilege: "He thought bitterly of the house that had been lost for him" (*CS*, p. 419)—a house which clearly had been bought by the blood of slaves. He even contemplates marrying a black woman so he can rub his mother's face in the action. Though the story may have begun in the good of Julian's social enlightenment, it surely shifts as it unfolds, and it ends with Julian's corrupt nature.

If we see his initial action—the attempt to change his mother's racial bias—as "good," we must soon recognize his "good" actions are, nevertheless, in competition with his mother's good efforts—her support of him as a struggling young writer, her ability to laugh at herself over the irony of wearing the same hat as a black woman, and her genuine affection for certain black people in her life—her childhood nurse, Caroline, and the boy on the bus, Carver. Even so, it is not until his mother succumbs to her health failures, with a stroke, that Julian has any clue about his own competing evil. "The tide of darkness seemed to sweep him to back to her [his mother], postponing from moment to moment his entry into the world of guilt and sorrow" (*CS*, p. 420). It is neither his "goodness" nor his mother's, her "evil" nor his own which account for the eventual shift, but the complex interplay of competing evil and competing good that allow for God to bring Julian to a place of human rectification. In O'Connor's terms, the system that allows the existence of the negotiation of these forces is a Divine one.

No story holds greater ability to reveal the good/good evil/evil competition than the story "Revelation." A common reading of the story might go something like this: Ruby Turpin, a biased bigot, is accosted in a doctor's office one day, while stewing in her self-satisfaction. An emotionally-unstable, pock-marked, overweight young woman, who acts as an avenging angel, throws a book (*Human Development*) at Ruby, knocking her out of her smug complacency. As a result of her experience, Ruby is propelled toward an eventual revelation of her own fallen nature and the prevenient Grace which equalizes all human life.

O'Connor herself validated her friend Maryat Lee's claim that she made "Mary Grace" so ugly because she "loved her so much" (*HB*, p. 578). If we begin our understanding of the story with O'Connor's validation of Mary Grace, and read it as a competition between good and evil, then we must identify evil in the character of Ruby Turpin who is centered in the smugness and self-satisfaction. However, O'Connor has taken great pains to show us not only the battle and the events which lead up to it, but also the eventual vision of the source of that evil. Ruby enters the waiting room of the doctor's office, quickly pointing out a seat for her husband, Claud, whose leg has been injured by an accident involving one of their livestock. She is considerate enough to seat him, even though he makes a begrudging effort to give Ruby his seat. Claud at least attempts to show respect; others in the waiting room do not. There are at least six other people, including a young child, who do not offer or even acknowledge Ruby's need for a seat. If Ruby is, indeed, the worst example of humanity, how are we to categorize the others held up for comparison?

No one in the waiting room seems to offer anything other than judgment, and Mary Grace is not set apart from the others. She, too, has her own agenda: "The girl raised her head and directed her scowl at Mrs. Turpin, as if she did not like her looks. She appeared annoyed that anyone should speak while she tried to read" (*CS*, p. 490). Ruby's compassion for Mary Grace's physical attributes actually does seem to stem from her awareness of how harsh society can be to those who do not meet certain standards. Her response to Mary Grace is not one of revulsion, but instead, one which recognizes Mary Grace's plight. In fact, it is Ruby's preparation for the ultimate encounter that forces us to question Ruby's function in the good/evil world. Ruby may contemplate "who she would have chosen to be if she couldn't have been herself," but she moves away from that self-centeredness, and on to "naming the classes of people" (*CS*, p. 491). These are not classes that Ruby has created, but merely classes she recognizes, and the more deeply she considers these groups, the "complexity of it" begins to "bear in on her" (*CS*, p. 491). Ruby does not place herself at the top of the hierarchy; she recognizes the system that relegates humans to various positions of power, and she also recognizes how flawed the system is that cannot account for categories of nuance—well-mannered people of all races, people of stature without money, and so on.

While Ruby does indeed seem to be capable of thinking of the falseness of societal hierarchies, she is also a participant in the system, one which affords her power, however temporary, and one that demands her ability to keep that power if she is flexible within that system. She recognizes the changing social order and that she must accommodate the black people who work for her and Claud. While the "white-trash" woman debases Ruby for her negotiation of the cultural system (raising hogs instead of cotton, greeting the hired help) Ruby remains openly polite (*CS*, p. 494). However, her divine catalyst—Mary Grace—stews in her private fury at a woman whose flaws, or evil, we might say—barely seem intentional.

If Mary Grace is an avenging angel, one would expect her to maintain some redeemable qualities—something that might model "good" as well as point out "evil." However, all of Mary Grace's actions are more judgmental, more violent than Ruby's. Once Ruby and Mary Grace's mother agree that accepting changes in societal structures is necessary, Ruby begins to notice that Mary Grace's "peculiar eyes were still on her" (*CS*, p. 494). The hierarchy continues to unfold; admirably, Mary Grace's mother and Ruby both deflect the "white-trash" woman's declaration: "They ought to send all them niggers back to Africa...That's where they come from in the first place" (p. 495). While Ruby and Mary Grace's mother reveal their own fallen humanity in their responses, they do at least practice civility and flexibility; however, Mary Grace is as entrenched in her response to their bigotry, as the "white trash" woman is in her own. She and Mary Grace demonstrate no potential for change, and it is clear that Mary Grace has chosen Ruby's flaws as the target for her own personal dissatisfaction; thus, Mary Grace's own sense of humanity deteriorates before our eyes:

> As she said it, the raw-complexioned girl snapped her teeth together. Her lower lip turned downwards and inside out, revealing the pale pink inside of her mouth. After a second it rolled back up. It was the ugliest face Mrs. Turpin had ever seen anyone make and was looking at her as if she had known and disliked her all her life—all of Mrs. Turpin's life, it seemed too, not just all the girl's life. (*CS*, p. 495)

Mary Grace is rude to not only Ruby, but to her mother as well. As her mother's anger grows and she enlists the help of others in the waiting room to shame the girl, Mary Grace's indignation grows. In the midst of Ruby's praise and claims of thankfulness about her own life, Mary Grace's rage reaches her breaking point. She becomes inhuman, an animal—throwing her book into Ruby's face, flying across the table to attack her, sinking her "claws" into her flesh, and eventually writhing on the floor as she is captured by the doctor and others in the waiting room. Mary Grace's deterioration into animalism would seem the greater of evils when compared to Ruby's sin of smug self-satisfaction. However, when Ruby has a momentary vision, as if she were "looking through the wrong end of a telescope" (*CS*, p. 499), she realizes that Mary Grace is indeed a force to be recognized: "There was no doubt in her mind that the girl did know her, knew her in some intense and personal way, beyond time and place and condition" (*CS*, p. 500). When Ruby asks her what she has to say, Mary Grace tells her to "Go back to hell where you came from, you old warthog" (*CS*, p. 500). Ruby's subconscious seems to recognize the truth of Mary Grace's words, and the polite and pleasant "shell" that distinguishes Ruby from the fallen characters around her deteriorates. She rebukes the assistance of the doctor in the waiting room, "growl[ing]" under her breath at his attempt at levity and to care for her medically

(*CS*, p. 501). She and Claud return home to their farm, and though she attempt to verbally deny Mary Grace's label, her "denial has no force" (*CS*, p. 502) and her "ferocious concentration" does not change (*CS*, p. 503). The next day, her denial focuses on garnering sympathy from the black women who work on the farm. As she tells them of her experience, they offer sympathy and defense of her, but Ruby sees their words as hollow and informed by the system of manners and economic hierarchy, much as her own behavior was prior to her encounter with Mary Grace. As she peels back the layers of good behavior, her rage grows: "She knew how much Negro flattery was worth" (*CS*, p. 505). We find her, again, growling to herself as she makes her way toward the hog pen which will become, as the story suggests, the place of her ultimate revelation.

In the final moments of the story, O'Connor allows Ruby Turpin to reach a place of being which must register as "ultimate good." She moves outside her own narrow experience, outside the limitations of her cultural and society and becomes capable of more than just her own spiritual awakening. Her vision in the hog parlor moves her to the realm that O'Connor would call the "reality of distance." Ruby feels the vision coming on, and indeed, it has been coming on since her entrance into the doctor's office. The feeling is less of anticipation and more of inescapable destiny, and she absorbs its slow unfolding as "abysmal life-giving knowledge" (*CS*, p. 508). She never sees herself deprived of the characteristics which she holds to be virtuous—"having a little of everything and the God-given wit to use it right"—but the beauty of her vision is that she sees "good" as well as evil as having been "burned away" (*CS*, p. 508).

Jack Dillard Ashley considers this and other "theophanies" in O'Connor's work, and seeks to underscore the value of the Old Testament concept of appearance, manifestation, and revelation. Ashley claims that the term goes beyond the idea of "epiphany", which is associated with New Testament notions of spiritual awakening, and claims that the concept of theophany is a more powerful way of understanding the moments in O'Connor's fiction, as it is associated with "the macrocosm" in its focus on the concrete manifestations of God in the tangible world, and it arouses the emotions of "terror, awe, reverence and sorrow" instead of those associated with epiphany: "light, illumination, recognition, and elevation of reason" ("The Very Heart of Mystery: Theophany in O'Connor's Stories", p. 103). About "Revelation", Ashley has this to say: "Apparently, suffering by theophany was worth it for Ruby Turpin, since ordinary phenomena of macrocosm are transformed into the sonorous ecstasy of luminous Theocosm" (Ashley 2006, p. 109). He quotes Revelation's last paragraph as proof:

> At length she got down and turned off the faucet and made her slow way on the darkening path to the house. In the woods around her the invisible cricket choruses had struck up but what she heard were the voices of the souls climbing upward into the starry field and shouting hallelujah. (*CS*, p. 509)

This understanding of theophany serves to attest to the competitions among all forms of good and evil, where the battles are interesting, but the ultimate victory has already been secured. O'Connor makes her argument about theodicy in both of her novels and almost every story. She frames the battles of good and evil, but masks them as we try assigning them to simplistic categories. Good and evil are palpable, but they often appear in costumes that can be changed as the stage requires. Locating examples of clear evil and clear good is challenging, and for critics of her work even exasperating. O'Connor does not offer these challenges arbitrarily, in order to simply make her work obtuse. In her notes on craft as a guide to readers and writers, she explains: "From my own experience in trying to make stories 'work,' I have discovered that what is needed is an action that is totally unexpected, yet totally believable, and I have found that, for me, this is always an action which indicates that grace has been offered. And it is frequently an action in which the devil has been the unwilling instrument of grace" (*MM*, p. 118). She depicts the world she sees around her, one in which competitions between acts of good, competitions between acts of evil, and competitions between evil and good all end in the same place: in ultimate and Divine convergence. If we cannot name them and differentiate between them, it is because all these matters are in a state of flux; an awareness of that theological state of being should bring comfort as we move toward ultimate unity.

Acknowledgments: The author of this article wishes to acknowledge the support of editor, Jill Graper-Hernandez for her patience and incredible inspiration.

Conflicts of Interest: The author declares no conflict of interest.

References

Ashley, Jack Dillard. 2006. The Very Heart of Mystery: Theophany in O'Connor's Stories. In *Flannery O'Connor's Radical Reality*. Edited by Jan Nordby and Karl-Heinz Westarp. Columbia: University of South Carolina Press.

Coulthard, A. Ronald. 1987. 'A View of the Woods': A View of the Worst. *Notes on Contemporary Fiction* 17: 7–9.

Gentry, Marshall Bruce. 1986. The Demonic O'Connor: The Violent Bear it Away and the Lame Shall Enter First. In *Flannery O'Connor's Religion of the Grotesque*. Jackson: University Press of Mississippi.

McCarty, Doran. 1976. *Teilhard de Chardin*. Waco: World Books Publisher.

O'Connor, Flannery. 1962. *Flannery O'Connor; Mystery and Manners*. Occassional Prose Selected and Edited by Sally and Robert Fitzgerald; New York: Farrar, Straus, Giroux. [Referred to as *MM* in text].

O'Connor, Flannery. 1979. *The Habit of Being: Letters of Flannery O'Connor*. Edited by Sally Fitzgerald. New York: Farrar, Straus, Giroux, [Referred to as *HB* in text].

O'Connor, Flannery. 1987. *Flannery O'Connor: The Complete Stories*. New York: Farrar, Straus and Giroux. [Referred to as *CS* in text].

O'Connor, Flannery. 2009. Flannery O'Connor on the Catholic Novelist in the Protestant South. *The Chesterton Review* 15: 730–40. [CrossRef]

Savery, Louis, and Patricia Berne. 2015. *Teilhard Chardin's Seven Stages of Suffering: A Spiritual Path for Transformation*. Mahwah: Paulist Press.

Article

Margaret Cavendish, Feminist Ethics, and the Problem of Evil

Jill Graper Hernandez

Department of Philosophy, University of Texas at San Antonio, 10 Cocke Dr, San Antonio, TX 78249, USA;
jill.hernandez@utsa.edu

Received: 9 January 2018; Accepted: 10 April 2018; Published: 16 April 2018

Abstract: This paper argues that, although Margaret Cavendish's main philosophical contributions are not in philosophy of religion, she makes a case for a defense of God, in spite of the worst sorts of harms being present in the world. Her arguments about those harms actually presage those of contemporary feminist ethicists, which positions Cavendish's scholarship in a unique position: it makes a positive theodical contribution, by relying on evils that contemporary atheists think are the best evidence against the existence of God. To demonstrate that Cavendish's work should be considered as early modern feminist theodicy, this paper will briefly introduce the contemporary feminist worry about theodicy as a project, show that Cavendish shares the contemporary feminist view about situated evil, and argue that her theodicy aims for agreement about how to eradicate great moral evils while preserving free will—and so, carves out a space for future female philosophers of religion who aim to be agents of healing in the face of such evil.

Keywords: Margaret Cavendish; theodicy; problem of evil; free will; feminist ethics; atrocity paradigm; redemptive goods; divine justice

---

Contemporary feminist ethicists have argued that theodicy in analytic philosophy of religion is disconnected from the actual experiences of those who suffer, because theodicy primarily focuses on the logical necessity of evil. If theodicy cannot address the phenomenological impact of suffering, and distances the divine from culpability for the worst sorts of harm, theodicy also makes it difficult to account for human responsibility in bringing about preventable, culpable, atrocious harms.[1] Fueling the feminist worry is that since the time of Leibniz (the author of the early modern period's *Theodicy*), only men have been taken seriously as contributors to the philosophical project of theodicy[2], even though a number of female contemporaries of Leibniz made noteworthy strides in philosophy of religion, often writing in the guise of political treatises, or novels that emphasized civil rights.

There are two ways to rectify the problem: what counts as theodicy could be expanded to include unique arguments to demonstrate that the existence of a perfect God is compatible with evil; or, philosophy can expand the canon to include a diverse group of thinkers, who contributed to the theodical project despite not originally falling under the lofty appellation of "philosophers". This paper does both. It contends that the philosophical canon on theodicy should be widened to include Margaret Cavendish (1623–1673) as a philosopher of religion in the early modern period, although Cavendish does not write traditional philosophical treatises, does not have an orthodox conception of God, and does not set out to do theodicy. It also argues that our conception of theodicy should expand to incorporate Cavendish's arguments—she provides a traditional, free-will defense argument, but

---

1   The best examples are (Card 2002, 2010).
2   In philosophy, in the last twenty years, contemporary theists are reshaping the canon, including (Stump 2010; Adams 2006, 1999).

also develops a *participative redemptive theodicy,* in which creative human agency can combat evil and transform society. Although it is true that, compared to contemporary theists, Cavendish provides a thin evaluation of divine culpability for evil, she also chooses to focus on positive human creation in the face of evil.

Since Cavendish's aim is not even secondarily the philosophy of religion, we might think that she does not set out to pursue a project in theodicy; nevertheless, she does defend God against blame for pernicious evil, even as she attempts to minimize political injustice, against women in particular. Her work presages, then, the contemporary feminist emphasis on situated suffering, but also provides distinctive contributions to philosophy of religion. To make the case for Cavendish's early modern feminist theodicy, this paper will briefly introduce the contemporary feminist worry about theodicy as a project, will show that Cavendish shares the contemporary feminist view about situated evil, and will argue that her theodicy aims for agreement about how to eradicate great moral evils while preserving free will—and so, carves out a space for future female philosophers of religion who aim to be agents of healing in the face of such evil. Cavendish provides a view that is both consistent with those of her male counterparts (since God does not interfere with the moral order as long as we have freedom) and trailblazing in the philosophy of religion. She uniquely advances theodicy in the early modern period by relying upon concrete moral evils as her point of departure towards an evaluation of redemptive responses to the problem of evil.[3]

1. Cavendish, Morality, and Concrete Harms

Recently, scholars have begun to make progress on including female scholars in the early modern period of philosophy as philosophers of religion.[4] None, however, have yet focused exclusively on the scholarship of Cavendish as a philosopher of religion, working on the project of theodicy. One reason for this is Cavendish's own non-orthodox views of theology, and another must be that Cavendish contended that, whereas there is a supernatural being (Cavendish 1666, p. 17), the questions about the nature of God's existence were outside the scope of natural philosophy (Cavendish 1664a, pp. 3, 17).[5] Jacquelyn Broad explains that, for Cavendish, "There is simply no need to posit the existence of immaterial substances, or the interference of God's spiritual intermediaries, in order to account for the life, motion, and organization of natural things." (Broad 2007, p. 499)

Theodicy faces two main critiques from contemporary feminist ethicists: first, theodicy utilizes a sense of "evil" that is fully divorced from *atrocious harms* (i.e., the sorts of harms that eliminate human dignity and individual identity); and second, the problem of evil does not even require the concept of "evil", since the very idea of God creating an imperfect world suffices to "cast major aspersions on the character of the supreme being" (Card 2002, pp. 12–13). The first worry faults theodicy for not adequately taking up the suffering that results from systems of oppression. Theodicies treat atrocious evils as a mere theoretical possibility (since it is necessary that humans have the free will to choose to commit evil, but it is contingent that those acts be performed). But treating evil as an abstract, logical category removes agency (whether human or divine) from the most egregious sorts of harm. Agency is required not only to hold someone responsible (who is to blame, after all, if the possibility of evil must be necessary?), but also to fully understand the impact of suffering on the world. Bat-Ami Bar On writes: "One stops witnessing when one abstracts so much and gets away from the phenomenological experience of the suffering of real people. Abstractness undermines the work on . . . [which] a spectator depends in order to connect to embodied people in pain." (Bar On 2007, p. 196)

---

[3] There are many more women in the long early modern period who contributed to the philosophical projects about evil or divine perfection who, for space issues, cannot be discussed here.

[4] Hernandez (2016) focuses on Cavendish, as well as Catharine Macaulay, Mary Hays, Mary Astell, and Mary Wollstonecraft, but her treatment of Cavendish is underserved to make room for her discussion of transmuted goods.

[5] Cavendish's work cited in this paper will include: [BW] (Cavendish [1666] 2003a); [ODS] (Cavendish [1666] 2003b); [OEP] (Cavendish 1666); [PB] (Cavendish 2000); [PF] (Cavendish 1653); [PL] (Cavendish 1664a); [SL] (Cavendish 1664b); [WO] (Cavendish 1655).

The second level of contemporary critique against theodicy is a moral argument against God. Since humans who commit or allow atrocious evils could choose to do otherwise, and should choose to do otherwise, they are morally culpable for the harm brought about by them. Consider that citizens blame those in power for choosing not to prevent or limit suffering in the world when they are able. If human agents ought to be held responsible when they allow suffering they could have directly prevented, then all the more, God should be implicated by the presence of atrocious evil in the world. Theodicies, correlatively, fail to sufficiently account for God's perfection, since an all-good God would want to prevent atrocious evils, an all-knowing God would be able to see when and where they might occur, and an all-powerful God would be able to thwart those actions he sees and wants to prevent.[6]

However, for the positive impact contemporary feminists have had on focusing attention on foreseeable and preventable harm, the history of philosophy indicates that their views were presaged in important ways by female scholars in the early modern period, and Cavendish particularly. A focused treatment of her work reveals two shared traits between Cavendish and contemporary feminist ethicists: they both employ a concrete sense of evil, and the both reject traditional theodicy's messages of eschatological justice, which simply cannot be reconciled with the God of Christian Scripture (on Cavendish's view). If God is loving, God's created order would not mandate the suffering of the neediest, the most innocent, and the most oppressed.

On this hypothetical, Cavendish departs from contemporary ethicists. She believes that God is in fact loving, and spreads goodness on humanity, regardless of whether humans treat each other well:

> In truth, Generosity and Humanity is like the Sun and the Air, for Humanity doth like the Air spread equally to all, it enters every where, and fills up all Vacuities; and Generosity like the Sun, shines every where, and on every Creature, although not at one Time, yet in such a Compass of Time as it hath strength and motion to extend it self; also his Benefits are General, he Disputes not Who or What deserves his Light or Heat, but knows his Light and Heat is Beneficial to all Creatures. (Cavendish 1664b, p. LVIII).

God does not quibble about who should be the beneficiaries of his goodness—all who live in the created order receive his gifts. Nature itself is so guided by physical laws that there cannot be disorder. Any perceived irregularities within creation are "just a reflection of our limited perspective and our parochial interests and concerns" (Cunning 2016, p. 172). If nature is governed by laws of creation, and humans are natural animals of that creation, then human action should also be rule-guided and in harmony with the divinely-inspired creation.[7] Whatever divisions humans perpetuate within the created order are not flaws in the order itself, but a sign of disconnect between the rules and actions that are supposed to be governed by them. Rather, Cavendish writes, "those active Parts, being united into one Infinite body, cannot break Natures general Peace; for that which Man names War, Sickness, Sleep, Death, and the like, are but various particular actions of the onely matter; not, as your *Author* imagines, in a confusion, like Bullets, or such like things juggled together in a man's Hat, but very orderly and methodical . . . " (Cavendish 1664a, p. 146). Human action, then, even when it results in negative consequences and suffering (war, sickness, sleep, death, etc.) cannot erode the natural order,

---

6   For a more in-depth analysis of the difficulty of concrete evil facing theodicy from a feminist ethical account see, for example, Hernandez (2016, chp. 1).

7   Although Cavendish believes God created this particular world (i.e., planet), she is not committed to the view that God created all of nature: "You will say, the Scripture doth teach us that, for it is not Six thousand years, when God created this World. I answer, the holy Scripture informs us onely of the Creation of this Visible World, but not of Nature and natural Matter; for I firmly believe according to the Word of God, that this World has been Created, as is described by *Moses*, but what is that to natural Matter? There may have been worlds before, as many are of the opinion that there have been men before *Adam*, and many amongst Divines do believe, that after the destruction of this World God will Create a new World again, as a new Heaven, and a new Earth; and if this be probable, or at least may be believed that there have been other worlds before this visible World? For nothing is impossible with God; and all this doth derogate nothing from the Honour and Glory of God, but rather increases his Divine Power" (Cavendish 1664a, p. 15).

function, and unity of the world. Evil cannot overturn the orderly functioning of natural systems, but is instead evidence that sometimes humans make choices that run contrary to the guidance of morality.

Cavendish's emphasis that neither divine nor human interaction in the natural order can alter what occurs in nature has led some scholars to conclude that suffering and pain are natural consequences of human action within the natural order. It may seem, on their view, that Cavendish thinks that any attempt to attribute positive and negative value to the consequences of human action is empty. Cunning, for example, argues:

> [Cavendish] is committed to the view that there is a necessary connection between a cause and its effect and that, in a plenum, there is no possible way for things to unfold other than they do. There is no possible reality outside of the bodies of the plenum; there is simply no grid. There are epistemic possibilities that are a reflection of the limited information that we have about our surroundings, but these (imagistic ideas) are just bodies in the plenum as well. Cavendish is committed to saying that there is only one way that things can be at any given moment, and so she will not ever assert that things should be a certain way, or that there are aims and purposes that the constituents of the plenum should take on apart from the ones that it in fact does. She instead holds that the plenum is simply as it is. We do employ normative terms like "good" and "bad", but these are just a reflection, from our own point-of-view, of how the plenum accommodates our interests and concerns. Different constituents of the plenum are competing with each other to maintain their respective proportions of motion, and that is that. This is a theme that recurs throughout the Cavendish corpus. As we have seen, she holds that strictly speaking there is no disorder or irregularity in nature; the decay and destruction of particular beings is just among the things that happen as creatures struggle to remain in existence. (Cunning 2016, p. 271).

Here, Cunning's argument moves from Cavendish's fact of necessary connection in the world to the emotive moral conclusion that normative judgments simply reflect personal preferences.

Cunning does admit, a bit later, that Cavendish appears to change her mind, at least on whether it is appropriate to label certain events as *bad*, especially when human action constrains the freedom of women and results in war (p. 273), but it seems that Cunning's inference from Cavendish's metaphysics to morality is inconsistent with several of Cavendish's other texts, which discuss concrete suffering. For instance, although Cavendish notoriously provides contrasting positions on metaphysics and epistemology across her writings, she does not equivocate about her strong sentiments against certain morally repugnant atrocities, such as civil war. She writes, in *Sociable Letters*:

> ... or else it proceeds from Unwise Government, where many Errours gather into a Mass, or Tumor of Evil, which Rises into Blisters of Discontents, and then Breaks out into Civil War; or else Heaven sends it to Punish the Sins of the People. Besides, it is to be observed, that Vices Increase in a Civil War, by reason Civil Government is in Disorder, Civil Magistrates Corrupted, Civil Laws Abolished, Civil Manners, and Decent Customs Banished, and in their Places is Ra|pine, Robbing, Stabbing, Treachery, and Falshood, all the Evil Passions and Debauch'd Appetites are let Loose, to take their Liberty. (Cavendish 1664b, CXX)

Evil passions and debauched appetites are let loose when disorder in government occurs and civil war breaks out. This disorder can then lead to multifarious, terrible wrongs (like rape, robbery, and murder). Some scholars, like Cunning, infer from Cavendish's writings about civil war that she "might be a bit conflicted", but that she "cannot hold that there is a fact of the matter to the effect that there is something bad about the death of an individual, even one's own self; nor can she hold that there is something literally bad about the destruction of an entire human society. When such things occur, they are just among the things that happen" (Cunning 2016, p. 273). Cunning is right that Cavendish believes it is metaphysically true that events occur within a created order, but it does not pragmatically or morally follow from this that these concrete harms are determined and inescapable. Neither should we infer that, for Cavendish, human agents are morally inculpable when they do not prevent the occurrence of evil, or do not minimize their harm when they are able.

It may be appropriate to read Cavendish's metaphysics as precluding real categories of "good" and "bad" in place of "what is", as suggested by Cunning, but the same reading cannot be made of Cavendish's views of ethics and justice—even if those views are more difficult to pin down. Cavendish actually says something quite like this in *Sociable Letters,* where she contrasts the difficulty of changing the physical world with the ability of education and habit to change the trajectory of human behavior:

> for there is no Assurance or Certainty in the Effects or Influence of the Stars and Planets, there is more Assurance in the Educations, and Customs of Men, and Custom and Education hath Stronger Effects, for Custom and Education can Alter the Unaptness in Natural Capacities and Understandings, the Dull Dispositions, Froward, or Evil Passions of the Mind; also it oftentimes Tempers the Irregular Humours of the Body, and can Restrain the Unsatiable Appetites of the Body and Senses, and Long Custom Alters the Nature of Men. (Cavendish 1664b, CXXXVIII)

Here, Cavendish offers a striking contrast to Cunning's contention that there are no real moral categories. Cavendish actually presents an opposite view, that the moral has sway over the natural. If "custom" (i.e., habit and practice) and "education" can alter the inaptness, dullness, and evil passion of the mind, our actions can be morally better or worse, which makes us morally responsible to perform that best actions. Although not even the systematicity of nature (the "stars") can influence human nature, proper habituation, association, and education can yield an improved moral condition, and a better world, for us.

Deborah Boyle (2006), in contrast to Cunning, argues that we can find a pieced-together "consistent core" of political and ethical views in Cavendish's *Orations* (Cavendish [1666] 2003b). The orations address social issues and government, and are organized around shared themes of peace and stability (Cavendish [1666] 2003b, pp. 253–54). Perhaps most relevant to the question of concrete moral harms and goods, Boyle observes that Cavendish's moral project is grounded on identifying and eradicating immoral action—action that should be otherwise. Boyle observes:

> In other texts, when Cavendish praises or blames individuals for their actions, she typically appeals to how their actions have increased or decreased peace. For example, she criticizes Cato for killing himself over a change of government; the new government was likely to make the country safer and more peaceful, Cavendish says, so someone who truly cared for peace and safety would have supported the change. (Boyle 2006, p. 254).

Justice in the public square comes directly from governmental order, but Cavendish appeals to others to behave in peaceful ways. If you believe in peace, you ought to act peaceably, since consistent thinking produces consistent action—moral thinking must result in bringing about moral states of affairs. The result is that Cavendish does not believe that all states of affairs are equal and determined. Instead, action is valuable based on whether its consequences are peaceful and positive, and whether an action ought to be performed depends in part on the extent to which it allows us to enjoy rights and peace: "Wherefore your best way is, to Submit and Obey, to be Content, to be Ruled, and not seek to Govern, to enjoy your Rights, and to revenge your Wrongs by Law and Justice, and not to make War and Confusion to destroy your selves" (Cavendish [1666] 2003b, p. 122). Of course, as a monarchist, Cavendish believes that we are most able to pursue action that produces the best states of affairs under a strong monarch. Such a leader is positioned to allow us to pursue peace, Cavendish thinks, and to avoid war (which can enslave, entrap, suppress rights, and create a false peace.) If there is a despotic government, or if a citizenry is morally base and confused, the predictable evils of war are likely to result. Cavendish's strong warning against the vices of war and her view that peace is the protector of virtue are powerfully present in her poem "A Dialogue Betwixt Peace and War":

War.

Thou *Flattering Peace*, and most unjust, which drawes

The *Vulgar* by thy *Rhet'rick* to *hard Lawes*

Which makes them *silly Ones*, content to be,

To take up *Voluntary Slavery*.

And mak'st great *Inequalities* beside,

Some like to *Asses* beare, others on *Horsback* ride.

Peace.

O *War*, thou cruell *Enemy to Life*,

Vnquieted Neighbour, breeding alwaies *Strife*

I the *Parent* of *Learning* am, and *Arts*,

Nurse to *Religion*, and *Comfort* to all *Hearts*.

I am the *Guardian*, which keepes *Vertue* safe. (*PF*, 90–91)

As the guardian of virtue, peace is cast in the poem as something that can vanquish the injustices and concrete harms of war. We can strive for and attain peace, especially when we seek it in other endeavors, like religion, aesthetics, and moral education.

Cavendish does not only prop peace up as the aim for moral action, but she also explicitly repudiates vice as something to be avoided. She writes, "Vices are Vices, no otherwise but that they are Hurtfull or Destructive to Mankind, which makes them Vices, for the Gods Forbid them because of the Evil Effects" (Cavendish [1666] 2003b, p. 207). These are not the words of a thinker who conceives of human states of affairs as having univocal value, but of one who has thought carefully about ways in which people are responsible for goods and harms they reap on each other. Instead, she calls us to think of concrete harms as those which have pragmatic, deleterious effects on the government, and on individuals.

It cannot be maintained, then, that moral categories and values are vacuous for Cavendish. In her ethical and political writings, she remains, as ever, the eccentric scholar, but she is consistent about her beliefs about the abomination of war (and civil war, in particular), and that the political can be debated and can shape human action. Similarly, Cavendish is clear that political and civic harms relate importantly to religious beliefs and experiences. Her political work responds to horrors (Broad and Green 2009), depicts lived experiences of suffering, and is directly tied to the problem of evil. Cavendish writes, for example: "Rationally one would think that God should not take delight in shaven heads, or bare and dirty feet, or cold backs, or hungry stomachs" (Cavendish 1655, pp. 29–30).

If we fashion some systematicity to Cavendish's views on the problem of evil, we will see that Cavendish positions evil firmly in the concrete, in at least two distinct ways. First, moral evil comes about when we choose to do that which we know we ought not to do. It may seem basic for an ethical theory to identify evil with action that goes against what an agent is meant to do morally, but it is significant that Cavendish underscores the fact that immoral action ought not to occur. Karen Detlefsen, for example, highlights this facet of Cavendish's ethics when she points out that, for Cavendish, "We may even willfully and freely deviate from these best guesses (e.g., as did those who fomented the civil war through which Cavendish lived)" (Detlefsen 2009, p. 433), and that when we choose wrongly, injustices occur, and especially limit the ability of women to think for themselves. Concrete evil gains significance in relation to the injustices that result from them.

War is not the only venue through which concrete evil occurs. Instead, Cavendish believed that some of the most harmful incidents occur when women are not allowed to be educated, when they are disallowed from expressing or experiencing civil rights because of political abuses, and when domineering patriarchal domestic and civil rule suppress other freedoms for women. Marriage, for example, harbors the possibility that women will be subject to horrors, including, "'the very real threat of death in childbirth … but women also have to put up with abandonment, abuse, drinking, gambling, not to mention children who turn out to be disgraceful reprobates if they survive (Cavendish 2000, pp. 112–17). The Epilogue proclaims: 'Marriage is a Curse we find/Especially to Women kind (Cavendish 2000, p. 117).'" (Wilson 2007, p. 204). Apart from these potential sources of female suffering, Cavendish sought to "delineate the traits of a fanciful and witty dimension parallel to the masculine dominion of objectivity, where she manifested and realized the inalienable right of a woman to think within the intimacy of her mind and her house."[8] Freedom and, so, the ability to act morally, depend on, "the independent locus of feminine cognition and enfranchisement" (Mascetti 2008, p. 3), and Cavendish pointed out that many women suffer under domestic and political constraints that prevent them from being able to choose alternate actions. Women, if unfree, are also left unable to ever experience the intellectual and physical goods that are brought about from living a well-chosen path.

Indeed, for Cavendish, most suffering is originally sourced in some intellectual oppression. "We go wrong," Cavendish observes, "either because we are ignorant of the ends which we ought to pursue or because we know what ends we ought to pursue but we willfully deviate from them" (Cavendish 1664a, p. 509f). She was keen to pick out various social settings in which women suffer from being unable to pursue a life of the mind. She even thought women were limited in intellectual pursuits within religious practice: "I thought you had been either Jews, or Turks, because I never perceived any women in your congregations; but what is the reason you bar them from your religious assemblies?" (Cavendish [1666] 2003a, p. 20). Men of her time—who were citizens of the state, and so already had power beyond that of women—suppressed the ability of women to act, behave, and to think freely. When writing to men, Cavendish appeals to natural law (as well as female beauty[9]) to argue against the domestic, political, and religious oppression of women. She writes: "It is not only uncivil and ignoble, but unnatural, for men to speak against women and their liberties, for women were made by Nature for men, to be loved, accompanied, assisted, and protected; and if men are bound to love them by Nature, should they restrain them by force: Should they make them slaves, which Nature made to be their dearest associates, their beautifulest objects and sweetest delights?" (Cavendish [1666] 2003a, p. 247). But when writing to women, Cavendish speaks in starker terms about the phenomenological experience of being "Inferior Women": "but alas, men, that are not only our tyrants but our devils, keep us in the hell of subjection, from whence I cannot perceive any redemption or getting out; we may complain, and bewail our condition, but they will not free us; we may murmur and rail against men, yet they regard not what we say" (Cavendish [1666] 2003a, p. 248). The situation of women against men seems without hope, and the tears of women are compared to "puffs of wind" and "fruitless showers" (Cavendish [1666] 2003a, p. 248). Not only do women suffer, but no one takes their suffering seriously.[10]

---

8   Mascetti (2008, p. 3). Some feminists have worried that Cavendish's reticence to seek to directly abolish systems of patriarchy means that she was less committed to what we would now call a feminist project. Indeed, Cavendish equivocates on issues contemporary feminists would think are important—for example, whether married women really are free; Cavendish at points argues that they are because their natural beauty gives them power over their husbands. Yet at other points, "Cavendish shows a keen awareness of the fact that many early modern women do suffer from a debilitating loss of negative liberty in the patriarchal marriage state," Broad (2014, p. 113). Mascetti replies to this criticism by noting that Cavendish's "philosophical feminism was, therefore, carved out of a conscious and supportive acknowledgment of male hegemony, and not turned into a method of gendered opposition and subversion. The dimension of feminine fancy that she created was innocuously and respectfully parallel to that of male wisdom" (Mascetti 2008, p. 13).

9   Although, some scholars observe the tension with which Cavendish's poems describe the relationship between women (as objects of love) and men (who seek to objectify women through the love act.) Jennifer Low writes, "Cavendish displays both the cruelty and the power relations inherent in the Petrachan ideal through [her] lyric … . By literalizing the trope of lovers' pains, Cavendish brings new life to the convention of the cruel beloved" (Low 1998, p. 160).

10   Cavendish famously defends a monarchy as the proper government to better address civil inequalities. Broad and Green note, "For Cavendish, as for Hobbes, it is crucial that the sovereign's power be simple and undivided. This is the only way in which human beings might gain some unanimity in their opinions about right and wrong: that is, by subordinating their

This isn't to say that men are the sole oppressors and the only ones that can commit vicious acts. In *SL* (Cavendish 1664b) (IX), Cavendish entreats an imaginary interlocuter:

> though it is easier to do evil than good, for every fool can make an uproar, and a tumultuous disorder, such as the wisest can hardly settle into order again. But Women in State-affairs can do as they do with themselves, they can, and do often make themselves sick, but when they are sick, not well again: So they can disorder a State, as they do their Bodies, but neither can give Peace to th' one, nor Health to th' other; but their restless Minds, and unsatiable Appetites, do many times bring Ruin to the one, and Death to the other.

Women and men can wreak havoc on a government, on each other, and on themselves—and their actions can have consequences such that even the wisest people cannot "settle into order". If we are able to harm each other in ways that escape the healing touch of the wisest among us, we must be compelled to seek knowledge, control appetites, and (ultimately) for Cavendish *do what is good*.

Cavendish's exhortations against evil and towards good lead us to several conclusions. First, the metaphysical realm is treated differently for Cavendish than the moral order. The content and strictures of morality are purely about human moral action, and so, the moral order is susceptible to be negatively impacted by political and individual actors. But those same actors can bring peace through their moral choices. Cavendish values states of affairs which preserve peace, but not at the cost of vice and enslavement. True peace is obtained when individuals are able to experience civil and domestic rights (especially, of course, if individuals have the benefit of living under a strong, virtuous monarchy). However, peace often does not prevail, and the worst sorts of harm result when it does not. The harms cited by Cavendish are of the sort that contemporary feminist ethicists identify as that worthy of ethical analysis, and which most perniciously serve as evidence against the existence of God: atrocities.

Should the critic argue that the injustices named by Cavendish fall out of the realm of the atrocious harm category, it should be noted that the intellectual injustice Cavendish focuses on is systemic, pernicious, and denigrating, perhaps even more because the harms are not purely physical. Broad and Green observe that, for Cavendish, "Women are not free because they are, quite simply, coerced, threatened, or forced into obedience. In this way, men keep women in the subordinate position of children and fools—human beings without the full use of their reason" (Broad and Green 2009, p. 220). Husbands may have the natural authority to "direct and guide" women, Cavendish suggests, but they err if they interpret that to mean "ruling and governing" and use that interpretation to further limit women's freedom (Boyle 2013, p. 528). Keeping women indentured in the home leads to a continued oppression of women by men in the public sphere.

2. Free Will and Redemptive Goods

Margaret Cavendish's commitment to a positive view of moral goods and immoral harms that is grounded in the concrete impinges on the problem of evil in the early modern period, and belies a pragmatic and moral point for Cavendish as a theist: there are lived experiences of suffering and evil that must be made consistent with a loving, relational God. It is difficult to defend God's dual role in preserving justice and divine love. If God shares in our grief, who is responsible for inflicting it? How can there be justice if the innocent bears the punishment of the guilty, and how is justice administered if responsibility for divine suffering is transferred from humankind to God? (Walker 1988, p. 183).

Cavendish provides one explicit and one implicit account of divine perfection that should be called "theodicy": God had to create the world as he did, and concrete moral evil is a part of the world, but it does not mitigate against divine perfection. In *SL*, Cavendish gives one of the most traditional

---

judgement to the judgement of one individual. Thus in Cavendish's utopia, there is 'but one sovereign, one religion, one law, and one language, so that all the world might be as one united family'" (Broad and Green 2009, p. 212).

philosophical arguments in her corpus, when she argues that human freedom requires that God allow for evil in the world. In this long passage from *SL* CLXX, for example, Cavendish goes so far as to worry about the salvation of those who give up faith because of the problem of evil, and provides a strikingly traditional free-will defense of the problem of evil:

> Fear, for Moral Conscience, said she, is the most Tender Effect of a Fearful Passion, but Divine Conscience is an Effect of Grace, which the Common People hath but little of... I do believe, that the Great Omnipotent God is Good, Wise, Powerful, Knowing, Fore-seeing, and Just, as not to Damn a man for that which he could not possibly know, or for that which Nature made him to do, neither was he Ignorant, as not to Fore-see what Man could, or would do, and if Man could do nothing without Gods Permission, Gods Mercy would not Permit, or Suffer Man to Damn himself, for that would be to Make Man to that End, Knowing it before, as Fore-seeing it, and if he gave Man a Free-Will, that were to give away one of his Attributes, and so to make Man Great, and himself Less, and only to Impower Man to Damn himself; or for God to Make Man, and then Damn him, whereby to shew his Power, would neither stand with God's Justice nor Goodness; but certainly God could shew his Power other wayes, than by Damning those Creatures he Made, or Makes; and that God be as much, if not more Glorified by the Damned as by the Blessed, is but an Odd Belief, that Gods Glory should Arise from Torments, as if God had no other way to be Glorified, this would not Express Justice so much as Severity, if not Cruelty, as first, to Fore-see the Evil, then to make the Creature, and at last to Suffer that Evil, and to Damn the Creature for the Evil ... but most Men have Blasphemous Opinions, as to make God either Cruel, or Ignorant, as not to Fore-know, or else to Make to Damn. (*SL*, CLXX)

There are a number of distinct points in this text that lend themselves towards theodicy, mostly centered on the concept of divine justice. First, a good God will not punish humans for performing actions that they are unfree to perform, or are non-culpably ignorant in performing. Second, God's mercy is incompatible with a sort of moral necessitarianism. Finally, most people are comfortable thinking blasphemous thoughts about God, namely, that God is perfectly good, all-knowing, and just, but punishes his contingent creation for exercising free will that was given to humanity during creation. By providing a free-will defense, Cavendish provides an argument that is consistent with traditional theodicy in the early modern period. If we want to account for divine perfection and the presence of evil in the world, we need to remember that evil comes when people choose to act in a manner that is contrary to the guidance of the moral law.

Although Cavendish provides traditional justification for the compatibility of divine perfection and evil in the created order, her work also reveals that traditional theodicy is, by itself, insufficient to explain the suffering of the oppressed. Just as contemporary feminism faults traditional theodicy for its abstract conception of evil, Cavendish conceives of evil in concrete, situated terms, and would reject attempts to abstract evil away from the concrete. "Moral evil" is inseparable from actual experiences of suffering in society and in the home. If the purpose of theodicy is to demonstrate (or, more thinly, to explain) how divine perfection is consistent with evil in the world, theodicy ought also to address the plight of those who suffer domestically and socially.[11] In 21st-century parlance, culpable, preventable atrocities in the world pose a threat to divine perfection, especially divine benevolence.[12]

In the same way that Cavendish's work reveals difficulties with traditional theodicy, it also develops a unique conception of (what we would call today) "redemptive theodicy", as long as "redemption" is understood independent of an eschatology. Cavendish's view of redemption does not

---

[11] See, for example, Anderson (2009) especially Joy (2010).
[12] Card defines evil as "reasonably foreseeable intolerable harms produced (maintained, supported, tolerated, and so on) by culpable wrongdoing. So understood, evils have two irreducibly distinct components: a *harm component* and an *agency component*" (Card 2002, p. 5).

rely upon some unknowable, unseen, latter good, and so is not an eschatological event. Redemption is not some ideal that is provided to those who suffer, as a way of placating their anguish through something they can only hope for (but never fully experience until after death, when there will be a complete and just reckoning of the scales). Rather, redemption for Cavendish primarily indicates a civil (rather than specifically spiritual) restoration. Redemption transforms social, religious, and legal systems that have denied women's rights, perpetuated slavery, and waged war, and theodicy that ties the divine concurrence of evil with redemption ought to rely upon a concrete sense of justice (i.e., one that is accessible through the experiences of daily life). If harms are to be eradicated through concrete, just actions, a requirement of any theodicy is that society must be transformed. But, just as redemption is a civic enterprise, instead of a religious one, the transformation of society that must accompany any theodicy must come about by creative human agency.

It might be said that reading Cavendish's demand that redemption for acts of injustice must come through redemptive, restorative human action is simply not theodicy. Such a worry rightly focuses Cavendish's focus on positive human creation in the face of evil. It *is* true that, compared to contemporary theists, Cavendish provides a thin evaluation of divine culpability for evil (or for good in the world, for that matter). But this is not because she is not doing theodicy, but rather is largely due to her skepticism about what can be known about the nature of God. Cavendish is not a skeptic about whether God exists. She writes: "No part of nature can or does conceive the essence of God, or what God is in himself; but it conceives only, that there is a divine being which is supernatural" (Cavendish [1666] 2003a, p. 17). That God exists is not something to be skeptical about, since the natural order is a created one, but we ought to be reticent to claim to understand anything that transcends the scope of nature. It false to infer from her reluctance to pontificate about the nature of God that Cavendish entirely avoids the problem that evil poses to divine perfection. Cavendish thinks, for instance, that it would be absurd to think that God would permit Satan, "to have such a familiar conjunction, and make such contracts with Man, as to empower him to do mischief and hurt to others, or to foretell things to come, and the like" (Cavendish 1664a, p. 227). She confirms in an earlier *PL* (Cavendish 1664a) passage (that maps onto the *SL* theodical text), that:

> God's Mercy would not Permit or suffer Man to Damn himself, for that would be to Make Man to that End, Knowing it before, as Fore-seeing it, and if he gave Man a Free-Will, that were to give away one of his Attributes, and so to make Man Great, and himself Less, and only to Empower Man to Damn himself; . . . this would not Express Justice so much as severity, if not Cruelty, as first, to Fore-See the Evil, then to make the Creature, and at last to Suffer that Evil, and Damn the Creature of the Evil; neither, said she, can that Rational Part that God hath given me, perceive how it can stand with his Goodness and Mercy, or his Wisdom and Glory, to Suffer more Devils, than to Make Saints.

(Cavendish 1664a, p. 170)

This passage argues, a bit differently than the *SL* text, that divine goodness would prevent finite human sins to condemn us to eternal damnation. The benevolence of God—characterized here as mercy and justice—is juxtaposed against the concrete results of human evil, such as cruelty and suffering. Of course, there is a hint at a free will defense here as well, but that defense is strongly overshadowed by appeals to divine goodness. It is irrational, Cavendish's character asserts, to conceive of a good and fully wise God that would create humans who could eternally condemn themselves, just as it is irrational to conceive of a good God who could allow his creation to suffer. The interlocuter interjects, not to disagree, but to warn against anthropomorphizing God: "Man is so Presumptuous, as to Assimilize God, as also to Pretend to know what God sayes, making him to Speak like Man; also to Express him to have Passions; but if God be Absolute and Incomprehensible, it is High Presumption to Assimilize God to any Creature; besides, it is absurd and Ridiculous to Compare that which is Incomprehensible, for if he cannot be Conceived, how shall he be Express'd?" Cavendish (1664a, p. 170). If there is a God (and there is, for Cavendish), we cannot know anything about his nature. We can merely acknowledge that he is, and that he exists in the manner of perfection. An upshot to this interesting bit of philosophy of religion is that Cavendish thinks that what we can know of God indicates that he would be more interested in fostering the moral development of his creation rather than permitting rampant suffering within it.

A potential critique would come from our inability to know God's nature: if we are ignorant of divine essence (Cavendish 1664a, p. 107), how could Cavendish advocate for a moral response to the problem of evil—whether for humans, who must work towards moral improvement, or for God, who must limit evil in the world? An answer more than likely resides in Cavendish's view of faith, which can ground some substantial claims about God's nature (Cavendish 1664a, pp. 210–211), as well as God's creation. "So, she believes," Karen Detlefsen writes, "in accordance with faith because it is in keeping with Church and Scriptural authority, that God is immaterial, divinely infinite, and perfect" (Cavendish 1664a, pp. 186–187). Yet more regularly, and quite constantly in her mature works, "Cavendish says that God is the author not only of nature's perceptive, knowing capacity and therefore of nature's freedom, but also of nature's self-moving power." (Detlefsen 2009, p. 430)

Although God is the author of nature, Cavendish stops short of concluding that God is the author of moral evil. God creates the conditions under which humans can use their freedom, and his power does not rule the minute details of everyday life, "like as one wheel in a clock turns all the rest" (Cavendish 1666, p. 212). Detlefsen describes the relationship Cavendish sees between nature and God as "interaction through rational suggestion" (Detlefsen 2009, p. 439). If divine perfection morally guides created beings, then evil in the world is mitigated by reforming bad actions (that come, on Cavendish's view, from some false thinking and acting inconsistently with the best guidelines of morality). The hard human work of redeeming evil requires that individuals who perform evil actions, "be improved through good education, gainful employment, and exposure to models of virtue" (Boyle 2006, p. 260).[13]

Cavendish thus provides a redemptive account of evil, in which reformation is realized by transforming evil minds within peaceful society rather than by some heavenly escape from the trappings of the body. There is an original goodness in all people that is masked by the intellectual paternalism of the powerful. When we do the difficult work of opening access to free intellectual pursuits, oppression changes from the inside out. Rather than depending upon some otherworldly eschatology for redemption, Cavendish puts forward a picture in which human action can focus on broadening access to intellectual pursuits for women (and others who are not able to pursue them). Reason affords us the ability to change the intellectual suppression of others: "In Cavendish's scheme, philosophical civility is guaranteed by intellectual governance, a regulatory function she attributes to institutions that foster heterogeneity." (Barnes 2009, p. 54).

3. Conclusions

Divine justice, for Cavendish, is preserved when all wrongdoers partake in redemption as a natural part of God's creative order, whose completion is in our perfection. Her redemptive theodicy is grounded in a paradigm that mirrors the contemporary atrocity paradigm, and yet confirms the necessity of moral transformation, especially towards civil and domestic peace. The minimum result is that her work, which has its starting point in concrete, situated evil, and moves out to a defense of divine existence, ought to be considered within the corpus of philosophy of religion. Perhaps, too, the maximum result is a theodicy whose end—participative redemption—is available to all, independent of theistic belief. The accessibility of redemption underscores the normative force of Cavendish's philosophy of religion. The moral law is embedded into the created order, organized according to

---

13 Unsurprisingly, Cavendish thinks moral transformation can result from a *proper* authoritative structure within government, "Thus the role of government is not merely to control those with 'rude and wild natures' but to transform them" (Boyle 2006, p. 260).

the rules of reason, and functions for all people. The cycle of redemption and reformation can bring transformation and healing to the person who experiences and participates in it. Theodicy that ignores concrete evil misses the phenomenological significance of living in a world with pain and suffering.[14]

Conflicts of Interest: The author declares no conflict of interest.

References

Adams, Marilyn McCord. 1999. *Horrendous Evils and the Goodness of God.* Ithaca: Cornell University Press.

Adams, Marilyn McCord. 2006. *Christ and Horrors.* Cambridge: Cambridge University Press.

Anderson, Pamela Sue, ed. 2009. *New Topics in Feminist Philosophy of Religion: Contestations and Transcendence Incarnate.* Berlin: Springer.

Bar On, Bat-Ami. 2007. Terrorism, Evil, and Everyday Depravity. In *Feminist Philosophy and the Problem of Evil.* Edited by R. M. Schott. Bloomington: University of Indiana and Hypatia, Inc., pp. 195–205.

Barnes, Diana. 2009. Familiar Epistolary Philosophy: Margaret Cavendish's Philosophical Letters. *Parergon* 26: 39–64. [CrossRef]

Boyle, Deborah. 2006. Fame, Virtue, and Government: Margaret Cavendish on Ethics and Politics. *Journal of the History of Ideas* 67: 251–89. [CrossRef]

Boyle, Deborah. 2013. Margaret Cavendish on Gender, Nature, and Freedom. *Hypatia* 28: 516–32. [CrossRef]

Broad, Jacqueline. 2007. Margaret Cavendish and Joseph Glanvill: Science, religion, and witchcraft. *Studies in History and Philosophy of Science* 38: 493–505. [CrossRef]

Broad, Jacqueline. 2014. Women on Liberty in Early Modern England. *Philosophy Compass* 9: 112–22. [CrossRef]

Broad, Jacqueline, and Karen Green. 2009. *A History of Women's Political Thought in Europe, 1400–1700.* Cambridge: Cambridge University Press, p. 200.

Card, Claudia. 2002. *The Atrocity Paradigm.* New York: Oxford University Press.

Card, Claudia. 2010. *Confronting Evils: Terrorism, Torture, Genocide.* Cambridge: Cambridge University Press.

Cavendish, Margaret. 2003a. The Blazing World. In *Margaret Cavendish Political Writings.* Edited by Susan James. Cambridge: Cambridge University Press. First published 1666.

Cavendish, Margaret. 2003b. Orations of Divers Sorts. In *Margaret Cavendish Political Writings.* Edited by Susan James. Cambridge: Cambridge University Press. First published 1666.

Cavendish, Margaret. 1653. *Poems, and Fancies.* London: Text Creation Partnership.

Cavendish, Margaret. 1655. *The Worlds Olio.* London: Text Creation Partnership.

Cavendish, Margaret. 1664a. *Philosophical Letters, or Modest Reflections upon Some Opinions in Natural Philosophy.* London: Text Creation Partnership.

Cavendish, Margaret. 1664b. *Sociable Letters.* London: Text Creation Partnership.

Cavendish, Margaret. 1666. *Observations upon Experimental Philosophy, to which is Added, The Description of a New Blazing World.* London: Text Creation Partnership.

Cavendish, Margaret. 2000. *Paper Bodies: A Margaret Cavendish Reader.* Edited by Sara Heller Mendelson and Sylvia Bowerbank. Toronto: Broadview Literary Texts.

Cunning, David. 2016. *Cavendish.* London: Routledge.

Detlefsen, Karen. 2009. Margaret Cavendish on the Relation between God and World. *Philosophy Compass* 4: 421–38. [CrossRef]

Hernandez, Jill. 2016. *Early Modern Women and the Problem of Evil: Atrocity & Theodicy.* London: Routledge.

Joy, Morny. 2010. *Rethinking the 'Problem of Evil' with Hannah Arendt and Grace Jantzen.* Dordrecht: Springer.

Low, Jennifer. 1998. Surface and Interiority: Self-Creation in Margaret Cavendish's. *The Claspe. Philological Quarterly* 77: 149–69.

---

14 There are feminists and theologians who would disagree, of course, with a redemptive theodicy, whether grounded in abstract or concrete evil. Oppressive paternalistic regimes could, after all, continue their abuses of political power with the promise that their antics are necessary for the project of redemption to occur. Cavendish does not argue that political injustices are justified on the basis of whether they eventually strengthen the character of the person who suffers, but given that they are part of our cache of human experiences, we must then answer the question, "What now?"

Mascetti, Yaakov. 2008. A 'World of Nothing, but Pure Wit': Margaret Cavendish and the Gendering of the Imaginary. *Partial Answers: Journal of Literature and the History of Ideas* 6: 1–31. [CrossRef]

Stump, Eleanore. 2010. *Wandering in Darkness*. Oxford: Oxford University Press.

Walker, Michael. 1988. The Atonement and Justice. *Theology* 91: 180–83. [CrossRef]

Wilson, Karen Ross. 2007. Marriage and the Problem of Evil in Works by John Milton and Margaret Cavendish. Ph.D. dissertation, University of California-Davis, Davis, CA, USA.

Article

Souls in the Dark: Theodicy and Domesticity in *Home*

Mark S. M. Scott

Department of Religious Studies, Thorneloe University at Laurentian, 935 Ramsey Lake Road, Sudbury, ON P3E 2C6, Canada; mscott4@laurentian.ca; Tel.: +1-705-673-1730 (ext. 403)

Received: 17 October 2017; Accepted: 15 December 2017; Published: 19 December 2017

Abstract: Theodicy typically addresses the problem of evil in the public square, focusing on instances of paradigmatic evil that raise the issue broadly. Theodicy, however, also operates in the private sphere, where the conflict and chaos of family life raise doubts about God's goodness and power. Domestic suffering—here defined as the hurt, sorrows, and heartbreaks of family life, apart from domestic abuse, which belongs to a separate category—has often been neglected by theodicists. In this article, I will analyze Marilynne Robinson's fictional novel *Home* for insights into the problem of evil in the domestic realm. While it does not offer a domestic theodicy per se, Robinson's *Home* sheds light on the reality of suffering love and its bias toward hope, which charts new theological pathways in theodicy that have hitherto been underexplored.

Keywords: Marilynne Robinson; *Home*; Gilead trilogy; problem of evil; theodicy; suffering love; hope

---

"But the soul finds its own home if it ever has a home at all" (*Home*, 282)

Classic theological and philosophical treatments of the problem of evil cast the question onto a vast canvass, enumerating the most egregious examples of suffering around the globe, both historically and currently. Most often, these are infamous spectacles whose shockwaves were felt far and wide: the Plague, the Inquisition, the Lisbon Earthquake, the World Wars, the Holocaust, 9/11, and so on. These and other instances of public, superlative evils are nodal points for the problem of evil, and rightly so. But what about the problem of evil as it arises in private life, within the walls of our homes, in the complex, sometimes strained, sometimes severed relationships between immediate family members? More subtle than traditional instantiations, they nonetheless raise the problem in an important—often neglected—register. Hemingway notes the "intimate harm" that family sometimes inflict (Hemingway 1964, p. 88). Where would we begin an analysis of theodicy in the domestic realm, especially given its frequent invisibility?

Marilynne Robinson provides a portal through which to undertake an oblique analysis of theodicy in her novel *Home* (Robinson 2008), the second of her Gilead trilogy, interposed between *Gilead* (Robinson 2004) and *Lila* (Robinson 2014). All three novels shed light on the problem of evil, but from different vantage points. *Gilead* explores the interplay between beauty and suffering (Scott 2016). *Lila* ponders the mystery of suffering and grace (Scott 2017). *Home*, while absorbing these themes, hones in on suffering love and hope. My essay will analyze *Home* in three stages. First, I will select five portraits of pain from the novel that illustrate the problem of evil as the problem of suffering love. Second, I will briefly draw from theologians and philosophers to expound on the relationship between love and suffering in a world of woe. Finally, I will sound the notes of hope that temper the tragedy of *Home* without bypassing it.

1. Portraits of Pain: Five Vignettes

1.1. Jack Boughton: Troubled Soul

The problem of evil in *Home*, as in the entire Gilead trilogy, centers on Jack Boughton, the prodigal son of local Presbyterian minister Robert Boughton. All the other characters buffet and break against the rock of Jack's reprobation. He represents the problem of evil generally and specifically. Firstly, at a general level, it seems unjust that an all-loving, all-powerful God would inflict his family with the pain of his inexcusable misdeeds, which escalate in severity and significance as he gets older. As paragons of virtue, the Boughtons enjoyed the esteem of nearly all, but Jack's antics as "the black sheep, the ne'er-do-well" cast a shadow over their reputation (69). Why would God allow these good parents and siblings to be tormented by their often selfish and destructive prodigal son and sibling? Why would God not intervene to convert him or to change his character? Why would God allow them to suffer their whole life on his account?

But Jack also illustrates the problem specifically in his enduring experience of estrangement (85). From the moment he stands tentatively on the back porch, unsure of his welcome, until the time he leaves, he never feels at home (30, 318). He shies away from physical contact, avoids intimate conversation, and never enjoys the sense of full inclusion, always living on the outskirts of the family, asking permission for things that his father and sister insisted were his to enjoy as much as theirs. In one memorable moment, Glory gives Jack a haircut, at his request. Though unremarkable on the face of it, given Jack's aversion to physical contact, his request comes as a surprise. He fidgets uneasily at her touch, unused to it (171) and tears up in "exasperation": "I'm so tired of myself" (172). Unable to feel home with himself, he cannot feel at home with others, even in his family home, and so he remains inexplicably estranged (267).

Jack's self-estrangement and self-loathing eventuates in a botched suicide attempt in the barn, his hidden oasis from the joyful commotion of the Boughton family life since he was a boy. In a state of drunken despair, he stuffed his shirt and socks into the tailpipe of the DeSoto and courted oblivion, only forestalled by his inability to start the car without the keys, which he gave to Glory (243–44). It was the family's greatest fear: "Was this what they had always been afraid of, that he would really leave, that he would truly and finally put himself beyond the reach of help and harm, beyond self-consciousness and all its humiliations, beyond all that loneliness and unspent anger and all that unsalved shame, and their endless, relentless loyalty to him?" (247–48). After the initial shock of finding him, Glory discreetly washes him and helps him into bed, but the episode signals the end of Jack's hopes for happiness. He has given up on himself (208).

1.2. Robert Boughton: Tortured Soul

Jack's elusiveness and estrangement weighed heavily on his parents, who could never make him feel at home in the world (170, 230, 267). At every age, they tried to alleviate his alienation and loneliness. His father Robert Boughton constantly affirmed his love for Jack. When, as a child, a malicious neighbor sarcastically told Jack that his parents deserved him, his father responded graciously: "Well now, that was kind of her. I will be sure to thank her. I hope I do deserve you, Jack" (13). All they ever hoped for him was happiness, but Jack could never shake his "sadness" and "heavyheartedness" (115). If, as they say, you are only as happy as your saddest child, then their hopes were unrealized, so Robert "tried not to hope for anything at all, except that we wouldn't lose you. So of course we did" (116). For his whole life, Jack was an open wound for Robert Boughton and his wife: an unanswered prayer that darkened their otherwise sunny skies.

Despite his lifelong "posture of heroic and fatherly grace" (24), Robert finds himself unable to maintain his practiced magnanimity upon Jack's return, even though it was the answer to decades of fervent prayer. The years have taken a toll on him: "Kindness takes more strength than I have now ... Maybe I'm finding out I'm not such a good man as I thought I was. Now that I don't have the strength—patience takes a lot out of you. Hope, too" (274). Age and weariness interrupt the flow of his unlimited supply of grace to Jack. Near the end of his life, he reflects on his failure to protect Jack from himself: "You see something beautiful in a child, and you almost live for it, you feel as though you would die for it, but it isn't yours to keep or to protect" (294–95). In the end, as Jack extends his hand to bid his father farewell, Robert withdraws his hand and turns away from him in exhaustion, confusion, and despair: "Tired of it!" (317).

Crippled by age and diminished by disappointment, Robert's "posture of grace" finally wears out (45). Jack does not blame him, nor does he walk away in anger. He kisses his father on the brow, a hint of hope in an otherwise hopeless situation. Robert's inability to assume the role of the prodigal's father, ready to forgive and to celebrate the return of the prodigal son, was a failure of frailty, not of faith. But, unlike the parable (Luke 15: 11–32), where the older brother resents the father's welcoming reception of the son, Jack's older brother Teddy picks up the mantle dropped by their father, and gives him the parting embrace that his father denies him: "'I suspect I'll never see you again. In this life. I'd say take care of yourself, but I'm afraid you won't do that either. Well, never hesitate—' He held out his hand. When Jack took it, he touched his shoulder, then embraced him" (268). Teddy completes his father's legacy of grace to Jack.

1.3. Glory Boughton: Good Soul

Though heroic in his unflagging love for Jack, Glory emerges in *Home* as the true heroine of the story, and as the custodian of grace and hope for Jack. 38-year-old Glory returns to the family home in Gilead after a long and humiliating engagement to a married man (7, 22, 118, 149). Duped by him for years, she finally sees through the charade, left only with the memory of the love she imagined they shared. One night, she dumped her "fiancé's" 452 love letters and her "cheap ring" down a storm drain, a symbolic gesture of the end of their relationship and her illusions about him (119). As false tokens of feigned love, they were deposited where they belonged: down the drain: "It was all horrible enough to be funny, I suppose, Now that it's over" (119). Glory's innate honesty and soft-spot for hard-luck cases made her the perfect mark for her "ex-fiancé's" avarice or affection (or both), and now she finds herself unhappy at home (131).

When Jack returns to Gilead, it gives her a renewed purpose, but also new worries and problems. In their younger years, Glory felt a special bond with Jack, the most enigmatic of her seven siblings, and five years her senior. When he impregnated a local teenager, who gave birth to a daughter, Glory took great pains to help the mother and child. She wrote letters imploring Jack to come home and take responsibility for his daughter, but he never did (150). Nevertheless, her love for him was undiminished, and she expressed it in her attentiveness to his daughter. More than once, Jack affectionately calls Glory "a good soul" (118, 149). Although he would never know the kindnesses she did for him in those years (70), he appreciated her tender care for him now: "Everything would be so much harder if you weren't here. Impossible, in fact" (131; cf. 316). Despite all the sorrow Jack caused in the past and present, she loves him selflessly.

Glory's inexhaustible, altruistic love for Jack takes on epic proportions, however, in her decision to stay in Gilead—in a town she hates, in a house she does not want—because Jack loved it in his own way (299–300, 323). The memory of his presence in it, both when they were younger and now, endows it with a sacredness she chooses to cherish. His wistfulness for it and the stories he told his wife Della about it augment its value to her (104, 320). She also keeps it as a haven of hope for Jack: "Now you know where to come when you need help . . . If you ever need to come home, I'll be here" (316–317). In an act of breath-taking sacrificial love, she commits to forgo her own hopes and dreams to keep the home fires burning for him, as a grand gesture of love and hope. "Good" falls far short of capturing the calibre of Glory's soul, but it is a soul forged in the fires of Jack's past and present abandonment of her and his responsibilities.

1.4. Baby Boughton: Lost Soul

The dark secret that haunted Jack was his abandonment of the child of his youth and her mother, Annie Wheeler, a poor teenager (233, 276). Jack confides his struggle with guilt to Glory: "Say you do something terrible. And it's done. And you can't change it. Then how do you live the rest of your life?" (99). His father Robert was "stunned" and "winded" by it, but he never failed to extend grace (7). Jack believed that his father found it unforgivable, which deepened his sense of estrangement: "I knew I had done something he couldn't forgive. He thought he could. He said he had, but he's a terrible liar. It shocked me that I could hurt him so badly. It scared me" (277). Thus began Jack's 20-year self-exile from Gilead. Glory filled in for Jack as best as she could, herself only a teenager, but in the end the baby died of an infection, perhaps the fault of negligence—poor living conditions—or perhaps simply the nature of human frailty (234).

The unnamed child was the collateral damage of Jack's selfishness and irresponsibility. Though lost to the world before her time, she brought joy to her mother, Glory, and presumably both sets of parents, despite the scandal that caused her existence in the first place. Loved in life and in death, she remained for Glory and Robert part of the family. For Jack, however, she only reminded him of his misspent youth and his moral failings. For Glory, the mere mention of Annie Wheeler or her child brings tears to her eyes, but she does not regret their existence (150). They brought joy to their life, and she wants Jack to know that, to ease his conscience. The affair demonstrates the interconnectedness of suffering: Jack's actions ripple through two families. But at the center of the devastation was an innocent little girl who never knew her father, never knew family stability, and ultimately fell victim to conditions she did not create and could not prevent.

1.5. Robert Boughton, Jr.: Restless Soul

We do not learn of the secret treasure of Jack's heart until the final pages of *Home*, although readers of *Gilead* will remember: "Jack Boughton has a wife and a child" (Robinson 2004, p. 217). Guarded and distrustful, as well as protective of their feelings, Jack never told them about his son, but when Della visited their home with her boy, Glory suddenly realized: "Jack had a beautiful child, a beautiful son" (322). He plays baseball and wants to be a preacher, and he loves his father, who has disappointed him again by his absence. We do not know much else about him (*Gilead* fills out the picture), but we can reasonably infer that he will always wonder about his father, even if he has a fine step-father one day. He will ask himself why his father left them, why he could not hold a job, and why his life was so hard. Jack's absence plants a seed of restlessness that might one day set him on a journey to discover the answers, such as they are.

2. Theodicy and Domesticity: A Theological Analysis

2.1. Suffering Love: "Love is Tears"

These five vignettes illustrate the reality of suffering love, especially in family life, often the site of our most intimate and immediate encounters with sorrow. All the characters suffer because of their love for Jack, whose estrangement taints their happiness and whose despair imperils their joy. Does Robinson's attention to the inexorable connection between love and suffering in the novel constitute a nascent domestic theodicy? No, but it does draw our attention to an important facet of theodicy, found especially in cruciform theodicies, that love suffers (Scott 2015, pp. 145–72). Poets and playwrights have understood this inescapable principle of life, and it opens theological vistas into the mystery of suffering, even if it does not solve the problem of evil. If her foray into domestic suffering might leave the analytic philosopher unsatisfied, it might at least stimulate an analysis of the theological implications of suffering love for theodicy.

First, to love is to suffer: live long enough, love deeply enough, and life will break your heart into a thousand pieces. Jürgen Moltmann argues that divine love entails divine suffering: "The God who is love, and who loves every one of his creatures with a love that is infinite, is bound to experience sorrow ... " (Moltmann 1993a, p. 39). God cannot be impassible because that would undercut love: "For a God who is incapable of suffering is a being who cannot be involved ... He cannot weep, for he has no tears. But the one who cannot suffer cannot love either" (Moltmann 1993b, p. 222). Nicholas Wolterstorff, reflecting on the death of his son, concurs: "Love in our world is suffering love ... God is love. That is why he suffers ... Suffering is the meaning of our world. For Love is the meaning. And Love suffers" (Wolterstorff 1987, pp. 89–90). In a poem, C. S. Lewis succinctly summarizes the correlation: "Love is tears" (Lewis 1964, p. 123).

The concept of *perichoresis* or *circumincessio* illuminates the theological grounding of suffering love (McGrath 2016, p. 453). Theological anthropology posits as its first principle that humans are created in the image of God (Genesis 1: 26). In finite, flawed ways, humans mirror the divine life. God, conceived as Trinity, exists in an eternal interplay of Father, Son, and Spirit where the three Persons are internal to one another. Perichoresis signifies the mutual indwelling or co-interpenetration of the Persons: in any one Person, the other two are eternally present. Thus, they exist in an indissoluble, ineffable unity. Humans mutually indwell each other too, not ontologically (as with God), but emotionally. Love creates room for another inside the self, which makes it vulnerable to the pain of loss, rejection, and disappointment. The other's pain, then, becomes internal to the self, since their well-being has merged with it, as we see in *Home*.

So suffering love signifies the human capacity to internalize the suffering of another. Insofar as it co-suffers compassionately and empathetically, it reflects the love of God, which suffers in solidarity with human suffering, for human sinfulness, and by human hands, as Moltmann explains: "The suffering of God with the world, the suffering of God from the world, and the suffering of God for the world are the highest forms of creative love, which desires free fellowship with the world and free response in the world" (Moltmann 1993a, p. 60). Suffering love, therefore, represents the highest manifestation of human love, often displayed in families. While the concept of suffering love in God and in human relationships does not formally solve the problem of evil, it charts a theological trajectory that takes theodicy in new directions (such the domestic realm) and contains new resources for reflection (i.e., redemptive suffering).

2.2. Hope: Souls in Waiting

After 20 years of worrying, Jack's father knew the intimate connection between love and suffering. The only possible way to alleviate his suffering was to sever his love, which he tried, unsuccessfully: "So many times, over the years, I've tried not to love you so much. I never got anywhere with it, but I tried. I'd say, He doesn't care a thing about us . . . . Your mother always said, You imagine some happiness is going to come out of all this, all this waiting and hoping, but it never will. So I tried to put an end to it. But I couldn't" (272–73). Robert could no more stop loving Jack than he could stop believing in the happy ending his wife warned him against. She died without knowing Jack's whereabouts or seeing him again (58), but Robert hung on to life long enough to see him again and, in his mind, that was vindication for hope, and of the "goodness of the Lord" (274), the verification of which awaited Jack's arrival, in his mind.

But hope seems in woefully short supply in *Home*. Old age and ill health prevent Robert from sustaining the grace he cultivated a lifetime to give to Jack. Jack attempts suicide, gives up on his dream of making a life together with his wife and son, and leaves town just before his brothers and sisters converge on Gilead to pay their final respects to their dying father. So there is no Boughton family reunion, no restoration of Jack to his wife and son, and the baby girl of his youth remains buried beneath the earth. His long-anticipated and celebrated return to Gilead after 20 years of unexplained absence yields no results—nothing has changed: Jack remains alienated from his family and himself, his misdeeds remain unredeemed, and his dreams are shattered. Domestic suffering does not always have happy endings, so it should come as no surprise that Robinson denies readers forced or facile resolutions in *Home*. Though grim, it is not hopeless.

Glory envisions a future where she stays at the family home as a gesture of hope and as a tribute to their love for Jack. She imagines Jack's boy, her nephew, returning as a young man, in search of his roots. "He will talk to me a little while, too shy to tell me why he has come, and then he will thank me and leave, walking backward a few steps, thinking, Yes, the barn is still there, yes, the lilacs, even the pot of petunias. This was my father's house. And I will think, He is young. He cannot know that my whole life has come down to this moment" (324–325). Glory embodies the hope that Jack's wife and son will find peace, which might bring him peace. And if Jack never finds peace with himself and others on the open road, if it eludes him until the end of his weary days, perhaps he will find peace on the other side of eternity, answering the unceasing prayers of his family, and completing their unrealized felicity (316). What else is heaven for?

3. Conclusions

It does not take a family reunion to realize the messiness of family life, although they inevitably underscore it. Most of us live it every day, in one way or another, to varying degrees of severity. Sometimes suffering love for family cuts to the bone. Relationships fail. Hearts break. Hope fades. Suffering love, however, refuses to give up, even when "there never was much hope . . . just a fool's hope" (Tolkien 1955, p. 83). But love always hopes, Paul tells us (1 Corinthians 13: 7), so hope refuses to let brokenness have the last word. When and how restoration finally comes remains a mystery, as Robinson's novel intimates with Glory's expectant waiting at the family home for Jack, for his son, and for peace, but it never gives up. In a world of relentless sorrow, we strive to make home a shelter from the storm, a refuge from the slings and arrows of life. Sometimes it is a haven, sometimes it is a hell, and sometimes it vacillates between the two.

Home illustrates a forgotten facet of theodicy: domestic suffering. For our purposes, domestic suffering refers not to the painful experiences of abuse that fit under the category of horrendous evils (Adams 1999), but to the ways families fail to save each other from their worst impulses, and how they light a candle of hope even after the failure. Domestic suffering denotes the suffering love of family life, and its bias toward hope. Theodicy often operates in the visible space of "paradigmatic evil": instances of horror that raise the problem of evil publicly (Scott 2015, pp. 49–51). But for many, the problem of evil surfaces invisibly in their private lives, in the hurt and heartache of broken relationships, in the unreachable pain of others that we internalize. Where is God then? Robinson's novel narrows the focus to the intimate experiences of suffering in family life, and to the inextinguishable love that guides souls in the dark to the light of hope.

Conflicts of Interest: The author declares no conflict of interest.

References

Adams, Marilyn McCord Adams. 1999. *Horrendous Evils and the Goodness of God*. Ithaca: Cornell University Press.
Hemingway, Ernest. 1964. *A Moveable Feast*. New York: Scribner.
Lewis, C. S. 1964. *Poems*. Edited by Walter Hooper. New York: Harcourt Brace & Company.
McGrath, Alister E. 2016. *Christian Theology: An Introduction*, 6th ed. Malden: Wiley-Blackwell.
Moltmann, Jürgen. 1993a. *The Trinity and the Kingdom: The Doctrine of God*. Translated by Margaret Kohl. Minneapolis: Fortress Press.
Moltmann, Jürgen. 1993b. *The Crucified God: The Cross of Christ as the Foundation and Criticism of Christian Theology*. Translated by R. A. Wilson, and John Bowden. Minneapolis: Fortress Press.
Robinson, Marilynne. 2004. *Gilead*. New York: Picador.
Robinson, Marilynne. 2008. *Home*. New York: Picador.
Robinson, Marilynne. 2014. *Lila*. New York: Farrar, Straus and Giroux.
Scott, Mark. S. M. 2015. *Pathways in Theodicy: An Introduction to the Problem of Evil*. Minneapolis: Fortress.
Scott, Mark S. M. 2016. Beauty from Ashes: Aesthetic Transformations of Suffering in *Gilead*. *CRUX* 52: 11–18.
Scott, Mark S. M. 2017. Wrestling with Existence: Pondering Suffering and Grace in *Lila*. *Toronto Journal of Theology*, 33, forthcoming. [CrossRef]
Tolkien, J. R. R. 1955. *The Lord of the Rings: The Return of the King*. New York: Ballantine Books.
Wolterstorff, Nicholas. 1987. *Lament for a Son*. Grand Rapids: Wm. B. Eerdmans Publishing Co.

Article

The Distance between Zurich and Todtnauberg

A. K. Anderson

Department of Religion, Wofford College, Spartanburg, SC 29303, USA; andersonak@wofford.edu

Received: 1 December 2017; Accepted: 27 December 2017; Published: 2 January 2018

Abstract: This paper focuses on two poems written by Paul Celan after first encounters he had with writers who held great significance for him. In 1960 Celan met fellow Jewish poet Nelly Sachs at the Stork Inn in Zurich, and afterwards recorded the event in the poem "Zürich, Zum Storchen". Seven years later, Celan visited Martin Heidegger at his hut in the German mountains. Celan's depiction of this encounter is found in the poem "Todtnauberg". In this essay, I make a two-fold argument regarding the Zurich poem. First I claim that "Todtnauberg" is clearly crafted in light of the earlier Sachs text, a fact that has been overlooked by previous scholarship. As such, it is only in placing the two texts side by side that a complete understanding of "Todtnauberg" comes into view. Second I will indicate how the Zurich poem reflects key elements of an approach to the problem of evil that I term an "enestological theodicy." Such a term needed to be coined, since this sort of theodicy does not fit in the more traditional narrative categories related to the problem of evil.

Keywords: Paul Celan; Nelly Sachs; Martin Heidegger; Todtnauberg; Zurichat the Stork; enestological theodicy

1. Introduction

It takes less than two hours to drive from Todtnauberg, Germany across the border to Zurich, Switzerland. However, in the world of Paul Celan's poetry, these two sites seem utterly remote from one another. Both locations appear in poems he wrote about first meetings he had with writers who were particularly significant to him. After exchanging letters for a number of years with his fellow Jewish poet Nelly Sachs, Celan met her for the first time in May 1960 when she came from Sweden to receive a literary award in Germany—her first return to that country since 1940 when she fled the Holocaust. Celan depicted their initial meeting at the Stork Inn in Zurich in his poem "Zürich, Zum Storchen."

Celan's life, like Sachs', was shattered and haunted by the Holocaust, as he lost both of his parents in the Shoah, and he himself spent time in labor camps. As such, his first meeting with Martin Heidegger in July 1967 was very different than the interaction with Sachs. While both men had admired the work of the other from a distance, Celan approached their first encounter with an understandable ambiguity, given Heidegger's links in the 1930s to National Socialism. Nevertheless Celan ventured to Heidegger's mountain hut, and afterwards presented his version of the interaction in "Todtnauberg."

This later poem has received extensive attention over the years, much more than "Zürich" has. This essay, however, will focus in particular on this less famous poem, in order to make a two-fold argument about it. First I will claim that "Todtnauberg" is clearly crafted in light of the earlier Sachs text, a fact that has been overlooked by previous scholarship. As such, it is only in placing the two texts side by side that a complete understanding of "Todtnauberg" comes into view. Second I will indicate how the Zurich poem reflects key elements of an approach to the problem of evil that I term an "enestological theodicy." Such a term needed to be coined, since this sort of theodicy does not fit in the more traditional narrative categories related to the problem of evil.

I will go about this in four primary steps. The first three are based on comparing sections of the poems. Part one will consider parallels between the first two portions of each text. Part two will focus on the longest section of each text (in each case it is the third section). It is here that the connection between the two poems is clearest, as Celan uses similar wording to craft parallels between the respective responses of the Jewish God and Heidegger to the Holocaust. Part three will then turn to the remainder of the poems, which is where the texts diverge most clearly. Finally, part four will provide an explanation of key aspects of the enestological type of theodicy, especially notable in the "Zürich" poem.

2. On the Day of an Ascension

ZÜRICH, ZUM STORCHEN [Section 1 and Section 2]
Für Nelly Sachs

Vom Zuviel war die Rede, vom
Zuwenig. Von Du
und Aber-Du, von
der Trübung durch Helles, von
Jüdischem, von
deinem Gott.

Da-
Von.
Am Tag einer Himmelfahrt, das
Münster stand drüben, es kam
mit einigem Gold übers Wasser.

[ZURICH, AT THE STORK
For Nelly Sachs

Our talk was of Too Much, of
Too Little. Of Thou
and Yet-Thou, of
clouding through brightness, of
Jewishness, of
your God.

Of
that.
On the day of an ascension, the
Minster stood over there, it came
with some gold across the water.][1]

TODTNAUBERG [Section 1 and Section 2]
Arnika, Augentrost, der
Trunk aus dem Brunnen mit dem
Sternwürfel drauf,

in der

---

[1] All translations of Celan's poetry in the text are by John Felstiner (Celan 2001, pp. 140–41, 314–15). Full versions of both poems, with Felstiner's attendant translations, are provided as an Appendix Λ.

Hütte,

[TODTNAUBERG
 Arnica, Eyebright, the
drink from the well with the
star die on top,

in the
hut,]

      Both of these poems are written about encounters occuring under the shadow of the Shoah, but
the titles hint at the different directions these meetings eventually take. The "stork" reference in
"Zürich" suggests more than the literal location where Celan and Sachs meet. It points to Celan's
sense of new life emerging from the encounter (the content of this new life will be explained in section
four below). By contrast "Todtnauberg" suggests the opposite outcome. The *"Tod"* in Todtnauberg
hints at an interaction that will ultimately result in a form of death, not in new existence. Further,
the personal dedication to Nelly Sachs in the "Zürich" text stands in stark contrast to the indirect,
impersonal reference to Heidegger in "Todtnauberg" as *"Denkenden"* ("The thinking one").
      The direction of these initial contrasts then seems to be undercut in the first section of each poem.
"Todtnauberg" begins with a sense of hope, recovery, and serenity, as it describes the water found in
the well outside Heidegger's hut, as well as two flowers linked to healing: arnica, which soothes aches
and bruises, and eyebright, which, per its German equivalent *Augentrost*, is thought to provide comfort
to one's eyes. However, this peaceful scene also emphasizes silence, at least in terms of the absence
of human voice. By contrast, the human voice is immediately apparent in "Zürich", with its early
reference to talk (*"die Rede"*). The discussion seems more monotonous and exhausting than hopeful, as
evidenced by the seven separate uses of "von" ("of") in the first eight lines. Much is talked about, but
the result is dissatisfying, either "too much" or "too little". Whatever the problems are in the meeting
with Sachs, silence is not one of them.
      Despite the different beginnings, both poems are suffused with religious references. The beginning
sections of both poems evoke the people of Israel. The reference is explicit in the Sachs poem with its
mention of *"Judischem"*, but it is also implicit in "Todtnauberg" when Celan notes the star die or cube
above the well outside Heidegger's hut. In Celan's poetry in general, references to stars bring to mind
the Star of David, even if no specific reference to Israel is made.
      Further, both sections deal with architecture of a religious or spiritual sort. In "Todtnauberg" the
term used for Heidegger's hut (*"Hütte"*) is also the word for tabernacle (as in another Celan poem,
"Hüttenfenster"). The duality of this term fits the quasi-spiritual meaning with which Heidegger
endowed the building. As Adam Sharr (Sharr 2006, p. 103) notes, Heidegger "responded to the hut and
its mountains through a routine of almost monastic subsistence, affirming there his belief in a liturgy
of being and delineating life by its passage in routine". This was Heidegger's church of nature, linking
him to the "power of creation" apart from the mediation of any tradition (ibid., p. 65). In contrast to
this nature temple, Celan meets with Sachs in the city, across the Limmat River from the Grossmünster
Cathedral. Celan was not a Christian, nor a believing Jew, but both he and Sachs found a meaning in
being able to see the shining gold of the church reflected in the water from where they sat at the Stork
Inn across the river. Such Christian imagery is not unusual in Celan's poetry since "Christian topoi
are as important an imaginative resource for Celan as traditional Jewish ones, and often the two are
simultaneously invoked" (Bernstein 2000, p. 106).
      In this section of the "Zürich" poem, the most significant Christian reference is to the Day of
Ascension, the day on which Celan and Sachs meet at the Stork. In the broad Christian narrative of
history, three key higher times involve creation (protology), the life and actions of Jesus (Christology),
and the end of time (eschatology). While these all clearly diverge in their focus and meaning, what
they, as traditionally viewed, share is that the main action in each is initiated and carried out by the

divine. The Day of Ascension inaugurates a different era in this grand narrative, namely a period between the times where the focus is on human action, albeit action inspired by God. In the Ascension, the direct divine presence on earth departs, leaving humans in the ongoing present to act as witnesses to this higher presence. While protology, Christology, and eschatology are well-established terms for talking about this broad Christian view of history, there is no parallel word for this post-Ascension period of the ongoing present. As such, I have coined "enestological" to serve as the companion term for talking about this phase in the Christian narrative. This word is derived from the Greek ενιστημι, which means "to be at hand" or "to be present". In this poem, Celan chooses to emphasize that he and Sachs meet on a day that highlights that humans have been left in the here and now, and the responsibility for the future is in our hands.

3. "Death-Rattled" Words

ZÜRICH, ZUM STORCHEN [Section 3]

Von deinem Gott war die Rede, ich sprach
gegen ihn, ich
liess das Herz, das ich hatte,
hoffen:
auf
sein höchstes, umröcheltes, sein
haderndes Wort—

[ZURICH, AT THE STORK

Our talk was of your God, I spoke
against him, I let the heart
I had
hope:
for
his highest, death-rattled, his
wrangling word—]

TODTNAUBERG [Section 3]

die in das Buch
—wesen Namen nahms auf
vor dem meinen?—
die in dies Buch
geschreibene Zeile von
einer Hoffnung, heute,
auf eines Denkenden
(un-
Gesäumt kommendes)
Wort
im Herzen,

[TODTNAUBERG

into the book
—whose name did it take in
before mine?—
the line written into

this book about
a hope, today,
for a thinker's
(un-
delayed coming)
word
in the heart,]

While the contrast in the two poems' titles shows one way in which Celan wrote "Todtnauberg" as a companion to "Zürich", it is the third (and longest) sections of each poem that provide the clearest evidence that the Heidegger poem was in part constructed using the model found in the earlier Sachs poem. In both poems the third section provides the key moment of transition, as it moves the text from the initial, introductory stage to its concluding point. In both cases, this is done by focusing on similar themes, with variations of three key terms (word, heart, and hope) proving central in each.

It is in these respective sections that the evil of the Holocaust emerges clearly. In "Zürich" Celan uses "*umröcheltes*" as one of the three modifiers he applies to the response he seeks from Sachs' God. "Death-rattled" suggests that any possible reply by the Jewish God would have to be impacted in a shattering way by the Shoah. In the third section of "Todtnauberg" by contrast the focus is not on those who suffered but on the perpetrators, or at least those who endorsed the ideology behind the horror that was inflicted on millions of people. While the previous section ends with reference to the seemingly serene "*Hütte*" out in nature, this portion of the poem begins inside the hut, where a more insidious side is revealed. As Celan signs Heidegger's guest book, he wonders about others who have visited before him, especially those who would have met with Heidegger when he was associated with National Socialism.

This past link to the Nazis is an overriding concern of Celan's during his visit to Todtnauberg. The words "word", "heart", and "hope" emerge at this point in the narrative, in reference to Celan's reaction to Heidegger's past. As Celan writes in the hut's guestbook he expresses his own hope for some words of acknowledgment, confession, and explanation from Heidegger ... words that would either come from Heidegger's heart, to Celan's, or both ("*einer Hoffnung, heute, auf eines Denkenden [...] Wort im Herzen*").

Just as Celan hopes for an accounting from Heidegger for his actions and inactions during the time of the Nazis, so, too, does he seek a response from the God Sachs continues to believe in despite the horrors of the Holocaust. Celan takes on the role of a modern Job, challenging the Jewish God, and demanding an explanation for the atrocities carried out against God's chosen people. Celan protests against the unfathomable scale of the destruction to lives and hearts brought about by the Nazis. However, despite Celan's non-belief, he nevertheless admits he left his heart open to some revelatory response, a word from the beyond ("*ich liess das Herz, das ich hatte, hoffen: auf sein [...] Wort*").

As such, in both poems hope exists for receiving an explanation for silence in the face of the Holocaust. It should be noted, however, that while these poems are so tightly linked in these ways, a crucial difference is in place at the end of the third sections of "Zürich" and "Todtnauberg". While language makes its first appearance in the narrative of "Todtnauberg", it is only in writing done by Celan himself—no words have been spoken by either Celan or Heidegger. By contrast, the third section of "Zürich" again emphasizes the interaction and debate taking place between Sachs and Celan (as in the first line: "Our talk was of your God, I spoke [...]"). This central distinction between the poems is crucial to note, since it lays the groundwork for understanding the concluding sections of each work.

4. We Really Don't Know What Counts

ZÜRICH, ZUM STORCHEN [concluding sections]

Dein Aug sah mir zu, sah hinweg,
dein Mund
sprach sich dem Aug zu, ich hörte:

Wir
wissen ja nicht, weisst du,
wir
wissen ja nicht,
was
gilt.

[ZURICH, AT THE STORK

Your eye looked at me, looked away,
your mouth
spoke toward the eye, I heard:

We
really don't know, you know,
we
really don't know
what
counts.]

TODTNAUBERG [concluding sections]

Waldwasen, uneingeebnet,
Orchis und Orchis, einzeln,

Krudes, später, im Fahren,
deutlich,

der uns fährt, der Mensch,
der's mit anhört,

die halb-
beschrittenen Knüppel-
pfade im Hochmoor,

Feuchtes,
viel.

[TODTNAUBERG

woodland turf, unleveled,
Orchis and Orchis, singly,

crudeness, later, while driving,
clearly,

the one driving us, the man
who hears it too,

the half-
trodden log-
paths on high moorland,

dampness,
much.]

The division between these two sections can be narrowed down to two words, one from each text: the unified "we" of Sachs and Celan in the Zurich poem and the "singly" walking Celan and Heidegger in "Todtnauberg". While the "Stork" in the title refers in part to the Inn at which Celan and Sachs meet, it also suggests new life and the birth of a connection that is evident in the solidarity exhibited at the end of that poem. Likewise, while Todtnauberg is the actual location for the Celan/Heidegger encounter, but the "*Tod*" (death) in the title also applies to the lack of renewal and unity that results from Celan's pilgrimage to Heidegger's hut. This section will focus on how these differing results come about in the poems.

In the concluding section of "Todtnauberg" the omission of the human voice is finally broken, albeit only in a single instance, in a solitary word. "*Krudes*" is the term used to describe the conversation that takes place between Heidegger and Celan as they ride together. While John Felstiner translates the term as "crudeness" (as above), a more accurate sense of the term in this context might be "blunt" or "raw", older meanings discussed by James Lyon (Lyon 2006, p. 183).[2] In a letter to his wife about the Heidegger meeting Celan writes "in the car we had a very serious conversation in words that were unmistakable on my part" (ibid., p. 163). Celan does not mention Heidegger's response, but his use of "unmistakable" suggests his own words were "raw" or "blunt" as he questioned Heidegger about his past. The poem, too, gives no indication of a response by Heidegger, and this fits with what Anne Carson (Carson 1999, p. 34) writes regarding this poem: "Heidegger had long been master of 'the danger-free privilege of silence'". This aloof response to Celan's "raw" emotions and speech is underscored by Celan's reference to the driver of the car (Gerhard Neumann), who actually "hears" ("*anhört*") Celan's words and the human cry and hope within them in a way that Heidegger does not. As such, Neumann is referred to as a full-fledged human being in the poem ("*der Mensch*"), while Heidegger is only described in his capacity as a thinker ("*Denkenden*").

Likewise, hearing is central to the conclusion of "Zürich". In this case, however, the one who hears is Celan himself, and what he hears from Sachs is an admission of shared perplexity when recalling the memory of extreme suffering (a contrast to the entrenched silence in the face of the same, as seen in "Todtnauberg"). Despite the trauma of the Holocaust, Sachs remained a believer, unlike Celan. Sachs, who was in Switzerland to receive the Droste Prize, said in her acceptance speech, "'Everything counts' in God's eyes" (Felstiner 1995, p. 159). As such, she was broadly asserting knowledge of the divine plan and purpose, even after the horror that the Jews endured at the hands of the Nazis. However, in her meeting with Celan, she steps back from such assurance, and meets him halfway by acknowledging human finitude and doubt. Up until this concluding section, the poem has been one of opposition and separation: the "I" of Celan against Sachs' "you". The first mention of "We" therefore signals a change, as a point of solidarity is reached. Recalling the pivotal third section of the poem, when Celan expresses his hope for a reply from God about the Holocaust but receives none, this final section could indicate that Sachs' words are a stand-in for that divine word. If nothing else, this serves as a fitting end to a poem rooted in the Day of Ascension. The divine may have been present, but in the ongoing moment between the times, the focus is on human agency and interaction. Here there is a moment of genuine human connection, one based on an expression of vulnerability and

---

2   While finding Lyon's discussion of this term from the poem useful, I disagree with his general interpretation of the Celan/Heidegger encounter. He thinks Celan was relatively satisfied with their meeting, but for the reasons I am articulating in this essay, such a stance goes against the overall sense and feel of the text, especially when read in the context of the "Zürich" poem.

ignorance. Such is the new life signaled by the poem's title, which provides a stark contrast to the isolation and figurative death that suffuses Celan's "Todtnauberg". In Celan's poetry, it turns out, the distance between Zurich and Todtnauberg is an abyss.

5. A Particularly, But Not Uniquely, Modern Theodicy

Regarding the history of attempts to address the problem of evil, Marjorie Suchocki (Suchocki 1988, p. 1) writes that "religious thinkers have sought the reason and resolution of those sorrows at the edges of history—in protology and eschatology". This quote clearly covers a significant part of the history of theodicy, as many thinkers have sought to discern the "Why?" of the origins of evil, or tried to riddle out the transhistorical redemption of evil. Within the Christian tradition another method has been to view the suffering of the world through a Christological lens and to address the reality of evil via the person and work of Jesus. Whatever differences these three positions may have, they share two key things. First, they deal with the matters of suffering and injustice through turning to the grand narrative of a tradition (with that narrative ranging from creation to the end of time). Second, their focus is on what God has done or will do vis-à-vis evil, that is to say, the emphasis is on specific divine action regarding these horrors. While these three ways of approaching the theodicy question all have venerable histories, they do not exhaust all the primary narrative approaches to this topic.

As noted above, protology, Christology, and eschatology are all well-established terms for discussing major moments in particular faith narratives, but there is no comparable companion word to refer to the category of the ongoing present. This is significant because one of the major developments in the modern period is the growing agreement among some writers that God's action in the present is what must be stressed when discussing evil, rather than putting one's attention on the distant past (protology or Christology) or the remote, uncertain future (eschatology). It is for this reason that I have coined the term enestological to express this general position. The need for such a category is seen in the fact that a whole host of modern writers do not easily fit primarily either into the protological, Christological, or eschatological types of theodicy. Among these include a variety of feminist, womanist, black, and other liberation thinkers, as well as process theologians. Key elements typical of this enestological outlook, albeit in a highly condensed form, are evidenced in Celan's "Zürich" poem.[3]

Three related facets combine to make the text a reflection of such a present-oriented approach to the problem of evil. First, there is Celan's protest in the face of the enormity of the suffering and injustice wrought in the Holocaust. While, of course, unspeakable acts and horrors suffuse history, the modern period has brought with it even greater capacity for humans to enact such havoc and destruction on others. In turn, protests such as Celan expresses in this poem have grown in number and intensity. It is such awareness of the modern increase for the capacity to unleash evil that serves as a, if not the, impetus for the enestological outlook. One paradigmatic enestological writer, Emmanuel Levinas (Levinas 1998, p. 97), articulates this viewpoint when he states that "The disproportion between suffering and every [traditional] theodicy was shown at Auschwitz with a glaring, obvious clarity". As such, a new approach to evil and suffering needed to be developed.

In light of this, second, the poem expresses dissatisfaction with and a distance from explanations and justifications of the existence of evil. While Sachs may have some sense that for God "everything counts", she backs off this simple, blanket statement in light of the back and forth she has with Celan. If she did not do so, she would be saying both "Too Much" and far "Too Little" regarding the Holocaust, and, by extension, endless other moments of horror. The stance they share in the face of the enormity

---

[3] Since Celan himself was not a believer, the claim here is not that he himself was consciously, deliberately articulating a theodicy or an approach to the problem of evil. Rather, the point is that his poem, suffused with religious concepts as it is, ends up expressing key elements of this sort of theodicy.

of human suffering is one of mutual ignorance regarding ultimate answers: "we really don't know what counts". Sarah Pinnock (Pinnock 2002, p. 125), another paradigmatic example of this type, speaks against the simple attempts to construct solutions so that we can feel the evils of existence have been resolved: "Evil must remain a surd, with no resolution, no atonement".[4]

This leads, third, into what is expressed in the poem by the reference to the Day of Ascension. Humans find ourselves in the here and now, we regularly encounter new instances of evil around us, and the responsibility for addressing these lies in our hands. As such, as in the Zurich poem, humans can work in the present moment to alleviate suffering and bring solace to the hurting. In the enestological perspective, the divine is working through these deeds of humanity, but unlike with the protological, Christological, and eschatological stances, the primary action in this viewpoint is on the part of humans. A prime process representative of this type, David Griffin (Griffin 1991, p. 33), echoes this thought when he writes that "process theology agrees with the poem, 'God has no hands but our hands'".

While the enestological type of theodicy has emerged with a particular significance and force in the modern period, it found expression in earlier times as well. An example from the Jewish tradition is the prose conclusion to the Book of Job.[5] While Job 42:7–17 often is dismissed as providing a simplistic, Hollywood ending to a story of extreme suffering and loss, these verses actually contain a complex picture of the relation between divine and human action in the face of evil. While the text portrays God as being, somehow, the ultimate source behind the events of the narrative, the emphasis is on human actions and decisions in the present, and this is seen in three ways in this passage. First, through divine guidance, Job is led to pray on behalf of his three friends, despite the fact that they failed so miserably in their role as comforters to him in his time of need. Second, while God is credited in a general sense with restoring Job's fortunes, the text highlights the fact that the direct means through which Job gets back on his feet is the gifts and assistance of family and friends. Finally, God is described as blessing Job's later life, which includes the birth of ten new children. In this, however, the portrayal is not of a miraculous divine intervention that produces in an instant an entirely new family. Rather, what is shown is Job and his wife coming to a renewed appreciation of the gift of life, and this leads them to the desire to bring new offspring into the world. This embrace of creation and the wonders it contains comes in light of the divine revelation of the glories of existence in Chapters 38–41, and is evidenced in the conclusion by the references to nature in the names of Job's new daughters, translated by Robert Alter (Alter 2010, p. 179) as Dove, Cinnamon, and Horn of Eyeshade. Throughout this concluding prose section of the Book of Job, human activity in the present moment is at the forefront, while divine guidance serves as the backdrop and impetus for that activity.

In sum, Wendy Farley (Farley 1990, p. 127) writes from an enestological perspective that "in the very heart of suffering and oppression" human "resistance to evil is possible; in this resistance divine compassion becomes incarnate". Such incarnation comes about only through human action, and Celan's "Zürich" poem presents a concrete example of such incarnated compassion in the face of loss and grief. If, however, the alternative model found in "Todtnauberg" is the path that humans instead choose to trod, then: the rest is silence.

Acknowledgments: The author thanks Elizabeth Anderson for her careful reading of and helpful feedback on an earlier version of this text.

Conflicts of Interest: The author declares no conflict of interest.

---

[4] It is to be noted that some enestologically-oriented writers take a different stance on this general point. Process theologians, for example, do attempt to provide an explanation for the existence and origin of evil, while nevertheless placing their ultimate stress on the need for humans to act against evil in the present moment.

[5] This is just one way of approaching the problem of evil within the Jewish tradition among many. Elliot Dorff points out others (Dorff 1999, pp. 116–20), including more protologically oriented free-will theodicies, as well as Jewish writers who stress the importance of an eschatological solution to evil based on belief in the afterlife.

Appendix A. Full Versions of "Zurich" and "Todtnauberg"

ZÜRICH, ZUM STORCHEN

Für Nelly Sachs
Vom Zuviel war die Rede, vom
Zuwenig. Von Du
und Aber-Du, von
der Trübung durch Helles, von
Jüdischem, von
deinem Gott.

Da-
Von.
Am Tag einer Himmelfahrt, das
Münster stand drüben, es kam
mit einigem Gold übers Wasser.

Von deinem Gott war die Rede, ich sprach
gegen ihn, ich
liess das Herz, das ich hatte,
hoffen:
auf
sein höchstes, umrocheltes, sein
haderndes Wort—

Dein Aug sah mir zu, sah hinweg,
dein Mund
sprach sich dem Aug zu, ich hörte:

Wir
wissen ja nicht, weisst du,
wir
wissen ja nicht,
was
gilt.

[ZURICH, AT THE STORK
For Nelly Sachs

Our talk was of Too Much, of
Too Little. Of Thou
and Yet-Thou, of
clouding through brightness, of
Jewishness, of
your God.

Of
that.
On the day of an ascension, the
Minster stood over there, it came
with some gold across the water.

Our talk was of your God, I spoke

against him, I let the heart
I had
hope:
for
his highest, death-rattled, his
wrangling word—

Your eye looked at me, looked away,
your mouth
spoke toward the eye, I heard:

We
really don't know, you know,
we
really don't know
what
counts.]

TODTNAUBERG

Arnika, Augentrost, der
Trunk aus dem Brunnen mit dem
Sternwürfel drauf,
in der
Hütte,

die in das Buch
—wesen Namen nahms auf
vor dem meinen?—
die in dies Buch
geschreibene Zeile von
einer Hoffnung, heute,
auf eines Denkenden
(un-
Gesäumt kommendes)
Wort
im Herzen,

Waldwasen, uneingeebnet,
Orchis und Orchis, einzeln,

Krudes, später, im Fahren,
deutlich,

der uns fährt, der Mensch,
der mit's anhört,

die halb-
beschrittenen Knüppel-
pfade im Hochmoor,

Feuchtes,
viel.

[TODTNAUBERG

Arnica, Eyebright, the
drink from the well with the
star die on top,

in the
hut,

into the book
—whose name did it take in
before mine?—
the line written into
this book about
a hope, today,
for a thinker's
(un-
delayed coming)
word
in the heart,

woodland turf, unleveled,
Orchis and Orchis, singly,

crudeness, later, while driving,
clearly,

the one driving us, the man
who hears it too,

the half-
trodden log-
paths on high moorland,

dampness,
much.]

References

Alter, Robert. 2010. *The Wisdom Books: Job, Proverbs, and Ecclesiastes.* A Translation with Commentary; New York: WW Norton.

Bernstein, Michael Andre. 2000. *Five Portraits: Modernity and the Imagination in Twentieth-Century German Writing.* Evanston: Northwestern.

Carson, Anne. 1999. *Economy of the Unlost (Reading Simonides of Keos with Paul Celan).* Princeton: Princeton University.

Celan, Paul. 2001. *Selected Poems and Prose of Paul Celan.* Translated by John Felstiner. New York: WW Norton.

Dorff, Elliot. 1999. Rabbi, Why Does God Make Me Suffer? In *Pain Seeking Understanding.* Edited by Margaret Mohrmann and Mark Hanson. Cleveland: Pilgrim Press.

Farley, Wendy. 1990. *Tragic Vision and Divine Compassion: A Contemporary Theodicy.* Louisville: Westminster Press.

Felstiner, John. 1995. *Paul Celan: Poet, Survivor, Jew.* New Haven: Yale University.

Griffin, David. 1991. *Evil Revisited: Responses and Reconsiderations.* Albany: SUNY Press.

Levinas, Emmanuel. 1998. Useless Suffering. In *Emmanuel Levinas: Entre Nous.* Translated by Michael Smith, and Barbara Harshav. New York: Columbia Press.

Lyon, James. 2006. *Paul Celan and Martin Heidegger: An Unresolved Conversation, 1951–1970*. Baltimore: Johns Hopkins.

Pinnock, Sarah. 2002. *Beyond Theodicy: Jewish and Christian Continental Thinkers Respond to the Holocaust*. Albany: SUNY Press.

Sharr, Adam. 2006. *Heidegger's Hut*. Cambridge: MIT Press.

Suchocki, Marjorie. 1988. *The End of Evil: Process Eschatology in Historical Context*. Albany: SUNY Press.

Article

The Multiverse and Divine Creation

Michael Almeida

Department of Philosophy and Classics, University of Texas at San Antonio, San Antonio, TX 78249, USA; michael.almeida@utsa.edu

Received: 2 November 2017; Accepted: 22 November 2017; Published: 24 November 2017

Abstract: I provide the account of divine creation found in multiverse theorists Donald Turner, Klaas Kraay, and Tim O'Connor. I show that the accounts Kraay and Turner offer are incoherent. God does not survey all possible worlds and necessarily actualize those universes in the (on balance) good worlds or the worthy worlds. If God necessarily actualizes the multiverse, we have no idea which universes are parts of that multiverse. I show next that Tim O'Connor's multiverse account of creation is also incoherent. I argue that a preferable multiverse would include a much greater variety of universes than are included in Turner, Kraay or O'Connor. In the last section I offer some concluding remarks.

Keywords: creation; philosophy of religion; multiverses

1. Introduction

Among the advantages of the theistic multiverse is that it aims to satisfy the principle of plenitude. According to A.O. Lovejoy, the principle of plenitude entails that creation is as extensive and abundant as possible:

> ... the extent and the abundance of the creation must be as great as the possibility of existence and commensurate with the productive capacity of a 'perfect' and inexhaustible Source (Lovejoy 1932).

There are infinitely many universes in the theistic multiverse. Multiverse theory further ensures that the plenitude of creation is consistent with being the best possible world. Indeed, the theistic multiverse is the uniquely best world.

The theistic multiverse provides, in addition, a powerful theodicy. There is not a single instance of gratuitous evil anywhere in the entire multiverse—indeed there is not a single instance of contingent evil in the multiverse. There are plenty of instances of evil—there might well be vast amounts of undeserved suffering, horrendous moral evil, and terrible natural disasters in many universes—but there is not a single instance of evil that is not metaphysically necessary. And since every instance of evil is metaphysically necessary, it is impossible to actualize the best possible world without permitting every instance. It is simply impossible that any evil in the multiverse should be reduced, mitigated, or eliminated.

For all of the theoretical advantages of the theistic multiverse—and there are certainly many—it offers an account of divine creation that is impossible. The account of creation according to which God necessarily actualizes all of the good-enough—or the on balance good or worthy or threshold-surpassing—universes from all of the simple or complex worlds is not a coherent view. If God necessarily actualizes the best multiverse, the correct account of divine creation does not involve any choice at all among possible universes. There is indeed no reason to believe that the theistic multiverse includes any universes that are on balance good or worthy or threshold surpassing.

In Section 2 I provide the account of divine creation found in multiverse theorists Donald Turner, Klaas Kraay, and Tim O'Connor. In Section 3 I show that the accounts Kraay and Turner offer are incoherent. God does not survey all possible worlds and necessarily actualize those universes in the (on balance) good worlds or the worthy worlds. If God necessarily actualizes the multiverse, we have no idea which universes are parts of that multiverse.[1] In Section 4 I show that Tim O'Connor's multiverse account of creation is also incoherent. In Section 5 I argue that a preferable multiverse would include a much greater variety of universes than are included in Turner, Kraay or O'Connor. I offer some concluding remarks in Section 6.

2. Creating the Theistic Multiverse

There is a widely shared view that the extent of divine creation must be proportional to the maximal greatness of God. Giordano Bruno, philosopher and theologian, expressed the following "heretical" views on the creation of an infinite divine power.

> I hold the universe to be infinite as a result of the infinite divine power; for I think it unworthy of divine goodness and power to have produced merely one finite world when it was able to bring into being an infinity of worlds. Wherefore I have expounded that there is an endless number of individual worlds like our earth. I regard it, with Pythagoras, as a star, and the moon, the planets, and the stars are similar to it, the latter being of endless number. All these bodies make an infinity of worlds; they constitute the infinite whole, in infinite space, an infinite universe, that is to say, containing innumerable worlds. So that there is an infinite measure in the universe and an infinite multitude of worlds. But this may be indirectly opposed to truth according to the faith.[2]

Bruno's ontology reverses the order of worlds and universes, or at least seems to. Universes include an infinity of worlds rather than worlds including an infinity of universes. But he insists on an infinite creation from an infinite divine power. Similar views on divine creation are expressed in Kant's *Universal Natural History and Theory of the Heavens*:

> But what is at last the end of these systematic arrangements? Where shall creation itself cease? It is evident that in order to think of it as in proportion to the power of the Infinite being, it must have no limits at all ... the field of the revelation of the Divine attributes is as infinite as these attributes themselves (Kant 1969).

A creation that is in proportion to the power of an infinite being, according to Kant, must itself be infinitely or limitlessly large. More recently, Paul Draper has expressed similar thoughts concerning what a perfectly good God of limitless resources would create:

> ... a perfectly good God of limitless creative resources would be likely to create vastly many worlds, including magnificent worlds of great perfection as well as good but essentially flawed worlds that are more in need of special providence .... For by creating valuable worlds, God adds to the excellence of reality and also provides for the expression of divine benevolence, divine justice, and other virtues (Draper 2004).

These views all seem to express some logical or metaphysical relationship between maximal greatness and the principle of plenitude. We noted above that the principle of plenitude is most closely associated with Arthur Lovejoy. The principle of plenitude, according to Lovejoy, states that no genuine potentiality can remain unfulfilled:

> ... the extent and the abundance of the creation must be as great as the possibility of existence and commensurate with the productive capacity of a 'perfect' and inexhaustible Source ... the world is the better the more things it contains (Lovejoy 1932).

---

[1]   I will argue in what follows that God should actualize every possible universe. This perhaps follows trivially on the account of multiverse creation under discussion.
[2]   See (White 2002). See also (Munitz 1951).

The principle of plenitude is also invoked in the explanation of the theistic multiverse. According to Donald Turner, it is God's love that explains why he creates anything at all. Divine love also explains why God creates every valuable cosmos.

> But why would God be committed to the Principle of Plenitude? In fact, why should God create anything at all? . . . .God is a loving God, and while he does not need anyone to show his love to, nonetheless, his love leads him to create beings to show his love to.
>
> . . . . So God creates a cosmos full of beings. But why stop there? The same considerations that lead him to create this cosmos would lead him to create any valuable cosmos (Turner 2014, p. 11).

According to the multiverse account of creation, the theistic multiverse is composed of an important subset of the possible universes in metaphysical space. A maximally great being creates *all and only* those universes that meet a certain standard of value.

> . . . Thus I claim that God ought to actualize that complex possible world which contains cosmoi corresponding to every simple possible world above some cut-off line—for example, every simple possible world with a favorable balance of good over evil.[3]

According to Turner's account of creation, God surveys all possible worlds—perhaps all of the simple possible worlds—and selects for creation the cosmoi of all of those possible worlds that are on balance good. The theistic multiverse therefore includes all and only those cosmoi that are on balance good. It is easy to see that the theistic multiverse, on Turner's account, is the best possible world. It is God's perfect goodness, omnipotence, and love that explain why God actualizes the best possible world—the theistic multiverse.

Klaas Kraay offers several plausible principles that aim to explain the divine creation of the theistic multiverse.

> Pushed to their logical limit, these considerations suggest that an unsurpassably powerful, knowledgeable, and good deity will create every universe that is worth creating. I suspect that this way of thinking is motivated by a principle of plenitude . . . [4]

Since it also true that God cannot create a universe that is unworthy of creation, God must create all and only the universes worth creating. The universes that God selects from are instantiations or concretizations of possible worlds.[5] So, just as God can survey possible worlds and evaluate them according to their good-making and bad-making properties, God can survey the universes and evaluate them according to their good-making and bad-making properties.

> The axiological framework for possible worlds discussed [above] can now be applied, mutatis mutandis, to universes . . . . As we earlier restricted our attention to possible worlds actualizable by God, let's now restrict our attention to universes creatable by God. Finally, just as there are three candidate hierarchies of possible worlds . . . so too there are three candidate hierarchies of universes: either there is exactly one unsurpassable universe, or else there are none, or else there are infinitely many.[6]

On Kraay's picture of divine creation, God surveys all of the possible universes we find in possible worlds. God evaluates the universes according to their good-making and bad-making properties. Finally, God creates all and only the universes that are worthy of creation in the theistic multiverse. Indeed, God *necessarily* creates all and only the universes that are worthy of creation.

---

[3] Ibid., p. 11.
[4] See (Kraay 2010, p. 361).
[5] Kraay's terminology is that universes 'comprise' worlds. In Kraay's metaphysics, possible worlds are maximal states of affairs. So it is perhaps better to see universes as actualized or concretized maximal states of affairs.
[6] Ibid., p. 360.

If there is a unique unsurpassable world ... there is good reason to think that it would be morally unacceptable for God to allow any other world to be actual. But if it is morally unacceptable for God to permit any world other than the unique best to be actual, it seems that this is the only world that could be actual—which is just to say that it is the only possible world ... (Kraay 2011)

According to Tim O'Connor, God creates a superuniverse containing every single universe that meets his own standard of goodness.

More likely ... is that God would elect to create that super-universe containing every single universe at or above [some goodness threshold] τ ... [7]

According to O'Connor, the superuniverse that results would be infinitely valuable. Indeed, God would have a choice among such infinitely valuable superuniverses. And, again, for O'Connor, the principle of plenitude explains the creation of the superuniverse.

... So God has reason not to settle for creating a superuniverse that has only one universe as a member. Nor will it help for God to create two or three-membered superuniverse, or in fact an n-membered superuniverse, for any finite value n. But it would appear to help if God were to create an infinitely membered superuniverse, provided there is no finite upper limit on the value of its members.[8]

According to O'Connor, God surveys all of the universes existing in all possible worlds and creates all and only those universes whose value exceeds some value τ.

3. Incoherent Creation: Turner and Kraay

Both Turner and Kraay maintain that it follows from the principle of plenitude and God's essential perfection—God's maximal greatness—that God actualizes the best possible world. The best possible world, according to Kraay and Turner, is the theistic multiverse. Turner urges that God *ought to actualize* the theistic multiverse and since, necessarily, God does what he ought to do, God necessarily actualizes the theistic multiverse.

Kraay also concludes that God—a maximally great being—necessarily actualizes the theistic multiverse.

theists should maintain that the actual world is a multiverse featuring all and only universes worthy of being created and sustained by God, and—more controversially—it recommends that theists embrace modal collapse: the claim that this multiverse is the only possible world.[9]

But if both Turner and Kraay are right that God necessarily actualizes the best possible world—the theistic multiverse—then both of their accounts of divine creation are flatly incoherent.

Reconsider Turner's account of the divine creation of the theistic multiverse. According to Turner, God surveys the cosmoi of all simple possible worlds and selects for creation those cosmoi whose value is on balance good. The theistic multiverse is composed of all and only those cosmoi that are on balance good. And the theistic multiverse is therefore the best possible world.

But if God necessarily actualizes the theistic multiverse, then this account of divine creation is obviously not possible. If God necessarily actualizes the theistic multiverse, then *there are no simple possible worlds*. If God necessarily actualizes the theistic multiverse, then the theistic multiverse

---

[7] Ibid., p. 117.
[8] See op. cit. (O'Connor 2008, p. 117).
[9] (Kraay 2011, p. 361).

is the only possible world.[10] Therefore, there exist no simple possible worlds whose cosmoi God created in actualizing the best possible world. If God necessarily actualizes the theistic multiverse, then necessarily he does not create cosmoi corresponding to any cosmoi in any simple possible world. It would be impossible for God to do so.

So, if God necessarily actualizes the theistic multiverse, then God creates whatever universes happen to exist in the theistic multiverse. There is nothing else it is possible for him to do. Whatever universes exist in the theistic multiverse are the only universes that exist, full stop. Are all of those universes on balance good? Perhaps they are, but then perhaps not. It is another infelicity in Turner's account of divine creation of the theistic multiverse that he assumes that God actualizes the best possible world only if God creates all of the on balance good cosmoi. If God necessarily actualizes the theistic multiverse, then he actualizes the best possible world *no matter how good or bad* the universes happen to be that compose the theistic multiverse. If God necessarily actualizes the theistic multiverse, then God necessarily actualizes the best possible world. The intrinsic value of universes composing the multiverse is irrelevant to the question of whether the multiverse is the best possible world.

Reconsider Kraay's account of the divine creation of the theistic multiverse. According to Kraay, God creates all of the universes, or sets of universes, that are worthy of creation. All of these universes or sets of universes comprise possible worlds. So, the theistic multiverse is composed of all and only those universes that are worthy of creation. And the theistic multiverse is therefore the best possible world.

But, according to Kraay, God necessarily actualizes the theistic multiverse. So, again, this account of divine creation is not possible. If God necessarily actualizes the theistic multiverse, then *there exist no possible worlds apart from the multiverse*—there simply are no possible worlds except the multiverse. If God necessarily actualizes the theistic multiverse, then the theistic multiverse is the only possible world, full stop. Therefore, there exist no other possible worlds whose universes God surveyed and then created or duplicated in actualizing the best possible world. If God necessarily actualizes the theistic multiverse, then necessarily he does not create all of the worthy universes existing in other possible worlds. That cannot be how divine creation occurs.

How could divine creation occur, if God necessarily actualizes the theistic multiverse? If God necessarily actualizes the multiverse, then God creates whatever universes happen to exist in the theistic multiverse. The universes that comprise the multiverse might all be worthy of creation. But perhaps many of them are not worthy of creation. Perhaps many of them are intrinsically bad worlds. None of these questions matter to whether God actualizes the best possible world. No matter what their intrinsic value or disvalue, God necessarily actualizes the best possible world.

It is an infelicity in Kraay's account of the creation of the theistic multiverse that he assumes that God actualizes the best possible world only if God creates all of the universes worth creating. If God necessarily actualizes the theistic multiverse, then he actualizes the best possible world no matter how worthy or unworthy the universes happen to be that compose the theistic multiverse. If God necessarily actualizes the theistic multiverse, then God necessarily actualizes the best possible world. The intrinsic value of the universes composing the multiverse is not relevant at all to the question of whether the multiverse is the best possible world.

The accounts of divine creation in Turner and Kraay are not coherent. It is impossible that God necessarily actualizes the theistic multiverse and that he creates all of the on balance good or worthy cosmoi existing in all other possible worlds. If God necessarily actualizes the theistic multiverse,

---

[10] Turner updates his views in (Turner 2014). His revised view, which he assimilates to Leibniz's views, is that there are possible worlds that God cannot actualize. To make the revised view work it would have to be true that God actualizes some worlds as a matter of metaphysical necessity and nonetheless there are possible worlds that he cannot actualize. But there could be no possible worlds that it is metaphysically impossible for God to actualize. Alternatively, Turner could hold, with Leibniz, that it is not metaphysically impossible for God to actualize a less-than-ideal world. If that is true then it is hard to see why we need the theistic multiverse.

then there exist no other possible worlds whose universes God might have duplicated or created. If God necessarily actualizes the theistic multiverse, then there is no requirement that the universes composing the multiverse be on balance good or worthy of creation. The theistic multiverse is the best possible world no matter the intrinsic value or disvalue of universes composing that world.

4. Incoherent Creation: O'Connor

According to Timothy O'Connor, God would not create any single membered superuniverse or any finitely membered superuniverse, since there is, for each of them, infinitely many better superuniverses.

> ... it is plausible that God, intending to create, would not wish to settle for a universe than which there are an infinity of better universes, whose increase in value over our universe stretches without limit as we go up the series .... So God has reason not to settle for creating a superuniverse that has only one universe as a member. Nor will it help for God to create a two or three-membered superuniverse, or in fact an n-membered superuniverse, for any finite value n. But it would appear to help if God were to create an infinitely membered superuniverse, provided there is no finite upper limit on the value of its members.[11]

But even the infinitely membered superuniverses are not sufficiently good for God to actualize any one of them.

> More likely ... is that God would elect to create that super-universe containing every single universe at or above [some goodness threshold] τ ... [12]

But, again, O'Connor refines God's principle of selection from among the infinitely valuable worlds.

> ... notice that [as] we go up the scale of superuniverses (unlike universes), eventually the values become infinite, in such a way that the hierarchy seems to 'flatten out'. The superuniverse God creates is one of these equally top-valued members, the choice between them to be decided on grounds *in addition to* objective value.[13]

The additional criteria are measured along three qualitative dimensions of value. First, for each universe, we can assess the intensive value of each of the basic objects. Using criteria for the perfection of each kind of object, this measure concerns the perfection of each object in the universe. Secondly, there is the aggregate value of objects taken collectively. Finally, there is the organic value of each universe, and perhaps the organic value of its subregions.

> The total value of a universe appears then to be a point in three-space. Given that none of a universe's objects may have infinite intensive value, its value in this regard ... will typically not be infinite ... And crucially a universe's organic value will always be less than maximal. Even allowing for infinite aggregative value, then, no single universe will be of maximal value ... Hence, there is a natural impetus for a perfect being to create an infinitely membered superuniverse whose members are ordered by value without an upper bound.[14]

According to O'Connor, then, a perfect being will actualize some rich and infinitely value superuniverse.

---

[11] See (O'Connor 2008, p. 117).
[12] Ibid., p. 117.
[13] Ibid., p. 117.
[14] Ibid., p. 118.

I have argued that all the possibilities deemed creation-worthy by a perfect Creator would conform to a rich structure. Even so, an infinity of options satisfies these constraints, and there is no reason yet uncovered to suppose that any highly particular sort of universe will be deemed necessary.[15]

No highly particular sort of universe is necessary, according to O'Connor, but it is necessary that God actualize a possible world that satisfies the criteria he has set forth. *Necessarily*, God actualizes an infinitely membered, partial ordered superuniverse for which there is no finite upper bound on the intensive value on the objects in each universe and no finite upper bound on the organic value of its universes, all of which exceed the threshold τ.

But O'Connor's account of divine creation of the superuniverse is incoherent. According to O'Connor, God would elect to create that superuniverse containing every single universe at or above some goodness threshold τ. There are superuniverses, according to O'Connor, that contain a single member, a single universe. And there are superuniverses that include n universes for every finite number n. Some of those universes have a value that exceeds some goodness threshold τ and some do not. What God does is survey all of the single (and presumably, finite numbered) universes in the superuniverses. God then elects to create all of those universes that exceed the goodness level τ. And the result is a superuniverse that has infinite value. God chooses to actualize a superuniverse that is among the infinitely valued ones.

But if God necessarily actualizes an infinitely membered, partially ordered superuniverse for which there is no finite upper bound on the intensive value of the objects in each universe and no finite upper bound on the organic value of its universes, all of which exceed the threshold τ, then there *exist no single membered superuniverses*. Indeed, there could not be a superuniverse that is even finitely membered, since God must choose to create a superuniverse from among a subset of the infinitely membered superuniverses.

The picture of divine creation according to which there are sufficiently good universes in various superuniverses that God chooses to create in the top-superuniverses is not a coherent one. It simply cannot be what occurs in divine creation, if it is true that, necessarily, God chooses to actualize a superuniverse that meets the specific criteria that O'Connor specifies. Most of the universes that feature in O'Connor's account of divine creation are necessarily non-existent. So, it is impossible that God should have chosen to create any of them in the divinely preferred set of superuniverses.

5. On Creating All Metaphysical Reality

Multiverse theorists in general restrict the universes composing the theistic multiverse to those meeting some standard of goodness. O'Connor requires that the universes in the superuniverse exceed the threshold τ, Kraay requires that the universes in the theistic multiverse all be worth creating, and Turner requires that the cosmoi in the theistic multiverse all be on balance good. Other multiverse theorists place similar restrictions. Hud Hudson suggests that God would actualize a multiverse that includes a plenitudinous hyperspace that includes every 'world' worth actualizing.

> ... I am suggesting ... that the many independent regions of a plenitudinous hyperspace provide [the hyperspace] theorist with the resources to affirm a perfectly good sense in which God creates the best world and our own world is not the best. The sense in question amounts to the double claim that at least one of the independent three-dimensional subregions of hyperspace is as valuable as any three-dimensional subregion could be, and that the particular three-space in which we find ourselves is not the fortunate one ... [P]lenitudinous hyperspace ... also provides the resources to maintain a ... sense

---

[15]   Ibid., p. 120.

in which God creates absolutely every world worth creating, even if their number is indenumerable.[16]

Peter Forrest, too, suggests that God would create every possible world meeting some standard of goodness.

> In the absence of arguments to the contrary, it is reasonable to assume the Principle of Compatibility and that God can create one version of every possible good world. It follows that God never chooses between one possible world and another; rather, God examines all possible worlds and, for each possible world, decides whether to create it or not.[17]

The theistic multiverse, by any of these accounts, is not plenitudinous. The theistic multiverse does not include possible worlds or universes that correspond to every way things (non-skeptically) might have been. The multiverse includes only those possible worlds that meet or exceed some standard of goodness.

But if God necessarily actualizes the theistic multiverse, then the multiverse is identical to *all of metaphysical reality*. There are no possible worlds, objects, events, or states of affairs that are not actual worlds, objects, events, and states of affairs. If God necessarily actualizes the theistic multiverse, then the theistic multiverse at least nominally satisfies the general principle of plenitude.

> The most general form of the principle of plenitude does not distinguish among *possibilia*. If there are possible objects, kinds of objects, events, kinds of events, states of affairs and so on, then the general principle entails that every possible object, kind of object, event, kind of event, state of affairs and so on *exists* at some time or other where the existence of merely possible objects, kinds of object, events, kinds of event, states of affairs and so on do not differ ontologically from the existence of actual objects, kinds of object, events, and so on.[18]

In the theistic multiverse, every possible object, event, etc. exists at some time or other where the existence of these possible objects, events, etc. does not differ ontologically from the existence of actual objects, events, etc. There is no ontological difference between possible objects and actual objects, since the possible objects *just are* the actual objects. The theistic multiverse does not make the distinction between actual worlds, objects, events, states of affairs and possible worlds, objects, events, and states of affairs. The theistic multiverse is the only existing possible world, so God actualizes every possible world.

It is nonetheless an important criticism of the theistic multiverse that it is not plenitudinous. It nominally satisfies the general principle of plenitude, but there are many ways things non-skeptically might have been that are not represented in the theistic multiverse. There are, for instance, no on balance bad worlds in that multiverse. There are no worlds in which there is pervasive suffering and injustice. And there are no worlds in which the level of goodness falls just below the standard of goodness for universes in the theistic multiverse.

---

[16] See (Hudson 2005, p. 166 ff). The plenitudinous hyperspace Hudson describes is similar to a possible big world that Lewis proposes. See (Lewis 1986, p. 72).

[17] (Forrest 1981). On Forrest's ontology, possible worlds are collections of individual objects.

> A world is a set of material objects and/or minds (excluding God) connected by chains of causal, temporal or spatial relations, but to which no other material object or mind is so connected (except via God). By an individual, I mean a human being's life, considered as a four-dimensional entity (also the life of any animal capable of experiencing evil). By a world-version (or individual-version) I mean a complete description of a possible world (or individual). How does one classify world-versions? One can consider kinds of worlds: our kind of world is one in which there are regular laws with few exceptions and these laws are like the ones in our world. I assume the Principle of Compatibility, namely that any two worlds of different kinds might both exist. If this principle is correct, one can define a possible world to be an incompatibility class of world versions, that is, two versions are of the same world if they cannot both exist. Are any two world-versions compatible? If they are, there is the odd possibility that in another actual world everything is exactly like this world but for one grain of sand missing. Thus it seems that the same possible world has several different versions.

[18] See (Almeida, chp. 1, sct. 1.4.2).

It is important to note that it is open to defenders of the theistic multiverse to argue that God creates all of metaphysical reality, more broadly understood. The theistic multiverse might include universes corresponding to every way a universe non-skeptically might have been. There is, it might be argued, one possible world, but that possible world includes every possible universe.

But, the universes in the theistic multiverse, whatever universes they are, must be compossible. Compossible universes are more accurately described as isolated parts of one scattered universe in one big world. But, the defender of the theistic multiverse might argue, the isolated universe-parts or quasi-universes might be *close enough* to complete universes to represent them. Here is Lewis on big worlds:

> One big world, spatiotemporally interrelated, might have many different world-like parts. *Ex hypothesi* these are not complete worlds, but they could seem to be. They might be four-dimensional; they might have no boundaries; there might be little or no causal interaction between them. Indeed, each of these world-like parts of one big world might be a duplicate of some genuinely complete [Lewis] world.[19]

There are several ways in which there might be a big world. The theistic multiverse theorists generally elect to have all of the actual universe-parts spatiotemporally isolated. But there is really no reason to isolate the world-like objects into clearly demarcated regions of metaphysical space. There is no theoretical advantage to doing so. Perhaps the world-like objects all fall into epochs in an infinite temporal sequence.

> Time might have the metric structure not of the real line, but rather of many copies of the real line laid end to end. We would have many different epochs, one after another. Yet each epoch would have infinite duration, no beginning, and no end. Inhabitants of different epochs would be spatiotemporally related, but their separation would be infinite . . . [20]

However the one big world is structured, it would include infinitely many world-like objects. Those world-like objects are parts of the vast, temporally infinite, universe. The defender of the theistic multiverse might argue that—contrary to what we might have thought—the one big world comprises all of metaphysical reality, and the totality of the world-like objects in the theistic multiverse represent every way things non-skeptically might have been.[21]

David Lewis has offered this style of argument against the position that there might be possible worlds that include island universes—that there might be possible worlds that include as parts spatiotemporally isolated universes.

> If you thought, as I did too, that a single world might consist of many more or less isolated world-like parts, how sure can you be that you really had in mind the supposed possibility that I reject? Are you sure that it was an essential part of your thought that the world-like parts were in no way spatiotemporally related? Or might you not have had in mind, rather, one of these substitutes I offer? Or might your thought have been sufficiently lacking in specificity that the substitutes would do it justice?

The multiverse theorist might argue analogously that if you thought there was a possible world for every way things non-skeptically might have been, how do you know you are not thinking of world-like objects? How do you know that you are not thinking that there is a *world-like object* for every way things non-skeptically might have been? If the theistic multiverse includes an infinity of world-like objects, and if the theistic multiverse—the one big world—is all there is to metaphysical

---

[19] See (Lewis 1986, p. 70 ff). All of the bracketed material is my own.
[20] Ibid., p. 72.
[21] Certainly multiverse theorists run into the problem of such worlds being a part of metaphysical reality. But we do have some evidence from modal imagination that there is a rich variety of possible worlds in the pluriverse.

Religions **2017**, *8*, 258

reality, then we might be moved to conclude that metaphysical reality is in fact plenitudinous or close enough.

6. Conclusions

The accounts of divine creation in Turner, Kraay, and O'Connor are not coherent. If God necessarily actualizes a multiverse, then divine creation cannot be other than the necessary creation of some multiverse or other. The intrinsic value or disvalue of the multiverse could not be relevant to God's decision to actualize it. Divine creation could not be—as the multiverse theorist envisions it—a moral decision reflecting the perfect goodness of a creator. That is not at all what transpires during creation. The necessarily actualized multiverse—for all multiverse theorists can coherently tell us—might include nothing but intrinsically bad universes.

Conflicts of Interest: The author declares no conflict of interest.

References

Almeida, Michael J. Forthcoming. *Theism and Modal Realism*, Unpublished manuscript, under review.

Draper, Paul. 2004. Cosmic Fine-tuning and Terrestrial Suffering: Parallel problems for Naturalism and Theism. *American Philosophical Quarterly* 41: 311–21.

Forrest, Peter. 1981. The Problem of Evil: Two Neglected Defenses. *Sophia* 20: 49–54. [CrossRef]

Hudson, Hud. 2005. *The Metaphysics of Hyperspace*. Oxford: Clarendon Press.

Kant, Immanuel. 1969. *Universal Natural History and Theory of the Heavens*. Translated by W. Hastie. Ann Arbour: University of Michigan Press.

Kraay, Klaas. 2010. Theism, Possible Worlds, and the Multiverse. *Philosophical Studies* 147: 355–68. [CrossRef]

Kraay, Klaas. 2011. Theism and Modal Collapse. *American Philosophical Quarterly* 48: 361–72.

Lewis, David. 1986. *On the Plurality of Worlds*. Oxford: Blackwell.

Lovejoy, Arthur O. 1932. *The Great Chain of Being*. Cambridge: Harvard University Press.

Munitz, Milton K. 1951. One Universe or Many? *Journal of the History of Ideas* 12: 231–55. [CrossRef]

O'Connor, Timothy. 2008. *Theism and Ultimate Explanation: The Necessary Shape of Contingency*. Hoboken: Wiley-Blackwell.

Turner, Donald. 2014. Revising the Many-Universes Solution to the Problem of Evil. In *God and the Multiverse: Scientific, Philosophical, and Theological Perspectives*. Edited by Klaas Kraay. New York: Routledge.

White, Michael. 2002. *The Pope and the Heretic: The True Story of Giordano Bruno, the Man Who Dared to Defy the Roman Inquisition*. New York: HarperCollins.

Article

One Philosopher's Bug Can Be Another's Feature: Reply to Almeida's "Multiverse and Divine Creation"

Klaas J. Kraay

Department of Philosophy, Ryerson University, Toronto, ON M5B 2K3, Canada; kraay@ryerson.ca

Received: 14 December 2017; Accepted: 4 January 2018; Published: 12 January 2018

Abstract: Michael Almeida once told me that he thought we were just a couple of hours of conversation away from reaching deep agreement about some important topics in the philosophy of religion pertaining to God, multiverses, and modality. This paper represents my attempt to move this conversation forward and to seek this common ground. Specifically, I respond to Almeida's paper entitled "The Multiverse and Divine Creation". In the first four sections, I record my disagreement with him concerning some smaller matters. In Section 5, I try to persuade him that what he considers a 'bug' in the theistic multiverse is actually a feature—and a desirable one at that. In Section 6, I close by identifying some points at which our views seem to converge.

Keywords: God; evil; universe; world; multiverse; Almeida

1. The Principle of Plenitude

Almeida begins his paper by saying that an advantage of the theistic multiverse is that it aims to satisfy the Principle of Plenitude. As A.O. Lovejoy states, this principles includes

> ... not only the thesis that the universe is a *plenum formarum* in which the range of conceivable diversity of *kinds* of living things is exhaustively exemplified, but also any other deductions from the assumption that no genuine potentiality of being can remain unfulfilled, that the extent and abundance of the creation must be as great as the possibility of existence and commensurate with the productive capacity of a 'perfect' and inexhaustible Source, and that the world is better, the more things it contains (Lovejoy 1932, p. 52)

Later, Almeida chides Donald Turner, me, and Timothy O'Connor for developing models of theistic multiverses that fail to deliver all of the abundance promised by the Principle of Plenitude. Specifically, Almeida complains that our models do not include on-balance bad or otherwise unworthy universes (8).

But neither Turner, nor I, nor O'Connor ever intended our models to include such universes, and so Almeida's complaint misses the target. It is true that Turner discusses the Principle of Plenitude favourably in his paper, and that he says that it "motivates" his model (Turner 2003, p. 147). But Turner is quite clear that his multiverse only includes universes that are "above some cut-off line—for example, every [universe] with a favourable balance of good over evil" (Turner 2003, p. 149; and see also (Turner 2015)). As for me, it's true that I also explicitly harnessed considerations about plenitude when devising principles which posit that God will create and sustain *all* those universes that are worth creating and sustaining. But I also introduced further principles which posit that God will create and sustain *only* those universes that are worth creating and sustaining (Kraay 2010, 2011). As for O'Connor, he too thinks that " ... presumably there is some goodness threshold τ below which God would not create [universes]" (O'Connor 2008, p. 117).

I suspect that Almeida's deeper concern here is that there is independent reason to think that on-balance-bad or otherwise unworthy universes really do exist—necessarily—in modal space, and that the multiverses defended by Turner, me, and O'Connor therefore really ought to include them.

But, as we will see below, in Section 5, it is highly controversial whether, *given theism*, modal space includes such universes.

2. The Theistic Multiverse and the Problem of Evil

Almeida says that another advantage of the theistic multiverse is that it furnishes "a powerful theodicy" (1). This is not quite right, and can be a little bit misleading, as I will try to explain. Following Alvin Plantinga, let's say that a theodicy specifies God's actual reason for permitting evil or for [actualizing] a world that contains evil (Plantinga 1974, p. 10). Now, Turner's theistic multiverse includes only universes that are 'on-balance good'; mine includes only universes that are 'worth creating and sustaining', and O'Connor's includes only those universes 'at or above some goodness threshold τ'. These phrases represent, so to speak, overall criteria governing God's choice.

But these criteria could be filled out in various ways. Some might hold, following Mackie (1955), that only universes featuring *no evil whatsoever* meet these criteria—and evidently, such a strict variant could not furnish a theodicy in Plantinga's sense.[1] Presumably, however, Almeida has something different in mind. Suppose that a proponent of the theistic multiverse holds that some universes that meet these general criteria do indeed contain evil. In what sense could such a view furnish a theodicy? Clearly, it would not itself constitute a specific account of God's goals within a universe, or what goods God aims to bring about within a universe (etc.) by permitting any type or token of evil. At most, such a view could offer a highly abstract and formulaic account of why God actualizes a world containing evil: the theistic multiverse is such a world, and all of its universes that contain evil nevertheless meet the stated overall axiological criteria. But this is a theodicy only in a very limited sense.[2]

Moreover, the claim that theistic multiverse theory furnishes a theodicy is liable to be read as suggesting that it can successfully be invoked in responses to arguments from evil.[3] And indeed, some of its proponents have held exactly this, although they differ about how significant a contribution the view can make to such responses. Some think that its contribution will only be modest (e.g., O'Connor 2008). Others think it has the resources to significantly enhance existing response strategies (e.g., Hudson 2005; Schrynemakers 2015). The limit case is Megill (2011), who believes that the bare epistemic possibility of a theistic multiverse completely defeats all arguments from evil, past and present. But all these claims are controversial. Draper (2004), Almeida (2008, chp. 8), and Monton (2010) have argued, in various ways, that theistic multiverse theories cannot defeat arguments from evil, and I have argued likewise (Kraay 2011, 2012).

Here is my way of seeing the matter. Defenders of theistic multiverses posit that if God exists, then the actual world is a multiverse that includes only those universes that meet or exceed their preferred axiological criteria. Most arguments from evil, meanwhile, involve an a posteriori claim to the effect that our universe contains (or probably contains) types or tokens of evil that disconfirm God's existence. In the context of the theistic multiverse, such claims can be taken to assert that our universe fails, or probably fails, to meet the axiological standard preferred by the critics of theism. And so the discussion begins. As I have written elsewhere:

> Defenders and critics of multiverse-theism can work together to find a mutually-agreeable threshold [at or] above which universes should be deemed worthy of inclusion in a theistic multiverse. They may well subsequently differ on the a posteriori question of whether our universe surpasses the agreed-upon threshold. Considerations about the existence, variety,

---

[1]   Here is a related concern. Almeida states that "there might well be vast amounts of undeserved suffering, horrendous moral evil and terrible natural disasters in many universes" (1). But whether this is so also depends upon how these general criteria are fleshed out. On some precisifications of these criteria, universes in the theistic multiverse could not feature any such events.

[2]   To see the contrast, consider Plantinga's own theodicy, which specifies the exact goods—Incarnation and Atonement—for the sake of which God permits evil (Plantinga 2004).

[3]   I rather doubt Almeida intends this, but the point is nevertheless worth clarifying.

magnitude, duration, scope, distribution, types, or intensity of evil in our universe could be appealed to in defending the claim that our universe is (probably) not worthy of inclusion. And defenders of multiverse-theism could either try to show that our universe (probably) is worthy of inclusion, or—more modestly—they could try to defeat or undermine arguments to the contrary. In short, the typical moves in the debate concerning the problem of evil can easily be reframed to apply to multiverse theism. But this, by itself, will not furnish an advantage to either side (Kraay 2012, pp. 157–58.)

For this reason, theistic multiverse models alone cannot defeat, undermine, or otherwise diminish the probative force of arguments from evil.

3. Axiological Properties of Universes and of Worlds

Almeida criticizes Turner and me for assuming that the best possible world will contain all and only those universes that surpass the relevant axiological threshold. With respect to Turner, Almeida says:

If God necessarily actualizes the theistic multiverse, then he actualizes the best possible world no matter how good or bad the universes happen to be that compose the theistic multiverse. If God necessarily actualizes the theistic multiverse, then God necessarily actualized the best possible world. The intrinsic value of universes composing the multiverse is irrelevant to the question of whether the multiverse is the best possible world (5).

And with respect to me, Almeida says:

If God necessarily actualizes the theistic multiverse, then he actualizes the best possible world no matter how worthy or unworthy the universes happen to be that comprise the theistic multiverse. If God necessarily actualizes the theistic multiverse, then God necessarily actualizes the best possible world. The intrinsic value of the universes composing the multiverse is not relevant at all to the question of whether the multiverse is the best possible world (5).

Unsurprisingly, I disagree. Here are two arguments for my preferred way of seeing the matter. First, consider these four principles, which I have discussed elsewhere (Kraay 2010, 2011):[4]

P1   If a universe is creatable by an unsurpassable being, and worth creating (i.e., it has an axiological status that [meets or] surpasses some objective threshold t), that being will create that universe.

P2   If a universe is sustainable by an unsurpassable being, and worth sustaining (i.e., it has an axiological status that [meets or] surpasses some objective threshold t), that being will sustain that universe.

P3   If a universe is not worthy of creation (i.e., it has an axiological status that fails to [meet or] surpass some threshold t), an unsurpassable being will not create that universe.

P4   If a universe is not worthy of being sustained (i.e., it has an axiological status that fails to [meet or] surpass some threshold t), an unsurpassable being will not sustain that universe.

Jointly, these principles suggest that that God will create and sustain all and only those universes that meet or surpass a certain axiological threshold. The result, I have argued, is the best possible world.[5] But of course this means that, contra Almeida, the best possible world simply cannot feature any unworthy worlds.

---

4   I have added, in square brackets, an additional qualification to each principle. This both clarifies my proposal and makes it consistent with the way that O'Connor speaks about his favoured axiological threshold.

5   This claim will need some qualification, which will come in Section 6, below.

A second way to motivate my way of seeing the matter is by considering connections between the axiological properties of universes and of worlds. I have argued that the axiological status of universes can be expressed as some complex function of the universe-good-making-properties (UGMPs) and universe bad-making properties (UBMPs) that universe exhibits, and the degree to which it exhibits them. I have also argued that the axiological status of worlds can be expressed as some complex function of the world-good-making-properties (WGMPs) and world-bad-making properties (WBMPs) that world exhibits, and the degree to which it exhibits them (Kraay 2010). I take it that, ceteris paribus, worlds are better to the extent that they include more universes at or above the relevant axiological threshold. I also take it that, ceteris paribus, worlds are worse to the extent that they include universes below the axiological threshold. So it is a mistake to think, as Almeida does, that the axiological status of a multiverse has *nothing* to do with the axiological status of the universes it contains. For the same reason, I disagree with Almeida's claim that "If God necessarily actualizes the multiverse, we have no idea which universes are parts of that multiverse" (2). On my view, principles P1–P4 give us a rather good idea.

I should clarify three small additional points about the axiological properties of universes and of worlds, in order to forestall any confusion. First, I do not hold that the theistic multiverse contains only universes and nothing else. Worlds can and do contain non-spatiotemporal entities, and clearly these cannot be housed inside universes, which, after all, are concrete spatiotemporal entities. Paradigmatically, of course, *God* is a non-spatiotemporal entity, and so God cannot be said to inhabit a universe, but can be said to exist in a world.[6] Some non-spatiotemporal entities, (like God and numbers) exist necessarily. Others (like angels, perhaps) are continent beings. The fact that worlds can include non-spatiotemporal objects matters because it helps to underscore the point that there is an important distinction between WGMPs and UGMPs (and, equally, between WBMPs and UBMPs). After all, some WGMPs and WBMPs have nothing whatsoever to do with universes, since they refer to the presence or absence of non-spatiotemporal entities in a world, and the resulting axiological effects in that world.

Second, while the overall axiological status of a world depends upon the WGMPs and WBMPs it exhibits, it may that be certain good-making properties cease to make worlds better past a certain point, or in certain combinations. (The same goes, *mutatis mutandis*, for WBMPs.) So, while the goodness of a world or a universe depends upon the axiological properties it exhibits (or fails to), this dependency may not be simple.

Third, someone might object to theistic multiverse theory on the grounds that universes should not be treated as the primary locus of value in our axiological theorizing. This complaint might hold, for example, that *persons*, or perhaps *creaturely lives*, should be treated as the primary locus of value, and should accordingly be given greater prominence than universes in axiological theorizing. I would respond by saying that an account of WGMPs, WBMPs, UGMPs and UBMPs could be developed to harness these intuitions. Someone might say, for example, that a universe is worth creating, or a world is worth actualizing, *only if* the persons it contains lead lives that are overall worth living. To generalize the point: talk of the good- and bad-making properties of universes and worlds represents only a sort of schema that can be fleshed out in various ways to accommodate different axiological and ethical views.

4. Almeida on O'Connor

Almeida claims that O'Connor holds that "God would elect to create that superuniverse containing *every single universe* at or above some goodness threshold τ" (7, emphasis added). But, although O'Connor does include this very proposition in his book (O'Connor 2008, p. 117), it is not quite right to characterize his considered view in this fashion. First, we need some context. O'Connor prefaces

---

[6] I here set aside distinctive Christian claims about the Incarnation, and I also set aside the attribute of omnipresence (which, I think, should be interpreted non-literally).

this claim by saying merely that it is *more likely*—more likely than the scenario he set out immediately beforehand, namely that God would create *every* possible universe. Let's set likelihoods aside, since it's difficult to know how to construe this claim probabilistically. I take it that O'Connor really means to say that it is *more plausible* to think that God will create every universe at or above axiological threshold τ than it is to claim that God will create every universe simpliciter. (I agree, and will say about this below.) But, of course, it doesn't follow from the fact that an author regards position X as more plausible than position Y that the author's considered view is indeed X.

Second, and contra Almeida, the next few moves clearly reveal that it is not O'Connor's final view that God would create *every* universe above threshold τ. After noting that God could achieve infinite overall aggregate value by creating every threshold-surpassing universe, O'Connor immediately points out that God could achieve the same result by creating every second, third, or *n*-th universe at or above threshold τ. O'Connor regards these all as "adequate choices" (p. 117). But then O'Connor notes that there is no highest transfinite cardinal, and, hence, no upper bound on how many universes God could create. So while there are many ways for God to bring about *infinite* aggregate value in creation, none of these would bring about *maximal* aggregate value. This does not trouble O'Connor, however, since he thinks it " ... doubtful that a perfect being would desire to pursue maximal aggregate value at all" (p. 119).[7] O'Connor ultimately favours the view that universes can be grouped into *kinds* or *value-types* (p. 120), and he thinks that God would create at least some universes from each of these, without attempting to creating all of the universes that there are in modal space. In the end, then, O'Connor's considered view comes to this:

> I have argued that all the possibilities deemed creation-worthy by a perfect creator would conform to a rich structure. Even so, an infinity of options satisfies these constraints, and there is no reason yet uncovered to suppose that any highly particular sort of universe will be deemed necessary. Hence, for all we've seen, the extent of alternatives open to a perfect creator will be wide indeed (120).

So, Almeida is mistaken when he claims that O'Connor's God will create *every* universe at or above threshold τ. But, Almeida is quite correct to say that there are some things that O'Connor's God cannot do. In particular, O'Connor's God cannot: (a) refrain from creating;[8] (b) create any universe whose axiological status is below threshold τ; (c) actualize a possible world that contains only one universe—in other words, he cannot refrain from creating a multiverse; (d) create a multiverse comprised of merely finitely many universes; and he cannot (e) refrain from creating at least one universe from each *kind* or *value-type*.

5. "It's not a Bug; it's a Feature!"[9]

I now turn to the central disagreement between Almeida, on the one hand, and Turner, O'Connor, and me on the other. Almeida states:

> It is nonetheless an important criticism of the theistic multiverse that it is not plenitudinous. It nominally satisfies the general principle of plenitude, but there are many ways things non-skeptically might have been that are not represented in the theistic multiverse. There are, for instance, no on balance bad [universes] in that multiverse ... And there are no [universes] in which the level of goodness falls just below the standard of goodness for universes in the theistic multiverse (8).[10]

---

7   In my view, O'Connor's God turns out to be a satisficer—and for my criticisms of divine satisficing, see Kraay (2013).
8   O'Connor (2008) seems persuaded by the thought that God inevitably creates (p. 113).
9   Turner (2015) also uses this apt phrase in his response to Almeida (p. 120).
10   This quotation elides the following claim: "There are no [universes] in which there is pervasive suffering and injustice." I leave it out for two reasons. First, the vagueness of 'pervasive' makes it unclear to me whether such universes would really be below the axiological threshold. On some precisifications, they would be; on others, they wouldn't. Second, and relatedly, I take it that certain degrees or levels of suffering and injustice would bring a universe below the axiological threshold, but that others would not.

So, Almeida thinks that these theistic multiverses are not fully furnished, since they fail to include universes that really do exist, necessarily, in modal space. As a result, Almeida further objects that theistic multiverse models incoherently represent God as choosing some universes over others to create and sustain. In particular, if God necessarily chooses only those universes that meet or surpass some axiological threshold, then universes below the threshold are in fact metaphysically impossible, and so cannot coherently be represented as possible objects of God's choice. All of this is the chief 'bug' that Almeida detects in theistic multiverse theory.

This 'bug' is sometimes referred to as 'modal collapse'—the idea that on a given theoretical model or ontology, modal space turns out to be rather less capacious, or more restricted, than it really ought to be.[11] Now, one philosopher's 'bug' can be another's 'feature', so to speak—and indeed, can be a desirable feature. In the remainder of this section, I will explain why I think that the restriction that Turner, I, and O'Connor agree on—namely, that God will not create worlds below a certain axiological threshold—should be thought a desirable feature, rather than a bug. The central idea begins with this simple modus tollens:

(1)　If God creates and sustains any universe that is below a plausible axiological threshold, God is not essentially unsurpassable.

(2)　God is essentially unsurpassable.

(3)　It's not the case that God creates and sustains any universe that is below a plausible axiological threshold.

Now, given theism, nobody but God is in the business of creating and sustaining universes, and no actual universes lack a creator and sustainer. It follows that, given theism, no universes below the threshold are possible. They are, in fact, logically self-contradictory, because, from the vantage point of those universes, they both have and lack a creator and sustainer who is essentially unsurpassable.[12] Given theism, then, modal space just cannot be as capacious as it might, meta-modally speaking, otherwise be. In Thomas Morris' phrase, God is "a delimiter of possibilities" (Morris 1987, p. 48); as Brian Leftow puts it, God leaves a "modal footprint" (Leftow 2005, p. 96; 2010, p. 30).

Now, of course, Almeida may wish to insist that the universes below this axiological threshold really *are* logical possibilities. But I think it is illicit, in this dialectical context, to rely solely on, or even privilege, modal intuitions that bracket God. Here is Thomas Morris again:

> If there is a being who exists necessarily, and is necessarily omnipotent, omniscient, and good, then many states of affairs which otherwise would represent genuine possibilities, and which by all non-theistic tests of logic and semantics do represent possibilities, are strictly impossible in the strongest sense. In particular, worlds containing certain sorts of disvalue or evil are metaphysically ruled out by the nature of God, divinely precluded from the realm of real possibility (Morris 1987, p. 48)

Alvin Plantinga, incidentally, holds a similar view:

> [A]ll possible worlds ... are very good. For God is unlimited in goodness and holiness, as well as in power and knowledge; these properties, furthermore, are essential to him; and this means, I believe, that God not only has created [i.e., actualized] a world that is very good, but that there aren't any conditions under which he would have created a world that is less than very good ... The class of possible worlds God's love and goodness prevents him from actualizing is empty. All possible worlds, we might say, are eligible worlds: worlds that God's goodness, mercy, and love would permit him to actualize. (Plantinga 2004, p. 8)

---

[11]　For more on this, see Kraay (2011).

[12]　The same sort of reasoning, but with respect to worlds rather than universes, can be found in Guleserian (1983).

Morris and Plantinga here speak of worlds, rather than universes, but of course this makes no difference, since they would both hold that worlds that include universes that fail to surpass a plausible axiological threshold are not genuine possibilities.

So, why is this a desirable feature rather than a bug? Well, it is desirable for the defender of theistic multiverses, since it neatly avoids casting God—an essentially unsurpassable being—as the creator and sustainer of any worlds below the relevant axiological threshold. It is also desirable for those with a high view of divine sovereignty, because there is an important sense in which God is sovereign over modal space on this view.

6. Modelling Possibility With and Within the Theistic Multiverse

Toward the end of his paper, Almeida says this:

> In the theistic multiverse, every possible object, event, etc. exists at some time or other where the existence of these possible objects, events, etc. does not differ ontologically from the existence of actual objects, events, etc. There is no ontological difference between possible objects and actual objects, since the possible objects just are the actual objects. The theistic multiverse does not make the distinction between actual worlds, objects, events, states of affairs and possible worlds, objects, events, and states of affairs. The theistic multiverse is the only existing possible world, so God [trivially] actualizes every possible world (8).

I have three points to make in response.

First, this is not an accurate description of O'Connor's theistic multiverse. O'Connor thinks that there are no universes below threshold τ in the theistic multiverse. But, as we have seen, O'Connor takes pains to argue that God can still sensibly be thought to choose between genuine metaphysical possibilities, despite this constraint. This is because there is no greatest transfinite cardinality, and, accordingly, there is an infinite array of metaphysically possible super-universes (each including only universes at or above axiological threshold τ) from which God can choose, while still bringing about infinite value in creation.

Second, strictly speaking, my view does not require me to say that the theistic multiverse is the only possible world. Technically, my view is just that God will create and sustain all and only those universes that are worthy of being created and sustained. Perhaps there are several worlds that all meet this description, but that nevertheless differ with respect to the contingent non-spatiotemporal entities they lack or contain. But I won't insist on this point—in fact, I will ignore it in what follows.[13]

So, on Turner's view, and mine, it is the case that God necessarily actualizes the theistic multiverse, and so Almeida's description here might seem apt. But, again, perhaps not entirely—and this is my third point. One might follow Donald Turner (and others) by distinguishing between two sorts of possibility. As Turner puts it, the first sense holds that "the internal consistency of a world is determined without reference to whether it is a world the actualization of which is consistent with God's character" (Turner 2015, p. 121). In this sense, worlds other than the theistic multiverse *are* possible. But in the second sense, according to which the internal consistency of a world is determined without bracketing considerations pertaining to God's character, such worlds are *not* possible. Relatedly, one might

---

[13] And here's why. Suppose, first, that there are multiple unsurpassable worlds that feature all and only those universes worthy of being created and sustained, but that nevertheless differ with respect to their contingent-but-non-spatiotemporal features. In this scenario, I don't think God could have a rational basis for choosing one over the other—and this is a problem for theism, which needs to hold that God is unsurpassably rational. (Almeida, incidentally, agrees.) Next, suppose that there is, instead, an infinite hierarchy of increasingly better theistic multiverses, each of which includes all and only the worthy universes, but which nevertheless differ with respect to their contingent-but-non-spatiotemporal features. This would make the theist vulnerable to William Rowe's problem of no best world. I think this problem is a very serious worry for theism, given certain plausible assumptions. (Almeida, incidentally, does not.) So this inclines me to think that the theist should hold that there is one unique best of all possible worlds, where that world features all and only those universes that are worthy of being created and sustained, and all and only those contingent non-spatiotemporal entities that are worthy of being actualized.

picture possible worlds in the former sense as mere ideas in God's mind—really and truly there for inspection, but not really and truly furniture in modal space. If a move like along these lines is plausible, then Almeida's description above will not be entirely accurate.

Finally, I turn to concerns judgments of possibility *within* the theistic multiverse. Elsewhere, I have written:

> If the only possible world is the theistic multiverse, the claim "nothing could possibly be other than it is" is ambiguous. Taken to mean that there could not possibly have been anything other than the array of universes worth creating and sustaining, this claim is true. But expressed from a vantage point within a universe, and taken to refer to that universe, it is false. From this perspective, to say that things could be otherwise is just to say that there is another spatiotemporally distinct universe in which things *are* otherwise. Universes ... can vary in all sorts of ways. They may differ in their laws of nature and in their histories, and these variances can perhaps anchor many of the familiar modal claims whose intelligibility seemed threatened by the claim that there is only one possible world. In fact, this picture of modality—on which modal claims are understood to refer to concrete, spatiotemporally isolated universes—is strikingly similar to a well-known theory of modality: David Lewis' modal realism. So while the claim that there is only one possible world on theism seemed an affront to our modal intuitions, once it is seen that this world is the theistic multiverse, it may be that familiar modal claims can be parsed in terms of universes instead of worlds. Modal collapse may not be so bad after all. (Kraay 2011, pp. 366–67)

Almeida considers the idea that in actualizing the theistic multiverse, God creates all of metaphysical reality. Echoing Lewis, he dubs the result "the one big world" (Almeida 2017, p. 9; and see (Lewis 1986, 70 ff)). And, interestingly, Almeida then quickly offers the following suggestion:

> However the one big world is structured, it would include infinitely many world- like objects. Those world-like objects are parts of the vast, temporally infinite, universe. The defender of the theistic multiverse might argue that—contrary to what we might have thought—the one big world comprises all of metaphysical reality, and the totality of the world-like objects in the theistic multiverse represent[s] every way things non-skeptically might have been (9).

This suggestion seems very similar in spirit to my proposal, and so I welcome it, with only two small caveats. First, I must quibble with the second sentence, since I don't see why the 'one big world' should be regarded as either a universe (it's a multiverse) or as temporally infinite (it is not a spatiotemporal entity at all, although it contains spatiotemporal entities). Second, I would add the modifier "given theism" to the end of the final sentence, to capture the idea, discussed in Section 5, that God leaves a footprint on modality.

Almeida imagines a critic insisting that there *must be* possible worlds other than the theistic multiverse that represent ways things might have been. He then suggests the following reply:

> The multiverse theorist might argue ... that if you thought there was a possible world for every way things non-skeptically might have been, how do you know you are not thinking of world-like objects [within the multiverse]? How do you know that you are not thinking that there is a world-like object for every way things non-skeptically might have been? If the theistic multiverse includes an infinity of world-like objects, and if the theistic multiverse—the one big world—is all there is to metaphysical reality, then we might be moved to conclude that metaphysical reality is in fact plenitudinous or close enough (9–10).

I welcome this idea as well, although I again want to underscore the constraint that theism places, in my view, on plenitude.

It remains to be seen, of course, whether this conception of metaphysical reality is robust enough to meet our modal requirements. But it strikes me as promising—and as desirable for the theist.

Religions **2018**, *9*, 23

Moreover, it is not really that different from Almeida's own view: theistic modal realism. On my view, concrete spatiotemporal world-like objects—universes—are created by God and can plausibly anchor many familiar modal claims. On his view, concrete spatiotemporal objects—worlds—exist in modal space and ground familiar modal claims. While we differ on how many of these objects there are, given theism, there does seem to be some important convergence between our views. Perhaps Almeida and I will ultimately find agreement after all.

Acknowledgments: I am grateful to Michael Almeida for many discussions of these topics over the years.

Conflicts of Interest: The author declares no conflict of interest.

References

Almeida, Michael. 2008. *The Metaphysics of Perfect Beings*. New York: Routledge.

Almeida, Michael. 2017. The Multiverse and Divine Creation. *Religions* 8: 258. [CrossRef]

Draper, Paul. 2004. Cosmic Fine-Tuning and Terrestrial Suffering: Parallel Problems for Naturalism and Theism. *American Philosophical Quarterly* 41: 311–21.

Guleserian, Theodore. 1983. God and Possible Worlds: The Modal Problem of Evil. *Noûs* 17: 221–38. [CrossRef]

Hudson, Hud. 2005. *The Metaphysics of Hyperspace*. Oxford: Clarendon Press.

Kraay, Klaas. 2010. Theism, Possible Worlds, and the Multiverse. *Philosophical Studies* 147: 355–68. [CrossRef]

Kraay, Klaas. 2011. Theism and Modal Collapse. *American Philosophical Quarterly* 48: 361–72.

Kraay, Klaas. 2012. The Theistic Multiverse: Problems and Prospects. In *Scientific Approaches to the Philosophy of Religion*. Edited by Yujin Nagasawa. London: Palgrave MacMillan, pp. 143–62.

Kraay, Klaas. 2013. Can God Satisfice? *American Philosophical Quarterly* 50: 399–410.

Leftow, Brian. 2005. The Ontological Argument. In *The Oxford Handbook of Philosophy of Religion*. Edited by William Wainwright. New York: Oxford University Press, pp. 80–115.

Leftow, Brian. 2010. Necessity. In *The Cambridge Companion to Philosophical Theology*. Edited by Charles Taliaferro and Chad Meister. Cambridge: Cambridge University Press, pp. 15–30.

Lewis, David. 1986. *On the Plurality of Worlds*. Oxford: Blackwell.

Lovejoy, Arthur O. 1932. *The Great Chain of Being*. Cambridge: Harvard University Press.

Mackie, J. L. 1955. Evil and Omnipotence. *Mind* 64: 200–12. [CrossRef]

Megill, Jason. 2011. Evil and the Many Universes Response. *International Journal for Philosophy of Religion* 70: 127–38. [CrossRef]

Monton, Bradley. 2010. Against Multiverse Theodicies. *Philo* 13: 1–23. [CrossRef]

Morris, Thomas. 1987. The Necessity of God's Goodness. In *Anselmian Explorations: Essays in Philosophical Theology*. Notre Dame: University of Notre Dame Press, pp. 42–69.

O'Connor, Timothy. 2008. *Theism and Ultimate Explanation: The Necessary Shape of Contingency*. Oxford: Wiley-Blackwell.

Plantinga, Alvin. 1974. *God, Freedom, and Evil*. New York: Harper and Row.

Plantinga, Alvin. 2004. Supralapsarianism, or 'O Felix Culpa'. In *Christian Faith and the Problem of Evil*. Edited by Peter van Inwagen. Grand Rapids: Eerdmans, pp. 1–25.

Schrynemakers, Michael. 2015. Kraay's Theistic Multiverse. In *God and the Multiverse: Scientific, Philosophical, and Theological Perspectives*. Edited by Klaas J. Kraay. New York: Routledge, pp. 129–48.

Turner, Donald. 2003. The Many-Universes Solution to the Problem of Evil. In *The Existence of God*. Edited by Richard Gale and Alexander Pruss. Aldershot: Ashgate, pp. 1–17.

Turner, Donald. 2015. Revising the Many-Universes Solution to the Problem of Evil. In *God and the Multiverse: Scientific, Philosophical, and Theological Perspectives*. Edited by Klaas Kraay. New York: Routledge.

Article

God, Evil, and Infinite Value

Marshall Naylor

Camino Santa Maria, St. Mary's University, San Antonio, TX 78228, USA; marshall.scott.naylor@gmail.com

Received: 1 December 2017; Accepted: 8 January 2018; Published: 11 January 2018

Abstract: Prominent approaches to the problems of evil assume that even if the Anselmian God exists, some worlds are better than others, all else being equal. But the assumptions that the Anselmian God exists and that some worlds are better than others cannot be true together. One description, by Mark Johnston and Georg Cantor, values God's existence as exceeding any transfinite cardinal value. For any finite or infinite amount of goodness in any possible world, God's value infinitely exceeds that amount. This conception is not obviously inconsistent with the Anselmian God. As a result, the prominent approaches to the problems of evil are mistaken. The elimination of evil does not, in fact, improve the value of any world as commonly thought. Permitting evil does not, in fact, diminish the value of any world as commonly thought.

Keywords: god; evil; infinite value; the problem of evil; Anselmianism

---

1. Introduction

Prominent approaches to the problems of evil assume that even if the Anselmian God exists, some worlds are better than others, all else being equal. One proponent, JL Mackie, argues that all possible evils are pointless evils. A world where God prevents pointless evils from occurring would be a better world than if he had not prevented it. An opposing view by Alvin Plantinga challenges Mackie and argues that it is possible that some evils are not pointless. God permits evil because preventing evil makes a better possible world. In his own approach to the problems of evil, William Rowe argues that God has a reason to prevent pointless evils but not evils that at least entail greater goods. It is worlds where he prevents pointless evils from occurring that are better than if he had permitted them.

But the assumptions that the Anselmian God exists and some worlds are better than others cannot be true together. Indeed, if the Anselmian God exists, it is necessarily false that any possible world is better than any other possible world. The Anselmian God is conceived as omnipotent, omniscient, omnibenevolent, and a necessarily existing being. One description, by Mark Johnston and Georg Cantor, values God's existence as exceeding any transfinite cardinal value. For any finite or infinite amount of goodness in any possible world, God's value infinitely exceeds that amount. This conception is not obviously inconsistent with the Anselmian God. As a result, the prominent approaches to the problems of evil are mistaken. The elimination of evil does not, in fact, improve the value of any world as commonly thought. Permitting evil does not, in fact, diminish the value of any world as commonly thought.

In Section 2, I discuss the Anselmian conception of God as it figures into Mackie, Rowe, and Plantinga's approaches to the problems of evil. Section 3 explains the assumption that it is possible that worlds differ in overall value from one another as Mackie, Rowe, and Plantinga assume. Section 4 introduces and defends the view that God's omnibenevolent nature is such that it exceeds any transfinite cardinal value and that this conception does not contradict the Anselmian conception of God. Section 5 argues that if the Anselmian God exists, the prominent approaches to the problems of evil are mistaken, as no world is better than any other world. As a result, the standard reason why God permits or prevents evil—for the betterment of a world—is also false is presented in Section 6.

2. Traditional Conception of God

The initial assumption in the problems of evil is that God is, necessarily, omnipotent, omnibenevolent, omniscient and necessarily existing.

> TCG. Necessarily, God is omnipotent, omnibenevolent, omniscient, and a necessarily existing being.

TCG is the traditional conception of God. God is perfectly powerful, all-good, knows everything there is to know, and exists in every possible world. It is a divine being that is maximally great. This conception of God is found in early Christian thinkers including Saint Anselm.

According to Anselm, God is a being than which none greater can be conceived. The greatest conceivable being has the properties of omnipotence, omnibenevolence, omniscience, and necessary existence as a matter of conceptual fact.

> And surely that than which a greater cannot be thought cannot exist only in the understanding. For if it exists only in the understanding, it can be thought to exist in reality as well, which is greater. So if that than which a greater cannot be thought exists only in the understanding, then the very thing than which a greater cannot be thought is something than which a greater can be thought.[1]

> And it so truly exists that it cannot be conceived not to exist. For it is possible to conceive of a being which cannot be conceived not to exist; and this is greater than one which can be conceived not to exist. Hence, if that, than which nothing greater can be conceived can be conceived not to exist, it is not that than which nothing greater can be conceived. But this is a contradiction. So truly, therefore, is there something than which nothing greater can be conceived, that it cannot even be conceived not to exist.

> And this being thou art, O Lord, our God.[2]

Anselmian arguments are familiar. Consider two divine beings: DB_1 and DB_2. DB_1 is certainly divine. He possesses all the omni-properties but exists merely in the understanding. But another divine being, DB_2, possesses all the omni-properties but exists, as Anselm puts it, in reality. Assume that existence is a positive property of a being. DB_1, though divine, is not a maximally great being. DB_1 is surpassable in greatness. There is another being, DB_2, which is greater than DB_1. Furthermore, God—as a conceptual fact—cannot be conceived as not existing. It is a logically necessary truth.[3]

Anselm's conception of a maximally great being says that there is no conceivable being as great as God.

> 1 Necessarily, a being is maximally great if and only if that being is omnipotent, omnibenevolent, omniscient, necessarily existing and there is no conceivable being B* such that B* is greater than or equal to TCG.

If it is possible that there is a conceivable being B* whose properties equal or surpass that of TCG, then B* is TCG. But, according to Anselm, it is impossible to conceive of a being B* that is as good as or greater than TCG. Necessarily, God is a maximally great being such that there is no conceivable being who possesses omnipotence, omniscience, omnibenevolence, and necessary existence which is as good as TCG. TCG is a maximally great being (1) according to Anselm.

In their approaches to the problems of evil, Mackie, Rowe, and Plantinga assume the same equivalency. Mackie conceives God as TCG who is such that, necessarily, God eliminates evil as far as

---

[1] (Williams 2007).
[2] (Williams 2007).
[3] (Malcolm 1960, p. 45).

he can and that there are no limits to what God can do. Mackie is sometimes of the view that God can do even what is logically impossible.[4] The possible existence of any evil, then, is inconsistent with the existence of God. If there is an instance of evil in some possible world then there is no TCG, and theists should revise their belief in the traditional God.

> There may be other solutions which require examination, but this study strongly suggests that there is no valid solution of the problem which does not modify at least one of the constituent propositions in a way which would seriously affect the essential core of the theistic position.[5]

One way to resolve the problem is to modify or weaken the conception of God found in TCG. Perhaps there is no divine being that is both at least omnibenevolent and omnipotent. But then, as Mackie concludes, the traditional God does not exist.

Rowe explicitly conceives God as TCG at the outset of his evidential problem of evil. His argument is against those who believe in the traditional God.

> By theist in a narrow sense I mean someone who believes in the existence of an omnipotent, omniscient, eternal, supremely good being who created the world ... In this paper I will be using the terms "theism" ... in the narrow sense.[6]

And in his famous response to the logical problem of evil, Plantinga makes it clear that his concern is with the consistency between God as a TCG and evil.

> The Free Will Defence is an effort to show that (1) God is omnipotent, omniscient, and wholly good (which I shall take to entail that God exists) is not inconsistent with (2) There is evil in the world. That is, the Free Will Defender aims to show that there is a possible world in which (1) and (2) are both true.[7]

These prominent approaches, and most other approaches to the problems of evil, share the same conception of the Anselmian God. It is indeed the traditional conception of God that seems to generate the problems of evil. As Mackie observes, genuine solutions to the problems of evil require us to weaken our conception of the most perfect being.

3. Diversity of Value Assumption

The prominent approaches to the problems of evil assume that some worlds are better than others. More specifically, there is diversity of overall value among possible worlds.

> DVA. Necessarily, there is a diversity of value in the full in range of possible worlds.

DVA entails that the overall value of possible worlds varies. There are possible worlds with very little value and possible worlds with an abundance of value. Value would have to include at least moral and aesthetic value. Moral value in a world might include instances where significantly free beings exercise such qualities as compassion, care, generosity, concern, sympathy, and so on. It also could include the deontic features of a world.

> The good-making properties might include the fact that the requirements of justice are always observed in a world or the fact that basic rights are always respected in a world. Justice might require a distribution of social goods according to need or merit. Justice might

---

[4] (Mackie 1955, p. 203).
[5] Ibid., p. 212.
[6] (Rowe 1970).
[7] (Plantinga 1974, p. 165).

require an equal distribution of social goods. Justice might also require that no inhabitants of a world benefit excessively from the chance possession of natural or social goods. Of course, the good-making and bad-making properties will also include the overall value of a possible world or the proportion of value to disvalue in the traditional axiological sense of value.[8]

Mackie relies on DVA to defend his logical problem of evil when he claims that God's failure to avail himself of making a morally perfect world serves as strong evidence against the proposition that God exists.

[I]f God has made men such that in their free choices they sometimes prefer what is good and sometimes what is evil, why could he not have made men such that they always freely choose the good? If there is no logical impossibility in a man's freely choosing the good on one, or on several, occasions, there cannot be a logical impossibility in his freely choosing the good on every occasion. God was not, then, faced with a choice between making innocent automata and making beings who, in acting freely, would sometimes go wrong: there was open to him the obviously better possibility of making beings who would act freely but always go right. Clearly, his failure to avail himself of this possibility is inconsistent with his being both omnipotent and wholly good.[9]

According to Mackie, it is not the case that, necessarily, God was in a situation in which he could actualize only one of two sorts of worlds. Possible worlds in which automata–beings always do the right thing but are not significantly free–exist, or possible worlds in which significantly free beings exist but sometimes do wrong. Instead, Mackie urges that it is broadly logically possible that God had available to him the opportunity to actualize a better sort of world, in which every significantly free being always do the right thing.

Minimally, DVA affords Mackie the metaphysical picture that at least possible worlds with differing overall value exist. Without DVA, Mackie could not construe a situation in which God fails to create a morally perfect world that he might have created.

William Rowe relies on DVA in order to argue that we have reason to believe that God has good reasons to permit some evil in a world but not all evil in every possible world.

An omniscient, wholly-good being would prevent the occurrence of any intense evil it could, unless it could not do so without thereby losing some greater good or permitting some equally bad or worse evil.[10]

This standard formulation is Rowe's definition of gratuitous or pointless evil. God permits only evils such that they entail greater goods, the prevention of worse evils, or the prevention of evils equally bad. The first condition implies that Rowe relies on DVA in his evidential problem of evil.

According to Rowe, God permits evil if, necessarily, evil E entails a greater good G, and G & E is overall more valuable than ~G & ~E. There is a possible world, w_1, in which God permits E and, necessarily E entails G, and the occurrence of G & E is overall more valuable than a possible world, w_2, where ~G & ~E occur, all else being equal. Let > signify greater in overall value. So it is true that $w_1 > w_2$, in spite of the evil that occurs. God is justified in permitting the lesser evil E for G because G is unobtainable without E.[11]

DVA affords Rowe opportunities to explain various circumstances across a diversity of possible worlds in which God permits evil. In possible worlds in which lesser evils entail greater goods,

---

[8] (Almeida 2017).
[9] (Mackie 1955, p. 209).
[10] (Rowe 1970, p. 336).
[11] (Rowe 1970).

God permits the lesser evil. It is a better overall world than a world in which it had not occurred, all else being equal. In possible worlds in which a lesser evil entails the prevention of a greater evil, God permits the lesser evil.

Rowe does go on to argue that it is reasonable to believe there is some actual evil that does not entail greater goods, nor prevents evil. It is this justified belief that makes it the case that God probably does not exist. However, without DVA, Rowe could not explain why it is the case that pointless evils, not all evils, are a problem for the belief that God exists.

In his famous Free Will Defense, Alvin Plantinga relies on DVA in order to argue that God is justified in permitting some evil, against Mackie's argument that no evil is justified. Plantinga argues that it is possible that it is necessary that in all worlds free beings exist in, they sometimes do what is wrong. It is also true that it is not within God's power to cause them to always choose to do what is right. There is no world God could actualize in which every significantly free being always does what is right. However, there are possible and actualizable worlds where significantly free beings overall do more right actions than wrong actions. Additionally:

> A world containing creatures who are sometimes significantly free (and freely perform more good than evil actions) is more valuable, all else being equal, than a world containing no free creatures at all.[12]

So, God is justified in actualizing a possible world with some evil in it. The lesser evil of significantly free beings choosing to do what is wrong entails the greater overall good of those significantly free beings' existence and those beings mostly doing right. A possible world in which significantly free beings perform more good than evil actions is overall more valuable than if they did not exist.

DVA provides an opportunity for Plantinga to formulate a response to Mackie's problem of evil. There are at least two possible worlds with differing overall value. One possible world, w_1, contains significantly free beings who perform more right actions than wrong actions overall. In possible world, w_2, there are no significantly free beings performing more right actions than wrong actions. The existence of and actions of significantly free beings are among the good-making properties of w_1. These are goods that w_2 lacks since no significantly free beings exist there, all else being equal. On Plantinga's view, it is the case that $w_1 > w_2$. God is justified in permitting evil.

DVA is an important initial assumption in the problems of evil. Mackie uses DVA to argue that God could have created a morally perfect world such that its overall value exceeds the value of other possible worlds. Rowe uses DVA to argue that God is justified in permitting some evils. Worlds which lack those lesser evils that entail greater goods are, overall, less valuable than they could have been. Plantinga uses DVA to argue that God is justified in permitting the evil that significantly free beings create. The existence of those significantly free beings in spite of the moral evil that they create contributes positively to the overall value of that world such that its value exceeds that of possible worlds had they not existed.

4. Unsurpassable Value Assumption

But the initial assumptions of DVA and TCG both cannot be true. If TCG is false and DVA true, then there might not be any problem of evil. Mackie is direct when it comes to this possibility.

> If you are prepared to say that God is not wholly good, or not quite omnipotent, or that evil does not exist, or that good is not opposed to the kind of evil that exists, or that there are limits to what an omnipotent thing can do, then the problem of evil will not arise for you.[13]

If God is not wholly good, then it is possible that there is evil in a possible world such that God would not prevent it. He may be sufficiently powerful but not morally perfect and therefore fails to

---

[12] (Plantinga 1974, p. 169).
[13] (Mackie 1955, p. 200).

prevent evil. However, if God is not omnipotent, then it is possible there is some evil in a possible world such that God could not eliminate or prevent that evil. God would not be morally required to do the impossible. These solutions acquiesce in the existence of evil. But rejecting TCG is not an outcome many theists would readily agree to. But if TCG is true, then DVA is false. Indeed, DVA is necessarily false.

But exactly how is it that DVA is necessarily false? It certainly seems plausibly true. If there are possible worlds w_1 and w_2, and E occurs in w_1 but not w_2, all else being equal, w_1 has an instance of disvalue that w_2 lacks. The lowering of value of w_1 makes it such that $w_1 < w_2$, or w_1 is overall less valuable world than w_2. Consider the value of a very great good G that occurs in world w_1 but not in the nearly identical world w_2, which lacks that G. The increase in value of w_1 over w_2 makes it such that $w_1 > w_2$ or that w_1 is overall more valuable than w_2. DVA does not preclude the possibility of duplicate worlds.[14] DVA does not preclude worlds have identical overall value *in toto*. It seems that DVA is true.

Recall that TCG entails that God is a maximally great being and a maximally great being is maximally great if it meets the conditions of (1).

1   Necessarily, a being is maximally great if and only if that being is omnipotent, omnibenevolent, omniscient, necessarily existing and there is no conceivable being B* such that B* is greater than or equal to TCG.

There will be no conceivable being that surpasses God's omnipotence, omniscience, and omnibenevolence, according to Anselm. Additionally, it is a plausible characterization of (1) that a maximally great being at least entails possessing goodness that it is both unsurpassable and undiminishable.

UNG. Necessarily, God's goodness is unsurpassable and undiminishable.

This assumption has found support by Thomas Aquinas, Mark Johnston, Georg Cantor, and in some similar degree, Alvin Plantinga.

Aquinas conceives God as supremely good.

Since it is as first source of everything not himself in a genus that God is good, he must be good in the most perfect manner possible. And for this reason we call him supremely good … he alone exists by nature, and in him there are no added accidents (power, wisdom, and the like which are accidental to other things belonging to him by nature, as already noted). Moreover, he is not disposed towards some extrinsic goals, but is himself the ultimate good of all other things. So it is clear that only God possesses every kind of perfection by nature. He alone therefore is by nature good.[15]

Johnston is explicit about the Anselmian conception of God as an absolutely, infinitely good being.

God is absolutely infinite goodness. Accordingly, he has by his essence every positive value or perfection it is possible for him to have simply (i.e., not in virtue of some relation to other things) and in manner that is unsurpassable and undiminishable. Moreover, his goodness considered *in toto* is unsurpassable and undiminishable.[16]

This is the view of God that is reminiscent of Cantor's philosophical work on the conception of the *Absolute*.

The transfinite with its abundance of formations and forms, points with necessity to an Absolute, to the "truly Infinite," to whose Magnitude nothing can be added or

---

14   (Monton 2010).
15   (Aquinas 1964), Question 6, Article 3.
16   (Johnston 2015, p. 4).

subtracted and which therefore is to be seen quantitatively as an *absolute* Maximum. The latter exceeds, so to speak, the human power of comprehension and eludes particularly mathematical determination.[17]

What surpasses all that is finite and transfinite is no 'Genus'; it is the single and completely individual unity in which everything is included, which includes the 'Absolute' incomprehensible to the human understanding. This is the 'Actus Durissimus' which by many is called 'God'.[18]

This view also is found in very recent work of Plantinga.

... We are considering just the worlds in which God exists; for present purposes, let's assume that traditional theism is true, and that these are all the worlds there are. The first thing to note, I think, is that all of these worlds—all possible worlds, then are very good. For God is unlimited in goodness and holiness ... [b]ut what is the force of 'unlimited' here? I take it to mean that there are no nonlogical limits to God's display of these great-making properties: no nonlogical limit to his goodness, love, knowledge and power. From this it follows, I believe, that any state of affairs containing God alone—any state of affairs that would have been actual had God not created anything at all—is also in a sensible sense infinite in value ... [19,20]

Aquinas conceives God as supremely good and the source of all goodness overall. Johnston conceives God's goodness as essentially, unsurpassable and undiminishable. They are part of his property of being perfect in virtue of the kind of being he is. Cantor, too, sees God's value is such that nothing can either be added or subtracted from it. His value exceeds any finite and transfinite. Plantinga conceives God at least as a being of unlimited goodness—without at least finite limit, presumably—regardless of the states of affairs that obtain and with no non-logical limitations to his great-making properties including his goodness.[21] According to Anselm, God is a being than which none greater can be conceived. Plantinga, Cantor, Aquinas, and Johnston's view of God as UNG is consistent with TCG, the Anselmian God. TCG is a maximally great being such that no being is greater than it which is consistent with (1). UNG is a plausible description of God's *omnibenevolent* nature.

UNG entails that there is no finite amount in which the absolute value of God can be diminished. Consider some transfinite cardinal $\aleph_n$, and suppose the cardinality of God's value = $\aleph_n$. It is true that compared to even very large finite numbers n, the transfinite cardinal $\aleph_n$ is infinitely larger. God's value therefore exceeds every finite value. But it is also true that for every transfinite cardinal $\aleph_n$, there is an even larger transfinite cardinal $\aleph_{n+1}$. So, God's value is infinite, but also surpassable. And, of course, for a $\aleph_{n+1}$ there is an even larger $2^{\aleph_n+1}$. So, no matter what infinite cardinality measures God's value, it is a surpassable value. Now, according to Cantor, God is a being who transcends all finite and infinite measures. God's value is unsurpassable and undiminishable. Consider the possibility of some finite value n added to God's value $\aleph_j$.

$$(i) \ \aleph_j + n = \aleph_j$$

$$(ii) \ \aleph_j \times n = \aleph_j$$

---

[17] (Cantor 1994). See a letter from Georg Cantor to A. Eulenberg, February 28, 1886. This account of Cantor's conception is endorsed by Michael Almeida and Mark Johnston, as well. See (Almeida 2017, p. 157; Johnston 2015, p. 4).

[18] (Dauben 1979).

[19] (Plantinga 2008, p. 6).

[20] Ibid., 6.

[21] Though Plantinga conceives God greatness as unlimited, it is notable feature of his view that the Incarnation and Atonement are among the greatest contingent states of affairs that can occur in any possible world. If the view I argue for is correct, even worlds with Incarnation and Atonement are overall equally good as worlds without them.

No n is such that it increases the value of God. For any finite n, God's value infinitely exceeds that n. Arithmetic is uneventful between God's absolute infinite value and some finite value n. But the same can be said for the infinite amounts $\aleph_i$ subtracted from God's value.

$$\text{(iii)} \; \aleph_j - \aleph_i = \aleph_j$$

$$\text{(iv)} \; \aleph_j / \aleph_i = \aleph_j$$

It is also true that no $\aleph_i$ is such that it decreases the value of God. For any infinite $\aleph_i$, God's value infinitely exceeds that $\aleph_i$. Arithmetic is uneventful given God's absolute infinite value and the infinitely smaller infinite value. God's absolute infinite value surpasses any value whatsoever. It has no upper bound.

Though the functions of addition and subtraction are employed to explain God's value, the Cantor/Johnston view does not entail that God's value is conceived merely quantitatively. It is true that Cantor sees God's magnitude as immeasurably infinite that nothing can diminish or surpass it. But recall that it is also true that Cantor conceives God as the source of all things and lacking no perfection. Johnston also conceives God as having every possible perfection such that they are unsurpassable and undiminishable *en toto*. The Cantor/Johnston view is consistent with Thomist and Anselmian conceptions of God. God is the greatest conceivable being and has every perfection perfectly. God is the source of all things and, by nature, good. God's omnibenevolence is an absolute infinite value. God's goodness is such that it is unsurpassable and undiminishable. No finite or infinite value—quantitative nor qualitative—can increase or decrease it.

5. DVA is False

Recall that it has been argued that TCG is consistent with (1). It has also been argued that the value of God is UNG. UNG is consistent with both TCG and (1). Note that because God is necessarily existing, God exists at every possible world. It is also true then that DVA is necessarily false and prominent approaches to the problems of evil are mistaken.

Mackie argues that one way the problem of evil arises is because God failed to avail himself the option of creating a better world where free creatures that always do right exist in contrast to a world where they sometimes do right, or a world where there are automata. There is a world w_1 where automata exist rather than significantly free beings. In world w_2, there are significantly free creatures that sometimes go wrong. And in world w_3, there are significantly free creatures that always go right freely. The existence of and the actions of these creatures bear on the overall value of the world. As a result, Mackie assumes DVA is true and argues that $w_3 > w_2$ or w_1. God's failure to create w_3 is evidence of his non-existence.

But Mackie is mistaken. Among the valuable beings in these worlds is God. As a necessarily existing being, God's existence also bears on the overall value of a world. That value is an absolute infinite value. Furthermore, no finite or infinite value can either surpass or diminish God's value. It is not the case $w_3 > w_2$ or w_1. The prevention of any finite or infinite evil cannot either increase or decrease the overall value of any world. So, it is impossible that God was in a situation in which he failed to avail himself the option of creating a better world, as Mackie argues.

Recall that Rowe assumes DVA is true and argues that there are evils God permits because they entail greater goods. These are greater goods that God would want to occur rather than prevent. Take w_1 where some justified suffering occurs, E, and world w_2 where God prevents that E. It is also true that E entails a greater good G. w_1 is an overall better world than w_2 in spite of E because of G. So God permits that E.

But, necessarily, DVA is false. w_1 is not an overall better world than w_2. As a necessarily existing being, God's existence also bears on the overall value of a world, all else being equal. That value is an absolute infinite value. Furthermore, no finite or infinite value can either surpass or diminish God's value. w_1 does not yield any greater value if God permits E than in w_2 where God prevents it.

Likewise, the prevention of a pointless evil does not yield a better world compared to a world where it occurs. But then Rowe's approach to the problems of evil is mistaken. The reason Rowe gives for God permitting or preventing evil is necessarily false.

Recall Plantinga's famous defense and his assumption of DVA. God is permitted to create significantly free beings that sometimes do evil because they do more right than wrong, overall. It is a better world with significantly free beings existing than if they did not exist. Take w_1 where significantly free beings exist and world w_2 where they do not. It is true on Plantinga's view that these worlds differ in value. It is true on Plantinga's view that w_1 is greater in overall value than w_2.

But Plantinga is mistaken. DVA is necessarily false. As a necessarily existing being, God's existence also bears on the overall value of a world, all else being equal. That value is an infinite absolute value. Furthermore, no finite or infinite value can either surpass or diminish God's value. There is no world w_1 where significantly free beings sometimes go wrong but overall do what is right that is better than a world without them. Counter to Plantinga, God does not have a reason to permit significantly free beings for its added value to the world.

The prominent approaches to the problems of evil are mistaken. If TCG is true, UNG is also plausibly true. But if UNG is true, then DVA is necessarily false.[22] But DVA is a crucial assumption when engaging the problems of evil. The prominent approaches to the problems of evil then are mistaken.

6. Preventing or Permitting Evil

Recall that the prominent approaches to the problems of evil argue that God's reasons for preventing or permitting evil are based on the overall value of those possible worlds evil creates. But if UNG is true, no world is overall better than any other world regardless of whether God permits or prevents any evil. The reasons Mackie, Rowe, and Plantinga attributed to God for permitting or preventing evil are necessarily false. The prevention or permission of evil are not justified as Mackie, Rowe, and Plantinga see it.

Mackie urges that if God were to exist, his reason to prevent evil would be that he could actualize a morally perfect world such that it is overall better than a world where automata exist or where evil exists as the product of human free actions, all else being equal. Not creating that morally perfect world, Mackie urges, is inconsistent with God's omnipotence and being wholly good. But if UNG is true, no world is overall better than any other world. It is impossible that God could actualize a morally perfect world such that it is overall better than a world where automata exist or where evil is the product of human free actions. The world with automata or significantly free beings that sometimes go wrong have the same infinite absolute value as a world where humans always freely act rightly. It is true that God could actualize a world where significantly free beings always go right; however, that world would not even be overall slightly better than a world with automata instead. Indeed, a world where significantly free beings always go right would not even be overall slightly better than any world whatsoever. It is necessarily false that God's reason to prevent evil is to actualize a morally perfect world that is overall better than any world. The existence of evil then is not inconsistent with God's omnipotence and being wholly good with respect to Mackie's approach to the problems of evil.

Rowe argues that God has good reason to permit evil because of the great goods it creates or the equally bad or worse evils it prevents. Any instance of evil that does not meet at least one of

---

[22] It is also true that we can rank worlds from better or worse while granting that their overall value is the same, as an anonymous referee observes. For example, it is true that the contingent, created part of world w_{34} with much more evil in it is intuitively worse than an otherwise similar world, w_{85}, with less evil in it. Or, similarly, it is true that w_{34} might have less contingent, good-making properties than w_{85} such that w_{34} is ranked worse than w_{85}. But it is also consistent to say that w_{34} and w_{85} have the same overall value with respect to the existence of God. God is one of the good-making properties in those worlds. Klaas Kraay has briefly suggested that a problem of evil might then be refocused on deriving an inconsistency between the existence of God and the existence of evil in the contingent, created part of worlds. See (Kraay 2017).

these conditions is evidence that God does not exist. But if UNG is true, no world is overall better than any other world. It is impossible that God could permit or prevent evil such that it makes any world overall better. It is impossible that God could permit evil E such that the entailing great good G results in an overall better world than a world where ~E & ~G occur. It may be true that God could actualize a world where E entails G but it would not be even overall slightly better than any world whatsoever. It is necessarily false that God has a reason to permit evil because of the great goods it creates. Furthermore, the prevention of evil would not make any world even overall slightly better. It is not the case that the prevention or permission of any evil makes any world overall better or worse. It is necessarily false that God's reason to permit evil or prevent evil is to the betterment of any world. The existence of evil then is not inconsistent with God's omnipotence and being wholly good with respect to Rowe's view of the problems of evil.

Plantinga argues that God has a reason to permit evil because, in spite of the evil that it creates, a world with significantly free beings is a better world than without them. Furthermore, Plantinga recognizes that the worlds in which God exists are very good worlds and, since God exists at every world, all the worlds are very good. But if UNG is true, all worlds are more than very good; they are of absolute infinite value. No world is overall better than any other world. It is impossible that there is a world in which significantly free beings are mostly doing right that is overall better than a world where those significantly free beings do not exist. It may be possible that God could actualize a world with significantly free beings, but that world would not even be overall slightly better than a world without those beings or any world whatsoever. It is necessarily false that God has a reason to permit evil because, in spite of the evil that they create, a world with significantly free beings is a better world than without. It is impossible for God to have created significantly free beings for the overall betterment of any world.

The reasons the prominent approaches to the problems of evil attribute to God in preventing or permitting evil are mistaken. No world is overall better than any other world regardless if God permits or prevents any evil. Unlike Mackie's view, God does not have a reason to prevent evil for the betterment of any world. Unlike Rowe's view, God lacks the reason to permit and prevent any evil for the betterment of any world. Unlike Plantinga's view, God lacks the reason for permitting evil perpetuated by significantly free beings for the betterment of any world.

7. Conclusions

In this paper, I argue for the thesis that the prominent approaches to the problems of evil are mistaken. The Anselmian God is TCG, a maximally great being as described in (1). The Anselmian God is consistent with UNG, a conception found and defended by Aquinas, Anselm, Johnston, Cantor, and (to some degree) Plantinga. But if God is UNG, then DVA—a common assumption across the prominent approaches to the problems of evil—is false. There is no possible world with overall greater value than any other possible world. The standard reasons God prevents or permits evil as supposed by the prominent approaches to the problems of evil are mistaken.

Conflicts of Interest: The author declares no conflicts of interest.

References

Almeida, Michael. 2017. *Theistic Modal Realism*. San Antonio: University of Texas at San Antonio, p. 155, forthcoming.

Aquinas, Thomas. 1964. *Summa Theologia: Volume 2*. Translated by Timothy McDermott. New York: McGraw-Hill Book Company.

Cantor, Georg. 1994. On the Theory of the Transfinite. *Fidelio* 3: 104.

Dauben, Joseph Warren. 1979. Georg Cantor, Letter to G. C. Young, June 20, 1908. In *Georg Cantor: His Mathematics and Philosophy of the Infinite*. Cambridge: Harvard University Press.

Johnston, Mark. 2015. *Why Did the One Not Remain in Itself?* New Brunswick: Rutgers University, forthcoming.

Religions **2018**, *9*, 20

Kraay, Klaas. 2017. God and Infinite Value. Paper presented at 2017 Brackenridge Symposium, San Antonio, TX, USA, October 12–13.

Mackie, John L. 1955. Evil and Omnipotence. *Mind* 64: 200–12. [CrossRef]

Malcolm, Norman. 1960. Anselm's Ontological Arguments. *The Philosophical Review* 69: 41–62. [CrossRef]

Monton, Bradley. 2010. Against Multiverse Theodices. *Philo* 13: 113–35. [CrossRef]

Plantinga, Alvin. 1974. *The Nature of Necessity*. Oxford: Claredon Press.

Plantinga, Alvin. 2008. Superlapsarianism or 'O Felix Culpa'. In *Christian Faith and the Problem of Evil*. Edited by Peter van Inwagen. Grand Rapids: Eerdmanns, pp. 1–25.

Rowe, William L. 1970. The Problem of Evil and Some Varieties of Atheism. *American Philosophical Quarterly* 16: 335.

Williams, Thomas. 2007. *Anselm: Basic Writings*. Indianapolis: Hackett Publishing Company.

Article

Actualizing Unique Type and Token Values as a Solution to the Problem of Evil

Atle Ottesen Søvik

Department of Systematic Theology, MF Norwegian School of Theology, P.O.Box 5144 Majorstuen,
0302 Oslo, Norway; Atle.O.Sovik@mf.no; Tel.: +47-2259-0536

Received: 30 November 2017; Accepted: 22 December 2017; Published: 24 December 2017

Abstract: Concerning the problem of evil, I suggest that God's goodness and omnipotence causes God to want to actualize many different values and things, not solely angels in heaven, but also type unique values like independence, self-formation, creativity, and surprise, and token unique goods like animals and human beings. Such a universe as ours, though, requires undisturbed indeterministic self-formation as actualized by a good God to give those token unique beings access to those type unique values and allow them the opportunity to live forever with God after completion of this self-formation.

Keywords: the problem of evil; type and token values; indeterminism

1. Introduction

In this article I suggest the following solution the problem of evil: God is good and omnipotent, and as good, God wants to actualize many and many different values in the world. More precisely, God wants to actualize values that are type unique in being different kinds of good, and token unique in being instantiations of values at different times and places. This has the consequence that God not only wants to create a heaven with angels and no suffering, but also a universe like ours, which actualizes type unique goods like independence, self-formation, creativity, and surprise, and token unique goods like the actual animals and humans that live here. Bringing forth a universe like ours requires indeterminism, which also has the negative effect that suffering becomes possible. There is no other way to bring about a highly independent, self-formed, creative and surprising universe with the token unique individuals living there than through undisturbed indeterministic self-formation. This is the only way for the individuals living there to come into being and have the opportunity to live forever with God (after self-formation), and thus it is good that God actualizes such a universe.

In the following, I shall unpack these claims and defend them against objections. I have previously written a book on the problem of evil defending a similar theory (Søvik 2011). In the book I focused on independence, but here the focus is instead on actualizing type and token unique values, which was not a distinction made in the book. I have not seen anyone else use this distinction to solve the problem of evil. The discussion of types of values, their relation, and why God would actualize these is new to this article.

The article is divided into four parts. Part one is the introduction. In part two, I start by discussing how to understand values and the distinction between type and token unique values. I then argue that the goodness of God implies that God wants to actualize many and many different types of values. In part three, I present some specific values that I suggest God wanted to actualize in our universe, and what the conditions are for bringing forth such values. I end this part by arguing that it is good for God to create our universe with these conditions. In part four, I answer objections.

2. Values

How should values be understood? In meta-ethics, cognitive realists hold that moral judgments are beliefs that can be true. This means that there are true statements of the form "X is good", "X is just", etc. Among cognitive realists, there are three different groups offering three different explanations as to what gives moral judgments truth value; the supernaturalists, non-naturalists and naturalists. Supernaturalists refer to the mind of God to explain the truth value of moral judgments, so it is true that X is good if X is the will of God. Non-naturalists refer to values having their own (platonic) existence, or at least as being something which cannot be given a naturalistic definition, as famously argued by G. E. Moore (Moore and Baldwin 1903, § 13). Naturalists argue that values are something natural, for example, that what is good is that which produces the most pleasure (Bentham 1988, chp. 1).

The classical objection to supernaturalists is the Euthyphro dilemma: is something good because God wants it, or does God want it because it is good? (Allen and Plato 1970, part two). The classical objection to non-naturalists is that such values are queer entities, and that it is more plausible to believe that they do not exist (Mackie 1977). Classical objections to naturalism are Moore's open question argument and that naturalism seems to take the normative force out of ethics (presented further below).

There is not room in this article to discuss the ontology of values, but I will offer a brief defense for a naturalistic approach. This naturalistic approach avoids the Euthyphro dilemma. It also avoids the objection of queerness, since there are no queer entities. It further has the advantage of explaining ethical supervenience. All seem to agree that ethical facts supervene upon descriptive facts, in the sense that there cannot be an ethical change without a descriptive change. Differently put, there cannot be two identical universes except that in one of them murder is wrong and in the other murder is good. But this seems to favor a descriptive understanding of norms. For if values are something that have their own existence, it seems we should be able to have two identical universes, except that we add one value to one of them. How are values connected to the natural world if they are not identical to something natural?

Moore's open question argument against naturalistic ethics is as follows: It is a fallacy to give a descriptive definition to the term "good", since it is always an open question whether the definition given is actually good. For example, if "good" is defined as that which maximizes pleasure, we can still openly and meaningfully ask whether that which maximizes pleasure is good. According to Moore, this showed that the term "good" could not be given a descriptive definition.

Several counterarguments have been offered against Moore. It is meaningful to ask whether H_2O is water even if (most) water is H_2O. The argument is question-begging since it assumes that any definition of "good" is not right, and the argument proves too much since it seems that we can meaningfully discuss many definitions of terms (like knowledge) without concluding that they are undefinable. I believe that the reason we feel that we can meaningfully ask of any definition of "good" whether it is good is that we have a vague/general/non-conscious intuition about what goodness is. It does not follow that there is actually more to say, or something undefinable about it, or a correct answer beyond how we choose to define the term.

When it comes to Hume's charge that one cannot derive an *ought* from an *is*, the naturalist can respond that the "ought" has been given an "is" definition, so that ethical norms derive an is from an is. But if ethical norms are given descriptive content, it seems to take away the normative force of these ethical norms. Ethical norms commend or prescribe a certain action; they motivate people for action. How could this be understood if what is good is something natural?

This "normative force" can be understood in different ways. In itself, a *should* claim or an *ought* claim is a means to reach something considered good. Thus, when saying that people should or ought to do a moral act, it means that if they want to reach something good, then that is a means to that goal. But that alone does not seem to commend the goal in a way that normative claims seem to commend actions for people.

I believe that this commending aspect comes from people saying that something is good or should be done. If one accepts that something is good or should be done, one accepts that this is something one ought to try to reach. Different people will feel different degrees of normative force when facing different norms. If there is a God, most people would probably feel an extra weight from the fact that something was willed by the omnipotent creator of the universe, but even this could be rejected.

This may still seem too weak. Is there a normative force regardless of what people think or feel? Can we say that objectively you have reason to act in such and such ways, regardless of whether you want to or not? You cannot have a reason without a goal. It is the good as a goal that gives us reason to act, but that presupposes the goal first. Of course, there can be many reasons for acting morally—that it is good, that it is consistent and rational, that it is in your own self-interest, etc. These reasons will give different force to normative claims, but there is no ontological normative force coming from ethics itself beyond what is described here.

This was a brief and general defense of a naturalistic approach, which is also more ontologically parsimonious than non-naturalism and supernaturalism. However, the theodicy to be presented below does not depend on one accepting naturalism about values as long as one accepts ethical supervenience. A defense of this approach is nevertheless included in order to present a detailed theodicy.

After this general defense of naturalism about values, the time has come to ask what values are. In line with the goal of parsimony, I suggest that value or something good should just be understood as anything that is valuated/appreciated/considered good by anyone. However, we should distinguish between three different meanings of the term value/good, where the basic meaning is that something is good in the sense that it is valuated by an individual, and we could refer to this valuation as individual-good. This is then to distinguish from ethical-good, which is when we try to sum up all the individual-goods into what would be valuated most by the most. And this again could be distinguished from the sense in which the things or events being valuated are good, which we could call potential-good, since the value of something lies in its potential for being valuated by someone.

These different aspects of what is good relate in the following way: The most fundamental part is that someone valuates something. When someone valuates something—not instrumentally, but for its own sake—this does not have a deeper explanation than to just be valuation. I may watch comedies because I like to laugh, and there is no deeper explanation for why I like to laugh—I just like it. This valuation (individual-good) is the basis for ethical-good, since ethical-good is the most individual-good for the most individuals. And this valuation (individual-good) is also the basis for the value that things, people and events have (potential-good). That does not mean that something does not have value if it is not valuated, but that it would not have value if no valuation existed at all.

Again, there is no room to discuss this definition of values in this article, but I include it as a precise presentation of what values are. I now move on to the distinction between unique type and token values. A type value is a value that can be instantiated at several times and places, e.g., joy. A type value is unique if it has intrinsic properties different from other values, e.g., fun is a type unique value in virtue of having different intrinsic properties than peace, love etc.[1] A token value is an instantiation of a type value *at a certain time and place*, e.g., the joy of attending the party yesterday at my neighbor's house. Thus, the joy I experience as I write this article is token unique from my joy yesterday at the neighbor's house.

Having now defined values and the distinction between type and token values, the next question is whether God would want to actualize many and many different type and token values. One could imagine that God only created one type of potential good, such as harp music or clouds, and then just created one type of individual who could valuate it, such as angels. God could then increase the amount of potential good and individual good by increasing the number of clouds or harp songs or angels or the amount of time, and this would be ethically good since it brought about more individual good.

God could also increase the number of type values, creating different potential goods, such as stars. This would bring about more variation in what could be valuated, and the variation in itself

---

[1] The term "intrinsic properties" here refers to all characteristics other than spatio-temporal location.

would be a good that could be valuated. God could also create different kinds of individuals that could valuate different kinds of things, like animals and humans. These different types of individuals could valuate not only different things, but also each other. Again this would be an ethically good increase of individual good in the world. In addition, it would be sharing of goods in a relationship, which is also ethically good.

However, it is not necessarily ethically good just to create as many individuals as possible, since it depends on how their lives are overall. What we have seen so far is that it is prima facie ethically good of God to actualize many types of potential goods and many types of individuals who can valuate the goods and the variation itself, but there are other relevant things to consider as well in order to judge whether God's creation is good, for example, the place of suffering. In the next part, we shall make such a broad consideration of our universe.

3. Our Universe

God could have created animals and humans in many different ways. They could have been created without capacity for suffering. Perhaps God already has created such individuals in another universe, and at least it is a part of Christian faith that humans will have an afterlife which is like that—and some include animals in that vision.

The theodicy presented in this article suggests that God in our universe has actualized the following unique type values: The universe is independent in the sense of a partly self-creating universe which brings forth living individuals in a creative and surprising way, and these individuals are also independent in the sense of being partly self-creating. The individual animals and humans in this universe are themselves token values of a certain type, as just described.

The mentioned type values come in degrees: there can be different degrees of how independent, self-creating, creative and surprising something is. This theodicy proposes that these values come in a high degree in our universe: it is independent, self-creating, creative and surprising to a high degree.

The mentioned values have a common requirement, which is indeterminism. Indeterminism denies that the world is determined, which would mean that there is only one possible content of the future. Instead, indeterminism means that the content of the future is open. There can be different reasons why the universe should be determined, such as laws of nature, God, destiny, or something else. There can also be different reasons why the universe should be indetermined, such as causeless events, probabilistic laws of nature, or something else.

Even if the universe is indeterministic, it is not given what space of possibilities such indeterminism happens within. The future can be open but with a very limited set of possible futures, or it can be very open with a great variety of possible open futures. For example, indeterminism could be confined to the micro level of quantum physics or also apply to the macro level of human interaction, and it could have all sorts of other constraints.

The theodicy here presented proposes that our universe is genuinely indeterministic, which means that it occurs within a large space of possibilities. God knows what the possibilities are, but does not know which possibilities will be actualized. This genuine indeterminism gives the universe its high degree of independence, self-creation, creativity, and surprise.

While indeterminism is a condition that makes these mentioned values possible, genuine indeterminism has the negative side effect that it makes suffering possible. It can cause mutations and diseases, and it can cause natural disasters such as storms, earthquakes, volcanic eruptions etc. As a condition for a strong degree of libertarian freedom, it can also make people abuse this freedom to cause others pain. In order to be used as an explanation for suffering, indeterminism cannot be very restricted, but must have occurred within a large space of possibilities from the beginning of the universe. In addition, God's goal of a highly independent universe must make God generally refrain from interfering.

We shall consider many objections below, but here I ask the following question: Do we have reason to believe that our universe is genuinely indeterministic? The most common place to go for support is quantum mechanics. Quantum mechanics can be given indeterministic interpretations (like Copenhagen and GRW) and deterministic interpretations (like deBroglie-Bohm and Everett). Nevertheless, all interpretations will agree that the guiding laws are merely probabilistic, saying only that something will occur with a certain probability (Ney and Albert 2013). This still leaves open whether there is a determinism at a deeper level and whether indeterminism at the micro level of elementary particles can be scaled up to the macro level of human interaction.

James Ladyman argues that micro indeterminism obviously can be scaled up to the macro level of humans since humans interact with quantum indetermined processes. For example, a scientist may decide to invite his female colleague to lunch if he gets a click on his Geigerteller before 12 o'clock. Geigerteller clicks are undetermined events, and this decision may make them have lunch, fall in love and get married—or not. The world may then be very different in the future depending on undetermined events (Ladyman et al. 2007, p. 264).

However, one can also turn to classical Newtonian physics to find support for indeterminism at the macro level of human interaction. In such physics, indeterminism at the macro level occurs, for example, if three identical particles with the same speed collide (Earman 1986, pp. 30–32).[2] The question of whether our universe is deterministic or not will probably never be given a certain answer since there could always be a deeper level we have not discovered. But for the time being, there seems to be more support for indeterminism than determinism.

When it comes to the space of possibilities within which indeterminism takes place, it is hard for science to say much. When I propose that this is a large space, it must be considered as a metaphysical hypothesis, to be judged by the coherence of the worldview it implies. As explained above, this theodicy needs the space of possibilities to be large in order for indeterminism to work as an explanation of suffering.

The time has come to consider whether it would be good of God to actualize the mentioned values in our universe on the condition that indeterminism can cause suffering that God does not prevent. It is commonly said that a theodicy must meet two requirements: the necessity condition and the outweighing condition (Wahlberg 2015, p. 38). The possibility of suffering must be shown to be a necessary means to a sufficiently outweighing good.

When it comes to the necessity condition, this theodicy only works on the presupposition that substance ontology should be replaced by an ontology that prioritizes relations, such as relational ontology, structuralistic ontology, process ontology, or trope ontology. If substance ontology is right, what gives individuals their identity is fundamentally the substance that they are, and God could have actualized this substance in another universe. In other words, if substance ontology is right, God could have created you or me in another universe or directly into heaven.

If substance ontology is wrong, however, and one of the mentioned alternative ontologies are right, then what makes us into the individuals we are are our life stories and relations. Then I could not have had other parents, since other parents would not have given birth to me, but to another. And God could not have created me in another universe or directly into heaven since what makes me into me is the fact that I was born when I was, by those parents, and have formed my life through the events and relations that I have.

In other words, for God to actualize the token individuals of our universe, of the type that they are, God had to create a genuinely indeterministic universe governed by laws and independent from God's interventions, such as our universe is. We cannot complain that God should have created us in another universe since this would be logically impossible.

This claim requires also that it is not God who decides whether substance ontology or relational ontology is the correct metaphysics of the world, but that this is a fundamental fact about reality,

---

[2] Earman also gives other examples from Newtonian and relativity physics. Important examples are briefly summarized in (Sklar 1992, p. 203).

including God. There must necessarily be several facts about the world that are not the result of God's will, since God could not have chosen God's own being before God's own existence. That there are structures in reality that are not chosen by God is thus a logically necessary part of any theory of God.

The possibility of suffering is thus a necessary requirement for bringing about the individuals of this universe, and the outweighing good is the eternal life of happiness that God offers us after death. God could not ask us before we were born if we wanted to come into existence on these conditions, but had to make the choice for us. God knows that the suffering can be outweighed, and hopefully God also knows that we will think that it was worth it.

The theodicy here offered is the theory that God could only actualize the token and type values of this universe by creating this kind of universe, and that the suffering will be outweighed in the afterlife. It is argued that it is good of God to actualize many different type and token values. While God could just have created angels in heaven, God chose to actualize more types of individuals who could valuate more types of goods. This lets God valuate more types of good as well, such as having another kind of relationship with another kind of individual. Since this is our only possibility to have an eternal life with God, it is good for us that God created us—even on the condition that suffering is possible—and thus it is good that God created our universe.

4. Objections

There are plenty of objections that could be raised against this theodicy, and there is only room to answer the main objections. I will discuss some objections which apply to theism in general, and some objections which apply to a Christian concept of God in particular. The objections are the following: God could have reached the same goals without giving us libertarian free will and then indeterminism would not have been necessary; genuine indeterminism contradicts that God knows the future; animals suffer without having their suffering outweighed; offering a theodicy is immoral; God could have created a universe with indeterminism but where pain and suffering were nevertheless impossible; the theodicy does not explain the hiddenness of God; if not all are saved, some people will not have their suffering outweighed; since God did many miracles in the time of Jesus, God should prevent more suffering now; there is no support in the Bible that God wanted to create such an independent universe; God wants relationship with humans and not to leave them alone. Since I do not have space for a full discussion of these objections, I will briefly indicate my response in order to show the direction that a larger defense could take. Most of these objections are discussed in my book on the problem of evil (Søvik 2011).

Could not God have reached the same goals without giving us libertarian free will? Then indeterminism would not have been necessary? God could have created a universe which was determined and where we had only compatibilist free will. This would have been a weaker form of free will, since whatever happened would be determined before we were born. The universe would have contained different values, since it would have been less independent and less surprising, and it would have contained different token individuals. God could have done so, and could have created a good universe, and maybe God has. But the argument here is that God did not have to choose between making us and someone else, but that it is good that God has created us in addition to the good heaven-world and all the other universes God may have created.

Does not genuine indeterminism contradict that God knows the future? This theodicy implies that God does not know the future. That raises a lot of questions which cannot be discussed here, but there is a rich literature discussing the topic of God and time. I side with those who defend an understanding of God in time, such as Richard Swinburne, or the position of open theism.

Do animals suffer without having their suffering outweighed? We do not know which animals have a conscious experience of being an individual over time, which makes them capable of conscious suffering. It may seem obvious which animals suffer, but contrary to appearances, almost all actions can occur non-consciously, so it is not obvious which animals suffer. Anyway, God knows, and this theodicy does not work unless animals which experience being individuals over time also get a good afterlife, and so this is presupposed.

Is it not immoral to offer a theodicy? Offering a theodicy can sometimes create more suffering for people who suffer. But other times it can give comfort and hope to people who suffer. Searching for truth in itself is not immoral, but one must be context sensitive when actually presenting a theodicy to someone. Not publishing theodicies at all since sufferers might get hurt by them is not a good enough reason, since pursuit of truth and the possibility of helping sufferers are good consequences of publishing theodicies. There are obviously better ways to help sufferers than to publish theodicies, but it is not wrong to publish a theodicy even if there are other things that are more important.

Could not God have created a universe with indeterminism but where pain and suffering were nevertheless impossible? I wrote above that God created in our universe the space of possibilities that indeterminism takes place within, but I also wrote that there are some basic structures of the world that God has not created. That suffering at all is possible in the world is not a choice made by God. God cannot have chosen the basic possibilities of the world, since the basic possibilities must be there in order for anything to be actual at all.

God has chosen the restrictions that apply to our universe, but it seems plausible to me that there is a necessary link between genuine indeterminism and the possibility of pain and suffering, given genuine indeterminism. This means that God could have restricted indeterminism so much in our universe that pain and suffering could never occur. But this would have been a very limited indeterminism. If God wanted a high degree of independence in our universe, it would require an indeterminism with few limits, and then pain and suffering is one of the possibilities that genuine indeterminism can actualize.

Does this theodicy explain the hiddenness of God? The hiddenness of God is explained by the independence of the universe that God wanted to actualize. The independence of this universe is again explained by this being one of the many diverse values that God wants to actualize here while actualizing other types of values elsewhere. Many discussions of the hiddenness of God assume that God chooses, from situation to situation, to hide, whereas this theodicy makes it a part of the choice God made from creation on. I find such a choice by God far easier to defend than to claim that God should have reasons to hide from situation to situation.

Will some people not be saved, and then not have their suffering outweighed? This theodicy does not presuppose that all have an afterlife, since some may want not to live forever. But it does presuppose that all who have a capacity for freely choosing to reject God get a real choice to do so. Hopefully, none will choose that, but I leave the possibility open. As long as all have a real opportunity to have their suffering outweighed, this seems enough to defend the goodness of God.

If God did many miracles in the time of Jesus, why does not God prevent more suffering now? While God wanted to create an independent world, God also wanted there to be a trustworthy revelation available for those who seek it. God thus had a strong reason for offering a revelation and verifying it as a revelation from God by putting a divine signature on it in the form of miracles—especially the resurrection of Jesus. A high degree of independence does not mean that God can never intervene, but it does mean that God can *almost* never intervene.

If God can intervene, why does not God intervene in the worst cases of suffering? God has created a very independent universe with indeterminism playing a big role even from the beginning of the universe. Intervening to prevent great evils is a big intervention with great consequences for everything that happens later, and there are many great evils that should be prevented if God prevented all evils of a kind. Our universe has a degree of indeterminism and independence where God does not make such interventions. It would certainly have been easier to believe in the existence of God if our universe was different in this regard.

Is there any support in the Bible that God wanted to create such an independent universe? Gen 1: 26–28 says that humans are created in the image of God, and that God asked them to dominate the earth.

Since we are in fact highly independent, it is a coherent interpretation of the Bible to think of this as the will of God.

Does not God want relationship with humans and not to leave them alone? Relationship with humans is the ultimate goal for God, but in our universe there is an independent period first where, to a large degree, we shape our own lives. We may use our independence to seek and have relationship with God, but again, to a large degree, God remains hidden as long as the universe continues in the conditions it works under today.

5. Conclusions

The possibility of suffering in our universe can be explained by God wanting to actualize many different type and token values, and that among the values actualized in our universe are independence, self-formation, creativity, surprise and the token individuals of this universe. This solution has many presuppositions, among the more important being that there is genuine indeterminism in our universe, that there is an afterlife for humans and animals, and that substance ontology is wrong. These presuppositions have been briefly defended in this article which, although brief, offers a new theodicy to the larger discussion.

Conflicts of Interest: The author declares no conflict of interest.

References

Allen, Reginald E., and Plato. 1970. *Plato's 'Euthyphro' and Earlier Theory of Forms, International Library of Philosophy and Scientific Method*. London: Routledge & K. Paul.

Bentham, Jeremy. 1988. *The Principles of Morals and Legislation*. Great Books in Philosophy Series; Buffalo: Prometheus Books.

Earman, John. 1986. *A Primer on Determinism*. University of Western Ontario Series in Philosophy of Science; Boston: D. Reidel Pub. Co.

Ladyman, James, Don Ross, David Spurrett, and John Gordon Collier. 2007. *Every Thing Must Go: Metaphysics Naturalized*. Oxford: Oxford University Press.

Mackie, John L. 1977. *Ethics: Inventing Right and Wrong*. Pelican Books: Philosophy; New York: Penguin.

Moore, George Edward, and Thomas Baldwin. 1903. *Principia Ethica*. Cambridge: Cambridge University Press.

Ney, Alyssa, and David Z. Albert. 2013. *The Wave Function: Essays on the Metaphysics of Quantum Mechanics*. Oxford: Oxford University Press.

Sklar, Lawrence. 1992. *Philosophy of Physics*. Dimensions of Philosophy Series; Boulder: Westview Press.

Søvik, Atle Ottesen. 2011. *The Problem of Evil and the Power of God*. Studies in Systematic Theology. Leiden: Brill.

Wahlberg, Mats. 2015. Was Evolution the Only Possible Way for God to Make Autonomous Creatures? Examination of an Argument in Evolutionary Theodicy. *International Journal for Philosophy of Religion* 77: 37–51. [CrossRef]

Article

Mystical Body Theodicy

Joshua C. Thurow

Department of Philosophy and Classics, The University of Texas at San Antonio, One UTSA Circle, San Antonio, TX 78249, USA; joshua.thurow@utsa.edu

Received: 1 December 2017; Accepted: 25 January 2018; Published: 31 January 2018

Abstract: In this paper I develop a new theodicy–Mystical Body Theodicy. This theodicy draws on the Christian doctrine of the mystical body of Christ to argue that some evil can be defeated by a set of three goods connected with increasing the unity of humanity through love. This theodicy also helps three other prominent theodicies avoid objections.

Keywords: problem of evil; theodicy; Marilyn Adams; Richard Swinburne; mystical body

1. Introduction

At the highest level of abstraction, the problem of evil goes like this:

(PE1) There are evils of type F.
(PE2) If God existed God would not allow evils of type F. Therefore,
(PE3) God does not exist.[1]

There are many instances of this argument pattern. Each new substitution for 'F'—e.g., gratuitous evils, horrendous evils, natural evils, sufferings of non-human animals before there were humans, etc.—gets you a new argument, and there are a legion of such arguments.

What's a theist to do with (from his perspective) all these weeds? He'll first have to decide whether to take a **targeted** or **global** approach to eliminating the weeds. Can each argument be handled one at a time (or a few at a time), each requiring unique and carefully formulated treatments? This is the targeted approach. Or, can the whole lot of them be eliminated with one special treatment—the philosophical equivalent of Roundup to keep your theistic lawn clean? This is the global approach. He'll then have to decide whether to **attack** the weeds directly, i.e., argue that at least one of their premises are false, or to **defend** against the weeds by taking away what they need to grow, i.e., by arguing that there isn't good reason to believe their premises.

Skeptical theism is currently the most discussed and most popular response to the problem of evil.[2] It goes for the most economical response to the problem: a global defense. As such, it argues that one special treatment—a certain degree of skepticism about what is good and right and about what reasons God might have for acting—undermines reason to believe at least one premise of every instance of the above argument (usually PE2, but sometimes PE1 depending on how the evil is described). No need to look at each instance one-by-one. And no need to try to argue against a premise in each; arguing that p is false is often harder than arguing there aren't good reasons to believe p.

In this paper I want to explore perhaps the most prominent general alternative response: theodicy. A theodicy, as I shall understand the term, is an account of why, if God exists, God might allow evil. Theodicies can be targeted or global—that is, they can give accounts of why God allows a *certain set* of

---

[1] This is a deductive formulation, but obviously it also could be formulated probabilistically.
[2] See (Bergmann 2009; Dougherty and McBrayer 2014; Howard-Snyder 1996; McBrayer and Howard-Snyder 2013) for introductory and state-of-the-art essays on skeptical theism.

evils, or *all* evils.[3] Theodicies can also be weak or strong—that is, they can assert merely that, if God exists, God *might* have these reasons for allowing evil or they can assert more strongly that, if God exists, God *probably* has these reasons for allowing evil. Theodicies can thus respond to the problem of evil in either a targeted or global manner, and through either an attack or a defense. Thus some theodicies can, like skeptical theism, offer up a global defense. What distinguishes theodicies from skeptical theism is the manner of response: theodicies propose that God might allow evils for such-and-such reasons, whereas skeptical theists (qua being skeptical theists) make no such proposal.

What can the theodicist reasonably draw on in construction of such proposals? Marilyn McCord Adams's answer to this question vastly expanded the territory for theodicy, enabling her to develop her own detailed, theologically sophisticated, and justly-celebrated theodicy. She argues that much work on the problem of evil assumes the Myth of Shared Values—that value theory is religiously-neutral, thus common ground for both an atheist and a theist. This myth would, if taken seriously, imply that a theodicy must appeal to goods that are shared between theist and atheist. Adams persuasively argues that this myth is false; not only is there considerable disagreement in normative ethical theory among atheists, but theists believe in goods that the atheist rejects—most notably God, a being of supreme goodness (Adams 1999a, pp. 11–12). Those additional goods endorsed by theists may alter their overall value theory, thus giving them additional resources for explaining why God allows evil. Furthermore, it is appropriate for theists to use those additional goods in their theodicies because it is *their* beliefs that are being attacked by the problem of evil. If you want to argue that somebody's god doesn't exist, you need to target *their* god—including all of that God's important characteristics, concerns, and actions—not some abstraction of their god. If you just target some abstraction of their god, they can easily respond, "sure, *that* god (or a god that had merely those abstract features) may not exist. But that's not the god I believe in. I believe in *this* one. Tell me why this one doesn't exist." So theodicists can reasonably appeal to both shared values (such as there are) and values that are distinct to their theistic belief system.

Although Adams's insight here has led to the production of richer theodicies—her own is a fine example—I think that there are still gains to be made. Like Adams, I will work from within the Christian tradition to develop a theodicy for the Christian God. In this paper I present what I call Mystical Body Theodicy. It draws on the Christian doctrine of the mystical body of Christ according to which all those who follow Jesus become part of his mystical body with him as the head of the body. The whole body is a union, bound together in love through the action of the Holy Spirit. This theodicy helps explain in a distinctive way why God might allow some evils and it also helps to repair some problems with other theodicies. I argue that mystical body theodicy, combined with other popular theodicies, offers a very broad theodicy (not narrowly targeted), but not quite a global one. It is at least a weak theodicy and thus a defense, but I shall also argue that there are reasons to think it is a strong theodicy, and so may ground an attack. Furthermore there are some virtues to offering a strong theodicy that have been obscured in analytic philosophical discussion of the problem of evil. Indeed, they are somewhat obscured by Adams's rejection of the myth of shared values.

Here then is a roadmap of what is to come. In section two I criticize three prominent theodicies—those of Swinburne, Hick, and Adams. In section three I explain the doctrine of the mystical body of Christ. In section four I draw out some of the implication of this doctrine for theodicy, one such being that it can protect Swinburne, Hick, and Adams from the criticisms leveled against them in section two. In section five I discuss some limitations of mystical body theodicy, and in section six I conclude the argument and develop one final advantage of mystical body theodicy that comes from approaching it as a strong theodicy.

---

[3] My notion of a global theodicy is thus different from Marilyn Adams's notion of a 'global approach' to the problem of evil (Adams 1999a, chp. 2). Her notion has to do with accounting for evil by looking at the global balance of good and evil. Mine has no such association. Her 'global approach' is one way to offer a global theodicy (in my sense), but it isn't the only way.

2. Some Contemporary Theodicies: Swinburne, Hick, Adams

Richard Swinburne, John Hick, and Marilyn McCord Adams have carefully developed distinct theodicies. Each theodicy highlights a certain sort of good that, they propose, is present in the world or in humans, is connected in some sort of intimate way with various evils, and is such that a good God might well allow these evils given those goods exist that are intimately connected with these evils. Each theodicy has come under criticism. I shall present some of their main criticisms here. I do so not to show that mystical body theodicy is superior to these theodicies. Rather, I aim to show that mystical body theodicy can strengthen these theodicies. Theodicies are not usually in competition; they can be intertwined like strands in a durable cord.

2.1. Swinburne, Free Will, and the Good of Being of Use

Swinburne's theodicy of moral evil—evil that results from agency—builds on the classic free will defense. He takes it that libertarian free will to perform morally serious acts is a great good because such freedom is required to be able to have responsibility for oneself and others, which is itself a great good (Swinburne 1998, p. 88ff). But of course humans may freely choose to do bad or wrong things. God must allow humans to make such bad choices in order to allow them to have serious free will. Being the victim of a bad action is thereby bad, but also in a certain way good because "it is also a good thing to be of use, to help, to serve, either through freely exercising power in the right way, or through doing it naturally and spontaneously, or even by being used as the vehicle of a good purpose" (Swinburne 1998, p. 101). Victims are of use as an arena in which the perpetrator exercises significant free will, which is a great good. So, their being of use in this way is itself a great good.

Some will balk at this claim. Swinburne himself admits that "we do not, most of us, think that most of the time" (Swinburne 1998, p. 101). Plausibly, how good it is to be of use to end A depends upon the value of A itself. Although most people grant that free will is good, there is considerable disagreement about how good it is. And even if the having of free will is a great good, it doesn't follow that every exercise of free will is good. Plausibly, the good of exercising free will is at best minor when you use it to do something bad. If the good of being of use in doing A depends upon how good A is, then the good of being of use in exercising free will in such a case is minor. Surely it isn't large enough to outweigh the badness of the wrong action. So the good of being of use in others' exercise of free will isn't a significant enough good to play much of a role in a theodicy.

Later on I show how mystical body theodicy offers a more significant good that we—including victims of bad free choices—can be of use for.

2.2. Hick, Soul-Making, and Dysteleological Evils

John Hick's theodicy builds on the Irenaean idea that humans begin their existence as immature. God molds and shapes their souls by arranging the human environment so that they are pushed to become more virtuous. This molding and shaping can continue on into the afterlife. Evils induce some of that transformation. People become more courageous by facing real dangers (both natural and moral); they become more prudent by performing and witnessing others perform bad acts, seeing their consequences and thereafter deciding to turn away from them; they acquire temperance by wrestling with temptations, sometimes failing and learning ways to avoid future failure; they become loving by suffering through the pains of relationships and by having compassion on those who have suffered. Humans have to freely cooperate with and engage in this process; it wouldn't be good for God to force each transformation on them.[4]

Hick acknowledges that there are evils that appear not to contribute to soul making—"dysteleological evils," he calls them. But dystelological evils as a class, he argues,

---

[4] See (Hick 1966) especially Sections III and IV for the full account of his soul making theodicy.

are thereby mysterious and their mystery helps us to more fully sympathize with those who suffer them, as we are less likely to sympathize when we can see that suffering leads to the person's good. Dysteleological evils thus in fact contribute something to soul making!

Adams criticizes Hick on this point, arguing that this can't be a full explanation for why a good God would allow dysteleological evils (Adams 1999a, pp. 52–53). For God must also be good to those who have suffered evils, and the benefit Hick describes seems too generalized to count as being good to the victim; granted perhaps God is good to humanity in allowing them. Hick, she grants, might suggest that God gives those who have suffered dysteleological evils an opportunity in the afterlife to see how their suffering has led to the soul making of others; they embrace how they have been of use to others and thus become more virtuous and Godlike. In this way God is good to them. Adams thinks something is still missing. "Would not Divine Love focused on created persons lend positive meaning, not only to the individual's life as a whole, but also to any careers in which he or she participates in horrors?" (Adams 1999a, p. 53). Perhaps God has been good to the sufferer in her life as a whole, from the standpoint of the afterlife, but Adams thinks God should also be good to her in the phase of her life when she suffers. That she will learn a lesson later in the afterlife isn't apt for the suffering phase. Adams concludes, "to give this life, or any career involving participation in horrors, positive significance, some parameter of positive meaning for horrors other than 'educational' benefit must be found!" (Adams 1999a, p. 53).

Later on I show how mystical body theodicy offers another benefit that constitutes a way of being good to sufferers of dysteleological (and other) evils during the suffering phase of their life.

2.3. Adams, Redemptive Suffering, and Social Evil

According to Adams other theodicies such as Swinburne's and Hick's do not resolve the problem of evil because they do not adequately account for horrendous evils. A horrendous evil is an evil "the participation in which (that is, the doing or suffering of which) constitutes prima facie reason to doubt whether the participant's life could (given their inclusion in it) be a great good to him/her on the whole" (Adams 1999a, p. 26). Elsewhere she says horrendous evils have "power prima facie to degrade the individual by devouring the possibility of personal meaning in one swift gulp" (Adams 1999a, p. 29). A good God would be good to participants in horrendous evils. To be good to them he would need to restore personal meaning and give them reason to think their life is a great good to them. To do this, horrendous evils need to be defeated in the context of a person's life; that is, they must be given "positive meaning through organic unity with a great enough good within the context of his/her life" (Adams 1999a, p. 31).

Horrendous evils can be defeated by being a vehicle of unity with God—the greatest possible good, incommensurate with any other goods—or a means through which God honors us. Being honored by the greatest possible good and being unified with that being are both great goods sufficient to defeat evil. Adams offers various models to show how such defeat is possible. First, God honors us by suffering with us and having compassion on us. Our suffering thus acquires symbolic value as a dimension of God-likeness. In addition, through suffering we resemble God in bringing about human redemption by absorbing rather than striking out against evil. Second, suffering is a vision into the internal life of God, enabling us to see the depths of his love for us. Third, God will welcome us into heaven and thank us for the sufferings we went through while participating in his creation project. He will also "publicly compensate us for what we have undergone" and these rewards will "bring everlasting honor and unending joy" (Adams 1999a, p. 163). Fourth, God not only redeems but honors humanity by becoming incarnate and himself suffering horrendous evils. Those who participate in horrendous evils can thus identify with God, giving them a unique relationship with God and appreciation of the depths of his love and mercy.[5] Again, a core assumption of all of these

---

[5] She offers a fifth model inspired by Jurgen Moltmann. I leave it out for the sake of space.

models is that being honored by and being unified with a perfect and incommensurately good God is itself incommensurately good, and thus can defeat horrendous evils as long as the participant in such evils acknowledges and internalizes that honor and unification.

Philip Quinn argues that Adams' theodicy fails to account for social evils. She can explain how God might redeem horrendous evils individuals participate in, but what about evils that societies participate in, e.g., "the system in this country that permits the homeless to spend winter nights huddled on the subway grates of Manhattan while others live in decadent luxury" (Quinn 1993, p. 192)? Quinn takes it that social evils are sometimes horrendous and are not reducible to a set of individual evils. All of the four models above involve individual—not social—participants in horrendous evils being honored or unified with God. Those models are thus inapplicable to social evils.

John Cobb (Cobb 1997) offers a quite different criticism, aimed at the fourth model. Adams is a universalist about salvation: everyone eventually will experience God in a beatific vision in the afterlife. But if everybody ends up getting the beatific vision—in which God unifies with us and honors us—how can it be an adequate compensation for those who have participated in horrendous evils? It seems like those participants should get something better, but they don't because all experiences of God are incommensurate. Adams does say that those participants will have a distinct kind of experience of God exactly because of their having experienced horrendous evils (as Jesus did); their relationship with God will have a special sort of intimacy. But does that specialness suffice for making adequate compensation when the alternative is to not participate in horrendous evils, maybe participate in some lesser evils, and experience a different, somewhat analogous, intimacy with God? It's not so clear.

Later on I show how mystical body theodicy can both explain how social evils are redeemed and also incorporate participation in horrendous evils more tightly into a relationship with God; tight enough to plausibly overcome Cobb's objection.

3. The Doctrine of the Mystical Body of Christ

The doctrine of the mystical body of Christ is built on the idea that humanity was intended by God to be, in some respects remains, and yet in other respects has fallen from being a unity. Redemption consists in part in reincorporation into the proper unity intended for humanity. As Henri De Lubac writes, "the redemption being a work of restoration will appear to us by that very fact as the recovery of lost unity—the recovery of supernatural unity of man with God, but equally of the unity of men among themselves" (De Lubac 1988, p. 35). This unity is more than a likeness in faith, will, and value; it is a social unity that is spoken of as being like the unity of a body.

This theme of humanity's intended unity shows up right at the beginning of the Bible in the story of creation and fall. In the second creation story in Genesis 2 Adam—whose name means 'humanity'—is the entirety of humanity. But "it is not good for the man to be alone" (Gen 2:18), and so God creates Eve from Adam.[6] A little society is created from one being. And the two are meant to continue to live in some sort of unified existence—"a man will leave his father and mother and be united to his wife, and they will become one flesh" (2:24). Part of the problem with sin is that it sunders the unity amongst humanity; after eating the forbidden fruit they realize their nakedness and put on clothes, thus hiding themselves from each other. Adam tries to shift responsibility onto Eve for their sin, breaking unity of purpose. Soon sin divides their family. Cain's jealousy of Abel leads him to kill Abel; as punishment God sends Cain away and he becomes "a restless wanderer on the earth" (4:14). The theme is clear: humanity begins as a single entity, is to remain a unity even as it divides and multiplies, but sin damages humanity by tearing apart its unity and thus preventing humanity from

---

6   All Bible quotations are taken from the NIV translation.

being what it was meant to be. Augustine highlights this theme with a memorable metaphor: "Set in one place, [Adam] fell and, as it were, broken small, he has filled the whole world."[7]

God's restoration project through Abraham aims to restore this lost unity. Abraham isn't chosen to be a lone guru who follows God, perhaps inspiring others to do so also. He is called to be the father of a nation of people, Israel, who are collectively God's chosen people. The nation is called to be holy (Lev. 11:44–45; 20:7), thus manifesting the image of a holy God. And God tells Abraham at his calling that "I will make you into a great nation," and that "all peoples on earth will be blessed through you" (Gen 12:2–3). Abraham is thus thought of as the father of a nation and through that nation the world will be blessed. How? By being a witness to the holy God, but also by representing what that God wants for humanity: a collective unity that is holy like God. Isaiah makes it clear that all are welcome to bind themselves to the Lord, follow the law, "hold fast to my covenant" (Isa. 57:4) and receive God's blessing. "My house will be called a house of prayer for all nations" (Isa. 57:7).

From a Christian perspective, God's restoration project needs another layer of divine assistance—the incarnation of the Son of God, Jesus. Jesus doesn't come just to save a set of individuals; he comes to save humanity by saving the nation of Israel. According to the gospel of Luke, when Jesus is brought to the temple for circumcision, Simeon, who "was waiting for the consolation of Israel" was promised by God to see the Christ. When he does, he proclaims "my eyes have seen your salvation . . . a light for revelation to the Gentiles and for glory to your people Israel" (Lk. 2:25, 30, 32). Anna, a prophetess, after seeing Jesus "spoke about the child to all who were looking forward to the redemption of Jerusalem" (Lk. 2:38). The gospel of John expresses this theme very clearly. The gospel writer says that the high priest Caiaphas "prophesied that Jesus would die for the Jewish nation, and not only for that nation but also for the scattered children of God, to bring them together and make them one" (Jn. 11:51–2). Later in the gospel Jesus prays for the unity of his disciples: "Holy Father, protect them by the power of your name—the name you gave me—so that they may be one as we are one" (Jn. 17:11).[8] Since Christians believe that Jesus and the Father are two persons in one God (two of the three Trinitarian members), this is indeed a strong statement of unity.

The book of Acts and the various New Testament epistles describe how the early Christians went about becoming one and how they thought of their unity. Acts describes the followers of Jesus as being "one in heart and mind, . . . [sharing] everything they had" (Acts 4:32). Paul makes a complicated argument in Romans 9–11 that God's promise to Israel has not been violated because he has saved Israel through a remnant—namely, the followers of Jesus, the Church, to whom gentiles have been grafted. In Ephesians he argues that the gentiles were once "separate from Christ, excluded from citizenship in Israel" (2:12), but that now Jesus has "made the two one . . . his purpose was to create in himself one new man out of the two, thus making peace, and in this one body to reconcile both of them to God through the cross" (2:14–6). In First Corinthians 12 Paul famously depicts the followers of Jesus as being parts of one body: "Now you are the body of Christ, and each one of you is a part of it" (1Cor 12:27). Each member has a different role to play, contributing to the good of the body. Jesus "is the head of the body, the church" (Col. 1:18). The head, Jesus, supports, holds together, and grows the body (Col. 2:19). The word of Jesus, the head, dwells in the parts of his body (Col. 3:16). All of his people in his body "will in all things grow up into him who is the Head, that is, Christ" (Eph. 4:15). Christians thus ought to imitate Christ and God (Eph. 5:1–2). As a result of growing up into the Head, "from him [that is, Christ] the whole body, joined and held together by every supporting ligament, grows and builds itself up in love, as each part does its work" (Eph 4:16). This love that binds the parts of the body together is to be modeled on the love of Christ—"live a life of love, just as Christ loved us and gave himself up for us" (Eph 5:2). The author of 1John elaborates on the nature of this love: "This is how we know what love is: Jesus Christ laid down his life for us. And we ought to

---

[7] From *On Psalm 96*, quoted in De Lubac (1988), p. 376.
[8] This is the dominant theme of Jesus' prayer. See also Jn. 17:21, 22, 23, 26.

lay down our lives for our brothers. If anyone has material possessions and sees his brother in need but has no pity on him, how can the love of God be in him?" (1Jn 3:16–17).

Paul finally brings us full circle, comparing the love of Christ for his body, the church, to the love of a husband for his wife who (and here he quotes Genesis 2) is united with him in one flesh (Eph. 5:28–32). The unity of the body of Christ—redeemed humanity—is thus modeled on the sort of unity humanity was intended to have by God at the very beginning. In contrast to his metaphor of Adam being broken and spread through the whole world, Augustine pictures the church as "One man . . . that reaches to the end of the world."[9]

The doctrine of the mystical body of Christ thus includes the following claims:

(MB1) Redemption involves restoring humanity to a proper unified state.

(MB2) The Church is the group of redeemed humans.[10]

(MB3) The redeemed humans in the Church form an organic body of sorts (the body of Christ), with Christ as the head of that body, guiding and growing it into the proper unified state.

(MB4) The members of the body of Christ ought to be unified with each other through love and acts of love.

Although different Christian sects may disagree about the details of how to understand the mystical body of Christ, these four claims are endorsed across the Christian tradition—by Roman Catholics, Protestants, and Eastern Orthodox.[11]

4. Theodical implications

The doctrine of the mystical body of Christ thus envisions humanity being intimately united by bonds of love, with the character of that love modeled on Jesus's love for humanity—a love that led him to be willing to lay down his life for humans. This unity will be a community of sorts.[12] Forming such a community is a very great good, both from a Christian and a secular perspective. From a secular perspective, most agree with Aristotle that a human is by nature a political animal. We humans flourish best in communities, especially in communities in which we are loved. Loving relationships are great intrinsic goods, but they are also great extrinsic goods because of how love helps us to develop in our youth, conquer obstacles, survive threats to our life and well-being, achieve our goals, and connect emotionally with others.[13] The Christian perspective incorporates and expands beyond these secular reasons. To love, and be loved, in a community of persons is a way of being like God who, on the Christian view, is a Trinitarian being, three persons bound by love. Resembling God—the perfectly good being—is itself a very great good (Adams 1999b, p. 28ff). Humans in such a community will not just resemble God, on the Christian view, but will also be united to God, through Jesus, who is himself a member—indeed the head—of the community. Being united with God, the greatest possible being, in a community of love is an immensely good thing.

Evil, both moral and natural, can increase (or provide opportunities for increasing) the bonds of unity among humanity. When Sally is injured in a natural disaster family, friends, and strangers may work individually or together to help Sally recover: binding her wounds, being with her in her suffering, bringing her food, offering her a place to stay, giving her work, helping resolve her insurance claims, etc. Through all of these acts, bonds of love are tightened and various people are wound more tightly together into a community of love. When Derek is unjustly beaten by another person

---

9   From Augustine, *On Psalm 86*.
10 For the purposes of this paper I will stay neutral about whether the Church—redeemed humanity—will ultimately include all humans (i.e., about whether salvific universalism is true).
11 See (Pius XII 1943; Berkhof 1941, pp. 447–53; Zizioulas 2006, pp. 286–307) respectively. (Mersch 2011), originally published in 1936, is still the best discussion of the history of the doctrine from scripture and the Church fathers through the scholastics.
12 It could be a community of communities. We can stay neutral about the structure this community will take.
13 For some concerns about whether a certain kind of neo-liberal secular viewpoint will regard this sort of unity of humanity as good, see (White 2016).

family, friends, and strangers may work individually or together to help him: binding his wounds, being with him in his suffering, helping him to recover emotionally and physically, helping to bring him some justice from the law, and perhaps working to change laws or aspects of the culture that allow or encourage acts like what Derek suffered. Once again, through all of these acts, bonds of love are tightened and various people are wound more tightly into a community of love.

These are just two hypothetical (but realistic) examples; many more are readily constructed. One point they illustrate is that both moral evils (in Derek's case) and natural evils (in Sally's case) can increase the unity of humanity. The mystical body theodicy can thus explain evils of both sorts (many theodicies only apply to one or the other). They also illustrate that bonds of love can be tightened in a variety of ways. Individuals can come to love each other better, but also societies can change in ways that both enable societies to love their members and enable members of the society to love each other better. Take Derek's case for instance. If laws and policing practices were to change to prevent abuse of the sort he suffered, then society as a whole would treat its people better; society as a whole could then be said to love certain members better than in the past. And those laws and practices would enable individual lawyers and police to perform more loving acts to the members of the community.

I haven't said whether Sally or Derek have been incorporated into the body of Christ. But whether they are or aren't, evils suffered have in their cases led to goods of unity. If they aren't incorporated into the body of Christ, they still have become more unified in bonds of love to other people and to a human society. As mentioned above, there are secular reasons to think that these are very good things. And MB1 implies that these are very good things as well. If Sally and Derek are incorporated into the body of Christ, in addition to all of these goods they may also become more tightly bound to Christ if, e.g., they begin to pray to him and rely on him more, or the Church manifests the love of Christ by loving them, or they see the good deeds and love of others as God's means of working in the world. Even if Sally and Derek aren't Christians, the love that other people show them could well be God's means of drawing them to him as a manifestation of divine love.

On the Christian view there are two additional goods to be gained in situations in which an evil suffered brings about the goods of human unity. First, one who suffers such an evil imitates Christ. Paul expresses a deep desire to know "the fellowship of sharing in his sufferings, becoming like him in his death" (Php. 3:10). When one suffers and one's suffering increases the unity of humanity, one resembles Christ by suffering for the redemption of humanity (see again MB1). To be sure Christ's suffering for the redemption of humanity is unique: only he offers a sacrifice for the sins of humanity. But he offers that sacrifice to bring about an end result—the reconciliation of God and humanity, the latter united into a body with Christ as the head. When one's suffering increases the unity of humanity, one's suffering also (to some degree) brings about an aspect of the same end result. Imitating Christ by suffering for the redemption of humanity is in some ways a great good. Imitating a perfect being and playing a role in his redemptive goals are great goods. Being willing to play this role brings about the second additional good: becoming more tightly unified with Christ, and thus directly contributing in one's own person to the unification of humanity.

Marilyn Adams has persuasively argued that a good God wouldn't simply balance out the amount of good and evil in the universe. She writes, "Divine love would not subject some individual created persons to horrors simply for the benefit of others or to enhance cosmic excellence" (Adams 2006, p. 45). He would also be good to each person in his creation. Sally and Derek in my examples above both get to enjoy the tighter bonds of love that result from the suffering they undergo; arguably God can be said to be good to them despite allowing these sufferings. But there will be many people who do not enjoy the tighter bonds of love that result from their sufferings: some will die in the midst of their suffering, others will be too damaged physically or emotionally to participate in those bonds of love. Like Adams, I say that God can be good to these sorts of people by giving them an opportunity to subjectively appropriate the threefold goods (described above) of (a) increased unity of humanity, (b) imitation of Christ by contributing to the redemption of humanity, and (c) increased unity with Christ. To subjectively appropriate these goods one must recognize that they are good and endorse or enjoy one's role in producing or participating in them. The wretched depths of suffering and its effects in this life imply that God will need to provide some people an opportunity to appropriate the threefold goods in an afterlife.[14]

Mystical body theodicy is closely related to, but distinct from soul making theodicy. Their distinction lies in their account of how evils contribute to good. According to soul making theodicy, evils contribute to the good of individuals becoming more virtuous. According to mystical body theodicy, evils contribute to the unity of humanity in love (and to imitation of and unity with Christ). For soul making theodicy, the good is an individual good. For mystical body theodicy, the good is a social good. Of course, social goods tend to result from and require individual goods. When humanity becomes more united, almost assuredly some people are becoming more virtuous. But the unity of humanity is distinct from those people becoming more virtuous. For people can become more virtuous without humanity becoming unified; we can become more virtuous in the desert with little human interaction. Perhaps some human interaction is required since, as Aristotle argues, a person's virtue cannot be a mere disposition—it must be exercised. Even so, far less exercise is required for the possession of virtue than is required for love of another or for the unity of humanity.

Evan Fales has an objection to Eleonore Stump's theodicy which might also apply to mystical body theodicy.[15] He claims that it is unjust for a person A to put someone, B, through suffering S even if A knows that B will benefit from and even be happy to have gone through S because of some good G that results (Fales 2013, pp. 353–54). So it is unjust for God to put a person through suffering even if that suffering results in the threefold goods and that person subjectively appropriates those goods. I reject this argument for two reasons. First, according to mystical body theodicy God doesn't put humans through suffering; he allows such suffering in part because he can redeem it with the threefold goods, so there's an important doing/allowing distinction here. Second, following Swinburne, I think because God is humanity's creator and benefactor God has a right to allow humans to endure suffering as long as (i) that suffering produces goods for some part of the family of his creation and (ii) God can be good to the sufferer in his suffering (Swinburne 1998, pp. 223–36). Fales himself seems to grant that this objection carries little force, for he quickly develops the objection in a slightly different direction: what is unjust is the distribution of suffering. Plausibly suffering isn't distributed in a way that best fulfills "the greatest good for each of those individuals [i.e., those who suffer]" (Fales 2013, p. 356). Maybe this objection applies to Stump, but it doesn't apply to me. Mystical body theodicy does not assume that evils suffered that produce the threefold goods fulfill the greatest good for the sufferers. Rather, it assumes only that the threefold goods are great goods and that, when subjectively appropriated, one's life is a great good for oneself, and thus that God can be good to one through one's sufferings (that is, the sufferings that produce the threefold goods).

We are now in a position to show how mystical body theodicy can help Hick, Swinburne, and Adams avoid objections to their theodicies. Each discussion will also deepen our understanding of mystical body theodicy.

Hick's soul-making theodicy seemed unable to fully explain dysteleological evils—evils that appear to not contribute to soul-making. Hick argues that these evils can contribute indirectly to soul-making if people find such evils mysterious and are thus motivated to have compassion toward those who suffer them. Adams argues that God needs to be good to those who suffer dysteleological evils during the phase of their life in which they suffer and he doesn't do that just by giving them an opportunity in the afterlife to become more virtuous and Godlike by embracing how their suffering has led to the soul making of others.

Mystical body theodicy can say that God is good to them during the time of their suffering: he is allowing them to play a role, through their suffering, in the redemption of humanity by encouraging

---

[14] See (Adams 2006, pp. 205–41) for further defense of this point.
[15] Stump's theodicy is presented most fully in (Stump 2010).

humanity to become more unified. The sufferer may only come to subjectively appropriate and so value this role in the afterlife, but nevertheless from the afterlife the sufferer can look back and accept that God was good to him/her at that time of his/her life by giving him/her this role to play. To take this perspective the sufferer must come to personally value[16] several things: God, unification with God, imitation of God, and the unity of humanity. God surely has the resources to guide people to this perspective.

Swinburne's theodicy proposes that suffering moral evil carries with it the good of being of use to the perpetrator's exercise of free will. The problem with this proposal is that the good of being of use for A depends upon the value of A and it doesn't seem that freely performing a wrong action is all that valuable.

Mystical body theodicy suggests that there is another, much more valuable, end that we can be of use for when we suffer: the good of helping to increase the unity of humanity. For the reasons mentioned earlier, the unity of humanity is a very great good; surely much greater than the good of exercising free will wrongly. There may be some good in the latter; mystical body theodicy doesn't aim to replace Swinburne's proposed good with another, but rather to enliven the idea that it can be good to be of use by suggesting an additional good that is often served when a person suffers. It is also worth emphasizing that according to mystical body theodicy one is not merely of use, when one suffers, for increasing the unity of humanity. Remember the threefold goods. The sufferer himself also imitates Christ and has an opportunity to develop a greater unity with Christ.

Lastly we turn to Adams's theodicy. Mystical body theodicy draws on some of the same ideas that Adams uses in her theodicy, most notably that unity with Christ is a great value and that suffering can be a vehicle to greater unity with him. I've also incorporated her claim that in his goodness God would be good to people who have suffered evils. The other aspects of her theodicy mentioned earlier are consistent with (even if they are not directly incorporated into) mystical body theodicy.

Mystical body theology can help Adams respond to the two worries facing her theodicy: Quinn's concern that social evils are not redeemed and Cobb's worry that a special sort of intimacy with God, through suffering, isn't sufficient compensation given Adams's universalist assumption. Mystical body theodicy is well-equipped to explain how social evils can be redeemed—the redemption of humanity consists (in part) in humanity forming a unified body, with Christ as head, that is bound together by love. This body, the Church, is a society. That society, fully redeemed, will not be possessed by social evil. All social arrangements will be motivated by, and will embody, the love of Christ. The suffering, even horrendous suffering, of individuals due to social evil provides an opportunity for that social evil to be overcome, or at least combatted, by groups of people coming together in love to change their society. Human societies this side of paradise will no doubt continue to be tainted with social evil, and many—perhaps all—human societies will pass away in paradise and be replaced by something more divine.[17] Probably the USA, the UK, the Boy Scouts, and the NFL (just to take a few randomly-chosen examples) won't continue on in the fullness of redeemed humanity. But it is nevertheless good for humanity to become more unified in temporary societies like these. For surely the unity of love is good wherever it is found, and traces of it will endure through societal transformation and replacement.

In her later work, Adams briefly discusses the doctrine of the mystical body (not under that description, just as the idea that the Church is the body of Christ with Jesus as head) in the context of her theodicy. She says that humans are social animals and that part of what makes us human is that we have capacities for certain kinds of social interaction (Adams 2006, pp. 195–96). However, social systems produce horrors (p. 195). Divine indwelling, once one is opened up to it, bears social fruits by coordinating and harmonizing the transformation of each person, moving them into a "wholesome

---

[16] Rather than merely acknowledge the value of these things.
[17] As Adams herself notes in a very brief reply to Quinn (Adams 1993, p. 186).

community" (p. 163). These people thus grow to become "functional organs of Christ's body in the world" (p. 163). The primary functions of this Church, to be carried out by Christ's organs, are testimony and solidarity: testifying to the horrors we experience, and proclaiming God's love for us and his desire to defeat those horrors. Christians testify with words and with the example of their own lives in which horrors are being defeated by solidarity with Christ. Christians also stand in solidarity with humans—helping those who have suffered horrors (p. 202). The Church's efforts will not be completely successful in this age. The Church itself remains vulnerable to horrors, and indeed perpetrates horrors (p. 203). So we must trust primarily in the head of the Church, Christ, to eventually defeat all horrors. In the meantime we can participate critically in the efforts of the Church.

What she says here is good as far as it goes, but it doesn't go far enough. It is one thing to say that part of what makes us human is that we are capable of certain kinds of social interaction, and quite another to say we flourish best in, and so redeemed humanity will live in, a body-like community. The latter claim, central to the doctrine of the mystical body and so to mystical body theodicy, is what explains why the unity of humanity in love is a highly intrinsically valuable end, thus enabling us to explain how social evils can be defeated. They can be defeated, according to mystical body theodicy, in two ways. First, like Adams's view, social evils[18] can be defeated in the lives of individual persons; that is, the evils individuals have suffered because of social structures can be defeated in those individuals' lives. I've described above how such defeat comes about: by subjectively appropriating the threefold goods connected with suffering evil when that evil leads to (or provides an opportunity to lead to) an increase in the unity of humanity. Second, social evils are also defeated in humanity. Humanity is redeemed into a community (the Church), manifesting divine love, powered by the Holy Spirit, headed by Christ the redeemer. Humanity, through suffering social evils, participates in its own redemption when those social evils bring about greater unity.

An analogy might be helpful. If we, as a team, played poorly in a basketball game the best sort of redemption would be one in which the team is able to overcome the poor performance, responding to and defeating its previous weaknesses, in a new team performance. As humans we by nature seek to work together to accomplish various goods. And we fail together (each person participating in different ways). The best sort of redemption for humans would thus be in a community where we are able to succeed in pursuing these various goods together, responding to and defeating our previous weaknesses. The Church is the place where this happens.

Lastly, we turn to Cobb's objection to Adams's theodicy: intimacy with God, through suffering a horrendous evil, is an insufficient compensation for that evil given that, on her view, all will eventually be saved and experience intimacy with God. If I'm going to get intimacy with God eventually, why should I value going through a horrendous evil? Sure, it gives me a unique kind of intimacy with God, but is that worth it? Mystical body theodicy says that, in suffering evils, you may get more than a unique variety of something you were going to get anyway (i.e., intimacy with God)—you get to be a part of God's redemption of humanity and your suffering contributes to that redemption by increasing the unity of humanity. As argued above, the unity of humanity is a great good, and so contributing to that unity is also a great good. Notice the crucial point: salvific universalism doesn't imply that all will get to play such a role. Some will and some will not. Those who do experience a distinct and great good.

5. Limitations

Mystical body theodicy draws attention to a great good—the unity of humanity—that can plausibly contribute to explaining why God might allow evil. Mystical body theodicy is best combined with other prominent theodicies, yielding an explanation for a broader range of evils and, as argued in section four, patching some holes in other theodicies. But I don't think that mystical body theodicy,

---

[18] Horrors, more specifically, on her view. But I'll continue to speak more generally of social evils being defeated.

even combined with other theodicies, gives us a global theodicy. I doubt we'll ever have a plausible global theodicy. But we don't need a plausible global theodicy in order for theodicy to undermine the problem of evil. In this section I discuss some of the limitations of mystical body theodicy and some broader implications for whether theodicy undermines the problem of evil.

Mystical body theodicy helps explain why God might allow evils that in some way contribute to the unity of humanity. But many evils don't so contribute. The most obvious examples of such evils are the suffering of many animals, especially organisms that existed before humans evolved. Some contemporary animal suffering has contributed to the unity of humanity—the suffering of pets, livestock, and endangered species. Humans have worked to protect these animals and their efforts have drawn them together into a tighter unity of purpose, working towards good. But humans don't rally around all animal suffering; indeed probably a lot of animal suffering is simply unacknowledged by humans.

It is possible that one day humans will grasp the full range of animal suffering and as a result come together to better care for animals. If that were to happen, then mystical body theodicy might contribute to explaining why God allows animal suffering. But even so I don't think we'd have a plausible complete theodicy of animal suffering. Plausibly, God should be good to animals and if much of their suffering could only be justified by its contribution to the unity of humanity, then God wouldn't be good to all the animals that have suffered. He would be good to us through their suffering, but not good to them. In addition, surely the resulting good of the way humanity becomes unified in response to animal suffering could have been achieved with considerably less animal suffering. A lot less suffering could have happened before we evolved, for example, and plausibly our subsequent movement toward unity wouldn't have been affected one bit. So a lot of animal suffering would still appear gratuitous even if humans were to become aware of the extent of animal suffering and move toward greater unity as a result.

A similar line of argument goes for some human suffering. Some human suffering doesn't increase the unity of humanity. Some people die of diseases or natural disasters and nobody much cares about their loss. God might one day give us knowledge of all such cases and this knowledge might move us to greater unity, but again it isn't clear that we'd be moved any less by a lesser amount of such evil.

This is a familiar argument in discussions of the problem of evil, and indeed it is often leveled as a general objection to theodicies: even considering all of the possible goods connected with evil that are put forward by the best theodicies, it still seems that God could have gotten those goods with somewhat less evil. So there is gratuitous evil. God wouldn't allow gratuitous evil, so God doesn't exist. And if that argument is correct, then one might question mystical body theodicy as follows: "this is an interesting theodicy which points to an important good. But it doesn't help! There's still plenty of gratuitous evil, for the reason given in the argument I just gave."

I have two replies to this line of questioning. First, a theodicy can be valuable even if it doesn't completely explain why God might allow evil (or completely explain all of the remaining apparently unexplained cases). A theodicy is valuable if it explains more (or better explains) evils, or explains some of the previously apparently unexplained cases. Mystical body theodicy, for the reasons discussed in the previous section, does this. Second, even if the combined force of our best theodicies can't explain all evil, we shouldn't automatically conclude that there is gratuitous evil. For we can think of the existence of God plus the theodicies as a theory. Theories commonly face anomalies—phenomena that seem difficult to square with the theory—but the mere existence of anomalies doesn't justify rejecting the theory. There will inevitably be some anomalies given human error in data collection and analysis; such error is certainly present when thinking about why an event might justifiably occur since discerning whether it is justifiable depends upon discerning its effect on the world in the near term and far term. Our grasp of this information is limited and subject to mistake in assessment. So, to conclude that there are gratuitous evils and thus that God does not exist we would need to think carefully about whether the apparently gratuitous evils are merely anomalies; making such a determination is quite challenging.[19]

6. Conclusions

Mystical body theodicy proposes that God might allow some evils in part because those evils contribute to increasing the unity of humanity, a unity woven by the bonds of love. This unity is a great good from a secular perspective, since we are social creatures and flourish by working together and by living in loving relationships. It is also a great good from a Christian perspective, which says that salvation consists in part in humanity becoming unified in a body with Christ as the head. Those who suffer evils that contribute to the unity of humanity may be compensated with a threefold good: the good of helping to increase something of great good (the unity of humanity), the good of imitating Christ (who also suffered to bring about the unity of humanity in salvation), and if one subjectively appropriates the previous two goods, one obtains the good of becoming oneself more tightly bound into redeemed humanity, the Church. God is good to those who have subjectively appropriated these goods. Mystical body theodicy also immunizes three other prominent theodicies from various objections, thus filling gaps in their theodicies. I grant that there are limitations to mystical body theodicy, even if it is combined with other prominent theodicies. For some evils, it is difficult to explain why God would allow them. But mystical body theodicy does offer an additional explanation for many evils, and an explanation for some evils that otherwise might be difficult to explain. So mystical body theodicy positively contributes to theodical responses to the problem of evil. Whether the problem of evil is completely rebutted is difficult to judge; I've outlined some grounds for reservation about whether the remaining unexplained evils give good evidence against God's existence.

I want to conclude by pointing to one final advantage of mystical body theodicy. Most responses to the problem of evil are defenses—that is (according to my terminology) they argue that there isn't good reason to believe some premise of the problem of evil. This makes sense strategically—why do more than is necessary to ward off an objection? But it's one thing to merely ward off an objection to a claim T, and another to ward it off in a way that makes T more attractive. The latter, if you can do it, is more rationally valuable than the former. Strong theodicies—theodicies that attack a premise of the problem of evil, arguing that it is probably false—can make theism more attractive if it can be shown that a good God would probably allow evils for a reason R where R is clearly a great good even from a secular perspective. Theism can then be seen to be more coherent (rather than not seen to be incoherent) and committed to something of great value. Adams's rejection of the myth of shared values can obscure the fact that there are some shared values, and that there is an epistemic benefit to be gained for theism from capitalizing on those values to attack premises in versions of the problem of evil.

Arguably, from both a secular and Christian perspective, God probably would allow certain evils if they were redeemed by the threefold goods. The good of a unified humanity really does seem to be very great and we are already quite familiar with—indeed we honor—people who willingly sacrifice their interests or even their lives for the sake of a great good. Assuming I have shown that mystical body theodicy is in this way a strong theodicy, Christian theism will then be seen to be more coherent to nontheists who have read and bought my argument. Christian theism will also be seen to be committed to working toward the good of the unity of humanity in love; indeed the purpose of the Church is in part to increase this unity by redeeming many evils.[20] The mission of the Church will thus also be seen to be a great good from a secular perspective, making Christian theism more coherent, rationally attractive, and even morally attractive.[21]

---

19 See (Dougherty and Pruss 2014) for a more careful and thorough discussion of anomalies and the problem of evil.
20 To avoid Pelagianism we should add the following qualification: by and through the grace of Christ, the Head.
21 I dedicate this essay to the memory of Marilyn McCord Adams, whose work and character has inspired me and inspired much of the thought in this essay.

Conflicts of Interest: The author declares no conflict of interest.

References

Adams, Marilyn McCord. 1993. God and Evil: Polarities of a Problem. *Philosophical Studies* 69: 167–86. [CrossRef]

Adams, Marilyn McCord. 1999a. *Horrendous Evils and the Goodness of God*. Ithaca: Cornell University Press.

Adams, Robert Merrihew. 1999b. *Finite and Infinite Goods*. New York: Oxford University Press.

Adams, Marilyn McCord. 2006. *Christ and Horrors*. Cambridge: Cambridge University Press.

Berkhof, Louis. 1941. *Systematic Theology*. Grand Rapids: Eerdmans.

Bergmann, Michael. 2009. Skeptical Theism and the Problem of Evil. In *Oxford Handbook of Philosophical Theology*. Edited by Thomas P. Flint and Michael Rea. Oxford: Oxford University Press, pp. 374–402.

Cobb, John. 1997. Theodicy and Divine Omnipotence. In *Philosophy and Theological Discourse*. Edited by Stephen T. Davis. New York: St Martin's Press, pp. 199–203.

De Lubac, Henri. 1988. *Catholicism: Christ and the Common Destiny of Man*. San Francisco: Ignatius Press.

Trent Dougherty, and Justin P. McBrayer, eds. 2014. *Skeptical Theism: New Essays*. Oxford: Oxford University Press.

Dougherty, Trent, and Alexander Pruss. 2014. Evil and the Problem of Anomaly. *Oxford Studies in Philosophy of Religion* 5: 49–87.

Fales, Evan. 2013. Theodicy in a Vale of Tears. In *The Blackwell Companion to the Problem of Evil*. Edited by Justin McBrayer and Daniel Howard-Snyder. Malden: Wiley Blackwell, pp. 349–62.

Daniel Howard-Snyder, ed. 1996. *The Evidential Argument from Evil*. Bloomington: Indiana University Press.

Hick, John. 1966. *Evil and the God of Love*. London: Macmillan.

Justin P. McBrayer, and Daniel Howard-Snyder, eds. 2013. *The Blackwell Companion to the Problem of Evil*. Malden: Wiley Blackwell.

Mersch, Emile. 2011. *The Whole Christ: The Historical Development of the Doctrine of the Mystical Body in Scripture and Tradition*. Translated by John R. Kelly. Eugene: Wipf & Stock.

Pius XII, Pope. 1943. Mystici Corporis Christi: On the Mystical Body of Christ. Available online: http://w2.vatican.va/content/pius-xii/en/encyclicals/documents/hf_p-xii_enc_29061943_mystici-corporis-christi.html (accessed on 10 September 2017).

Quinn, Philip L. 1993. Social Evil: A Response to Adams. *Philosophical Studies* 69: 187–94. [CrossRef]

Swinburne, Richard. 1998. *Providence and the Problem of Evil*. Oxford: Oxford University Press.

Stump, Eleonore. 2010. *Wandering in Darkness*. Oxford: Clarendon Press.

White, Thomas Joseph. 2016. An Age of Discontent. *First Things*, November, 25–31.

Zizioulas, John. 2006. *Communion and Otherness*. London: T&T Clark.

Article

Theodicies as Failures of Recognition

Sari Kivistö [1] and Sami Pihlström [2,*]

[1]   Faculty of Communication Sciences, University of Tampere, Tampere 33014, Finland; sari.kivisto@uta.fi
[2]   Faculty of Theology, University of Helsinki, Helsinki 00014, Finland
*   Correspondence: sami.pihlstrom@helsinki.fi; Tel.: +358-40-5015535

Received: 10 October 2017; Accepted: 28 October 2017; Published: 1 November 2017

Abstract: This paper examines the ethical failure of theodicies by integrating the perspectives of philosophical argumentation and literary reading and analysis. The paper consists of two main parts. In the first part, we propose an ethical critique of metaphysical realism by analyzing its inability to recognize the perspectival plurality and diversity of suffering. As theodicies seek to explain how an omnipotent, omniscient, and absolutely benevolent God could allow the world to contain evil and suffering, it can be argued that metaphysical realism—i.e., the thesis that the world possesses its own fundamental structure independently of human perspectives of conceptualization and inquiry— is a problematic starting point of theodicism. We examine the failure of recognition of others' suffering inherent in theodicies as a failure based on the search for an overall reductive and objectifying picture (a "God's-Eye View") that is constitutive of metaphysical realism. The second part of the paper shows why we should include insights from imaginative literature in our attempts to understand the recognition failures of theodicies. Emphasizing the literary, philosophical, and theological relevance of various modern rewritings of the Book of Job, which has been a crucially important sub-text for many later literary works in which the protagonists render a particular kind of human experience—unmerited suffering—we turn more closely to some literary examples, such as Joseph Roth's novels *Hiob* and *Die Rebellion*. The tensions that are created around the moral controversy of the experiences of injustice and suffering and the human and religious reasoning and justification of violence are examined. The ambiguous ending of *Hiob* that adds an apparently hopeful and almost fairytale-like redemption to the story plays a crucial role in the interpretation provided in the paper. By analyzing some literary examples and their relation to the literary Job tradition, the recognition-failures of theodicist attempts to provide meaning into suffering—attempts based on metaphysical realism, as argued in the first part of the paper—are highlighted. Finally, we also critically consider the charge that theodicism could only be theoretically formulated and argue that a sharp distinction between theory and practice in this area is itself an act of non-recognition, or a failure to recognize suffering.

Keywords: suffering; theodicy; theodicism; antitheodicy; antitheodicism; realism; metaphysical realism; recognition; acknowledgment; literature; the *Book of Job*; Roth, Joseph

---

1. Introduction

Theodicies, seeking to justify "the ways of God to man," attempt to view human suffering from an overall metaphysical and/or theological perspective. From such a perspective, all apparently unnecessary and meaningless evil and suffering there seems to be in the world we live in is rendered in some sense "meaningful" or at least necessary for the overall goodness of the harmonious world system. While theodicies have been proposed by both classical and contemporary thinkers throughout the history of theistic thought (and there are, arguably, also secular theodicies available in the discussion), there is a growing tradition of moral criticism of theodicies drawing attention to their arguably striking insensitivity to human suffering (see, e.g., Betenson 2016). This tradition deserves further philosophical scrutiny, but it also needs to be carefully examined what the peculiar insensitivity typical of theodicies actually consists of.

Therefore, a key aim of this paper is to offer an ethical critique of *metaphysical realism* by analyzing its inability to recognize the perspectival plurality and diversity of suffering, interpreting the failure of recognition of others' suffering inherent in theodicies as a failure based on the search for an overall reductive and objectifying picture (a "God's-Eye View") arguably constitutive of metaphysical realism. In addition to engaging theodicies and their metaphysically realist background assumptions by philosophical argument and criticism, we will show why it is vital to include insights from imaginative literature in serious attempts to understand the recognition failures of theodicies. Emphasizing the literary, philosophical, and theological relevance of various modern rewritings of the Book of Job, a crucially important sub-text for many later literary works addressing unmerited suffering, our paper more closely analyzes some literary examples, such as Joseph Roth's novels *Hiob* and *Die Rebellion* that take a critical stand on any overarching perspective on individual suffering.

Arguing that theodicism typically (though not strictly speaking logically) presupposes metaphysical realism, as both assume the availability of a "God's-Eye View" theory of why there is evil and suffering (i.e., God's reasons for allowing the world to contain apparently meaningless and unnecessary evil and suffering on the massive scale familiar to us on a daily basis), we will not only argue against theodicism by criticizing its background assumptions but also (indirectly) against metaphysical realism itself by providing reasons for rejecting its (typical) consequence, theodicism. Metaphysical realism and theodicism will then ultimately collapse hand in hand. However, we should also to observe that this collapse does not lead to a rejection of realism *tout court*. Rather, *antitheodicism*—the view that abandons the entire project of theodicy, as will be explained in more detail below—needs a moderately realist understanding of humanly speaking objective reality and truth, but it is precisely the human dimension of this need that is not adequately available within metaphysical realism.

Let us start with some conceptual preliminaries made explicit in some of our earlier work, especially *Kantian Antitheodicy* (Kivistö and Pihlström 2016). We propose to define *theodicy* and *theodicism* simply with reference to the attempt to provide a justification for apparently senseless (meaningless, absurd) suffering. Generally, we may say that theodicies seek a justification, legitimation, and/or excusing of an omnipotent, omniscient and absolutely benevolent God's allowing the world (His creation) to contain evil and for allowing humans and other sentient beings to suffer. Classical formulations of theodicies can be found, for example, in Augustine's and his numerous followers' appeals to God's having created human beings with freed will as the reason why there is evil, and in G.W. Leibniz's position, formulated in his famous *Théodicée* (1710), according to which God could not have created any better world than the one that he, as omnipotent and absolutely good, did create; according to this Leibnizian theodicy, we live in "the best possible world," and while there is indeed some evil there, it is necessary for the overall good. Leibnizian theodicies are good examples of purely metaphysical attempts to explain the place of evil within the absolute divine harmony of the world; it does not aim at a moral justification of God's allowing suffering but at a metaphysical excuse explaining why even the best possible world may include some evil—or even quite a bit.

More recent examples of theodicies include attempts to revive "free will theodicies" and "soul-making theodicies" by major philosophers of religion such as Richard Swinburne and John Hick. Classical atheist arguments based on the problem of evil and suffering have, in turn, been presented by philosophers like David Hume and J.L. Mackie, while several contemporary thinkers have proposed "defenses" intended as more moderate than theodicies proper, suggesting that there is a possible world in which God has good reasons to create and maintain a world in which humans and other sentient beings suffer horribly, without necessarily claiming that possible world to be actual, or claiming that we would be able to know God's actual reasons (cf., e.g., Van Inwagen 2006).

Now, by "theodicism," we may refer to all those attempts to deal with the problem of evil and suffering that regard theodicy as a desideratum of an acceptable theistic position, irrespective of whether they end up defending theism or rejecting it. The theodicist can, then, very well be an atheist, insofar as they conclude that God does not exist (or probably does not exist, or that there is no justification for the belief that God exists) precisely because the theodicist desideratum cannot be fulfilled. Also those who propose a mere "defense"—instead of a theodicy proper—can be regarded as theodicists in the sense that they also seek to defend God and account for God's justice by arguing that, for all we know, God *could* have ethically acceptable reasons to allow the world to contain evil and suffering, even the kind of truly horrible evil and suffering familiar to anyone with adequate moral sensitivities in the world we live in. By "antitheodicism," in contrast, we may mean the rejection of any such, or indeed *any*, theodicies, or better, of the very project of delivering a theodicy or the attitude of encouraging or requiring engagement in such a project.

Theodicism and *evidentialism*—that is, the view that the rational acceptability of religious beliefs should be evaluated on the basis of the (religiously neutral) evidence that can be presented for and against them—are closely connected. As mainstream philosophy of religion today is (albeit with significant exceptions) relatively strongly evidentialist, at least in a broad sense, it comes as no surprise that it is also often strongly theodicist when dealing with the problem of evil and suffering. Accordingly, the existence of evil and suffering is in most cases formulated as an empirical premise challenging the theistic belief in an argumentative exchange searching evidence in support of, or against, the theistic hypothesis. This is so irrespective of whether the problem of evil is regarded as a logical or as an evidential problem (cf. Rowe 2001). The theistic goal is to respond to the atheists' "argument from evil." Just like theodicism is a normative view according to which any rationally acceptable theism ought to formulate a theodicy (or at least take steps toward the direction of a theodicy by formulating a more moderate "defense"), evidentialism is a normative epistemological view according to which any rationally acceptable theism ought to be defended by means of evidence, or rational considerations more generally. Theodicism is, then, a specific dimension of evidentialism: it tries to tell us how we *should* discuss the problem of evil when evil is regarded as a piece of evidence against theism that the theist needs to deal with.

A philosophical critique of theodicism is, therefore, a critique of the entire argument *from* evil and its use in both theistic and atheistic discourse. In this sense, again, our considerations in this essay will have a metaphilosophical dimension. It seems to us—though we cannot defend this view here (but cf. Kivistö and Pihlström 2016)—that the philosophically most interesting and profound disagreement lies not between theism and atheism or between religious believers and nonbelievers, but between the overall ethical and religious attitudes to suffering (and, hence, to reality generally) adopted by theodicism and antitheodicism.

While the link between theodicism and evidentialism seems to be relatively clear, the relation between theodicism and *realism*, especially *metaphysical realism*, has not been studied in any great detail in previous literature. We will try to argue that metaphysical realism is one of the most problematic background assumptions of theodicism—just as it is a problematic starting point in many other philosophical areas of inquiry, including various recent theories of the self, of death, and related matters (see Pihlström 2016). By metaphysical realism we may here simply mean the view that the world possesses its own fundamental ontological structure independently of our perspectives of conceptualization and inquiry and can, therefore, in principle be truly and completely described from an absolute standpoint (i.e., a "view from nowhere," or a "God's-Eye View," as it were). Metaphysical realism is, in fact, a conjunction of various more specific forms of realism, especially ontological, semantic, and epistemological.

After these introductory remarks and conceptual preliminaries, we may first turn to an analysis of the philosophical commitment to metaphysical realism as the background assumption of theodicism and then to interpretations of some literary manifestations of these ideas. As will be explained in the concluding section, our defense of antitheodicism is also in an important sense *humanistic*—and we may hope that this emphasis on humanism is (implicitly) highlighted by the heavy role played by literary reading and analysis in our argument.

2. Theodicy and Metaphysical Realism: Against Reductive Objectification

Let us briefly consider an example explicitly referring to the deep connection between realism and theodicism that we have only in a sketchy and introductory way invoked above. Peter Byrne (2003) argues that realism is needed in the philosophy of religion partly, or even primarily, because responding to the problem of evil by delivering a theodicy presupposes realism. Byrne suggests that theism needs to incorporate a "generic offer of a theodicy," and this requires a realistic conception of the divinity conjoined with moral teleology and a conception of a "final good" of human life (Byrne 2003, p. vii). Byrne's basic characterization of realism says that "the governing intent behind the concept of God is to refer to an extra-mental, extra-mundane, transcendent entity" (Byrne 2003, p. 6). While theodicies may not be explicitly invoked in realism discussions in the philosophy of religion, Byrne seems to maintain that the entire realism debate is largely motivated by the need to provide a theodicy—that is, by theodicism (as we have called it above):

> The need or problem is that of finding a response to evil. In particular, [religions] arise out of the human perception that the apparent order of the world around them is not a moral order; it is indifferent to the achievement of human happiness and the realisation of human goodness; it presents itself as blind and indifferent to justice. It is the job of a religion on this account to offer human beings a theodicy. (Byrne 2003, p. 17)

It is prima facie surprising to hear that *religions* should offer us theodicies, as one might think that this is the job of *theology* (or perhaps of the philosophy of religion) rather than religion itself. Be that as it may, Byrne insists that "a religion is any set of symbols (and associated actions, attitudes, feelings and experiences) providing human beings with a solution to evil by way of a theodicy"; more generally, religion is "that propensity in human beings (however grounded) to respond to evil by seeking the kind of meaning [...] associated with the enterprise of theodicy" (Byrne 2003, p. 18). Realism is needed for religion, because providing a theodicy invokes a "moral and providential causality in the world" transcending natural and human powers as well as a relational conception of the human good as "a matter of living in right relation to the source of the providential, moral order postulated as response to evil" (Byrne 2003, p. 18). The program of defending realism in the philosophy of religion thus includes, Byrne maintains, a critique of the very coherence of antirealist views of good and evil.[1]

Antitheodicism argues that the kind of theodicies Byrne and many other philosophers of religion defend—theodicies either seeking to philosophically justify or legitimize God's allowing apparently unnecessary and meaningless evil and suffering, or offering some secular proxy for this traditional theological project—amount to a colossal *ethical failure to recognize the suffering other* and the utter pointlessness of their suffering. Instead of taking others' suffering morally seriously, theodicies (as well as the only allegedly more moderate "defenses") arguably instrumentalize suffering in the service of some postulated or imagined overall good. Such an ethical argument for antitheodicism, focusing on the moral need to appropriately recognize the reality of suffering, or to take evil seriously, can draw from various sources, including William James's (1907) pragmatism, Wittgensteinian philosophy of religion (e.g., Phillips 2004), as well as post-Holocaust Jewish moral reflection exemplified by Emmanuel Levinas (2006) ethics of otherness, all of which can be interpreted as fundamentally Kantian formulations of antitheodicism (Kivistö and Pihlström 2016, chps. 3–5). These antitheodicisms are,

---

[1] On the other hand, atheist criticisms of theism, based on the argument *from* evil (e.g., J.L. Mackie's well-known logical argument), have also been attacked because of their commitment to axiological or moral realism, a standard assumption in the theodicy discourse. Consider especially (Carson 2007). Carson criticizes Mackie's problematic combination of moral error theory and assumption of moral realism in his formulation of the logical problem of evil. Mackie, a famous critic of moral realism and theism, seems to assume the truth of moral realism in his discussion of the problem of evil by (arguably) assuming that pain and suffering are mind-independently bad or evil. The issue, then, concerns the mutual (in)coherence of Mackie's views on ethics and religion (or atheism). This argument obviously targets Mackie in an *ad hominem* fashion, but it may teach a more general lesson of the need to consider the coherence among the various assumptions concerning realism and antirealism we make in different areas of philosophical inquiry.

we may suggest, "Kantian" not because they would necessarily explicitly refer to Immanuel Kant's own criticism of theodicies (or the Kantian theory of "radical evil," for instance) but because (i) their moral criticism of speculative metaphysics can (implicitly) be traced back to Kant's 1791 "Theodicy Essay" and its rejection of theodicies as violations of the limits of human reason (based on the general approach of Kantian critical philosophy), and (ii) they arguably seek to show that theodicies violate the necessary conditions for the possibility of adopting a moral perspective on the world and other human beings. (For other influential antitheodicist considerations in the contemporary discourse on evil, see, e.g., Bernstein 2002; Neiman 2002.)

Antitheodicists are usually not only non-evidentialists but also non-realists (at least in the sense of rejecting metaphysical realism), though *not* for that reason necessarily antirealists. This is so whether they start from Wittgensteinianism (e.g., Phillips), pragmatism (e.g., James), or Jewish post-Holocaust ethics (e.g., Levinas).[2] For example, Levinas seems to maintain that the metaphysically realist attempt to occupy a totalizing God's-Eye View on others' suffering is the source of theodicist immorality.[3] Phillips, in turn, regards transcendent theistic accounts of moral goodness as morally corrupting, as they do not acknowledge the "pointlessness" of evil. Byrne's (2003, pp. 132–35) metaphysical moral teleology and his theodicism based on metaphysical realism are thus diametrically opposed to Phillips's position. The bone of contention seems to be that while for Byrne goodness ultimately serves cosmic divine purposes, for Phillips goodness is non-teleological, "purposeless" (just like evil, analogously, is pointless) (Byrne 2003, p. 134). Metaphysical realism, then, is the key issue dividing these two thinkers and in its way explaining their divergence regarding theodicies. Furthermore, it can be argued that William James's (1907) pragmatist criticism of the "absolute" (and Hegelian monistic idealism, for him the paradigmatic form of metaphysical realism) is also primarily ethical; the metaphysical critique is based on the ethical unacceptability of the absolute yielding an irresolvable theodicy problem.

Why exactly is realism a key issue here? We propose that this is because metaphysical realism, at least typically if not inevitably, *reductively objectifies*—that is, tends to view as mere objects in the world—something that really cannot (and ethically *ought not to*) be viewed as mere objects among others "out there" in the mind-, practice-, and discourse-independent world: first of all God (easily, albeit perhaps not inevitably, leading to a kind of simplistic anthropomorphism) as well as, secondly, others' suffering (reduced into mere processes in the objective empirical world),[4] and hence also, thirdly, otherness itself. Such objectifications are in striking contrast with Levinas, in particular, for whom the other is more fundamental than any object-subject structure—and with (e.g., Jamesian) pragmatism, which also refuses to postulate a pre-structured reality independently of human valuational pursuits and practices. The crucial point here is that by reductively objectifying things that are beyond objectification, theodicism based on metaphysical realism also overlooks the diversity and perspectival nature of both suffering and human beings' individual (religious or non-religious) responses to suffering.[5] In other words, metaphysical realism and the theodicism based upon it are essentially *detached* views when it comes to responding to others' suffering; instead of being involved and engaged,

---

[2]   These different antitheodicisms are argued to not only belong to the Kantian tradition of antitheodicism but also to be indebted to Kant's (1791, Kant 1983) reading of the Book of Job (emphasizing Job's sincerity and truthfulness) in Kivistö and Pihlström 2016.

[3]   We are indebted to Panu-Matti Pöykkö's still mostly unpublished work on this feature of Levinas's thought.

[4]   Similarly, we may say that metaphysical realism objectifies human death and mortality into a mere empirical and factual events and states in the world, while a more Kantian-oriented transcendental approach to human mortality seeks to understand death as a limit phenomenon and horizon of life without which no worldly events would be humanly possible. Cf. (Pihlström 2016).

[5]   By diversity we here primarily mean the immense *individual* diversity of human beings' experiences of suffering and their responses to and ways of dealing with that suffering. Thus, we do not primarily intend this in the sense of social or cultural diversity, but of course such diverse backgrounds also crucially influence the ways in which individuals experience and respond to their experiences of suffering.

the theodicist relies on metaphysical realism in seeking to maintain a "view from nowhere" that puts suffering in its proper place in the overall clean and well-lighted picture of the universe.

From a Kantian point of view, we may say that the basic problem with metaphysical realism and its applications in theodicism—and everywhere else—is the tendency to seek a *theocentric* perspective, which is necessarily unavailable to us (or better, not just unavailable but something the pursuit of which remains humanly incoherent). It is arguably also an ethically problematic goal even to try to reach it precisely because it is ethically problematic to reduce others' experiences of suffering into mere objective processes and events in the world taken to be independent of our ethical acknowledgment of suffering in its meaninglessness irreducible to any alleged theodicist meaningfulness. A related problem in metaphysical realism is the attempt to make metaphysics prior to ethics, whereas the kind of critique of metaphysical realism and theodicism advanced here makes a meta-level case for the profound entanglement of these two areas of philosophy. However, the entanglement of ethics with metaphysics cannot itself be regarded as an objective fact in the world (based on metaphysical realism) but must be considered a feature of the human lifeworld and practices. It is in terms of such entanglement that we must see ourselves, and the world we live in, when we take seriously our irreducibly ethical pursuit of responding to suffering.

An antitheodicist ethics of acknowledgment thus cannot be based on any objectifying metaphysical realism; yet, it must maintain an ordinary notion of objective truth needed for the requirement of sincerity fundamental to Kantian antitheodicism.[6] Something like an ordinary concept of truth—not necessarily requiring any sophisticated philosophical elaboration—is needed simply in order for someone who has undergone experiences of suffering to be able to acknowledge the fact that that suffering actually took place; hence, such a notion of truth is also necessary for our antitheodicist purposes, because the antitheodicist must be able to argue that there is a sense in which theodicies with their "God's-Eye View" narrative structures overlook or neglect the truth about what really happened to an individual sufferer or how they experienced their suffering. *Failure of acknowledgment* is *the* crucial ethical failure in theodicist attempts to justify "the ways of God to man"; this is the antitheodicist's fundamental charge against theodicism.[7] These thoughts also lead us to appreciate why there should, and indeed can, be no argument *from* evil. This is precisely because arguing *from* evil, or responding to such arguments theodicistically, already presupposes metaphysical realism (and evidentialism), objectifying the very experiences of suffering that must not be objectified. (Note, however, that the presupposing relation can be bilateral: according to Byrne realism itself presupposes, as we saw, the project of providing a theodicy, as something that generically and essentially belongs to religions.) The very use of the empirical premise stating the reality of evil in the argument from evil—and theodicist responses to that premise and its atheist usage—insensitively objectifies as well as instrumentalizes suffering.

We should, furthermore, note that the nowadays fashionable position known as *skeptical theism* also problematically presupposes metaphysical realism. According to such a view, God is claimed to have (or possibly have) reasons for allowing suffering that we just do not or cannot know. The "divine hiddenness" discussion is yet another debate in contemporary philosophy of religion that is in a

---

[6] Cf. again Kivistö and Pihlström 2016, especially the analysis of the exchange between James Conant and Richard Rorty on George Orwell's *Nineteen Eighty-Four* (chp. 5).

[7] A more comprehensive examination of these issues would also critically explore the relation between recognition and acknowledgment. Recognition focuses on cognition (knowing), and is hence, arguably, ultimately based on metaphysical realism, while acknowledgment focuses not on knowing but on acknowledging, in a non-metaphysically-realist way. However, this idea needs considerable further development. (On the history of the issue of recognition in religion and theology, see Saarinen 2016.) Furthermore, the need to appeal to the "truth" of individual experiences of suffering in antitheodicist argumentation does not entail the subjectivist or relativist view that each individual account of such experiences would be as valuable as any other and that critical discussion across such perspectival interpretations of suffering would be impossible. Such discussion may be difficult, but certainly antitheodicism by no means precludes the possibility of acknowledging also the occasional failures of sufferers' own interpretations of their situations. On the other hand, such interpretive disagreements must always, for ethical reasons, be approached with utmost sensitivity.

questionable manner based on metaphysical realism. All these issues concerning the relation between God, human beings, and the world objectify God as well as otherness, presupposing that we can adopt a theocentric perspective on these matters, even though they are deeply human problems to which there is only a finite anthropocentric perspective available for us, amidst our ethico-religious human practices. Even the skeptical theist assumes that in principle a theocentric perspective could and should be available, while it merely de facto contingently is not. When the divine hiddenness issue is raised as a purely intellectual puzzle allegedly external to religious life itself, it differs crucially from the genuinely religious and/or existential anxiety associated with real-life experiences of the hiddenness of God (which may or may not lead to one's losing one's religion).[8]

It should be clear at this point that we believe metaphysical realism to be strikingly inadequate for exploring experiences and possibilities like this. Experiences of divine hiddenness and meaninglessness require an entirely different philosophical framework to be adequately addressed, and such a framework is unavailable in metaphysical realism. The purpose of this paper is not to articulate such an antitheodicist framework in any detail, but we have earlier (Kivistö and Pihlström 2016) argued that antitheodicisms continuing the Kantian tradition—including above-mentioned approaches such as Jamesian pragmatism, Wittgensteinian philosophy of religion, and Levinasian post-Holocaust ethics of otherness—are worth developing further in this regard.

3. Literary Examples of Unmerited Suffering: Modern Treatments of Job

We will now move on to a consideration of fictional literature as integral to our argument criticizing both theodicism and metaphysical realism as its presupposition. Any literary examination of antitheodicism must begin from the *Book of Job*, which is the traditional key text of useless and unmerited suffering. Job objects to theodicies that would explain his suffering in terms of just punishments for bad deeds, since in his own view he had never committed any crimes meriting such suffering. Job's friends, in turn, give rational explanations to his unwarranted suffering, thus representing false theodicy, that is, official and normative views of faith that try to justify God's reasons despite Job's concrete individual experience of the world. The friends offer traditional religious means of repentance and self-examination to heal Job's distress, although these interpretations of his condition actually increase his suffering by falsely attributing guilt to him.

Especially after the Second World War, critics have emphasized that narrative means can be ethically problematic in trying to make sense of individual suffering. Relying on this interpretative approach, Carol A. Newsom (2009) has analyzed how the friends falsely attempt to reduce Job's experience and also God's reasons to larger narrative structures, which would explain the causes and consequences of Job's unjust suffering. Newsom points out that in trying to integrate Job's experience of meaningless suffering by their traditional narrative patterns the friends perform an unethical act, since these patterns (e.g., stories of the bad fate of the wicked or the hope of the virtuous) fail to do justice to Job's present and particular situation and deny his own considerations

---

[8]   As against the mainstream analytic divine hiddenness discussion today, we may (again joining Wittgensteinian philosophers like Phillips) suggest that the experience of God's hiding, or being unavailable to human beings in prayer, for instance, is *internal* to a religious way of life, challenging the life and thought of a person engaging in religion from within—just as we may say that experiences of meaningless evil and suffering could be internal to religious life in an analogous way. Experiences of divine hiddenness could also challenge a non-believer, or an agnostic, to become more deeply engaged with an "awareness of what is missing" (see Habermas 2010). Indeed, it is possible that this is *the* form of religious experience available to a secular modern person, an experience possibly arising from a consideration of the problem of evil and suffering: it does not seem to be the case that God is really in charge of the world or history. At the meta-level, a secular yet religiously sensitive educated person might actually long for the possibility of (still) being part of the kind of meaningfulness or significance (internally belonging to a genuinely religious form of life) that makes possible the *religiously relevant meaninglessness* of a religiously experienced divine hiddenness. This meta-level question of meaningfulness and meaninglessness (which includes the ethical requirement of adequately acknowledging others' experiences of meaninglessness, especially the meaninglessness of suffering) is presumably the closest that reflective secular persons today can get to religious experience—and an awareness of the significance of the problem of evil and suffering, antitheodicistically formulated, might be crucial in reaching this meta-level acknowledgment.

of his condition. The friends suggest that by praying Job would attain an order in his affliction, but a meaningful moral order is precisely what Job is fundamentally lacking in his suffering. He insists that his suffering cannot be reduced to any meaningful storylines with initial causes and their effects, or relieved by therapeutic prayers or by the friends' consolations (cf. Job 16: 2–5). Nor can his suffering, as Newsom observes, be explained with reference to such conventional positive patterns as those of hope, transformation, or survival, which would help interpret Job's situation in the light of a meaningful whole, where the sense of wholeness and purposefulness is happily attained at the end of the story. Job's friends thus create conventional cultural patterns to present claims about the moral order and coherence of the world, but their fabrications are condemned by Job (as well as by Kant in his later theodicy essay: see again Kant 1983)[9]. Suffering does not take place in a world that is purposeful, ordered and teleological, since the lived experience denies such order and symmetry. As Newsom claims, Job questions the *narratability* of his violent experience. If modern philosophical terms had been available to Job, he might have resisted the metaphysical realism—the commitment to a "God's-Eye View" picture of a coherent world—that can be found at the background of the friends' theodicist suggestions.

The rejection of theodicies reappears frequently throughout modern literature and already before the Holocaust. In modern rewritings of Job, individual freedom is set against one or another overwhelming power of necessity crushing the individual agent and his or her freedom. What is also common to these figures is that none of them quietly accepts this condition, but they all ask for divine justice and soon also fight against the unjust forces around them. Like Job, who is an archetype of both unnecessary suffering and resistance, they object to theodicies that would explain their suffering in terms of just punishments for bad deeds, since in their own view they have never committed any crimes meriting such suffering. Among the famous literary characters who share this less patient basic reaction to suffering and turn to a rebellion against God is Franz Kafka's Josef K., who in *Der Prozess* (1925; see Kafka 1955) undergoes an experience, a mysterious condemnation, for which significance is hard to discover. Josef K. is arrested without having done anything wrong (*etwas Böses*), and he remains equally steadfast of his innocence as Job. Instead of accepting the existence of a moral balance in the world, both Job and Kafka's Josef K. start to challenge the idea of divine justice and soon also rail against God (or other powerful forces surrounding them). The protagonists' experience suggests that there is no moral order or harmony in the world unless humans themselves start to struggle for a morally better world. These literary works challenge the human project of making sense of suffering by providing meaning to suffering, and thus crucially develop the idea of antitheodicy that rejects such attempts of justification, suggesting that the problem of evil and disproportional suffering cannot be solved by theoretical reason or by appealing to such simple narrative or doctrinal patterns as punishment or reward.

In Kafka's novel God does not address man; the absence of the dialogue between humanity and God is the most agonizing feature in the novel. When Josef K. asks where the Judge is who could decide about his case and where the Court is that would discuss it, nothing turns up. The famous parable "Before the Law" at the end of the novel is a key passage that illustrates the human being's futile efforts to try to gain access to the Law and his repeated failure to be admitted. The parable is a metonymic illustration of the fact that Josef K. will never see the Judge or the Law he wishes to see and he is permanently left outside the doors, in the bewilderment of the meaning of his life. Thus, the story is a reversal of the *Book of Job* in which God does finally appear and address Job out of the storm-wind. Kafka refuses to fix meanings in any theological way and ground them in God. Josef K.'s story can be read as a mystery of human failure or a mystery of divine justice that is beyond the realm of human knowledge, but the latter view is less plausible if we read the novel in terms of

---

[9]   English translation by Allen W. Wood and George Di Giovanni in Kant, *Religion and Rational Theology*. Cambridge: Cambridge University Press, 1996.

antitheodicy (as we want to suggest). The absence of any certain answers from suprahuman forces is crucial here, but we should take it as a chance given to humans, instead of reading the novel simply as a pessimistic description of the despair of a modern secular person who will no longer be able to access the unity with God. Closed doors and the overall metaphysical emptiness that characterizes the world of the novel can be relieving to humans, since they encourage us to take responsibility for our actions, instead of trying to find some official instance or a higher power to judge our doings. This is how we can interpret the oft-noted Kafkaesque silence of the gods or the hermeneutic crisis; the openness and uncertainty and the missing totalizing view are ethically significant. That there is no visible sign of divine justice discernible to human beings does not mean that the human life would be therefore meaningless. On the contrary, the very absence of such signs may be a prerequisite for us humans to live a life that is deeply ethical. Similarly, we may say that the kind of rejection of metaphysical realism that we find necessary for antitheodicism is itself an ethically invigorating metaphysical move.

Samuel Beckett's *Waiting for Godot* (1952, in Beckett 2006) is another obvious key text here, as it explores the questions about the unfulfilled human desire for something to turn up, for signs of higher powers, some rational basis of things or a meaningful order that would suggest that the world does not end at the borders of the self. Yet the actual experiences of the protagonists record mere rootlessness and painful suffering; they mourn their situation basically in the same way as Job, although their suffering takes a different form of stasis and timelessness. In Beckett's antitheodicist works, the very existence of a super-perspective is suggested to be fundamentally illusory; such an illusion is maintained in order to hold back the suspicion that the world in which humans suffer is completely meaningless and that human beings are there alone. The protagonists would like to see evidence of transcendent powers in the smallest of events, and they would love to submit themselves to something larger than themselves, some extra-mental creature, but the mysterious Godot remains entirely absent, and keeping his distance Godot is merely produced in the conversations between the main characters. Again, the comprehensive God's-Eye View is not merely unavailable to human beings, but there simply *is* no perspective of that kind; there is no overall explanation or account of how things are. Nevertheless, it is only human to suppose there is, and the whole existence of the powerful figure of Godot is indebted to human belief, imagination and language that fill the silence.

Even language, when trying to reach for metaphysical heights, is drawn from the metaphysical for everyday use in absurd literature. The theatre of the absurd in general approaches the issues of personal guilt and responsibility by showing how the possibility of these concepts becomes obscure or impossible in a modern world. The use of these concepts presupposes an ordered world and meaningful human existence, which are called into question in absurd drama. As Friedrich Dürrenmatt has claimed in his essay "Theaterprobleme" (1955, in Dürrenmatt 1975), tragedy is possible only in an ordered world in which moral causalities take place and human beings bear responsibility for their actions; the tragic world is structured in a meaningful way. In his view, absurd comedy and grotesque are more useful concepts than tragedy in interpreting the current world, since they capture the ambiguous and paradoxical spirit of the age where causalities and personal responsibilities have disappeared and there is no connection to any transcendence. In absurd drama, human life is depicted as completely dissolute of any transcendent realm, and the experiences of meaninglessness and purposelessness stem from this sense of human isolation and dispossession.

While in our earlier work (Kivistö and Pihlström 2016) we studied the *Book of Job*, Kafka, Beckett, and Orwell for our antitheodicist purposes (suggesting that they interestingly correspond to, or aesthetically manifest, various post-Kantian philosophical antitheodicies), the novels we have now selected as the objects of our closer antitheodicist reading are two works by Joseph Roth. Roth's *Hiob: Roman eines einfachen Mannes* (1930, Roth 2012) is rather explicitly a rewriting of the *Book of Job*. The novel tells us a story of a simple man, whose life becomes special through his extraordinary suffering. The protagonist of the novel, Mendel Singer, relives the destiny of Job as his later incarnation and as if in a sort of textual possession that he cannot leave behind. We could talk about Job's existential immediacy in Roth's work that determines Mendel Singer's life course.[10] As is characteristic of Roth's writings, the first setting of the novel describes a rather fixed framework. The protagonist Mendel Singer is an ordinary, honest man who lives a happy life with his wife and children:

> He was pious, godfearing, and ordinary, an entirely commonplace Jew. He practiced the simple profession of a teacher. In his house, which was merely a roomy kitchen, he instructed children in the knowledge of the Bible. He taught with honourable zeal and without notable success. Hundreds of thousands before him had lived and taught as he did. (Roth 2012, p. 9; quoted in English in Fisch 1998, p. 104)

Soon after these initial notes that emphasize the hero's ordinary life, the situation suddenly changes and the stable framework collapses through a series of misfortunes. In the manner of other rewritings of the *Book of Job*, the novel is closely connected with the literary tradition that investigates the overwhelming reality of innocent and pointless suffering. It describes a situation in which the protagonist tries to reach for apparent meaning amidst a human life that is deeply unfair. His youngest son is seriously retarded, and the father tries to get into some contact with his son:

> He [Mendel] tried to guess what might be going on in that broad skull, to gaze in through the eyes as through a window in the brain, and by talking to him, sometimes loudly, sometimes softly, to draw from the stolid boy **some sort of sign**. He would repeat Menuchim's name ten times, moving his lips slowly so that the boy could see him say it if he could not hear. But Menuchim never responded.
>
> Then Mendel would take a spoon, strike it against a tea-glass, and immediately Menuchim would turn his head, and **a tiny light** would flame on his great, grey, liquid eyes. [...]
>
> "**Why** am I so afflicted?" thought Mendel, and he explored his conscience for sins but found none that was grave. (Roth 2012, pp. 45–46; quoted in English in Fisch 1998, p. 105; emphasis added)

Mendel here affirms his innocence and presents the essential question regarding the pointlessness of his existence and suffering (Why? Why Me?), and this is only one occasion that resembles the example of Job in the novel. Among the numerous disasters Singer has to face are the death of his wife and the demise of his children.[11] Travelling to America brings yet another disappointment to Mendel Singer's life, since he had hoped that America would offer an escape for his family (and for humankind) from the existential crisis, but these utopian hopes are never fulfilled. At this point Mendel turns to a rebellion against God: "His heart was angry against God, but in his sinews the fear of God still dwelt". Singer is not denying God but confronting him, and he refuses to pray: "'I shall not pray,' thought Mendel" (quoted in Fisch 1998, p. 107). His friends also explicitly compare him with Job. Roth's long account of irrational and constant agony creates a world without any moral balance that would guarantee that people receive what they deserve, and without any principle that would order that offenders are punished and the innocent stay free. As Hans Küng remarks in his essay "Religion in the Controversy over the End of Religion," "in suffering, especially in that of the innocent, man comes up against his extreme limit, comes to the decisive question of his identity, of the sense and nonsense

---

[10] On Roth's rewritings of Job, see (Hasan-Rokem 2015; Fisch 1998).

[11] This experience of radical disorder and despair also reminds one of Dostoevsky's Ivan Karamazov who is among the most famous similar descendants of Job, who returns his entrance ticket to heaven to God, not because he would not believe in God but because he cannot accept the unfair world God has created, longing for justice in the existing human world and not in some remote time to come, and morally refusing to accept any imaginable future reconciliation as a justification for innocent suffering. Posthumous glory and rewards in the afterlife are not something Ivan would be looking for, and the rosy promise of heaven is not satisfactory to him in a world in which innocent children suffer, since theodicy and future harmony simply collapse in the face of these victims. Ivan is not an atheist in any ordinary or straightforward sense; Dostoevsky called him deep, because he refuses to accept cheap solutions or consolations.

of his living and dying, indeed, of reality pure and simple" (Küng 1991, p. 234). Mental simplicity that appears in the subtitle of the novel can be read as a moral ideal stemming from the early (Hebrew) religion and thought, thus challenging overly rationalist perspectives on religion and suffering offered, for instance, by theodicy.

Roth's earlier novel, *Die Rebellion* (1924, Roth 2010), is another fictitious exploration of the problem of innocent suffering. Its main character Andreas Pum is a former soldier who has lost his leg in the war, but despite this major personal sacrifice he still believes in the sacred moral order of the world. At the beginning of the novel, Andreas is irritated by his comrades who complain and curse their future, as if they did not deserve their condition, but in Andreas's view all the suffering is likely to be necessary for some overall good. Andreas believes in a just god and some kind of business contract with Him, whereby He gives medals to those who have suffered in the war, and he rationalizes that the loss of one leg is not that bad if you get something better for compensation, as "the joy of receiving a medal was considerable" and "an invalid might enjoy the respect of the world" (p. 2). Pum believes not only in the justice of God, but also in the unfailing protection and support of the government that "overlies man as the sky overlies earth" (p. 2). The government represents here another fallacious overwhelming force that is the object of Pum's naïve expectation of a rationally ordered cosmos: "What comes from it may be good or ill, but it cannot be other than great and all-powerful, unknowable and mysterious, even though on occasion it may be understood by an ordinary person" (p. 2).

Instead of receiving an artificial leg, a medal, or a state employment for his services and sacrifices to his country, Andreas faces only unrest and upheaval. He becomes involved in a small scuffle that, in the manner of tragedies, leads to unexpected and disproportionate consequences and to a trial that sends him to prison. The sudden arrest, the legal process, and the trial scenes remind one of Kafka's missing legal order, and the little yellow church that Andreas visits for prayer also echoes the Kafkaesque silence of the gods; the church is empty and the winter sends its chilly breath into the house of God, which smells of snuffed candles that no longer give light. During all the distress, Andreas finally gives up his faith in a just world and questions God's goodness. While in prison he doubts whether God will look after the birds when he apparently does not care about the human beings; on the contrary, he punishes the innocent with suffering for no apparent reason. In the manner of Job, Andreas tries to examine hidden sins within his soul, with the idea that perhaps God knows some secret sin within him that he himself is not aware of, but he finds none that would be grave, and his worship changes into a rebellion against the world, its authorities, and God. He loses his belief in an inherent order that was grounded in his faith in God and the government.

The novel includes many elements that are familiar from the *Book of Job* and its later imitations, such as the self-examination of sins and the gradual awakening to the fact that the world is not governed by any moral balance or great justice that would reward loyalty and suffering with praise and honors. While nothing turns up to explain or reward the suffering, the protagonist finally starts to rebel against God. While in the beginning Andreas still claims that his own conscience is as clean as the china plate that is struck by a sunbeam as if by a check mark from Heaven (the symbol refers to some providential causality or presence in the world), he gradually loses his belief in such meaningful details and signs from transcendence as these turn out to be his own fantasies. The surrounding people and public authorities of society typically view his shortcomings from an objectifying perspective and nobody is engaged with or cares about his case. The officials love order and norms in various forms, and they objectify Andreas's case as a legal process independent of ethical considerations, whereas Andreas no longer assumes any social order and concludes that the world is much more complicated than any simple plot lines would suggest. There is no simple punishment and reward pattern according to which one could expect compensation for one's sacrifices or whereby everyone could achieve their own luck according to their merits; the world is governed by random luck alone. It is noteworthy that, in the manner of tragedies, the world continues its normal course regardless of the hero's collapse; it does not affect the broader picture or the life of the other people of the novel at all. In the end, Andreas's former friend and employer starts to look for another old soldier to take care of the dead man's duties as a lavatory attendant.

Unlike in Kafka's novels, which are full of meaningless details and whose atmosphere is dominated by the sense of pointless existence, in Roth's *Hiob* there is at least an apparent divine plot or purpose to the course of events (see also Fisch 1998, p. 108). There are channels of communication between the divine and the human (the prophecy in the beginning and the redemption at the end), and some finality (with an intention) in the form of the fairytale-like happy ending. Menuchim fulfills the prediction presented by a rabbi in the beginning of the novel, as he is made stronger through his suffering and finally healed. "The listening light" in Menuchim's eyes (see the quotation above) becomes meaningful in the story, anticipating the concluding miracle: Menuchim Singer has become a musical star (thus embodying the family name) and comes to meet his father in the final redemption scene. The unexpected turn of the plot seems to suggest that there is some final good in human life, but the harmonious conclusion is deeply ambiguous. On the one hand, it seems to offer the interpretative possibility that the true religious essence lies in the sense of mystery, and that finally all suffering receives its compensation, just like there is a happy ending in the *Book of Job* in which all Job's goods are restored. On the other hand, this (theodicist) understanding of the fairytale-like ending is not the only possible interpretation, since the unexpected turn brings yet another unpredictable element to the world that does not follow any patterns of justice or predictability. The sudden happy ending may feel unsatisfactory and disappointing precisely because it offers an unlikely and implausible conclusion to the novel, an ironic *deus ex machina* that seems to underline not so much the happy redemption but rather the fact that human suffering is not resolved in this world but only in some fictitious heaven that is also described in the end of *Die Rebellion*; only there is the protagonist finally able to meet his God and present his accusations against him. The human world remains deeply unjust and its problems remain unsolved, despite the happy ending and harmonious total picture that feel merely far-fetched when compared with all the preceding malaise.

Roth's *Hiob* thus also subverts the basic assumption of literary realism that the fictional reality rests on some intrinsic order. The sudden ending ironically underlines that it is not some cosmic force that creates and maintains meaningful order in the world; if there exists some chain of events or apparent mimetic order in the world, this order is completely fictitious and imposed on a chaotic world. Roth thus also challenges the basic idea of realism and the typical teleological plot of a realist novel, in which the fictional world usually follows an inevitable and irreversible cause-and-effect order of events. In realist novels, the immutable order usually remains, but here the seemingly simplistic fairytale ending complicates the picture by challenging the conventional intrinsic order characteristic of literary realism and privileging contingency over superimposed causality.[12] At the same time, this challenge to literary realism is—if our antitheodicist reading is correct—a challenge to philosophical (metaphysical) realism, insofar as the latter is presupposed by the theodicism that these rewritings of Job's story can be read as criticizing.

We will not go into further readings here, but we can briefly note that yet another, more recent novel that very interestingly complicates the simple punishment or reward model (defended by Job's friends, for example) is Philip Roth's *Nemesis* (Roth 2010). Its main character Bucky Cantor (yet another "singer") is a gym teacher who suffers from bad eyesight and some vague sense of shame owing to his physical weakness. In the main plot he fights against a sudden spread of polio, until he realizes that he has been spreading the infection himself. The virus has followed him from his school to the summer camp and more children are infected. In this sense the novel resembles a Greek tragedy, as the protagonist tries by all means to avoid the inevitable disaster but merely manages to advance the unhappy turn and cause more suffering. Like Oedipus, Cantor is ignorant of his guilt, but still guilty of

---

[12] On the tensions between realism and modernism in Roth's *Radetzkymarsch*, see (Landwehr 2003).

the disaster and the epidemic that infected his community; his lot is tragic, but not unfair, whereas Job was completely innocent.[13]

Cantor holds God accountable for all the suffering and looks for a deeper cause, while failing to grasp the broader picture. He accuses God of creating the virus and causing the deaths of innocent children: "His anger was provoked—not against whatever cause, however unlikely, people, in their fear and confusion, might advance to explain the epidemic, not even against the polio virus, but against the source, the creator—against God, who made the virus" (p. 127). He has serious difficulties in understanding the meaning of suffering and he also presents the ponderous why question familiar from other narratives of unmerited suffering: "Why does He set one person down in Nazi-occupied Europe with a rifle in his hands and the other in the Indian Hill dining lodge in front of a plate of macaroni and cheese? Why does He place one Weequahic child in polio-ridden Newark for the summer and another in the splendid sanctuary of the Poconos?" (p. 154)—"Why didn't God answer the prayers of Alan Michaels's parents? They must have prayed. Herbie Steinmark's parents must have prayed. They're good people. They're good Jews. Why didn't God intervene for them? Why didn't He save their boys?"(p. 170).

Job's opponents were his friends, but here the opponents are Bucky's naïve girlfriend, who advises him to seek relief in prayer, and the narrator, who turns out to be a former polio patient called Arnie (see also Batnitzky 2015, p. 220). He represents a secularist (or an atheist) view of life, stressing that one's life course is contingent and Bucky's stubborn posing of the why question is mindless, since Bucky should accept the tragic meaninglessness of suffering and not try "to convert tragedy into guilt" or "to find a necessity for what happens" (p. 265). But Bucky resembles Job in that he openly accuses God and sincerely tries to capture the sense of the suffering, yet without finding any overall picture. He speaks aloud and insists that his question must be heard and answered, but God remains silent.

In their different ways, all these literary examinations of antitheodicist thinking can be seen as presenting an essentially moral argument against theodicism, based on the idea that theodicies fail to adequately recognize the meaninglessness of individuals' suffering and typically (as a result of that non-acknowledgment) treat suffering human beings as mere means to some alleged overall good, thus also subordinating the suffering individual to some totalizing framework. Furthermore, there is an aesthetic dimension to this totalizing attempt. The aesthetics of antitheodicy, we might say, is an *aesthetics of disharmony*: the literary narratives briefly explored here can show that there may be no final harmonious justification, accommodation, or meaningfulness of evil and suffering, or, if there is, it is emphatically fictitious, as in Joseph Roth's novels. The world is not neat and harmonious: there is real evil, misery, suffering, and non-totalizable otherness. Disharmony is a central aesthetic category in all the literary works studied here. Job does not get any moral explanation from God but only a picture of a cruel, amoral creation; Josef K. finds no explanation for his case and never learns to know the actual reasons for his unexpected arrest. Beckett's tramps seem to live in a world that lacks meaning altogether.

If Beckett ridiculed the futile search for a rational universe, Joseph Roth took this quest more seriously. In Roth's novels, there is the assumption of there being an absolute super-perspective (a God's-Eye View), although it is unavailable to the protagonist, but it is a perspective of absoluteness that unethically neglects or reduces the significance of the protagonists' first-person individual human perspectives. There is a clash between the anthropocentric and the theocentric perspectives there, whereas in Beckett's *Godot* the very existence of such a super-perspective is suggested to be fundamentally illusory. Beckett shows us how human beings struggle in vain to find such a perspective, which simply is not there at all. There is no overall account of how things are; as suggested above,

---

[13] On Joban (tragic) themes in Roth's *Nemesis*, see (Batnitzky 2015).

it is only a human (and perhaps humanly understandable or even unavoidable) temptation or tendency to suppose there is, or to hope one could achieve such a perspective.

The literary works that deliberately elaborate on the *Book of Job* crucially contribute to the understanding of the problem of suffering that is at the heart of the theodicism versus antitheodicism controversy. What these works also illustrate is that disharmony also means multiple individual voices: the ethics and aesthetics of antitheodicy cannot be reduced to an overarching voice or an overall picture that would provide a single perspective on the world. In this sense, the rejection of metaphysical realism and the God's-Eye View exemplified by the antitheodicist literature studied here is also aesthetic.

4. Recognition, Theory, and Practice

Acknowledging reality—whatever we mean by that vague phrase—though necessary for adequate ethical acknowledgment of others' suffering, does not require metaphysical realism. On the contrary, metaphysical realism itself fails to acknowledge reality in its diversity, as it reductively objectifies everything into a single picture (as we have suggested). What proper acknowledgment requires is just a commitment to objective truth in an ordinary, philosophically unelaborated sense (see Section 2 above) rather than any overall assumption of metaphysical realism. Theodicies are of course only one specific, albeit ethically highly influential, example of a distorted non-acknowledgment of reality. Others include a quasi-Orwellian (or, perhaps today, "Trumpist") failure to acknowledge the very significance of truth and facts (as witnessed by the horrifyingly Orwellian pseudo-discourse of "alternative facts"), as well as popular self-help literature advancing various manipulative pseudo-therapies, self-branding, etc. There are profoundly problematic elements of *insincerity* in such cultural phenomena that are in interesting ways analogous to theodicist narratives with their postulation of a harmonious total picture. What we need as a remedy is not metaphysical realism with its imagined super-absolute facts but an ethical acknowledgment of humanly constituted and reconstructed reality and objectivity. It is part of this acknowledgment to also acknowledge the essentially contestable nature of any facts we may be committed to as well as the fragility of any meanings and meaningfulness we may find in our world.[14] When Richard Rorty (1989) tells us that if we take care of freedom, truth can take care of itself,[15] he needs to be reminded that this is true only if freedom is not just negative freedom from constraints but positive freedom that includes responsibility and a genuine commitment to acknowledgment, including the acknowledgment of human suffering, finitude, and fragility.

We have suggested that the realism discussion in the philosophy of religion, while apparently independent of the theodicy discussion, is actually very closely tied to the latter—to the extent that theodicism (typically, paradigmatically) presupposes a problematic form of metaphysical realism and should be criticized along with such realism. We have also suggested that antitheodicist literary works challenging literary realism can be read as also criticizing this philosophical form of realism. The collapse of metaphysical realism hardly directly entails the collapse of theodicism, but the antitheodicist should focus on attacking the metaphysically realist background assumptions of theodicism in addition to focusing on the main task of showing the colossal failure of moral acknowledgment in all attempts to justify others' suffering. This task can also be formulated in terms of the concept of *truth*. While metaphysical realism and theodicies seek the objective, absolute, and general truth—from a God's-Eye View—about suffering and its reasons, this search

---

[14] It can be suggested that if evil indeed is part of God's good creation, then the theodicy problem does not even arise, as its presuppositions are not fulfilled: it cannot even be coherently posed, because everything, as created by God, is by definition meaningful. (We are indebted to Akeel Bilgrami for this formulation.) The antitheodicist criticism of theodicies can also focus on the very availability of the theodicy problem in this sense—and on the assumption that there must be (somewhere) the kind of meaning postulated by theodicies.

[15] This remark, in the context of Rorty's reading of Orwell, is commented on in more detail in (Kivistö and Pihlström 2016, chp. 5). (See also Conant 2000; Rorty 2000.)

(we have argued) incorporates a failure to acknowledge the perspectival diversity of individual suffering and hence an inability to capture all the relevant truths that ethically demand our attention. A more perspectival pragmatic conception of truth is therefore to be preferred, for ethical reasons, to metaphysically realist correspondence truth (cf., e.g., Pihlström 2013).

The theodicy vs. antitheodicy issue is often seen as purely metaphysical (as in Leibnizian theodicies and their contemporary variants) or, alternatively, as primarily ethical (as in "moral antitheodicism" based on, say, Levinasian criticism of the immorality of justifying others' suffering, a criticism that claims to be more fundamental than any metaphysical theorization). We have tried to argue, at least implicitly, that both are too narrow ways of conceiving the matter. The issue we are dealing with actually exemplifies the deep entanglement of the moral and the metaphysical (as well as the aesthetic). One way to see the entanglement at the core of this topic is to note how deeply theodicies are committed to metaphysical realism. Antitheodicism, as has been suggested, is based on the ethical affirmation of the fundamental need to recognize or acknowledge—ontologically as well as ethically—individual sufferers' (or victims' of evil) perspectives in their distinctiveness and irreducibility. This requires that we reject metaphysical realism as a non-recognizing (and therefore at least potentially even morally corrupting) totalizing attempt to view the world as a totality from a God's-Eye View. This rejection is both ethical and metaphysical, with the two aspects inseparably present. Not only are the ethical and the metaphysical entangled here; similarly (and entangled with this entanglement), there is the entanglement of the unintelligibility or incoherence, on the one hand, and the ethical unacceptability, on the other, of the kind of metaphysics invoked by theodicies, based on metaphysical realism.

It could also be suggested that if metaphysical realism and thereby theodicism really are incoherent responses to the reality of suffering (or to reality generally), then we could not really be theodicists even if we tried. We would be in "bad faith"; we would in reality always already have acknowledged the moral status of the other person and thus also the irreducibility and unobjectifiability of their suffering, simply as a necessary precondition for our own moral subjectivity, and therefore the theodicy argumentation could not really get off the ground at all.[16] An engagement in theodicies, or a commitment to theodicism, would thus in a way be a self-denial, a concealment of one's inevitable commitment to moral acknowledgment. We may agree with this suggestion while also maintaining that it is important to emphasize the incoherence of theodicist and metaphysically realist thinking. Kant had to write hundreds of pages in defense of transcendental idealism while also maintaining that in some sense anyone who has experiences of objective objects and events must be a transcendental idealist (even against their own will), as its alternative transcendental realism is ultimately incoherent.

There is one more issue we need to deal with. A typical response to moral criticisms of theodicies in contemporary mainstream analytic philosophy of religion pursuing theodicies (or "defenses") starts from a sharp distinction between *theory* and *practice*. Theodicists can easily maintain that at the theoretical level their justifications for evil and suffering (or, more modestly, the defense according to which God might, for all we know, have acceptable moral reasons that would justify his allowing the world to contain apparently meaningless evil and suffering) may indeed fail to recognize the suffering other, or their experiences of meaningless suffering, while also maintaining that such a failure—based on (they might admit) metaphysical realism, as we have argued—does not matter philosophically or ethically insofar as the theodicist exercise indeed *is*, and remains, merely theoretical. Theodicists can (and arguably should) still avoid engaging in their theory-construction (backed up by metaphysical realism) when actually faced by suffering human beings and the practical need to comfort them. This practical task of consolation is to be clearly distinguished from the purely theoretical or intellectual task of constructing a theodicy argument or a "defense".

---

[16] We are here indebted to a suggestion made by Steven Crowell in relation to a related paper. Crowell formulated this as a Levinasian rejoinder to the kinds of worries raised here.

For example, Peter Van Inwagen (2006, p. 12) tells us that his examination of the problem of evil is "purely intellectual" and that his "defense" is not intended to even hypothetically comfort anyone (Van Inwagen 2006, p. 108); similar caveats are added by a number of other theodicists. Hence, it could be claimed that no failure of recognition is necessarily committed by the theodicist (or the one who seeks to offer a "defense") at the practical level of engaging with suffering human beings needing consolation (or, in a theological context, pastoral care). If the distinction between theory and practice is drawn carefully enough, theodicies and defenses may remain purely theoretical and intellectual, while comfort and consolation are practical matters to be dealt with separately.

However, it can now be argued—for example, from a *pragmatist* point of view (cf. Pihlström 2013, 2014), though this line of argument is certainly not restricted to pragmatism—that the very attempt to defend theodicism by drawing such a sharp theory-practice dichotomy *itself* (at a meta-level) constitutes a moral failure of recognition. The suffering other ought to be morally recognized precisely by *not* drawing such a dichotomy—that is, by not engaging in the theoretical argumentative exchange of purely intellectual ideas *pro* and *contra* theodicies at all. This, we may say, is where the metaphilosophical relevance of moral antitheodicism for the pursuit of philosophy of religion primarily lies. Again, antitheodicist arguments and positions as diverse as James's pragmatism, Phillips's Wittgensteinianism, and Levinas's insistence on the primacy of the other's face can be regarded as variations on this general theme, and so can the antitheodicist readings of the literature presented in the previous section. James (1907, James 1975, chp. 1) seems to base his entire pragmatic method on an antitheodicist refusal to attach any absolute or abstract metaphysical significance (either Hegelian or Leibnizian) to individual experiences of concrete suffering, while Phillips (2004) warns against the morally corrupting language of anthropomorphic accounts of God that seem to turn God into a monstrous agent calculating the advantages and disadvantages of allowing his creation to suffer. In a different but arguably analogously pragmatic strain, Levinas (2006) maintains that the justification of others' suffering is the foundation of all immorality. In their distinctive ways, these antitheodicist thinkers suggest that there is something deeply wrong—and non-recognizing— in the theory-practice dichotomy itself in this area.

It can be further argued that antitheodicism (exemplified by these very different thinkers), in insisting on not explaining away the meaninglessness of suffering, is needed precisely as a necessary condition for the possibility of adequately recognizing the other person as a (potential or actual) sufferer. It can be part of that adequate recognition to acknowledge that there is suffering that simply cannot be rendered meaningful in any morally acceptable sense. Therefore, there is a sense in which theodicist attitudes to others should *not* themselves be (philosophically, ethically) recognized as ethically appropriate attitudes, or perhaps not even tolerated, and this rejection of theodicism can be articulated in terms of pragmatism that is generally critical of any principled theory–practice dichotomies. If theory and practice are inevitably entangled, then the failure to recognize this entanglement again constitutes a failure to adequately engage in the practical task of recognizing otherness.

5. Concluding Reflections

It should thus be re-emphasized that a philosophical opposition to metaphysical realism, to reductive objectification, to what Kant called transcendental realism, and to various forms of reductionism and totalizing, on the one hand, and antitheodicism acknowledging individual suffering in its perspectival variety (defended in the literary works examined above, and in contrast to theodicist postulations of a totalizing overall perspective), on the other hand, are really two sides of the same coin. However, we should recognize a final reflexive problem here. Are we saying that this antitheodicism is a *generally* correct view to embrace? Are we betraying our own defense of irreducible perspectivalness, and the respect for diversity that goes along with it by failing to recognize the philosophical value of, say, monism and reductionism—or, indeed, of theodicism? We have no final answer to provide here. We are just tempted to point out that this criticism amounts to something comparable to the claim that one should, if one is tolerant, also tolerate intolerance; the only possible response to such a criticism in the end is "no, one should not." Yet, we should constantly examine our own temptations to reductionism, theodicism, and non-recognition.

The fact that we have to be reflectively self-critical in our pursuit of antitheodicism yields one final comment on what we might call the *humanism* of antitheodicism.[17] We should defend the individual human being's right and duty to take responsibility for creating moral meaning into her/his life and the world s/he lives in, in the absence of any transcendent, metaphysico-theological or theodicist grand narratives of the meaningfulness or significance of suffering. This is something that our reading of antitheodicist literature brings out very clearly. The human being stands in the center of this ethical project of constructing meaning; this is a human existential task that cannot be handed over to any (real or imagined) God. "Creating moral meaning" does not amount to discovering any ready-made meanings or moral truths (in a metaphysically realistic sense) but to living an open, possibly very difficult life fully aware of the significance of what Wittgenstein in the *Tractatus* (1921) called the "problem of life." Such creation of meaning may crucially need literary and other artistic perspectives on the world we live in. While fictional literature can hardly directly provide a knock-down argument against metaphysical realism or theodicism, it may be an essential, undetachable element of a sufficiently rich philosophical consideration of these issues—or so, at least, we have tried to suggest in this paper.

This "humanism of antitheodicism" is also, arguably, a humanism of a "de-selfing," disappearing subject: the ethically engaged person does not set her-/himself at the center but disappears into the world like the metaphysical subject of Wittgenstein's famous (albeit extremely controversial) solipsism in the *Tractatus* (Wittgenstein 1974, § 5.64; cf. Pihlström 2016, chp. 3). Such humanism is very different from the way in which the human being (one's own self) is placed at the center of things in contemporary popular "selfie" and self-help culture. The self-critically reflective antitheodicism we have defended in this paper contains the requirement of constant vigilance in *not* setting oneself first and thereby failing to recognize others' suffering. This is why it is important to fight against one's own theodicist temptations—and the related temptation to embrace the only apparently consoling absolute picture of metaphysical realism. Our criticism of theodicism and non-acknowledgment should first and foremost be self-criticism. Reading (and writing) creative literature drawing attention to *others'* suffering may be a fundamental element of such a campaign.

Acknowledgments: We are particularly grateful to Simo Knuuttila, Heikki J. Koskinen, Panu-Matti Pöykkö, and Risto Saarinen for helpful conversations on the topic of this paper. Thanks are also due to Jill Hernandez for her invitation to submit this paper to this special issue, as well as to the anonymous reviewer for helpful comments. We also gratefully recognize the significance of the Academy of Finland Centre of Excellence, "Reason and Religious Recognition" (hosted by the Faculty of Theology, University of Helsinki) for our work.

Author Contributions: The authors are jointly responsible for the entire article, though the literary sections were primarily written by Sari Kivistö and the philosophical sections by Sami Pihlström.

Conflicts of Interest: The authors declare no conflict of interest.

References

Batnitzky, Leora. 2015. Beyond Theodicy? Joban Themes in Philip Roth's *Nemesis*. In *The Book of Job: Aesthetics, Ethics, Hermeneutics*. Edited by Ilana Pardes and Leora Batnitzky. Berlin: De Gruyter, pp. 213–24.

Beckett, Samuel. 2006. *The Complete Dramatic Works*. London: Faber and Faber.

Bernstein, Richard. 2002. *Radical Evil: A Philosophical Interrogation*. Cambridge: Polity Press.

Betenson, Toby. 2016. Anti-Theodicy. *Philosophy Compass* 11: 56–65. [CrossRef]

Byrne, Peter. 2003. *God and Realism*. Aldershot: Ashgate.

---

[17] This fundamental humanism can, again, be regarded as a common feature shared by the different antitheodicisms briefly mentioned above. It should come as no surprise that such humanism is a trend in antitheodicisms that can be taken to be "Kantian" (cf. again Kivistö and Pihlström 2016), given Kant's insistence on the irreducible value of the human person.

Carson, Thomas L. 2007. Axiology, Realism, and the Problem of Evil. *Philosophy and Phenomenological Research* 75: 349–68. [CrossRef]

Conant, James. 2000. Freedom, Cruelty, and Truth: Rorty versus Orwell. In *Rorty and His Critics*. Edited by Robert B. Brandom. Oxford and Cambridge: Blackwell, pp. 268–342.

Dürrenmatt, Friedrich. 1975. *Der Besuch der alten Dame*. Stuttgart: Reclam.

Fisch, Harold. 1998. *New Stories for Old: Biblical Patterns in the Novel*. Basingstoke: Palgrave Macmillan.

Habermas, Jürgen. 2010. *An Awareness of What Is Missing*. Cambridge: Polity Press.

Hasan-Rokem, Galit. 2015. Joban Transformations of the Wandering Jew in Joseph Roth's *Hiob* and *Der Leviathan*. In *The Book of Job: Aesthetics, Ethics, Hermeneutics*. Edited by Ilana Pardes and Leora Batnitzky. Berlin: De Gruyter, pp. 147–71.

James, William. 1975. *Pragmatism: A New Name for Some Old Ways of Thinking*. Edited by Frederick H. Burkhardt, Fredson Bowers and Ignas K. Skrupskelis. Cambridge and London: Harvard University Press. First published 1907.

Kafka, Franz. 1955. *The Trial*. Translated by Willa and Edwin Muir. London: Penguin. First published 1925.

Kant, Immanuel. 1983. Über das Misslingen aller philosophischen Versuche einer Theodicee. In *Werke in zehn Bänden*. Edited by Wilhelm Weischedel. Darmstadt: Wissenschaftliche Buchgesellschaft, vol. 9. First published 1791.

Kivistö, Sari, and Sami Pihlström. 2016. *Kantian Antitheodicy: Philosophical and Literary Varieties*. Basingstoke: Palgrave Macmillan.

Küng, Hans. 1991. Religion in the Controversy over the End of Religion. In *Literature & Religion*. Edited by Walter Jens and Hans Küng. New York: Paragon House.

Landwehr, Margarete Johanna. 2003. Modernist Aesthetics in Joseph Roth's *Radetzkymarsch*: The Crisis of Meaning and the Role of the Reader. *German Quarterly* 76: 398–410. [CrossRef]

Levinas, Emmanuel. 2006. *Entre-Nous: Thinking-of-the-Other*. Translated by Michael B. Smith. London: Continuum.

Neiman, Susan. 2002. *Evil in Modern Thought: An Alternative History of Philosophy*. Princeton: Princeton University Press.

Newsom, Carol A. 2009. *The Book of Job: A Contest of Moral Imaginations*. Oxford: Oxford University Press.

Phillips, Dewi Zephaniah. 2004. *The Problem of Evil and the Problem of God*. London: SCM Publications.

Pihlström, Sami. 2013. *Pragmatic Pluralism and the Problem of God*. New York: Fordham University Press.

Pihlström, Sami. 2014. *Taking Evil Seriously*. Basingstoke: Palgrave Pivot.

Pihlström, Sami. 2016. *Death and Finitude: Toward a Pragmatic Transcendental Anthropology of Human Limits and Mortality*. Lanham: Lexington Books.

Rorty, Richard. 1989. The Last Intellectual in Europe: Orwell on Cruelty. In *Contingency, Irony, and Solidarity*. Cambridge: Cambridge University Press.

Rorty, Richard. 2000. Response to James Conant. In *Rorty and His Critics*. Edited by Robert B. Brandom. Malden and Oxford: Blackwell, pp. 342–50.

Roth, Joseph. 2010. *Rebellion*. Translated by Michael Hoffman. New York: Picador. First published 1924.

Roth, Joseph. 2012. *Hiob. Roman.*. Köln: Kiepenheuer & Witsch. First published 1930.

Roth, Philip. 2010. *Nemesis*. London: Vintage.

Rowe, William, ed. 2001. *God and the Problem of Evil*. Malden and Oxford: Blackwell.

Saarinen, Risto. 2016. *Recognition and Religion: A Historical and Systematic Study*. Oxford: Oxford University Press.

Van Inwagen, Peter. 2006. *The Problem of Evil*. Oxford: Clarendon Press.

Wittgenstein, Ludwig. 1974. *Tractatus Logico-Philosophicus*. Translated by Brian F. McGuinness and David F. Pears. London: Routledge and Kegan Paul. First published 1921.

 *religions*

Article

On the Question at the End of Theodicy

Anthony B. Pinn

Department of Religion, University of Rice, Houston, TX 77005-1892, USA; pinn@rice.edu

Received: 8 November 2017; Accepted: 1 December 2017; Published: 8 December 2017

Abstract: This article argues that theodicy provides an insufficient response to suffering - one that often further victimizes those who suffering most. In it's place, I argue for a moralist response based on Albert Camus and W. E. B. Du Bois.

Keywords: suffering; black lives matter; theodicy; race; racial disregard

> What did I do to be so black and blue.
>
> —Fats Waller

1. The Question: Theodicy and Racial Disregard

For the theistically inclined, the final court of appeal tends to be theodical in tone and content, the Job-like speaking to the "wind"[1]. Yet, there is a difference in the two narratives: Job questions and receives an angry and dismissive response that renders suffering a mystery to humans and a riddle understandable only by God, who keeps answers to God's self. On the other hand, the racially despised are met with more pain and deafening silence that means to crush. For Job, it was the loss of all that mattered (family, friends, dignity, agency, bodily integrity, and so on) due to a wager between God and other forces, and for the race-discarded, it is the irrational impact of non-biological markers on their movement through a death dealing society.[2] Nonetheless, despite obvious differences between Job and the racially disregarded, they share something related to the nature of suffering: social circumstances matter, and the graphic nature of this situation becomes more visible over time.

This is not to say current patterns of disregard point out new arrangements of life. Rather, they intensify and make more difficult dismissal of the destructive nature of the social codes directing collective life. Existential circumstances threaten the delicate sense of meaning and purpose that propel the human animal. It is a delicate balance indeed, and one grounded often in metaphysical assumptions and goals. For the religiously inclined, theological argumentations and hope(s) of a transcending variety provide a filler or glue between the gaps in life narratives.

What I point to is not simply the socio-political and economic disregard that makes life less than ideal based on color and its connotations. Although such connotations are death dealing in their own way, what I intend to highlight is a more elemental nudging toward meaninglessness that undergirds these more readily present challenges. Those challenges attack one's right to occupy physical time and space, and the underlying angst is produced by a deeper troubling not of occupation *of* time and space but to the significance of the human animal *in* that time and space.

This dilemma of rightful being *in* time and space promotes a particularly tenacious modality of anxiety tied to a sense that the pain and misery such circumstances entail has gone unnoticed, met with indifference. This situation often prompts a desire to prove worthiness through demonstrations of

---

[1] I would like to thank the reviewer who provided such valuable feedback on my essay. I have worked to provide attention to the insights and questions posed in that review, and I believe doing so has made this a better article.

[2] The Book of Job points to the questionable character of God—i.e., pride that sets up humans as pawns for play. I further interrogate the character of God in relationship to the story of Nimrod. See (Pinn and Callahan 2007).

spiritual and moral fitness. Standards of an assumed cosmic variety are difficult to meet, but even this failure when acknowledged and owned provides small comfort within a realm of suffering as those longing for righteousness await divine assistance. Or, as so many Christians are known to rehearse: "More like Jesus let me be . . . "

The asceticism, strength of soul, purity, and charity outlined and graphically illustrated in the African American collective context has often been the stuff of social existence. Of course, there are examples of African Americans—many in the 19th century—who embraced extreme markers of righteousness and perhaps some of this bleeds into more contemporary modalities of Pentecostalism, for example. But as a mainstay, these have presented themselves as religiously enacted elements of life premised on socio-economic and political need, resolved through a turn to the material world pushed to give more, to surrender more space. (That, surely, is a take away from black and womanist theologies.) The "what is to be made of me" is replaced by a "what is to be made of us?" In this context, the application of human standards involves attention to the construction of blackness, and what Cornel West, has called a genealogy of racism that allows the humanity of blacks as a contemporary—but troubled—recognition (West 1982). It, this narration of race prompting questions of "becoming", finds particular modes of saintliness wanting and tends to categorize much of this existential distancing as otherworldly confusion. In a word, such efforts are sustained not because they prove fruitful, but precisely because they do not—a failure that is absorbed and re/presented as a personal shortcoming that can, or should, be overcome through continued effort. It is, for example, a failure of will.[3]

Within religious quarters, the more fundamental nature of racial violence has prompted a range of theological and philosophical questions concerning the nature of embodied life—particularly related discourses of moral evil produced and encountered within the realm of human interactions. This is the realm of theodicy: what can be said about God in light of human suffering in the world? Despite common assumptions, theodicy does not always encourage an otherworldly orientation. Rather, my argument is theodical efforts have no choice but to promote redemptive suffering orientation within a historical framework.[4]

God is perceived as present in human history and concerned with the "good," and humans are real subjects of history whose existence is marked by injustice and misery. Furthermore, this misery and injustice are real—not an idea, not an illusion, but issues with material and historical consequences. These consequences are death dealing at worse and metaphysically deforming at best. Some type of resolution is necessary, one that acknowledges felt presence of all three—God, humanity, suffering. Herein lies the problem for some theists: if all three are real, and God is defined by at least a portion of what believers say about God, then God has some ability to act in the world.[5] God acting in the world would mean God is aware of injustice/misery and therefore must be "ok" with ongoing conditions. If God is "ok" with the condition of humans, and God is at least remotely good, then misery must have a cosmic rationale. Unless believers are willing to say God (1) endorses evil or (2) does not exist, there must be some merit (at least indirectly) in suffering.[6]

This is the wager suggested by the above: religion must encourage believers to surrender something. They must surrender certain modalities of experience, certain ways of knowing, and grant authority to an unproven but assumed to be concerned God. That is to say, they must find some

---

[3] I more fully develop this in (Pinn 2017).

[4] I make this argument in full: (Pinn 1995).

[5] I acknowledge, however, that some theists embrace a self-limiting God. However, this begs the question: What value does God see in suffering that God would limit God's self in order to allow it? This lends itself to redemptive suffering.

[6] The percentage of African Americans who hold to no notion of God would suggest some (and a growing number of "some") have moved in the direction of option two. Still, so many continue to believe and address the dilemma by saying that suffering might be deserved punishing. Some of the extreme examples of this include the assumption of many that natural disasters (e.g., Hurricane Katrina) are the result of sin. Others argue that God takes this situation and uses it pedagogically: we learn something from it. Theological wrestling with race-based misery is full of both examples—from the early years of the country pushing into the present.

type of merit in suffering. Mindful of this, theodicy can be addressed as truncating of a particular metaphysical substance (e.g., human integrity and agency) in that it seeks to find in some form a positive outlook on suffering. From my vantage point, to call suffering "redemptive" or to claim it has some merit is a challenge to the integrity of human life.

Through a looking "beyond" for the cause of disregard, for example, the human is reduced: the significance of human activity (e.g., movement in the world meant to maintain the integrity and dignity of life) is consumed through an appeal to cosmic determinations. As one might imagine, this requirement to surrender something disproportionately impacts those who have already faced violence. This is precisely my point: theistic effort to "save" God puts those who suffer most at greater risk. My statement is not an endorsement of this approach; it is a critique of theological responses to suffering that create greater disregard for those who already suffer disproportionately.

After all this, theodicy generates no answers that do not further beg the question or further challenge the integrity of those most prone to socially induced suffering. One might name this predicament theological absurdity—something akin to Albert Camus's philosophical absurdity, and both modes of absurdity pull at our existential arrangements and challenge our socialization regarding narratives of possible "Unity" and coherence of a deeply meaningful kind—e.g., metaphysical certainty concerning the meaning and outcome of life.[7] To the extent it can be argued that theodicy provides an answer to suffering, it does so at great risk to those who suffer most.

In the rest of this essay, I give consideration to the above problem of struggle-death viewed through a moralist discourse anchored by the likes of Camus and W. E. B. Du Bois, and I do so in light of recent US social developments.[8]

2. Social Circumstances and Black Lives: Pretext for a Question[9]

The situation cannot be overstated: we live a legacy of racial violence meant to confine and manage. The manner in which the US orchestrates this process of control has entailed the destruction of difference by brutalizing raced bodies whenever they are "out of place" or out of "time".[10] The terror involved in this process isn't simply the threat of death, but the inability to anticipate what will trigger violent response to blackness. As with Philando Castile in Minnesota—the land of "nice-ness"—compliance can be deadly. Any sign of struggle—even for one's breath—can be understood as a threat to the safety of law enforcement and, as was the case for Eric Garner, can result in death. The jail cell as a place of confinement can also be a death chamber, as Sandra Bland's demise makes clear.[11] There are no decipherable ground rules for survival if one happens to live in black flesh. Those black men and women who have been murdered by police officers died simply because they occupied time and space in a way considered threatening. They were in the wrong place, or they demanded respect and the exercise of their agency, or perhaps they were simply black in a land where white privilege codes all interactions. Yes, not all police officers hate blacks, women, and other "marginalized" groups, but those who do hate seem to operate without significant challenge.

The anger felt by so many is not simply the fact that some police officers have murdered, but that these murderers by and large have gone without consequences consistent with their senseless taking of life. No charges and limited reprimand after such killings produces disillusionment and agitation for good reason. So, many look for ways to speak to this injustice, to force change to a deadly system

---

7   By absurdity, I mean to point to Camus's framing of the concept: the unrequited effort of humans to gain answers to the
    circumstances of life from a world that is non-responsive. See: (Camus 1991a, 1991b).
8   This argument is more fully developed in an early draft of my William James lecture at Harvard Divinity School, March 2017.
9   Much of this material regarding examples of racial disregard is drawn from (Pinn 2016).
10 This articulation of right "place" and "time" is sensitive to Mary Douglas's use of these concepts. For instance, according to
    Douglas dirt can be understood as matter out of place. See (Douglas 1996). In *Body Matters*, Judith Butler extends the link
    arguing that some marginalized groups are identified within the social system as 'shit': (Butler 2011).
11 See for examples: (Ellis and Kirkos 2017; Baker et al. 2015; Nathan 2016).

because "Black Lives Matter". Still, the genius of white supremacy is that it mutates and transforms, and it gives up a little in order to present the illusion of fundamental change. It finds ways to blame victims for the violence perpetuated against them. There is a desperate effort to find something in the past of the victim that will justify murder as the safeguarding of order and wellbeing. At times, this something found is nothing more than the connotations blackness.

Racial violence has always been a prominent dimension of life in the United States. This is a country, truth be told, grounded and enriched through a vicious disregard for difference that allowed for the psycho-physical marginalization and brutalization of those deemed "out of place" (Douglas 1996). This is more than dynamic belittling (e.g., socio-cultural, political, and economic hostility justified through a physical marker of distinction such as race, gender, or class). Bodies are coded, and in this coding, all else is found. Social coding such as that of race is tenacious, and longstanding. Its impact is significant; it "colors"—so to speak—the outlook on life, the struggles encountered, and the range of options for resolution.

Activism toward change up to this point has been preoccupied with outcomes—measurable and permanent changes that promote wellbeing for all. Yet, while admirable in that people are putting themselves on the line, offering themselves for the sake of a larger purpose, such strategies have produced little fundamental change. There is an assumption this country can do better, that it wants to do better, that it is a good system used wrong. So, effort consistent and ongoing can make a difference. Such thinking is the basis for hope under girding ongoing protest and critique. This is not identical to, but rather draws its strength from an appeal to love. That is to say, it prompts a sense of the other that truncates the integrity of self. I would argue a prime example of this is the Christ Event embraced within the Christian tradition. This is not blaming the victim, per se, but it is a sacrifice that prompts a particularly positive depiction of suffering.

If it is love, what prevents the assumption it is the love of an abuser who damages without taking responsibility for the violence, instead preferring to believe the violence was forced by the abused? Isn't this logic found in some of the responses to the Black Lives Matter movement and other organized efforts for change? Isn't this thinking present in the vocalized assumption that protestors bring violence on themselves through their "disruptive" and divisive behavior? The idea that love is the guiding force serving to bring US citizens together is an old fallacy without historical evidence. This is theological slight-of-hand, a theologically driven wish without grounding. Where is the love in that?

I understand there is some sense of comfort—a type of space away from the chaos of life—in the claim that religion in the form of love-talk points to the answer. "If we can only get back to loving each other", so many lament in a variety of ways. This is said as if religion is a type of protective Teflon coating that has prevented hate, fear, and violence from actually penetrating the core values of the nation. And because of this coating, evil injustice is superficial and can be removed, the democratic process exercised, and life improved.[12] However, such thinking fails to really consider the biblical text from which its advocates claim it is drawn. What is to be made of the violence and the divinely sanctioned destruction of life that marks the sacred texts so quickly quoted (out of context)?

3. An Alternate Question: Life without Appeal?

The dogma and practices of churches do little to change the "folkways, habits, customs and subconscious deeds" that contribute to the condition of African Americans (Du Bois 1970, p. 222). If anything, church dogma and theology re-enforce some of the worst patterns of thinking and hence celebrate some of the worst modes of ethics.

---

[12] I develop this idea more fully in a variety of texts, including *The End of God-Talk: An African American Humanist Theology* (Pinn 2011).

Moving back in time, there is no adequate response to the theodicy question for Du Bois; the theological wishes expressed by many, from his vantage point, fail to highlight the depth of disregard marking the historical moment and instead seek resolution either as future restitution or divine intervention in the social dynamics of belief beyond the abilities of humans. Theodical interrogations go unfulfilled; there is no response given to the question of "why, God?"[13] Borrowing from Camus, I suggest, this line of questioning regarding human suffering is a mode of suicide—i.e., a surrendering of embodied integrity and agency. Instead of theodicy as a response to human suffering and misery, I prefer the question posed by the moralists: "Is life without appeal possible?" (Camus 1991a).

By this question, I aim to redirect inquiry—to push against effort to redress suffering by turning away from material life to an approach that grounds inquiry in the material, historical world. Such an arrangement urges confrontation with beliefs by pushing against comforting assumptions as one highlights and forces a view of human suffering without the affective and intellectual safeguard of theologically 'flinching' and ethically 'blinking' (Zaretsky 2013, p. 7). There is, then, no retreat from this predicament—no solace that will ultimately offer comfort (Zaretsky 2013, p. 8). For moralists, life is drowned in suffering. Questions regarding disregard, danger, and violence are met with the silence of the world (Du Bois 1995, p. 454).

Du Bois offers a response to theodicy, which is to reject theodicy and in its place offer philosophical-theological revolt.[14] I would propose this is his turn away from theodicy toward moralism and the absurd. It, then, is intellectually akin to Camus' interrogation of the plausibility of life without appeal. Cornel West, for one, seems to measure Du Bois' sense of the absurdity of life over against his strategies and promotion of sustainable structuring of hope. However, Du Bois concerns himself with a diagnosis of the condition premised upon a cultural climate or sensibility defined by structures and strategies of disregard. Not theodicy, but rather, "how does it feel to be a problem?" (Du Bois 1986; West 1989, p. 142). By means of this question, Du Bois shifts away from the dominant narrative of religious faith marked by a certain type of fatalism—sorrow and misery until the next world or a more aggressive theology of revenge. He raises the question of pain and suffering, but as a moralist-absurdist question that rejects the fall back of a grand unity of purpose. Instead, can life be lived without appeal? In raising this question, I want to draw attention to my critique of models of theodical response to suffering that connote redemptive suffering strategies. I find such a dilemma in various modalities of constructive and liberation theologies. Here, through this question, I want to redirect theological inquiry in such a way as to jettison redemptive suffering.

Related to the above reading of Du Bois, I offer a question posed by another moralist, Richard Wright, who proclaims, "ought one to surrender to authority even if one believed that that authority was wrong? If the answer was yes, then I knew that I would always be wrong, because I could never do it. Then how could one live in a world in which one's mind and perceptions meant nothing and authority and tradition meant everything? There were no answers". (Wright 1937, p. 182). To exist is to be caught in this cultural climate. In this sense, as Susan Mizruchi notes, death and blacks "have become synonymous in white minds" (Mizruchi 1999, p. 274).

Physical death, as noted by Du Bois, and highlighted by John Wideman, is ever present; but it is not a separate reality that can be managed and bracketed off. Rather, it is akin to life, tied to life. This is only one mode of death noted by Du Bois. He also highlights another and intense mode of death, what I will call a death as metaphysical irrelevance. He writes, "you might have noted only the physical dying, the shattered frame and hacking cough; but in that soul lay deeper death than that"

---

13 I have made this argument in various locations, including: (Pinn 1995, 2002).
14 As my earlier work—including (Pinn 1995) demonstrates, I am aware of the various arguments made within womanist and black theological circles. I understand their nuance. However, even their effort to rethink suffering lends itself to redemptive suffering models.

(Du Bois 1986, p. 162). This, he continues, is the "death that is more than death—the passing of a soul that has missed its duty" (Du Bois 1986, p. 162).

For instance, projection of blacks as death produced an extreme effort to control death through death.[15] Kristin Hunter Lattany argues killing and death are intrinsic to the logic of the nation. Writes Lattany, "we can see that America is not a glamour queen but a grisly skeleton, her only produce death ... her only lessons how to kill and how to die".[16] As I have argued elsewhere, such a take on death highlights the manner in which certain human communities are circumscribed—violently at times—so as to protect the status quo. For them, death bleeds into life and life into death. One can lament this situation and be consumed by a certain type of agony; lament this situation and struggle against it—but still maintain the dominant logic. Or, one can push against it embracing the tragic-comic nature of life. For instance, according to Black Lives Matter, like moralist Du Bois, the ever-present threat of death does not stimulate a sense of melancholy.[17] Instead, death is simply a dimension of what it is to live within the context of the cultural climate in President Obama's and now President Trump's "America."[18] The every present threat of death confronts all dimensions of life, and there is no relief available. This, I would argue, is the approach Job and his friends feared and his God fought against.

Circumstances—"Yes we can" and "Make America great again" narratives of national transformation—do not afford more than illusion. Following Camus, I would press the following point: "The absurd, godless world is, then, peopled with men who think clearly and have ceased to hope" (Camus 1991a, p. 92). Camus and Du Bois promote, and I advocated for over against theodicy, living into death without reconciliation but by means of comfort with vulnerability, incompleteness and awareness of the openness entailed. In a sense, the task is to confront the world and not be bent permanently and tamed by the weight of its silence.

Conflicts of Interest: The author declares no conflict of interest.

References

Baker, Al, J. David Goodman, and Benjamin Mueller. 2015. Beyond the Chokehold: The Path to Eric Garner's Death. *nytimes.com*, June 13. Available online: https://www.nytimes.com/2015/06/14/nyregion/eric-garner-police-chokehold-staten-island.html (accessed on 1 November 2017).

Butler, Judith. 2011. *Body Matter*. New York: Routledge.

Camus, Albert. 1991a. *The Myth of Sisyphus and Other Essays*. New York: Vintage International.

Camus, Albert. 1991b. *The Rebel*. New York: Vintage International.

Douglas, Mary. 1996. *Impurity and Danger*. New York: Routledge.

Du Bois. 1970. *Dusk of Dawn*. New York: Schocken, p. 222.

Du Bois, W. E. B. 1986. *The Souls of Black Folk*. New York: Vintage, p. 162.

Du Bois, W. E. B. 1995. *W.E.B. Du Bois: A Reader*. Edited by David Levering Lewis. New York: Henry Holt and Company, p. 454.

Ellis, Ralph, and Bill Kirkos. 2017. Officer Who Shot Philando Castile Found Not Guilty on All Counts. *cnn.com*, June 17. Available online: http://www.cnn.com/2017/06/16/us/philando-castile-trial-verdict/index.html (accessed on 1 November 2017).

---

[15] I have written about death in a variety of pieces, but the most substantial is the project I am currently completing: (Pinn forthcoming), scheduled for submission to press August 2018.

[16] (Lattany 1993), I further develop this attention to death in (Pinn 2017).

[17] I want to make a distinction between melancholy and nihilism. The former, I argue, involves a sense of loss—a mourning of sorts connected to circumstances lost. This isn't a rejection of life as meaningful or valuable—but rather the mourning of circumstances that reflect this meaning and value. Nihilism is the rejection of possibility. It isn't recognition of something or someone lost; rather, it is a rejection of life as having value.

[18] An extension and fine tuning of this argument will be published as, "In the Wake of Obama's Hope" in (Floyd-Thomas and Pinn).

Juan Floyd-Thomas, and Anthony B. Pinn, eds. Forthcoming; *Religion in the Age of Obama*. London: Bloomsbury Academic.

Lattany, Kristin Hunter. 1993. Off-Timing: Stepping to the Different Drummer. In *Lure and Loathing: Essays on Race, Identity, and the Ambivalence of Assimilation*. Edited by Gerald Early. New York: The Penguin Press, p. 164.

Mizruchi, Susan. 1999. "Neighbors, Strangers, Corpses: Death and Sympathy in the Early Writings of W.E.B. Du Bois". In *The Souls of Black Folk: W. E. B. Du Bois*. Edited by Henry L. Gates Jr. and Terri Hume Oliver. New York: W. W. Norton & Company, p. 274.

Nathan, Debbie. 2016. What Happened to Sandra Bland? *thenation.com*. April 21. Available online: https://www.thenation.com/article/what-happened-to-sandra-bland/ (accessed on 1 November 2017).

Pinn, Anthony B. 1995. *Why, Lord: Suffering and Evil in Black Theology*. New York: Continuum.

Anthony B. Pinn, ed. 2002. *Moral Evil and Redemptive Suffering*. Gainesville: University Press of Florida.

Pinn, Anthony B. 2011. *The End of God-Talk: An African American Humanist Theology*. New York: Oxford University.

Pinn, Anthony. 2016. On Struggle in Our Historical Moment. *Huffington Post Religion Blog*, July 12.

Pinn, Anthony. 2017. *Presence Together: Technology of Religion and the Interplay of Things*. New York: Oxford University Press.

Pinn, Anthony B., and Allen Callahan. 2007. God of Restraint: An African American Humanist Interpretation of Nimrod and the Tower of Babel. In *Book African American Religious Life and the Story of Nimrod*. New York: Palgrave Macmillan.

Pinn, Anthony B. Forthcoming; *Cold Blooded: Hip Hop and the Cultural Grammar of Death*. Durham: Duke University Press.

West, Cornel. 1982. *Prophecy Deliverance!* Louisville: Westminster/John Knox.

West, Cornel. 1989. *The American Evasion of Philosophy: A Genealogy of Pragmatism*. Madison: University of Wisconsin Press, p. 142.

Wright, Richard. 1937. *Black Boy*. New York: Harper and Row, p. 182.

Zaretsky, Robert. 2013. *A Life Worth Living: Albert Camus and the Quest for Meaning*. Cambridge: Harvard University Press, pp. 7–8.

Article

Do Not Despise the Discipline of the Almighty: God as Leather Daddy and Reading Job through Althaus-Reid

Joseph Rogers

School of Applied Sciences, University of the Incarnate Word, 4301 Broadway CPO #324,
San Antonio, TX 78209, USA; rogers@uiwtx.edu

Received: 4 August 2017; Accepted: 28 September 2017; Published: 1 October 2017

Abstract: The feminist queer theologian Marcella Althaus-Reid (1952–2009) wrote about what it meant to be an "indecent theologian" and claimed that sexual stories from the margins of society can help transform theological issues. What can "indecent theology" mean for the problem of evil specifically as it is addressed in the book of Job? This article will use Althaus-Reid's creative methodology, which engages in a dialogue between theology, sexual theory, politics, and personal narrative. This methodology will be applied to the hermeneutic of suffering in the book of Job. I propose that this engagement of theodicy through a queer lens and more specifically within the category of gay sadomasochism in particular, while not definitively addressing the broader problem of evil, can be a creative lens to reinterpret the book of Job. By queering Job, I offer an alternative understanding of the problem of suffering and evil that can find a space within contextual theology. The article concludes with a remark on how such a reading can be used as a liberating text for the queer community.

Keywords: theodicy; queer reading; gay studies; liberation theology; sadomasochism

1. Introduction

In her work, *Indecent Theology: Theological Perversions in Sex, Gender and Politics*, Marcella Althaus-Reid suggests that all theology "is a sexual ideology performed in a sacralising pattern" (Althaus-Reid 2000, p. 87) and that sexual urges and arousal is a categorical concept that should not be compartmentalized away from other forms of epistemological classifications. So much of theology, according to Althaus-Reid, has been either divorced from the realm of the erotic or has focused so exclusively on issues of sin and distortion that it has caused damage and violence in people's spiritual lives.

The task of the practical theologian is to reflect theologically on those areas of life that are commonly experienced. This paradigm "makes room for the reflection on experience and practice and for dialogue with the social sciences as it engages with the normative resources of the Christian faith" (Osmer 2011, p. 157). Althaus-Reid would add that this reflection is indecent. What she means by this is that a Systematic Theology that supports hegemonic constructs of sexual coercion or capitalistic or military power within the major institutions of society are labeled as "decent." Those theologies that undermine, subvert, and critically question these thought systems Althaus-Reid would be termed as "indecent." This would then ask the practical theologian to engage in indecent readings of scripture to both subvert and reorganize the relationships found within its pages. By freeing the voices in the sacred texts from the limits of heteropatriarchal structures, the writings can become focused on the outsider, the one who sits on the margins of sexual practice and social acceptance.

Althaus-Reid's work is imaginative and playful, making use of sexual double entendres in her writing often employing humor to address serious issues of oppression and marginalization. This methodology allows us to capture the joy of sexuality as embodied spirituality, while at the same time it disarms and challenges commonly held assumptions. Althaus-Reid calls on queer theologians to transform these unjust structures. Because all theology operates with a sexual ideology rooted in accepted forms of oppression that cause violence for marginalized people, the task of a robust queer theology is to embrace its status as an outsider, and to re-contextualize a theology of liberation that includes erotic desire from a subversive loci that disrupts popular orthodoxies. This breaks boundaries that allow theology to be located in experience, one that even allows for "doing theology in corsetlaced boots" (Althaus-Reid 2000, p. 148).

In this essay, I will first address the use of a queer hermeneutic including the limits and strengths of this approach. I will then position sadomasochism (S&M) within a gay experience and briefly touch on homoerotic S&M as a liberating power that evidences a relationship of social exchange that challenges status-quo hierarchies. I will then draw upon those two previous sections to undertake a queer reading of the book of Job in the spirit of the writing of Althaus-Reid, and investigate a narrative theodicy as it is viewed from a queer lens. I do not claim that my reading of Althaus-Reid is all encompassing nor even touches on every aspect of her work. I acknowledge as well that my use of Althaus-Reid's work is solely focused on one aspect of her thinking and that some elements of my interpretation of her work as it applies to a gay S&M reading from scripture could be interpreted differently by other readers and scholars of Althaus-Reid's theology.

It is important to note here that many contemporary theologians and philosophers have advocated an abandonment of a theoretical theodicy. As I will discuss in Section 5, attempts to reconcile the reality of evil and suffering with the traditional theistic ideas of a benevolent God often end in frustration or require readers to gloss over parts of the text. Rather than insisting on a satisfactory answer to the problem of evil, I will argue that a creative queer reading of Job's struggle with suffering can move the focus away from an attempt to solve an intellectual problem to one that embraces a theological praxis of transformation. In concentrating on the "theological language of the Queer Other" (Althaus-Reid 2003, p. 31), we are able to theologically reflect on a queer experience of suffering. What will conclude this essay is my analysis of Job using what Althaus-Reid would lovingly call "displacement techniques" (Althaus-Reid 2003, p. 3).

2. Queer Reading

Althaus-Reid's understanding of a theological dyad (Althaus-Reid 2003) is helpful to begin a cursory overview of queer scripture reading. Althaus-Reid argues that much of theology is based on an exclusively heterosexual ideology of twos. This is where binaries are emphasized; God and humanity, clergy and lay, Father and Son, sin and redemption, etc. These binaries are primarily heterosexual and often these binaries occupy a secretive space. According to Althaus-Reid, this is when, as a sexual ideology, an expression of heterosexual desire is defined by its own secretiveness "between twos; this is the logic of husband and mistress; or husband and boyfriend; or wife with her beloved" (Althaus-Reid 2003, p. 12). These secretive dyads act as a model in which desire is treated as something shameful, to be hidden or, even worse, transferred to an unhelpful theological reflection. These reflections have a direct impact on the lives of those who do not conform to the models of power this dyad establishes. The theologian who emphasizes heteronormative, theologically binary concepts is simply reinforcing the hegemony. The goal of the queer theologian, then, is to disturb and transgress this. In some theological concepts, Althaus-Reid would see this transgressive element already in place.

One example Althaus-Reid uses to explain this is the concept of the Christian trinity. "By believing in the Trinity, we mean that there is an acceptance that theology is not a symmetrical art (a dyadic, one-to-one relationship with issues of dogma and tradition) but is a twisted one, following a path of reflections marked by disruptions of dyads or scandals. For we are not saying that God is one, manifested in father–son relationship, but that God is a relationship of three" (Althaus-Reid 2003, p. 16). For Althaus-Reid, this third representative in the Trinity is an example of queerness. By highlighting the queerness of a theological concept, we destabilize the normative establishment networks of power that cling to a single narrative that resist any outside interpretation.

The argument can, and has, been made that interpretations of the Biblical texts themselves are narratives that shape a political, social, and sexual identity. The imaginative use of sacred stories to either forge an identity or to give hope to an oppressed people is not new. Samuel Hill refers to this as the politics of survival. In the context of the narratives in the Hebrew Scriptures and a Jewish identity, this hermeneutic is the process of "a people using narratives to construct a strong sense of national identity, against a background in which such an identity is being threatened by extinction" (Hill 2009, p. 42).

As the shift is made to give attention to a queer reading, it is important to acknowledge that many authors suggest that the term "queer" is not so much an identity but rather "something of the uncapturable or unpredictable trajectory of a sexual life" (Ahmed 2016, p. 489). This is certainly the understanding of "queer" as Althaus-Reid would suggest, although Althaus-Reid would be quick to point out that this trajectory be one that is "indecent," one that emphasizes its voice from the margins.

Some scholars like Amy Kalmanofsky often feel hesitant to "queer read." The legitimate concern is that using creative approaches to scripture could rob the text of its historical grounding. "I do not offer a queer reading of the biblical stories I analyze because I think a queer reading would disturb the integrity of these narratives by imposing an interpretation on these texts that cannot be supported" (Kalmanofsky 2016, p. 2). Kalmanofsky is correct in her caution but overstates, I believe, the danger. For Kalmanofsky, her goal is to demonstrate the Biblical text's deep connection to the sexual status-quo. A queer reading seeks to upend this as it acknowledges that the "integrity" of the historical context is a culturally conditioned one.

In exploring Schüssler Fiorenza's work on feminist hermeneutics, Robert Goss astutely points out her critique of theological institutions of higher learning. These academies, seminaries, and universities have so insisted on a "value neutral" biblical scholarship that considers the text's historical meaning, that any meaningful, contemporary reflection is either lost or is secondary. Goss applies this to a queer hermeneutic effectively arguing that the Bible "is a justice resource in the queer battle for Christian power/truth" (Goss 1993, p. 90). A queer reading is one that can simultaneously undo the scriptural texts that reinforce a harmful heterosexist model and at the same time make relevant to a queer audience a text that can act as a source of strength and hope. This model allows the Bible to be "critically read both as subversive and empowering practice" (Goss 1993, p. 90).

An imaginative reading of biblical texts, far from being a devaluation or a lessening of the integrity of scripture, is historically normative and has a long tradition within religious communities. Elaine Pagels has remarked about the ways in which Christianity has engaged the hermeneutics of sacred writing, an engagement that has recognized the reality that a "genuine interpretation has always required that the reader actively and imaginatively engage the texts. Through the process of interpretation, the reader's living experience comes to be woven into ancient texts, so that what was 'dead letter' again comes to life" (Pagels 1988, p. xxvii).

We must be able to reach a position where we understand the historical and theological context in which the narrative was written, and yet at the same time realize the possibilities that an erotic queer biblical sensibility can bring both to hermeneutical discourse and to the transformative potentials of the text upon the queer reader and her experience. This subverting of traditional forms of interpretation helps to delegitimize structural and ecclesial monopolies of what is considered "truth" as well as actively bringing scripture to life as a form of queer resistance.

3. Sadomasochism

Images of sexuality in popular culture have increased in the modern world, but these images still make clear demarcated lines between mainstream sexualities and marginalized sexualities. Mainstream culture has even begun to embrace the sadomasochistic subculture through popular novels and their film adaptations (*Fifty Shades of Grey* is one such example). This is not, however, to say that this mainstreaming of sadomasochism is necessarily positive. Eleanor Wilkinson has argued that, while we have seen an increase in the acceptance of sadomasochism in society, the existing narratives by which sadomasochism is framed come with very limited conditions (Wilkinson 2009, p. 182), thus reinforcing sadomasochism's otherness. In the case of *Fifty Shades of Grey*, for example, the kink of the main protagonist is depicted as an unhealthy personality quirk that needs redemption from the hands of a "good woman." Sexist and heteronormative power structures of oppression exist within S&M depictions in the culture that "often replicate wider power structures" (Wilkinson 2009, p. 188). That these communities can often be spaces where homophobia reveals itself is to be expected given that sadomasochistic stories are as diverse and varied as those who inhabit S&M spaces.

If sadomasochism represents an "other," then how much more so would a gay sadomasochism, especially one that often employs traditional heterosexual images of masculinity and subverts those very images? To exemplify this, one needs to turn to images of gay machismo like those made popular by artist Tom of Finland. These representations are not without their problems. While individuals like John Rechy admire that Tom of Finland's images are ones in which "gay sex is celebrated, proudly performed, never hidden ... they are proud outlaws" (Rechy 2006, p. 31), the critique nonetheless is that these images often depict men in Nazi uniforms, military gear, and using police props of punishment. These tropes are "representative of legendary heterosexual homophobic forces" (Rechy 2006, p. 32), thus reflecting a disturbing gay self-hatred that seeks punishment for gay desire. While Rechy correctly identifies a concern that is often raised with such images, I would contest this as not being a valid criticism given that Tom of Finland's images are ones in which both the sadist and the masochist revel in joy at each other as complementary in a theatre of role playing, a point that Rechy himself acknowledges. The question, to me, becomes whether these traditional representatives of oppressive, indeed horrid symbols of torture against queers can be subverted and redeemed. I would answer that they can. In the same way that black liberationists have made the link between the lynching tree and the cross, symbols can, paradoxically, be the conduit toward a theology of hope. "How did African Americans survive and resist the lynching terror and keep enough of their sanity to love and marry each other, to raise their children, and to teach them love and respect for each other? The answer is clear for many blacks: it was their faith in God and themselves that kept them emotionally and spiritually healthy ... Whites used Christianity to lynch blacks and blacks used it to survive and resist whites" (Cone 2013, p. 225).

As Jeremy Carrette rightly points out, the inclusion of S&M into theological discourse is done not for a sense of titillation or as an attempt at academic "shock and awe." S&M places itself as a "transgressive subcultural form of resistance to hegemonic sexual practices—in so far as it identifies pleasure outside the procreative act" (Carrette 2005, p. 14). In addition, this cohabiting of pleasure and pain and the relationship of power and submission to that power within a psychosocial context is key to a theological reading of sadomasochism. While Carrette's concern is to recognize the role of BDSM as it relates to a theological reflection on embodied forms of social exchange within a Western capitalist system and to point out its force as both liberating and oppressive, my goal here is to narrow this scope to the space of a particular biblical text. The focus will be a reinterpretation of a narrative theodicy that fits the need of a queer reading. To paraphrase Reginald F. Davis, the context of queer oppression will dictate the content of this theology (Davis 2005, p. 97). This will be a theology that articulates on the rapport between suffering and joy with sadomasochism as a referent. "For S&M requires something which commercial-theological productive sex does not require, that is a pleasure generated through an exchange of deep trust and intense intimacy—formative of communities. This is where sex gets dangerous, not in its glossy commodification but in its personal imaginative pains and enacted fantasy, with all the messiness of human suffering and our multiple polymorphous selves" (Carrette 2005, p. 23).

Gay sadomasochists as "deviants" and "perverts" seems to me a perfect place to locate a theological reflection on theodicy with an eye toward an Althaus-Reidian interpretation of scripture. It is toward this that I now turn.

4. An Indecent Reading of Job

Queering Job will require more than simply showing Job as a liberationist text for a gay audience. It will require an embrace of what has been marginalized and reviled as well as the full sexual deconstruction of God. My suggestion is to read Job as an exploration of the relationship between suffering and desire, as the subversion of the role of obedience along with a critical questioning of authority. By queering Job we are able to unmoor it from its vanilla nature tied to a vanilla theology (Althaus-Reid 2000). I think Althaus-Reid would be pleased with such a proposition, and while I admit that my focus is on one aspect of male-to-male gay sexual expression, it is one that can be appropriated toward an inclusive queer hermeneutic.

The book of Job opens by introducing its protagonist as an "upright" man, as one who is "perfect" (1:1). By all accounts, Job represents the very epitome of a decent theology and his life is a reflection of such a stable theological category. Prosperous, esteemed, and happy, Job's life is the status quo of which God is about to disturb. In queering Job's backstory I construct the patriarch as a "house faggot." In this context, such a term denotes a gay man who appeases and seeks to be validated by heterosexual social institutions. Such an individual undermines queer liberation, embraces heterosexist paradigms and even reviles members of their own queer community. This revision of Job as "house faggot" broadens the scope of the text to locate queer theory within the narrative and at the same time theologically reflect upon and question political and theological oppression within queer communities. Through locating Job within this queer reading, we are able to move the narrative from a broader exploration on the role of suffering to one that is localized. Job has often been used as a text to explore the larger questions of just vs. unjust suffering, the suffering of the "righteous" or the nature of faith in the face of a seemingly indifferent deity. Moving the narrative away from one that focuses on definitive answers to the question of suffering to one focusing on a liberationist orientation of the narrative, we are able to have it serve as a force of queer resistance. The efficacy of Job to speak authoritatively about the role of suffering will be addressed later, but it is important to point out here that the more interesting strength of the Joban narrative lies in its ability to be read as a subversive deconstruction of heterosexism and homophobia. Queering Job as a sexual story unpacks issues of homophobia within society, as well as examining eroticism as a form of communicating faith. The theologizing of sexual stories is an acknowledgment that sexuality, particularly one rooted in heteronormativity, informs "our economic, political and societal life ... Without a theology of sexual stories, the last moment of the hermeneutical circle, that is, the moment of appropriation and action, will always have a partiality and a superficial approach to conflict resolution" (Althaus-Reid 2000, p. 131). Having Job fill this narrative role within a queer fetish context helps enhance and inform both a theological and political struggle for justice and liberation.

In the prologue, Job's piety is emphasized. Transgressing the narrative, piety here is read as a totalitarian theology "which does not admit discussion or challenges from different perspectives" (Althaus-Reid 2003, p. 8, note 4). Job believes in his own goodness. His worldview and his moral obligations are ones in which he is confident. Like many who claim not to be homophobic and would embrace their classification as a "good person" but nonetheless rarely question their own heterocentered privilege, Job begins in the prologue with a preconceived notion of God, the Covenant, and his own place in the world. Content and self-satisfied Job begins the narrative centered in a heterosexist constructed ideology, and "it is this piety that the book as a whole, by way of the Satan's question, subjects to critique" (Ticciati 2005, p. 353). That Job is faithful to his own understanding of a commonly accepted religious sense of righteousness is without question. The friends who come to both mourn and console Job reinforce this and even remind Job that he himself offered such explanations to others (4:1–6).

As much as the friends of Job come to try and offer explanations for his suffering, they operate out of a particular ideology that, like Job in the prologue, seeks to strengthen the status quo. In the friends' minds, Job has transgressed the prevailing hegemony and is being punished by God as a result. The friends exist here as an attempt to represent traditional sexual orthodoxy as part of God's order for society. They represent a soft-core theology that, like soft-core pornography, looks toward a new horizon but still keeps boundaries sharp and careful. The friends already presume that they themselves are graced by God, thus justifying their heterosexist worldview as a reflection of their own piety. The fact that Job is suffering, they surmise, is a result of his violating this heterosocial code.

Job, of course, has done no such thing. In his mind, the friends are mistaken. Like a good "house faggot," he insists that he has toed the line and maintained the power structures of privilege. "Then Job answered: 'No doubt, you are the people, and wisdom will die with you; I am not inferior to you. Who does not know such things as these? I am a laughing-stock to my friends; I, who called upon God and he answered me, a just and blameless man, I am a laughing-stock'" (12:1–4). Job's internalized homophobia and his desire to preserve the status quo extends beyond his physical life. Even when Job laments his being born at all in Chapter 3, he envisions an afterworld in which everything and everyone would have an ordered place and all would fit into a purpose that does not challenge the binary, either/or logic of his own theology. Both Job and the friends are operating out of a faulty understanding of God, all the while the friends' speeches to Job evoke passages from the Psalms and the prophets. As Wesley Morriston has pointed out, given that God sharply rebukes the explanation of the friends, "it is fair to conclude that the poet means to reject the prevailing Hebrew view of the meaning of suffering" (Morriston 1996, p. 341, note 3).

When God finally addresses Job it is from the narrative construction of a "leather-daddy" dom–sub relationship. In fact, the opening of God's initial discourse from the whirlwind is one in which the wildness of creation is highlighted. Taking Job on a tour of creation, God utterly silences Job with a vision of ferocity, awe, and strength. This experience of God's preeminence is one that is harrowing in its vision. We certainly do not find a gentle pastoral scene of God's providence where everything is tenderly cared for, but rather a world in which all creatures have the reality of their existence, in all its glory, horror, and messiness embraced and affirmed. Creatures, both hunter and prey, exist in such a way that exposes the universe as arbitrary and indifferent to official religious classifications of justice. This is a cosmos not bound by logical argumentation but one that is free and transgresses the binaries humans impose on the world (39:5–12). Job's realization that God is not bound to any law collapses his worldview that there ever was a contract between humanity and the divine. Job's role as the "house-faggot" is disrupted and in a striking "coming out" moment, Job makes the bold step of admitting the errors of his cooperation with the status quo. "Then Job answered the Lord: 'See, I am of small account; what shall I answer you? I lay my hand on my mouth. I have spoken once, and I will not answer; twice, but will proceed no further'" (40:3–5). Job rightly realizes that the traditional Covenant has proven to be empty. God, it seems in these passages, is bound not by external religious systems of law, but God is driven by his desire for his creation. Like a dominant top, God has taken charge of creation assigning a role for each, even using fetish instruments and devices to do so (41:1–2). This Theophany is divorced from a soft-core, mainstream S&M with safe words and an end that is tidily resolved. God's address to Job does not bring answers nor even comfort to Job (nor to the reader). God is declaring that his domain is one that is wild and untamed.

On the one hand, God is such an alien outsider to Job that he is unable to even come close to grasping the immensity that God is, and yet on the other hand God takes an intense interest in Job. Like a bottom novice to the world of S&M, this leather-daddy God fills Job with awe and fear, and through this (indeed, perhaps because of this), Job also comes to embody his role in this top–bottom dynamic (40:3–5). It is precisely through his journey of pain that he is able to understand who he is in relation to God and the reality of what it means to be an embodied creature. In this reading, God is an erotic encounter, a leather daddy who is "adorned," who "brings down with a glance," and who "binds" (40:10–13). By encountering God in this role, the definition of what it means to be a man of integrity changes for Job. In this erotic play with the divine, Job is transformed. Ironically, his experience of pain has made Job realize that his obedience was to an external law, a law that God is not bound to. In his challenges and his erotic play with God, Job is transformed to see his obedience is now focused on relationships; integrity with himself and integrity within God's creation. This moves obedience away from the following of heterocentered laws and situates it as a grappling with reality in an attempt to be transformed by the liberating power of our sexual embodiment. This movement is one often fraught with pain as Job discovered, and yet it is trough this journey of pain that brings him insight.

The relationship between pain and insight is one explored in S&M discourse. Often men in S&M will discuss pain as a way toward some greater good, something that in the end some self challenge has been overcome. Staci Newmahr calls this "investment pain". This "discourse draws heavily on hyper- masculine narratives of pain ('No pain, no gain'). This discourse frames pain as an unpleasant stimulus that promises future rewards. Not surprisingly, men, whether bottom or topping, frame pain this way more often than women do" (Newmahr 2011, p. 138).

Job's worldview has been totally challenged and reordered. He has come to see his relationship with God as forming a new covenant. That God took an erotic interest in him has changed Job's previous understanding of the Covenant. This new, reordered relationship forms the basis of Job's emerging understanding of God and his own suffering. Job's revelation is truly one that is "libertine."

Althaus-Reid explains that "libertine" is a word often used by religious institutions to give name to their fears. It is a word used to speak of that which transgresses the limitations placed upon sexual behavior and relationships. Althaus-Reid speaks of the libertine act as one that is a covenant. This type of covenant is a practice in which relationships are "pacted and agreements are made amongst people on the sole basis of what is going to be acted. This covenanting in itself is a pleasurable praxis, in the way that it chooses and combines the flow of desires and then fixes them" (Althaus-Reid 2003, p. 27).

This, in the end, is Job's awakening. Job's initial shock and awe at having his worldview challenged through an experience of suffering has led him toward a new, transgressive relationship, a new transgressive covenant. Job's understanding of God, the Covenant, and his own theological idea about suffering has undergone a deep transformation and he has come to see God and life in a new way.

5. Conclusions

Terrence Tilley has concluded that Job's labyrinthine response to suffering may be irredeemable. "The book of Job makes no coherent claims. It provides no warrant for speaking of God or the meaning of human suffering. It gives no 'revelational data' for theologians to build on or transmit. It offers no solutions to problems of suffering. As a text for scholarly inquiry, its scramblings, ambiguities and uncertainties suggest that closure of the meanings of the texts or canonization of a 'final' text may not be possible. As part of the Jewish and Christian religious canons, it reveals that no way of speaking of God and suffering will do" (Tilley 1989, p. 268). Tilley's conclusion seems sound enough. Given the amount of debate and uncertainty among biblical commentators and scholars in striving for a sound theoretical theodicy, Tilley is correct that a final solution to the problem of suffering cannot be found within the pages of Job. An interpreter of Job who attempts to effectively reconcile traditional religious theism, particularly Christian theism, with a seamless God of moral order who stands on the side of the suffering should be prepared to encounter a number of logical inconsistencies.

I think, however, that Tilley overstates his claim that nothing of value about the nature of God and suffering can be found within the Job narrative. Queering Job as a deconstructive act of biblical hermeneutics can become a powerful resource for LGBTQ communities. As narratives that affirm both the struggle for personal transformation, and justice-making in the world, queer biblical reading transgresses those oppressive paradigms that keep queer people quiet and politically marginalized. By making the texts "obscene" and "indecent," one can claim the narrative as a queer liberative practice.

A biblical reflection on the nature of suffering within a queer context can affirm the role that political pain and the awareness of marginalization plays in the development of an energized hegemony of resistance. For LGBTQ communities, reading Job indecently means questioning the structures of heteronormativity that we as a queer people of faith have often been complicit in. Such an exercise becomes a queer faith practice that moves individuals to theologically reflect on the suffering of their experience, which is both personal and political, both private and communal.

Althaus-Reid holds that obscenity unmasks and exposes reality for what it is, thus setting it free. "Obscenity leads us toward a theology of exhibitionism, which is a very encouraging sign for the task of affirming reality and the suppressed aesthetics of Christianity" (Althaus-Reid 2000, p. 111). This act of "uncovering" has been seen in a number of liberationist movements as a gesture of resistance and as a way to expose the various forms of racism, sexism, classism, and homophobia in religious communities. By engaging in an erotic S&M meditation on the nature of suffering, theodicy is made obscene. Job declares "and after my skin has been thus destroyed, then in my flesh I shall see God" (19:26) as he attempts to interpret his experience. It is in his embodied, renewed sexual awakening that Job is able to transcend his old worldview and to reorder the comprehension of himself, his experience of suffering and the very nature of this alien God he thought he understood.

For a queer audience, Job's journey of wrestling with the nature of suffering and justice can be a powerful narrative of resistance. Reading this text through an "indecent" sexual lens means claiming it as our own. It embodies an embrace of sexual expression on the margins while at the same time offering a theological reflection on the role that heterosexism and patriarchy as expressed in ecclesial institutions applies to the lives of queer people. "Indecent people challenge precisely the unnaturality and abnormality of the present sexual ideology, in all the consequences of this sexual and political theology" (Althaus-Reid 2000, p. 131). By queering Job, traditional hermeneutical constructs of the text tied to the privileged are delegitimized and the experience of both an indecent God and an indecent theological reflection on life are affirmed.

Conflicts of Interest: The author declares no conflict of interest.

References

Ahmed, Sarah. 2016. Interview with Judith Butler. *Sexualities* 19: 482–92. [CrossRef]

Althaus-Reid, Marcella. 2000. *Indecent Theology: Theological Perversions in Sex, Gender and Politics*. London: Routledge.

Althaus-Reid, Marcella. 2003. *The Queer God*. London: Routledge.

Carrette, Jeremy. 2005. Intense Exchange: Sadomasochism, theology and the politics of late capitalism. *Theology & Sexuality* 11: 11–30.

Cone, James H. 2013. Wresting with the Cross and the Lynching Tree. *Theology Today* 70: 220–27.

Davis, Reginald F. 2005. African-American Interpretation of Scripture. *Journal of Religious Thought* 57: 93–105.

Goss, Robert. 1993. *Jesus Acted Up: A Gay and Lesbian Manifesto*. New York: HarperCollins.

Hill, Samuel. 2009. A hermeneutics of sexual identity: A challenge to conservative religious discourse. *Verbum et Ecclesia* 30: 38–43. [CrossRef]

Kalmanofsky, Amy. 2016. *Gender-Play in the Hebrew Bible: The Ways the Bible Challenges Its Gender Norms*. London: Routledge.

Morriston, Wesley. 1996. God's Answer to Job. *Religious Studies* 32: 339–56. [CrossRef]

Newmahr, Staci. 2011. *Playing on the Edge: Sadomasochism, Risk, and Intimacy*. Bloomington: Indiana Press University.

Osmer, Richard. 2011. Practical Theology: A current international perspective. *HTS Teologiese Studies/Theological Studies* 67: 156–62. [CrossRef]

Pagels, Elaine. 1988. *Adam, Eve, and the Serpent: Sex and Politics in Early Christianity*. New York: Vintage Books.

Rechy, John. 2006. Tom of Finland: Sexual liberator? *The Gay and Lesbian Review*, March 1.

Ticciati, Susannah. 2005. Does Job Fear God for Naught? *Modern Theology* 21: 353–66. [CrossRef]

Tilley, Terence. 1989. God and the Silencing of Job. *Modern Theology* 5: 257–70. [CrossRef]

Wilkinson, Eleanor. 2009. Perverting Visual Pleasure: Representing sadomasochism. *Sexualities* 12: 181–98. [CrossRef]

Article

The Problem of Evil and the Grammar of Goodness

Eric Wiland

Department of Philosophy, University of Missouri-St. Louis, One University Blvd, St. Louis, MO 63121, USA; wiland@umsl.edu

Received: 5 January 2018; Accepted: 20 January 2018; Published: 31 January 2018

Abstract: I consider the two venerated arguments about the existence of God: the Ontological Argument and the Argument from Evil. The Ontological Argument purports to show that God's nature guarantees that God exists. The Argument from Evil purports to show that God's nature, combined with some plausible facts about the way the world is, guarantees (or is very compelling grounds for thinking) that God does not exist. Both presume that it is coherent to predicate goodness (or greatness) of God. But if Peter Geach's claim that goodness is logically attributive is cogent, then both arguments fall to the ground.

Keywords: god; evil; goodness; religion

---

1. Here I consider two venerated arguments about the existence of God: the Ontological Argument and the Argument from Evil. The Ontological Argument purports to show that God's nature guarantees that God exists. The Argument from Evil purports to show that God's nature, combined with some plausible facts about the way the world is, guarantees (or is very compelling grounds for thinking) that God does not exist. Obviously, both arguments cannot be sound. But I argue here that they both are unsound for the very same reason.

2. Consider first the Argument from Evil. There are very many ways the Argument from Evil can be formulated. For the most part, these differences will not affect the issue at hand in this article. So here is one way of putting the Argument:

E1. If God exists, then a being who is all-powerful, all-knowing, and **perfectly good** exists.

E2. A being who is all-powerful, all-knowing, and **perfectly good** would not create a world in which there is (avoidable) evil.

E3. But there is (avoidable) evil in the world.

E4. God does not exist.

We are led to conclude that God does not exist, because if God did exist, then God would prevent the sorts of evils that we in fact see. We can be confident that God would prevent these evils, because that is what a perfectly good being who knew about these evils would do, if God could.

Consider next the Ontological Argument. There are many ways this argument can be formulated, but most of the differences between them will not affect the issue at hand in this article. (One variation *is* important. I will have something to say about this later.) Here is one rough but standard way the Ontological Argument is put:

O1. God is that than which no **greater** can be conceived.

O2. If God does not exist, then there is something **greater** than God that can be conceived.

O3. God exists.

We are led to conclude that God exists, because it is part of the very concept of God that God is as great as one can possibly be, and that existence is part of greatness. We can be confident that God exists, because we know that a being that can be conceived and actually exists is greater than a being that merely can be conceived but does not exist.

Notice that both arguments rely on premises involving the nature of God, and that both attribute evaluative properties to God. In the case of the Argument from Evil, we are to think that God is good. In the case of the Ontological Argument, we are to think that God is great. Here I will question whether it is correct to think about God this way.[1]

3. Why think that there is anything amiss in saying that God is good or great? It will be instructive as a point of comparison to briefly review the history of one of the most influential arguments in moral philosophy, G. E. Moore's Open Question argument, an argument whose cogency depends entirely upon the logical grammar of goodness. Moore held that it always makes sense to ask, of any natural property, whether something that has that property is good.[2] From this fact, Moore concluded that goodness is not identical with any natural property; for if the two were indeed identical, then it would *not* always make sense to ask whether something that has that natural property is good.

The lesson that Moore took away from this observation is that since goodness is not a natural property, it must be a nonnatural property. Noncognitivists, by contrast, typically conclude that goodness is, strictly speaking, not a property at all, and so moral language is to be understood as used to do something other than describing how the world is.[3] And Cornell realists point out yet another option: they argue that the Open Question argument does not rule out the possibility of *a posteriori* necessary moral truths, and so goodness might still be a natural property after all.[4]

But one typically overlooked response to the problem Moore poses originates in the work of Peter Geach.[5] Geach draws our attention to two different ways adjectives can logically function. Borrowing some terms from grammar, Geach distinguishes what he calls "predicative adjectives" from "attributive adjectives". Predicative adjectives attribute the possession of an independently identifiable property to the object of the adjective. Most adjectives seem to function as predicative adjectives. Consider color concepts. Because 'white' is predicative, the fact that the Washington Monument is a white building strictly implies that the Washington Monument is white. The noun that the adjective is modifying in the original claim can be dropped, and the adjective still can be truly predicated of the subject. (More formally, if F functions as a predicative adjective, then "x is a F K" implies that "x is F".)

But this sort of implication is not available in the case of the use of every adjective. Attributive adjectives modify the object of the adjective by specifying a way of being *that kind* of object. As a result, the adjective cannot be meaningfully and correctly detached from the specific generic noun it modifies. The adjective 'large' works this way. The fact that Y is a large microprocessor does not strictly imply that Y is large. The fact that Z is a heavy atom does not imply that Z is heavy. And, most importantly, the fact that N.N. is a good robber does not imply that N.N. is good. Attributive adjectives always, at least implicitly, need an associated generic noun to modify in order even to make sense. That is, we do sometimes say things like "Fido is large", this without explicitly mentioning any common noun. But context usually indicates that we do mean some common noun: we mean "Fido is a large dog" rather than "Fido is a large animal" or "Fido is a large noisemaker."

Note that we can 'trade' predicative adjectives in a way that we cannot attributive adjectives. If something is a white monument, and it is also a structure, then it must be a white structure.

---

1   Those who conceive of God as a *perfect* being nevertheless often understand this perfection to be a form of goodness. So what I say here about goodness also applies to the view that God is an Anselmian perfect being.

2   (Moore 1903).

3   (Stevenson 1944).

4   (Boyd 1988).

5   (Geach 1956).

But if something is a small whale, and it is also an animal, then it is not necessarily a small animal. Whether something counts as small depends upon the kind of thing it is modifying.

Mistakenly detaching attributive adjectives from the generic nouns to which they attach often results in contradictions. For it might both be true that a particular painting is a genuine van Meegeren and a fake Vermeer (to use a standard example). Yet it is nothing but confusion to say that some particular painting is both genuine and fake. Terms like 'genuine' and 'fake' mean something only when they at least implicitly modify some noun.

Now Geach proposed that the adjectives 'good' and 'bad' *always* function attributively. Nothing is simply good or bad, but instead is a good or bad instance of some kind or other. If N.N. is a good robber, and also a person, N.N. is not thereby a good person. And that is because there just is no property of goodness that can be identified independently of a goodness-fixing kind.

If Geach is right, then Moore was incorrect to hold that it always makes sense to ask, in response to the claim that some object has some natural property, whether it is also simply good. Rather, it *never* makes sense to ask of some object simply whether it is good (at least not unless the context implicitly makes some kind salient). That would be like asking whether it is large or heavy or genuine. *Nothing* is simply good. We can sensibly ask only whether something is a good K (where K denotes some generic kind), and then the answer to that question essentially depends upon *what* kind of thing is under discussion.

This is obviously so in the case of artifacts. It makes no sense just to say baldly that some particular object is good; rather, it makes sense to say that it is a good (or bad) music player, or a good (or bad) doorstop, or a good (or bad) theft deterrent, or a good (or bad) anniversary present, and so on. Something can be a good or bad instance of its kind (which themselves can be multiple), but nothing is good or bad *tout court*.

What does Geach's account of the grammar of goodness imply about morality? There are many possibilities, but his account fits very nicely with a view of morality developed by Elizabeth Anscombe, Philippa Foot, and Michael Thompson.[6] On this view, whether some *operation* or *state* of yours is good or bad depends upon the kind of creature you are. It would be a defect in *me* were I not to care for my offspring. Ignoring one's offspring is a bad human action. This has to do with natural facts about human beings. But it is not a defect in each and every fish were *they* not to care for their offspring. In their case, ignoring one's offspring is not a bad operation (at least for some species of fish). What counts as a good or bad operation depends crucially upon the kind of creature operating.

There are facts about how human beings live and operate, facts that set the standard of goodness for particular human beings. For instance, it is a natural fact that human beings have ten fingers. But Uncle Joe here has only six fingers. He is, for all that, a human being; but to that extent he is deformed or disabled. He is at least *missing* four fingers. It might not be a defect in some particular creature of some other kind to have six fingers, but it is for humans.

These natural facts are neither merely statistical nor purely normative. As Anscombe noted, human beings have thirty-two teeth, even if most of them do not.[7] And to say 'humans beings have thirty-two teeth' is not merely to say that they *should* have thirty-two teeth. For I might say of a rotary saw blade that I am now forging that *it* should have thirty-two teeth, and I would mean something very different by that utterance than I mean when I say that human beings have thirty-two teeth. In the case of the saw-blade, it would specify what I, its creator, intend. For humans, however, it specifies what kind of thing a human being *is*. (We can see the distinction at work by imagining a surgeon who says of her patient: 'This man, whose kind has two legs, should, due to gangrene in his foot, have one leg.')

Now there are natural facts not only about the number of fingers or teeth humans have, but also natural facts about their wills. And to the extent that my will differs from this standard, my will is

---

[6] (Anscombe 2006; Foot 2001; Thompson 1995).
[7] (Anscombe 1958).

thereby defective or bad. When we say that So-and-so is a (morally) bad person, we usually mean that So-and-so's will is a bad human will. Whether some feature or operation of me is a good or bad feature or operation never floats free of the kind (or kinds) of creature I am, but makes sense only in reference to this more general thing: my species.

I propose to take this account of goodness in general, and moral goodness in particular, very seriously. I admit that there are objections to this view, objections that merit careful consideration. Some of these objections seem *prima facie* powerful. This is not the place to weigh them, but I will head off a few misconceptions.

First, Geach's point is not about surface grammar. Very often, one says things like "That new Sopranos episode was good!", and everyone knows what one means. The listener typically has no trouble grasping that one means that it was a good *episode*, rather than a good soporific, or a good depiction of the typical American family.

Second, only some generic nouns imply standards of goodness. To say of some particular entity that it is a good molecule leaves one's listener scratching her head. For there is no such thing as a good molecule or a bad molecule, not without some special story about what one needs a particular kind of molecule for—in which case the relevant generic noun is not simply a molecule, but something more specific than that. Some but not all nouns are 'goodness-fixing kinds'.[8]

Third and finally, it is possible to agree with Geach in the main, but understand remaining stubborn predicative uses of the word 'good' expressivistically. While most surface predicative uses of the word 'good' can be understood by implicitly inserting some appropriate generic noun to which it is attached, we may interpret other predicative uses of 'good' as noncognitivists do. If Ellen says "That is good!", and she rejects all of our attempts to insert some generic noun into her thought ("A good party?" "A good meeting?"), then we should probably take her merely to be expressing her positive emotions about the subject of her sentence. While we can reject noncognitivism about most uses of evaluative predicates, such an account may be appropriate for other uses of them.

4. Now suppose Geach's view here is correct: goodness is a two-place relation between a particular and a kind, a kind of which the particular is a member. What follows from this account?

I will initially argue that (1) God is not a member of any kind; then, more modestly; (2) God is not a member of any kind that has standards of goodness internal to it; then, finally and sincerely; (3) God is not a member of any kind that has standards of goodness internal to it such that God would be defective with respect to said standards by failing to prevent suffering. (Similar claims about greatness will hold as well.)

First, consider the claim that God is not a member of any kind. There is no kind K of which God is a particular member. God is necessarily *sui* generis, which amounts to the claim that God isn't a member of any *generis* at all. On one conception of the divine, a particular god might be a member of the kind *gods*. This may be the proper way to understand certain mythological polytheisms. We might think that Mars, for instance, is a particularly good or bad god, because he has or lacks most of the characteristics gods have. But many theists can reply that God is instead *utterly unique*, without thereby committing any severe heterodoxy. Nor is God's uniqueness contingent, as is the uniqueness of, say, a particular British Guiana 1c magenta stamp, a kind of which there *could* have been more than one. God's uniqueness, by contrast, is necessary, a member of no genuine kind. And if there is *no* kind K of which God is a particular member, then, on the Geachean view of goodness, God cannot be a good (or bad) K.

It may be objected that there are indeed some true things that can be said about God. For instance, God has existed for more than four minutes. So God is a member of the kind of things that have existed for more than four minutes, just as you and I are. Thus it appears false to say that God is not a member of any kind whatsoever.

---

8   (Thomson 2003).

Nonetheless, this is not enough to establish what is needed for the Argument from Evil to work. This kind (more-than-four-minute-existents) does not give rise to *any* standards according to which a particular entity could be a good or bad instance of its kind. There is no such thing as a bad or good more-than-four-minute-existent. Any particular entity that has *not* existed for more than four minutes is not a bad more-than-four-minute existent. So while God may be a member of some kinds, God is not a member of any kind that has standards of goodness internal to it.

But it may now be objected that God is *indeed* a member of a kind that has standards of goodness internal to it. By any orthodox account, God is an intelligent being. An intelligent being is good qua intelligent being, in so far as it is knowledgeable, logical, and has all the other intellectual virtues. So it is indeed possible for God to be a good or bad intelligent being. Thus, the objector concludes, there are indeed standards of goodness that apply to God.[9]

Still, this is not enough to rescue the Argument from Evil. It is true that God would be a bad intelligent being by failing to be clever or rational or critical. God is indeed a member of *some* kinds that have standards of goodness internal to them. But even so, God is not a member of any kind for which alleviating avoidable suffering counts as a defect. That is, God is not a member of any kind of entity good instances of which must prevent avoidable suffering. So the kinds to which God *does* belong do not require eliminating our woes in order to be a good instance of those kinds. The fact that God can be a good K for some Ks does not mean God would thus wipe the world of pain and suffering.

Some will want to insist that God, like all humans, is a member of the class of Rational Beings, and as a result God is governed by exactly the same rules of rationality as are humans, and that these rules imply, among other things, that God should prevent suffering, and so on. I don't want to deny that God is a rational being. And I concede that if rationality alone demanded preventing avoidable suffering, my argument would fall to the ground. But there is little reason to think that rationality or rational agency demands this. A few philosophers have claimed that rationality itself indeed requires one to prevent avoidable suffering,[10] but all these arguments, alas, fail.[11] Rationality alone may require *some* things of agents—e.g., taking the necessary means to one's ends, deliberating in light of all the available evidence—but it does not require one to prevent avoidable suffering. Only a *specific* form of benevolence requires that.

The most important implication of this line of argument is that we have no grounds for saying that if God is good, God will not create a world in which there is suffering. For the antecedent, strictly speaking, makes no sense. God cannot be good or bad *tout court*, in just the same way that the number 3 cannot be good or bad, or that the set of molecules constituting this volume cannot be good or bad. Premises E1 and E2 are neither true nor false, but are ill-formed. And thus the Argument from Evil is not a sound argument.

My proposal here differs from classic responses to the problem of Evil. Some see a way out by radically altering what is meant by 'God'. Others, for instance, have thought that God has no interests or desires or aims, and that this is one reason why it does not make sense to say that God is good, for goodness is always relative to these things. But nothing I have said commits me to the thought that God is without interests or desires or aims. All I have held is that God is not a member of any kind whose goodness as a member of that kind requires one to minimize suffering.

Likewise, some have proposed what is called negative theology, the view that we can say only what God *is not*, not anything about what God *is*. Others have argued that God is hidden, and we just do not know why God would permit suffering unnecessarily. This may be true, but it too differs from what I have been arguing. We may know *exactly* what God is like. My proposal really requires no major revision in the traditional conception of God, only a revision in the common (but mistaken) conception of the grammar of goodness.

---

[9]   I thank George Streeter for raising this objection.
[10] See (Korsgaard 2009; Smith 2015).
[11] See (Enoch 2006) and Wiland (2012), among many other rebuttals.

My argument also differs from many recent responses to the Argument from Evil. It is not based upon the claim that evil is a result of the free will of human beings.[12] It is not based upon a theodicy of soul-making.[13] It does not depend upon the claim that suffering unifies us with God.[14] It does not cast doubt upon the thought that animals experience genuine suffering.[15] It does not depend upon (but does naturally cohere with) the thought that there is no best possible world.[16]

My argument does resemble Mark Murphy's recent response to the Argument from Evil.[17] We both agree that it is not true that God ('an Anselmian being') is ethically bound to promote the well-being of others. That is, even if it is ethically required for you and me to come to the aid of others, it isn't ethically required of God. Murphy concludes that the "argument from evil against the existence of an Anselmian being is effectively defanged by a proper understanding of the ethics of the Anselmian being" (p. 103).

I too think that a proper understanding of God—and of the nature of evaluative and ethical concepts—defangs the argument from evil. But my reasons are very different from Murphy's. Murphy still thinks that *some* sort of ethics applies to God; it's just not the same sort of ethics that apply to everyone else. By contrast, I'm calling into question the well-formedness of the very thought that God (or anything) can be judged to be good *simpliciter*. Only members of certain kinds can be evaluated, and God is not a member of any kind for which it is a defect not to prevent suffering. So, although we arrive at similar conclusions, Murphy's argument and my argument take very different paths to get there.

Even if I am correct that there are no standards of goodness or badness that apply to God, the problem of evil may return in some other form. Instead of predicating goodness of God, one might predicate omnibenevolence of God. The existence of evil seems to imply that there is no omniscient, omnipotent, omnibenevolent being. Does this show that God does not exist?

I do not think so. There is no reason for insisting that if God exists, God is omnibenevolent. Most religious traditions *do* hold that God *sometimes* acts benevolently. But these traditions (apart from their theologians) do not supply grounds for insisting that God must *always* does the *most* benevolent thing. God may be selectively benevolent, but not omnibenevolent. So shifting the focus from God's goodness to God's omnibenevolence will not enable to us to infer that God does not exist.

I concede it remains unclear why we should *worship* a being who does not always alleviate avoidable suffering. One might sensibly wonder why we should submit to the will of a being who could easily improve our lives, and yet sometimes does not. Although I do not have a solution to this problem, I suspect the most promising strategy is to focus not upon God's intrinsic nature (omnipotence, omniscience, etc.), but upon other *relations* between God and us. That is, even if God doesn't alleviate all of our suffering, God may still treat us in *other* ways that make God a worthy object of our worship. Not all ways of being worthy of worship involve abating suffering. Different religious traditions will spell out what makes someone worthy of worship in different ways.[18] Here, I merely assume that there might be *some* ways that God is related to us to be worthy of our worship.

I have suggested a way theists can reply to the Argument from Evil, a way to block the argument that God does not exist. The solution is heterodox in so far as I do not maintain that God is good. But we are still entitled to say that God is free of defect. God is without flaw. God is in no respect bad. Maybe that is all the orthodoxy we need.

---

12 (Van Inwagen 2006).
13 (Hick 1966; Dougherty 2014).
14 (Stump 2010).
15 (Murray 2008).
16 (Forrest 1981). See also (Alexander 2012), a book devoted to exploring some implications of the attributive account of goodness for various issues in the philosophy of religion. Although Alexander does skeptically reexamine the notion that there is a best possible world, he does not apply Geach's thoughts about attributive goodness to God directly, as I am doing. Thus my essay can be viewed as a supplement to his work.
17 (Murphy 2017).
18 Since Murphy's account of worship-worthiness rests upon the claim that God is intrinsically good, I cannot endorse his account.

5. The Ontological Argument suffers from similar problems, and here I will be even briefer. It begins by understanding God as great (or perfect); in fact, God is the greatest thing that can be conceived. This presumes that it make sense to say (baldly) that God is great. But is this correct?

I venture to say that all of the reasons for thinking that 'good' always functions attributively apply with equal force in favor of thinking that 'great' and 'perfect' always functions attributively. We often do *say* that something is (just plain) great, but this is usually because we expect the listener to use contextual cues to understand some generic noun as relevant. If Nicolas says "Beethoven was great", we presume that he means that Beethoven was a great composer, not a great joke-teller. When Muhammad Ali said "I am the greatest", we should not expect his confidence to waver if someone were to point out that there is an awfully large wall in China. Asking whether the Great Awakening was greater than the Great Depression misses the point. Greatness, like goodness, always logically functions attributively.

We *do* sometimes compare the greatness of one kind of thing with the greatness of a different kind of thing. People sensibly argue over whether Tiger Woods is greater than Michael Jordan, despite the fact that one is a golfer and the other is a basketball player (we should ignore Jordan's mediocre golfing and baseball careers). But this is only because (1) they are both athletes, and (2) it makes sense to talk of a great athlete. Such comparisons are possible only when the items that are being compared all fall under some category that implies criteria for being great. Not all categories *do* imply criteria of greatness: it makes no sense to speak of a great way of exerting a gravitational force. Thus it makes no sense to say that something is great unless some generic noun is thereby implied, or we are to understanding the locution in an expressivist fashion.

And so it is not true that God is great, much less greater than anything else conceivable. Premises O1 and O2 are not true, not because they are false, but because they are ill-formed. The Ontological Argument seemed to work only because it had appeared to make sense to say that God was great. Once we see that this does not make sense, the appeal of the Ontological Argument evaporates.

Can the Ontological Argument be revised so that it is sound? The most immediate way to repair the argument may be to find some kind of which God is a great instance. The theist will likely first try:

O1* God is that than which no **greater being** can be conceived.

O2* If God does not exist, then there is some **greater being** than God that can be conceived.

O3* God exists.

At least this argument uses 'great' attributively. Or it pretends to. For to say that one item is a greater *being* than another item merely amounts to saying that the first item is greater than the second item, which is to say nothing at all: being *a being* brings no specific criteria of greatness in tow.[19] In order to repair the Ontological Argument, one needs to find some *specific* generic noun of which God is the greatest possible instance.[20]

Perhaps we can do that. God is a great creator. God is a great provider. These are specific aspects of the orthodox notion of God. So consider:

O1** God is that than which no **greater provider** can be conceived.

---

[19] See Geach (1956, p. 41): " 'Event', like 'thing', is too empty a word to convey either a criterion of identity or a standard of goodness; to ask 'Is this a good or bad thing (to happen)?' is as useless as to ask 'Is this the same thing that I saw yesterday?' or 'Is the same event still going on?', unless the emptiness of 'thing' or 'event' is filled up by a special context of utterance."

[20] What is true of 'great' is also true of 'perfect', and so versions of the Ontological Argument formulated in terms of perfection face the same problem. What do a perfect gentleman, a perfect sphere, a perfect game, and perfect pitch all have in common? They have no *kind-relative* defects. A perfect game is a game whose pitcher allows no baserunners. A perfect sphere is an object whose shape deviates in no way from that of a sphere. What substantively makes a game a perfect game, and what substantively makes a sphere a perfect sphere, overlap not at all. As with 'good' and 'great', 'perfect' is arguably always an attributive adjective. And just as 'being' is not a goodness-fixing or a greatness-fixing kind, 'being' is not a perfection-fixing kind. Thus perfect-being theologies depend upon a mistaken conception of the concept of perfection. See, for example, (Rogers 2000).

O2** If God does not exist, then there is some **greater provider** than God that can be conceived.

O3** God exists.

Is this argument sound? A problem emerges. First, it is not obvious that a provider who exists is ipso facto a greater provider than a provider who does not, this for two reasons. First, it is arguable that existence is not really a perfection.[21] Second, even if existence *is* a good-making feature, consider explicitly who is the greater provider: Santa Claus, or my Uncle Daniel, who once gave me $10 for my birthday? It's true that Uncle Daniel exists, whereas Santa Claus does not. But Santa Claus gives presents to millions of children, while my Uncle Daniel is exceedingly flinty. The second consideration seems to outweigh the first. One provider is not always a greater provider than another provider simply because only the first one exists.

Still, perhaps a provider who exists is *ceteris paribus* a greater provider than one does not. And God is not simply a great provider. God is purportedly the greatest provider whom can be conceived. So maybe the argument is sound.

But is it true that God is the greatest provider that we can conceive? Is O1** true? I can conceive of a being who is exactly like God (call this being Schmod), except that (1) Schmod just provided me with a proof of the Goldbach Conjecture (or some other wanted thing that I have not in fact been provided with), and (2) Schmod does not in fact exist. Still, Schmod would seem to be an even greater provider than the greatest provider who actually exists. Or, if providing me with a proof of the Goldbach Conjecture is alone not enough to make Schmod a greater provider than the greatest provider who actually exists, then we can imagine Schmod also providing me and others with all sorts of things that no one actually provides us with. This should be enough to make Schmod a greater provider than the greatest provider who actually exists, much like Santa Claus is a greater provider than my Uncle Daniel. So O1** is false. And it appears that analogous moves could be made with any other generic noun that is inserted (in place of "provider") in the argument.[22]

Here's a second problem with the revised argument. Even if my argument of the previous paragraph fails, the revised argument shows only that greatest conceivable *provider* exists. It permits us to conclude nothing else about the nature of the being in question; in particular, we are not permitted to conclude that such a being has *all* the other characteristics typically attributed to God, such as omniscience—at least not unless it can *also* be shown that the greatest possible knower exists. So it is highly unlikely that the Ontological Argument can give the theist *everything* she wants. Still, I must confess that the Ontological Argument is less damaged by the logic of evaluative adjectives than is the Argument from Evil.

One might worry that while I have rejected some traditional definitions of 'God' (e.g., the best possible being, the greatest possible being), I have not offered an alternative definition. So, in what sense have I really shown that the theist can avoid the Argument from Evil? *What* exactly does a theist believe in?[23] Here I am *deliberately* underspecifying the nature of God, this so as to be maximally open to the widest range of theologies. I aim to exclude only those theologies whose claims about God are not well-formed. I assume that there are many *coherent* forms of theism. But, I acknowledge, I have not here shown that there are.

Furthermore, early on I hinted that there was a variation of the Ontological Argument that was importantly different from the version of it I consider here. This version is formulated not at all in terms of God's greatness, but instead in terms of God's necessity.[24] The thought behind these modal arguments is roughly that God, by definition, is not a contingent being. So if is possible that God exists, it is necessary that God exists. But it *is* possible that God exists. So God exists. Whether *this* argument

---

[21] See here (Lindeman 2017).
[22] This argument obviously bears affinities with Gaunilo's objections to one of Anselm's versions of the ontological argument.
[23] I thank an anonymous reviewer for raising this worry in particular, and for many other helpful suggestions.
[24] (Malcolm 1960; Plantinga 1965). If, however, some version of the modal argument is itself based upon the notion that God is good or perfect, the original problem reemerges.

is sound is a controversial matter; I raise it only to acknowledge that the logic of evaluative adjectives has no bearing upon it.

6. Evaluative adjectives such as 'good' or 'great' logically function as attributive adjectives, a fact that proponents of two standard arguments concerning the existence of God have overlooked to their own detriment. Many have been too quick to assume that we can determine whether God exists by exploring what good particulars of other sorts are like. But a good or great instance of one kind and a good or great instance of another kind need have nothing else in common. So reasoning analogically about God in these ways is likely to falter.

Conflicts of Interest: The author declares no conflict of interest.

References

Alexander, David. 2012. *Goodness, God, and Evil*. London: Continuum Press.

Anscombe, Gertrude Elizabeth Margaret. 1958. Modern Moral Philosophy. *Philosophy* 33: 1–19. [CrossRef]

Anscombe, Gertrude Elizabeth Margaret. 2006. Good and Bad Human Action. In *Human Life, Action and Ethics*. Exeter: Imprint Academic, pp. 195–206.

Boyd, Richard N. 1988. How to be a Moral Realist. In *Essays on Moral Realism*. Edited by G. Sayre-McCord. Ithaca: Cornell University Press, pp. 181–228.

Dougherty, Trent. 2014. *The Problem of Animal Pain: A Theodicy for All Creatures Great and Small*. Basingstoke: Palgrave Macmillan.

Enoch, David. 2006. Agency, Shmagency: Why normativity won't come from what is constitutive of agency. *Philosophical Review* 115: 169–98. [CrossRef]

Foot, Philippa. 2001. *Natural Goodness*. Oxford: Oxford University Press.

Forrest, Peter. 1981. The problem of evil: Two neglected defences. *Sophia* 20: 49–54. [CrossRef]

Geach, Peter. 1956. Good and Evil. *Analysis* 17: 33–42. [CrossRef]

Hick, John. 1966. *Evil and the God of Love*. Basingstoke: MacMillan.

Korsgaard, Christine. 2009. *Self-Constitution: Action, Identity, and Integrity*. Oxford: Oxford University Press.

Lindeman, Kathryn. 2017. Constitutivism without Normative Thresholds. *The Journal of Ethics and Social Philosophy* 12: 231–57. [CrossRef]

Malcolm, Norman. 1960. Anselm's Ontological Arguments. *Philosophical Review* 69: 41–62. [CrossRef]

Moore, George E. 1903. *Principia Ethica*. Cambridge: Cambridge University Press.

Murphy, Mark C. 2017. *God's Own Ethics: Norms of Divine Agency and the Argument from Evil*. Oxford: Oxford University Press.

Murray, Michael J. 2008. *Nature Red in Tooth and Claw: Theism and the Problem of Animal Suffering*. Oxford: Oxford University Press.

Plantinga, Alvin. 1965. *The Ontological Argument from St. Anselm to Contemporary Philosophers*. New York: Doubleday.

Rogers, Katherin. 2000. *Perfect Being Theology*. Edinburgh: Edinburgh University Press.

Smith, Michael. 2015. The magic of constitutivism. *American Philosophical Quarterly* 52: 187–200.

Stevenson, Charles L. 1944. *Ethics and Language*. New Haven: Yale University Press.

Stump, Eleonore. 2010. *Wandering in Darkness: Narrative and the Problem of Suffering*. Oxford: Oxford University Press.

Thompson, Michael. 1995. The Representation of Life. In *Virtues and Reasons*. Oxford: Oxford University Press, pp. 247–96.

Thomson, Judith Jarvis. 2003. *Goodness and Advice*. Princeton: Princeton University Press.

Van Inwagen, Peter. 2006. *The Problem of Evil*. Oxford: Oxford University Press.

Wiland, Eric. 2012. *Reasons*. London: Continuum Press.

Article

Evil and Human Suffering in Islamic Thought—Towards a Mystical Theodicy

Nasrin Rouzati

Religious Studies Department, Manhattan College, Riverdale, NY 10471, USA; nasrin.rouzati@manhattan.edu

Received: 13 December 2017; Accepted: 28 January 2018; Published: 3 February 2018

Abstract: This paper sheds light on the treatment of the 'problem of evil' and human suffering from an Islamic perspective. I begin by providing an overview of the term 'evil' in the Qur'an to highlight its multidimensional meaning and to demonstrate the overall portrait of this notion as it is presented in the Islamic revelation through the narrative of the prophet Job. Having established a Qur'anic framework, I will then provide a brief historical overview of the formation of philosophical and theological debates surrounding "good" and "bad/evil" and the origination of Muslim theodicean thought. This will lead us to Ghazalian theodicy and the famous dictum of the "best of all possible worlds" by one of the most influential scholars of Islamic thought, Abu Ḥāmid Ghazālī. The final section of this paper will explore the Sufi/ mystical tradition of Islam through the teachings of one of the most distinguished mystics of Islam, Jalāl al-Dīn Rūmī. The conclusion of the paper will attempt to bring about a new understanding of how the so-called "problem of evil" is not presented in Islam as a problem but rather as an instrument in the actualization of God's plan, which is intertwined with human experiences in this world—an experience that is necessary for man's spiritual development.

Keywords: problem of evil; theodicy; Qur'an; Job; good; evil; al Ghazālī; mysticism; Islam

1. Introduction

The 'problem of evil' or, as it is more often referred to, the cause of human suffering is perhaps one of the most debated questions in the history of the philosophy of religion.[1] Although the issue makes itself known to humankind in general, it gains particular attention in the context of monotheistic religions as it brings into question the main pillar of such religions, namely, the existence of a powerful and merciful God. In light of the enormous amount of evil in the world, especially in the case of undeserved suffering, the challenge becomes even more acute and begs for answers. According to Hick, pondering about the volume of afflictions and adversities that mankind is faced with, "we do indeed have to ask ourselves whether it is possible to think of this world as the work of an omnipotent creator who is motivated by limitless love ... this is indeed the most serious challenge that there is to theistic faith."[2]

This paper aims to shed light on the treatment of the 'problem of evil' and human suffering from an Islamic perspective. I will begin by providing an overview of the term 'evil' in the Qur'an to highlight its multidimensional meaning and attempt to demonstrate the overall portrait of this notion as it is presented in the Islamic revelation through the narrative of the prophet Job. Having established a Qur'anic framework, I will then provide a brief historical overview of the formation of theological

---

[1] The "Problem of Evil", in the context of Western scholarship, is generally identified in two main categories: *theoretical* and *existential*, and further divides the *theoretical* dimension into *logical* and *evidential*; the distinction between moral evil and natural evil is also underscored. For more on this see Michael L. Peterson, *The Problem of Evil, Selected Readings* (Peterson 2011), Alvin Plantinga, *God, Freedom, and Evil* (Plantinga 1974), and John Hick, *Evil and the God of Love* (Hick 2007).

[2] See John Hick, *An Interpretation of Religion* (Hick 2004, p. 118).

debates surrounding "good" and "bad/evil" and the origination of Muslim theodicean thought. This will lead us to Ghazālian theodicy and the famous dictum of the *"best of all possible worlds"* by one of the most influential scholars of Islamic thought, Abu Ḥāmid Ghazālī. The final section of this paper will explore the Sufi/mystical tradition of Islam through the teachings of one of the most distinguished mystics of Islam, Jalāl al-Dīn Rūmī. The conclusion of the paper will attempt to bring about a new understanding of how the so-called "problem of evil" is not presented in Islam as a problem but rather as an instrument in the actualization of God's plan, which is intertwined with human experiences in this world—an experience that is necessary for man's spiritual development.

2. Evil and Suffering in the Qur'an: An Overview

For more than fourteen hundred years the Qur'an has served as the foundation of the religion of Islam and continues to play a dynamic role in shaping and influencing the lives of its followers, regardless of their diverse cultural backgrounds. The Qur'an is also considered to be the highest source of Islamic scholarship and functions as the starting point for a major portion of scholarly works. Therefore, to understand the treatment of evil and suffering in Muslim thought, the journey must begin with studying the Qur'anic narratives where this concept makes itself known.

A cursory review of studies on theodicy reveals that the meaning of 'evil', for the most part, is assumed and is not negotiable—personal loss, illness, violence, natural disaster, etc. Although the term appears abundantly in both popular and scholarly works, there seems to be a conceptual ambiguity surrounding it: What exactly is evil? Furthermore, does human understanding of evil concur with the divine message?

A key term in Arabic that is translated as evil is *'sharr'* and it is presented in two distinct categories of Qur'anic narratives. The first category includes verses that fall in the semantic field of *sharr* and appears amongst the moral concepts of the Qur'an. The overall notion of good (*khayr*) and bad/evil (*sharr*) is a central theme in Qur'anic teachings and is emphasized in both Meccan and Medinan phases of the Islamic revelation.[3] Considering these narratives hermeneutically by applying an intra-textual contextualization method, whereby the Qur'an functions as its own interpreter,[4] seems to suggest that the most prominent meaning for the term *sharr* in this group of narratives is the situation that man creates for himself.[5] It is clearly stated in the Qur'an that when humankind, through his own volition, acts in certain ways and adapts to specific behaviors that are not in accordance with the divine plan, he situates himself in a condition that is referred to as *sharr* by the Qur'an. Some of the deeds that fall into this moral category include miserliness, unbelief/rejecting God, slander, and transgression.[6] The Qur'an noticeably upholds that the creation of the universe—and by extension, humankind—is purposeful and not in vain.[7] Man, therefore, must make a serious effort to live his life according to God's cosmic plan. By neglecting the purpose for his creation and the accountabilities that it entails, he creates an undesirable living condition for himself, that is, *sharr*. The purposefulness of man's creation and his responsibility as it pertains to suffering will be discussed later in the article.

The second category of Qur'anic narratives is more of an interest to us as it is directly related to human suffering and theodicy. This group of verses falls beyond the semantic field of *sharr* and is

---

[3] For information on the chronology of the Qur'an, see Neal Robinson, *Discovering the Qur'an: A Contemporary Approach to a Veiled Text* (Robinson 2003).

[4] Intra-textual contextualization is a methodology used in understanding Qur'anic verses according to the context in which they appear individually, as well as in relation to the overall theme of all the chapters in which they appear. For an excellent discussion on the interpretation of the Qur'anic terms, see Toshibiko Izutsu, *Ethico - Religious Concepts in the Qur'an* (Izutsu 2002).

[5] For example, see Qur'an, 3:180; 8:22; 24:11; 17:11. For an excellent exegesis on the Qur'an, see (Tabarsi 1350).

[6] For more information on various contexts of *sharr* in the Qur'an, see Tunbar Yesilhark Ozkan, *A Muslim Response to Evil. Said Nursi on Theodicy* (Ozkan 2015, pp. 19–35).

[7] Qur'an, 38:27

revealed in various historical contexts reflected in the Qur'an.[8] A careful scrutiny of these narratives demonstrates that the so-called problem of evil—and by extension, human suffering—is not treated in the Qur'an as a theoretical problem but rather as an instrument in the actualization of God's purpose. Most of these narratives illustrate that the underlying rationale for the existence of various forms of evil and suffering is that they serve as a trial (*ibtilā*) and test: "*We shall certainly test you with fear and hunger, and loss of property, lives, and crops; however, [Prophet], give good news to those who are steadfast.*" [9]

The purpose of human suffering and its role in God's overall cosmic plan may bring about two corollaries. First, there is no contradiction between the divine attributes of God and the fact that suffering exists; therefore, affirmation of the Qur'an regarding God's omnipotence is not under question: "*Say 'God, holder of all sovereignty, You give control to whoever You will, and remove it from whoever You will. You elevate whoever You will and humble whoever You will. All that is good lies in Your hands: You have power over everything.*"[10] Moreover, since God is undoubtedly in control of creation, suffering must also be allowed by him for God's plan to be fully executed. Second, if suffering is meant as a test and is regarded as a necessary component of life, then a Muslim must view the undesirable situations (illness, financial difficulty, loss of a loved one, etc.) as an opportunity to actualize his inner potential and move forward in his spiritual journey, becoming who he "is" as the fruit of the creational tree.

It may also be concluded that by presenting the notion of evil and suffering as part of the human experience and a necessary component of man's spiritual journey, the Qur'an refrains from articulating a systematic theodicy. Therefore, the objective is not to engage man in abstract ideas but rather to help him realize the purpose of suffering and offer guiding principles in how to overcome various forms of evil.[11] Here it may be noted that the notion of 'natural evil'—a distinct category under the umbrella of the 'problem of evil'—is not treated in the Qur'an. Although the Qur'an frequently makes references to nature and events in the natural world that might not be desirable by mankind, these are not referred to as 'evil'.

3. Overcoming Evil: Prophet Job (*Ayyūb*)—The Exemplar

The notion of prophethood (*nabuwwa*) and the descriptive narratives about the lives of the prophets constitute a major portion of the Islamic scripture. While the prophets serve as the conduits through which the divine message is communicated to addressee communities, they are portrayed as exemplars that inspire and guide people to the straight path of monotheism. The history of Qur'anic prophethood began with Adam, chosen to become the first prophet after the trial of eating from the forbidden tree, and includes many of the figures mentioned in Judaeo–Christian traditions. Although Islamic tradition speaks of 124,000 prophets in the history of mankind, the Qur'an mentions twenty-five by name and describes their challenges as they conveyed the prophetic message to their respected communities. Prophet Muhammad is mentioned as the final messenger and is referred to as the "Seal of the Prophets".[12]

The story of Job (*Ayyūb*), an eminent figure in Jewish and Christian tradition, is seen in the Qur'an to exemplify genuine devotion to God, gratitude through fortune and health, and patience when afflicted with illness and adversity.[13] Job's incomparable sincerity and submission to God's will in both

---

8 Discussing the historical, political, and social climate of Islam's normative period is beyond the scope of this paper; however, it needs to be noted that a large portion of the Qur'an is directly related to the circumstances that surrounded Prophet Muhammad and the early Muslim community.

9 Qur'an, 2:155. Also see 67:2 and 89:16.

10 Qur'an, 3:26, see (Abdel Haleem 2004).

11 For an extended discussion on the instrumentality of evil in the forms of *balā* see, Nasrin Rouzati, *Trial and Tribulation in the Qur'an: A Mystical Theodicy* (Rouzati 2015).

12 Qur'an, 33:40.

13 The story of Job in Judeo-Christian traditions is presented in the Book of Job and appears in the form of a dialogue between Job and his friends who try to explain to him the reason for his sufferings. A comparative study of the story between Judeo-Christian tradition and Islam is beyond the scope of this paper. For an excellent comparative review, see A.H. Johns, A Comparative Glance at Ayyub in the Qur'an (Johns 2008, pp. 51–82).

health and prosperity, as well as during affliction and hardship, are the reasons the Qur'an portrays him as "an excellent servant."[14]

According to Muslim exegesis, what distinguishes Job is the fact that despite his enormous fortune, he continually attributed the source of his blessings to God and remained humble as a servant who lacked ownership of his belongings. Similarly, when God tested him with a serious disease, he exercised patience and recognized that he was going through a test—a positive experience—and ascribed any negative feelings of despair to Satan.[15]

The Qur'anic narrative about Job demonstrates that trials and tests—whether in prosperity and health or illness and hardship—are part of the divine plan, so much so that even prophets are not exempt; it is through various experiences in life that man is able to actualize his potential and propagate his mission on this earth. As John notes, "the story of Job in the Qur'an is understood primarily as a reward narrative with an emphasis different from that of the story of Job in the Bible."[16]

4. Concept of Evil: Theological and Philosophical Development

One of the earliest problems in Muslim theological thought (*kalām*) was how to reconcile the divine attribute of omnipotence with the notion of human free will. The departure point for this discourse was the Qur'an and the diverse interpretations of its teachings on the divine names and attributes (*asmā' al-ḥusnā*).[17] The reconciliation of certain divine attributes, predominantly the aspect of an all-powerful God, with the idea of human free will—the broader frame with which human suffering was enclosed—was the first attempt to initiate a theodicy within the context of Islam.

The discourse presents itself at the core of the theological dialogue amongst various groups. The theologians who advocated for the attribute of omnipotence in its absolute and uncompromising form were of the opinion that the only agent in this world is God: He creates His own acts as well as the acts of all human beings. As this view raised serious concerns about the creation of "evil" acts by God, the debate developed further to question the validity of human free will—the concept that is deeply rooted in the Quran as it relates to man's responsibility and accountability, as well as divine judgment and reward and punishment. The dialogue crystallized between the Mu'tazilite and the Ash'arite, the two main schools of thought, with a divergence of opinion; both made a serious effort to win the argument according to their understanding of the Qur'an.[18]

The Mu'tazilite school of thought, also known as the rationalists, categorically opposed the idea that God creates human acts that include evil and advocated for human free will by emphasizing the importance of the divine attribute of justice (*'adl*). They upheld that God, in accordance with His attribute of (*'āadil*), cannot create evil and that evil is the direct result of man's freedom of choice. This view was challenged by raising questions such as: If God does not create evil, who, then, is responsible for human suffering caused by illnesses and disasters? And if God wills for illnesses and disasters in human life, how can He be just? The Mu'tazilites responded by affirming that illnesses and disasters, while may appear as "evil", are in actuality "good" that God creates and that serve a significant purpose in the creational cosmic plan. This seems to be the first appearance of the theory of instrumentality of human suffering in the divine plan. The notion of suffering, which included undeserved suffering by children and animals, continued to be discussed by the Mu'tazilite

---

[14] Qur'an 38:41–2 and 21:83–4.
[15] See Abubakr 'Tigh Neishabur Surabadi, *Tafsir Surabadi*, ed. Sa'Idi Sirjani (Surabadi 1381). Also, see Brannon M. Wheeler, *Prophets in the Qur'an, an Introduction to the Qur'an and Muslim Exegesis* (Wheeler 2002).
[16] See (Johns 2003, pp. 50–51).
[17] For more on this see Abdol Rahman Ibn Khaldūn, *Muqaddimah of Ibn Khaldūn* (Ibn Khaldūn 1375).
[18] For a comprehensive discussion on development of theology in Islam, see Harry Austryn Wolfson, *The Philosophy of Kalam* (Wolfson 1976).

theologians.[19] The Muʿtazilite's firm stress on God's justice, however, resulted in the group dividing, which finally gave birth to the Ashʾarite school of thought.

According to Ashʾarite theologians, God's law of justice applies only to human beings who have been obligated to act according to His laws. Applying the idea of justice to God, however, will put a limit on an all-powerful creator; therefore, God is not bound by His own laws. He is just in whatever He does.[20] Applied to suffering, this then means that all harm encountered by man is fair as it has been willed by God who is just in all His creation. The Ashʾarite thinkers were in sharp conflict with the Muʿtazilites who asserted that not only is God subjected to the same rules of justice but that, in fact, the obligation to act in just means is eternal and uncompromising for God. It is worth noting that a prominent Muslim philosopher, Ibn Rushd (Averroes, d. 1198), challenged these views and asserted that the element of justice may not be employed for God and man in the same manner: man, by virtue of being just, advances to a higher level of goodness; God, however, is just due to His perfection—a trait that requires Him to be just.[21]

In the final analysis, mainstream Sunnite theologians supported the Ashʾarite school of thought and emphasized that God creates all acts. In order to reconcile God's omnipotence with human responsibility, the doctrine of acquisition (*kasb*) was adopted: God creates all acts; humans freely acquire certain acts and, therefore, are accountable for the acquisition of good and evil acts.[22] Conversely, Muslim thinkers belonging to the Shiʾite branch of Islam—through the influence of rational element in the Muʿtazilite theology—remained in disagreement with the Ashʾarites. An example of this may be observed from the writings of an eminent Persian philosopher, Morteza Muṭahharī (d. 1979), who was of the opinion that the Ashʾarite outlook, while aimed at vindicating God from injustice, resulted in exonerating human oppressors of any wrongdoing.[23]

From the Muslim philosophical perspective, the notion of good and evil is enclosed within the wider ontological understanding of existence (*wujūd*) and nonexistence (ʿadam). Briefly put, good is defined as a positive entity that branches from existence; evil, on the other hand, stems from nonexistence and as such is viewed as a negative entity.[24] An example of the ontological interpretation of what constitutes good and evil may be seen from the works of two prominent Muslim philosophers who significantly influenced the shaping of Muslim philosophical thought: Ibn Sīnā, known as Avicenna (d. 1037), and Sadr al-Din Shirāzī, who was mostly recognized as Mullā Sadrā (d. 1636).

Ibn Sīnā formed a theodicy by distinguishing the various forms of evil such as "essential" evil (*sharr bidh-dhāt*), which is non-being or privation, and "accidental" evil (*sharr bil-ʿaraḍ*), which can be either being or privation. In his analysis, Ibn Sīnā concluded that it is the non-essential/accidental evil that is the leading cause of human suffering and that the total amount of good in the universe outweighs the amount of evil.[25] Mullā Sadrā, on the other hand, extensively developed this philosophical approach by an interest in combining theology with mystical insight. This approach, according to Rizvi, totally transformed the theory of existence as it pertains to Islamic metaphysics.[26] In Mullā Sadrā's view, explained in his major work called *Mafātiḥ Al-ghayb*, absolute existence is absolute good and since God is the only Necessary Being, He is the absolute good: perfection applies only to the

---

19 For a great discussion on the Muʿtazilite's view on pain and suffering see (Heemskerk 2000). For an extensive study on the notion of disability in Islam, see Mohammed Ghaly, *Islam and Disability: Perspectives in Theology and Jurisprudence* (Ghaly 2010).

20 See Wolfson, *The Philosopy of Kalam* (Wolfson 1976).

21 For more on his philosophy, see Ibn Rushd (Averroes), *The Philosophy and Theology of Averroes*, (Averroes 1921).

22 For more on theory of acquisition, see Wolfson, *The Philosopy of Kalam* (Wolfson 1976).

23 See (Mutahhari 1385, pp. 50–51).

24 For more on ontological aspects of good and evil, see Seyyed Hossein Nasr, *Islamic Philosophy from Its Origin to the Present* (Nasr 2006, pp. 65–68).

25 For more on Ibn Sīnā's theodicy, see Shams C. Inati, *The Problem of Evil: Ibn Sina's Theodicy* (Inati 2000).

26 See Sajjad Rizvi, 'Mulla Sadra', *Stanford Encyclopedia of Philosophy* (Rizvi 2009).

Necessary Being. Thus, the rest of creation—all contingent entities—lacks certain degrees of goodness; that is, evil and suffering are partial and negative.[27]

It may be concluded that Muslim philosophers[28] have mostly referred to evil as *privatio boni* "privation of good," which in turn provides a strong rationale for the doctrine of the optimum (*al-aṣlaḥ*). According to this principle, this world, regardless of the existence of evil and human suffering, has been created in perfect fashion by its Creator who is the Perfect One. Therefore, the amount of evil and human suffering is inconsequential in relation to the volume of good that is inherent in the makeup of creation.

5. Evil and "The Best of All Possible Worlds": Ghazālian Theodicy

As discussed previously, the instrumentality of human suffering—purposefulness and the greater good that it brings—is emphasized in the Qur'an and is also at the core of the Muslim theological and philosophical discourse. However, the practical and more tangible aspect of this theory becomes highly observable in the teachings of one of the most influential intellectuals of Islam, namely, Abū Ḥāmid al-Ghazālī (1058–1111). Al-Ghazālī's significant impact on advancing Muslim scholastic thought is the reason he is often referred to as "the proof of Islam" (*Ḥujjat al-Islam*). It is, however, his personal experience with suffering and, by extension, his powerful statement regarding the creation of the world—"there is not in possibility anything more wonderful than what is" (*laysa fī'l-imkān abda' mimmā kān*)—that is of special interest in this article.

Through a rigorous education in theology and jurisprudence, as well as Qur'anic and *hadith* (prophetic traditions) studies, al-Ghazālī's extraordinary abilities flourished at a relatively young age and earned him a professorship position at one of the most distinguished academic settings of his time, namely, Niẓāmīyah College in Baghdad. However, at the peak of his career, notwithstanding great achievements and recognition, al-Ghazālī became doubtful of the authenticity of his theoretical religious knowledge and resigned from his position to pursue a more interior path of piety. In Bowker's view, al-Ghazālī felt that his religious knowledge about God and the ability to describe Him with such articulacy was worthless if it did not bring him into a direct experience of God.[29]

In his spiritual autobiography *al-Munqidh min al-ḍalāl* (Deliverance from Error), al-Ghazālī describes his intellectual and emotional challenges that ultimately resulted in a major event in his life. After examining possible ways by which a deep religious knowledge and convention that is free from doubt may be attained, he affirmed that the mystic path of life where knowledge of God is grounded in direct mystical experience was the way he had to peruse. However, in preparation to travel on this path, he needed to disengage from all worldly attachments: the prestigious professorship position, family, and wealth, which in actuality proved to be much more difficult. This inner struggle lasted more than six months until he was faced with a serious illness—inability to speak, eat, or drink—that caused him afflictions and much suffering. In fact, it was through months of hardship and suffering due to unexpected physical and spiritual crises that al-Ghazālī transformed internally, leaving all of his possessions and departing to Damascus where he spent two years in contemplation and prayer in search of certitude and a personal experience of God that was free from doubtfulness.[30]

The positive impact of al-Ghazālī's encounter with his severe illness, which endangered his physical and mental wellness, appears in accord with the optimistic portrayal of hardship and

---

[27] For an excellent commentary on Mullā Sadrā's *magnum opus*, *Asfār*, see (Rahman 1975).

[28] As mentioned previously, Ibn Rushd (Averroës, d. 1198) is considered as one of the most influential Muslim philosophers. While he was greatly influenced by Ibn Sina, he made a considerable effort to highlight Aristotle's original roots in Islamic philosophy, and remove the Neo-Platonism influence that had entered years later. Several centuries later, Mullā Sadrā became known as the Shiite philosopher who added a mystical layer to philosophical and theological debates. For more on the development of Islamic philosophy, see (Nasr 2006).

[29] See John Bowker, *The Religious Imagination and the Sense of God* (Bowker 1978, p. 195).

[30] See Abū Ḥāmid Al-Ghazālī, *Al-Munqidh Min Al-Dalal, Deliverance from Error* (Al-Ghazālī 2006, pp. 52–55).

suffering presented in the Qur'an.[31] For al-Ghazālī, this apparent negative experience proved, in fact, to be positive and instrumental in the actualization of his intellectual and spiritual potentialities. As already mentioned, during his professorship in Baghdad, al-Ghazālī contributed greatly to shaping a variety of Muslim thoughts.[32] Still, the practical implications of much of his teachings, particularly the relationship between theological and mystical discourses, are clearly articulated in his writings following his departure and the years he spent in seclusion. As Zarrinkūb pointed out, the authenticity of religious knowledge that al-Ghazālī pursued through rational deductions for much of his life bore fruit after his illness and major mystical experience.[33] The reflections of al-Ghazālī's renewal are presented in his *magnum opus* called *Iḥyā' 'ulūm al-din* ("*The Revival of the Religious Sciences*"), composed during the next decade of his life. In this major work, al-Ghazālī illustrated through a highly detailed elucidation of personal religious experiences ways by which a profound inner life may be integrated with sound theological doctrines.[34]

The reflection of this worldview and much of what may be called Ghazālian theodicy is encapsulated in his famous dictum of the best of all possible worlds: "There is not in possibility anything more wonderful than what is" (*laysa fi'l-imkān abda' mimmā kān*). The statement presents itself in Book 35 of the *Iḥyā' 'ulūm al-din: Kitāb al-tawḥīd wa' l-tawakkul*, Divine Unity and Trust in God:

> Everything that God distributes among men such as sustenance, life-span *'ajal'*, happiness and sadness, weakness and power, faith and unbelief, obedience and apostasy—all of it is unqualifiedly just with no injustice in it, true with no wrong infecting it. Indeed, all this happens according to a necessary and true order, according to what is appropriate as it is appropriate and in the measure that is proper to it; nor is anything more fitting, more perfect, and more attractive within the realm of possibility. For if something was to exist and remind one of the sheer omnipotence of God and not of the good things accomplished by His action, it would be miserliness that utterly contradicts God's generosity and injustice contrary to divine justice. And if God were not omnipotent, He would be impotent, thereby contradicting the nature of divinity.[35]

Although a critical analysis of al-Ghazālī's statement is beyond the scope of this paper, it should be mentioned that he received much criticism from his opponents since taking this position—it is not possible for God to create a better world—is in conflict with the Ash'arite theological teachings relating to God's omnipotence.[36] However, it must be pointed out that the statement is embedded within a broader context of *tawakkul*, "trust in God," which is treated in the Qur'an extensively. In fact, *Al-Wakīl*, the trustee, is one of the divine attributes that the Qur'an references when it characterizes true believers, that is, those who hold full trust in God. This concept is also discussed by al-Ghazālī in his book called *The Ninety-Nine Beautiful Names of God*, '*al-Maqṣad al-asnā fī sharḥ ma'ānī asmā' Allāh al-ḥusnā*', where he provides a comprehensive discussion of the divine attribute of *Al-Wakīl*, and describes to his audience how God, in His essence, deserves to have matters entrusted to Him.[37]

Therefore, while certain elements of a classical theodicy are articulated in al-Ghazālī's maxim of "the best of all possible worlds," one may infer that his objective was to provide practical guidelines to reach a high level of trust in God despite the apparent imperfections of the world. Furthermore, prior

---

[31] For example, Quran, 2:216, " . . . you may dislike something although it is good for you, or like something although it is bad for you: God knows and you don't."

[32] For a comprehensive study on al-Ghazālī's thoughts, see Frank Griffel, *Al-Ghazālī's Philosophical Theology* (Griffel 2009). Also see Michael E. Marmura, 'Al-Ghazālī', in Peter Adamson and Richard Taylor (ed.), *The Cambridge Companion to Arabic Philosophy* (Marmura 2005).

[33] See Abdolhusin Zarrinkub, *Farar Az Madrasah - Life and Teachings of Al-Ghazali* (Zarrinkub 1387, p. 124).

[34] For more on this, see (Watt 2007).

[35] See (Al-Ghazālī 2001, pp. 45–46).

[36] For a detailed discussion on al-Ghazālī's statement, see (Ormsby 1984). It should be noted that several centuries later this statement was raised by Leibnitz in the context of a consistent theodicy. Also see (Kermani 2011, p. 58).

[37] See (Al-Ghazālī 1992, pp. 375–76).

to making the aforementioned statement about the perfectness of the world, al-Ghazālī engages in an in-depth discussion on the divine attributes of "wisdom" and "will" to highlight their connection, as well as the importance of viewing the world as the most excellent work of the Creator. From the Ghazālian perspective, the signs of God's will and wisdom are plentifully evident throughout His creation. Consequently, in order to fully trust in God that this world—including all of its seeming deficiencies—is the best of all possible worlds, one must be able to genuinely believe that the creation of the universe is planned and premeditated according to God's will and wisdom. It should also be mentioned that this level of trust, *tawakkul*, is one of the highest stations in the mystic path and plays a significant role in man's spiritual development.

As it may be inferred from the above discussion, al-Ghazālī's theodicy is established on a strong relationship between man and God and the need to reach an elevated level of trust in God in the face of the world's imperfections, adversities, and suffering. Nevertheless, it is in the teachings of Jalāl al-Dīn Rūmī, one of the most prominent thinkers of Islam as well as a mystic and Sufi poet, where the comprehensive elucidations of the constructive aspects of hardship and suffering in man's spiritual development come to light.[38]

6. Evil from the Muslim Mystical Perspective: Jalāl al-Dīn Rūmī

The mystical dimension of Islam, similar to other forms of religious mysticism discussed in Perennial Philosophy,[39] deals with the esoteric teachings of Islam and is traditionally represented by Sufism. Although the development of Sufism may be traced back to a century after the death of prophet Muhammad, the roots of its teachings go back to the Qur'an and the *Sunna* (normative behavior) of the prophet where contemplating on the spiritual realities of the universe is highly encouraged. That the external (*zāhir*) practices of Islam should guide to insight and inner realities (*bāṭin*) may be understood from the Qur'an where God is presented as both the Outward (*al-zāhir*) and the Inward (*al-bāṭin*).[40] Although the focus of Sufism is on the esoteric path (*tarīqah*) in order to reach a state of union with God, the doctrines and practices of the Sufi path are, nevertheless, founded on the exoteric framework specified in Islamic law (*sharī'ah*).[41]

One of the most influential Sufis of Islam is Jalāl al-Dīn Rūmī (1207–1273) who is known in the West for his mystical poetry. Rūmī was born in Balkh, the Persian province of Khorāsān, and received a high level of education under his father who was a distinguished jurisprudent and Sufi, as well as a formal trainee to the mastery level in Sufism from one of the most well-known Sufi masters of the time, Burhān al-Din Tirmidhī. Being educated in the traditional religious sciences in addition to Sufism gained him widespread recognition as a religious scholar and influential teacher in both exoteric and esoteric teachings of Islam. In Shafiei Kadkani's opinion, Rūmī is considered as one of the greatest intellectuals of the world mainly because of his extraordinary ability to engage with the mystical interpretation of some of the most difficult theological concepts, as well as their exposition in a poetic and inspirational language.[42] Although Rūmī's mystical elucidations are presented in much of his work, it is, however, his *magnum opus*, the *Mathnawī* that illuminates the mystical elements of the Qur'anic teachings, and is regarded as an esoteric commentary of the Qur'an.[43] In what follows, I will

---

[38] It is important to note that al-Ghazālī's mystical teachings have greatly influenced Rūmī's worldview. However, while the former emphasized more on God's majesty, the latter established his teachings more on the notion of God's love. For more on the mystical views of al-Ghazālī and Rūmī, see (Soroush 1379, pp. 33–37).

[39] Perennial Philosophy takes a universal approach in explaining the teachings of world religions, and brings to light a shared mystical vision among them. Viewed from this perspective, world religions and spiritual traditions, despite their cultural and historical differences, promote a deep understanding of the transcendent element, the Reality, which exists in the universe. For more on this, see (Huxley 2009, p. vii).

[40] Qur'an: 57:3, "He is the First and the Last; the Outer and the Inner: He has the knowledge of all things."

[41] For a comprehensive discussion about Islamic mysticism, see (Schimmel 1975). Also, see (Nasr 1987).

[42] See (Shafiei Kadkani 1388, p. 2).

[43] For more on the influence of the Qur'an in shaping Rumi's worldview, see (Zarrinkub 1388, p. 342).

attempt to summarize Rūmī's expositions on the notion of evil and human suffering as presented in the *Mathnawī*.

In Rūmī's worldview, the multiplicity that exists in this world is the effect of the manifestation of God's names (*asmā'*) and attributes (*sifāt*) that aim to reveal His creative power. In other words, while the form (*ṣūrat*) of the created entities is varied, their meaning (*ma'nā*), nevertheless, is indicative of One Reality.[44] Rūmī further expands the distinction between form and meaning to demonstrate that while man appears to be a being among other beings in the universe, the universe is, in fact, in man: " ... in form thou art the microcosm, in reality thou art the macrocosm."[45] He also identifies man as the "fruit" of creation and uses the analogy of a tree to describe this highly elevated status: "The only reason that the gardener plants a tree is for the sake of the fruit. Man is the goal of the creation; therefore, he is the last creature that comes into existence; yet, in reality, he is the first."[46]

The creation of Adam, as the exemplar of humankind in his ultimate closeness to God, is postulated at the center of Rūmī's teachings as it relates to the positive impact of trials and tribulations in man's spiritual development. According to Rūmī, the Qur'anic notion of the "knowledge of the names,"[47] taught to Adam upon his creation, reveals that humankind has the capacity to become the perfect mirror where God's names and attributes may be manifested. The knowledge of the names, Rūmī informs us, is not the external names of the created beings; rather, it is the mysteries and the inner meanings of the various elements within the creation of the cosmos. Man's responsibility is to live in accordance with his inner nature (*fitra*) and recognize that actualization of his potential is doable by his own volition, as well as the ability to differentiate between "form" and "meaning": to search for the truth behind the veils.

From the Rūmīan perspective, the most important phase in man's spiritual development is to get to know one's self, self-knowledge (*ma'rifat al-nafs*), and ultimately to recognize that he has been separated from his original Source (*aṣl*). By employing the analogy of a "reed," Rūmī explicates that this separation is the primary cause for humankind's unhappiness in this life.[48] Man tends to forget his divine origin and occupies himself with the worldly attainments; therefore, in order to awaken him from the state of negligence, he will be faced with adversities and sufferings. In other words, trials and tribulations are necessary as they assist man in self-purification (*tazkiyat al-nafs*), freeing him from material attachments and the inclinations of his ego. Rūmī expounds upon prophet Joseph's experience to describe the constructiveness of trials; Joseph's enslavement, as difficult as it was, freed him from slavery to other creatures so that he could become God's slave alone.[49] Furthermore, in Rūmī's scheme, when a person is faced with a negative *balā*, for example, a serious illness, his attitude and response towards his condition are of primary importance. The person whose goal in life is to satisfy the inclinations of his animal self will complain and bring to question the justice of God. On the other hand, a person whose goal is to purify the self (*nafs*), to go up the spiritual ladder, will find a deeper meaning in learning the lessons hidden within this experience.[50]

As it was alluded to previously, from the Qur'anic perspective, man's entire life on earth, in "good" (*khayr*) and "bad" (*sharr*), is viewed as a trial and a test; the purpose is to grant him the opportunity to flourish his inner potential by exercising freedom of choice (*ıkhtiār*) and to strive to find ways to return to his source. As Rūmī explains, mankind has the tendency to forget God in two situations: when he is granted wealth and during good health.

---

[44] See (Rumi 1926, VI:3172, 83).
[45] Ibid., IV:521.
[46] Ibid., III:1128–29.
[47] Qur'an: 2:30–37.
[48] See (Rumi 1926, I:1–2; 3; and 11).
[49] See (Renard 1994).
[50] See (Rumi 1926, III:682–68). For more on this, see (Zamani 1384).

Between God and His servant are just two veils and all other veils manifest out of these: they are health and wealth. The man who is well in body says, 'Where is God? I do not know and I do not see.' As soon as pain afflicts him he begins to say, 'O God! O God!', communing and conversing with God. So you see that health was his veil and God was hidden under that pain. As much as man has wealth and resources, he procures the means to gratify his desires and is preoccupied during the night and day with that. The moment indigence appears, his ego is weakened and he goes round about God.[51]

Rūmī further invites his reader to ponder about times of afflictions when his prayer in ending the suffering appears not to have been granted by God, and to recognize and appreciate that this is more beneficial for him: the longer the duration of the hardship, the longer he remains in this state of immanence to God.[52] Also, as Chittick observes, in Rūmī's view, "if a person tries to flee from suffering through various stratagems, he is, in fact, fleeing God. The only way to flee from suffering is to seek refuge from one's own ego with God."[53] Moreover, another positive impact of adversity and sorrow is that it transforms and purifies human character.

When someone beats a rug with a stick, he is not beating the rug; his aim is to get rid of the dust.
Your inward is full of dust from the veil of I-ness and that dust will not leave all at once.[54]

Finally, before closing the discussion on Rūmī's teachings, it should be pointed out that in his elucidations on the fruitfulness of hardships in man's life, Rūmī also provides practical guidelines that can be put to practice when one is faced with adversities. In an effort to benefit from spiritual growth, as well as overcome suffering without going into despair, Rūmī explicates two critical aspects of being a Muslim, namely, the Qur'anic virtues of patience (*ṣabr*) and trust in God (*tawakkul*). As trusting God is at the core of al-Ghazālī's teachings and has already been discussed in conjunction with the "best of all possible world" statement, we will now turn to a brief discussion on the concept of patience from the Rūmīan perspective.

In his explications of man's condition on this earth, Rūmī frequently sheds light on the virtue of patience. Nevertheless, it is in the parable of the "chickpea," one of the most well-known stories of the *Mathnawī*, where the importance of patience in the face of suffering fully comes to light. The story is about a fictional dialogue between a housewife and a chickpea that is being cooked as part of a meal. Similar to man at the time of his encounter with affliction, the chickpea complains to the housewife for cooking it in boiling water and it tries to escape by constantly jumping out of the pot. Finally, on realizing that it is not able to relieve itself from its misery, it desperately pleads with the housewife to take it out of the boiling water. The housewife then comes into a conversation to console the chickpea and help it learn that patiently enduring suffering is needed for its growth.

At the time of being boiled, the chickpea comes up continually to the top of the pot and raises a hundred cries,
Saying, 'Why are you setting the fire on me? Since you bought me, how are you turning me upside down?'
The housewife goes on hitting it with the ladle. 'No!' says she: 'boil nicely and don't jump away from the one who makes the fire.'
I do not boil you because you are hateful to me; nay, 'tis that you may get taste; this affliction of yours is not on account of you being despised.'
Continue, O chickpea, to boil in tribulation, that neither existence nor self may remain

---

51 See (Rumi 2004, p. 240).
52 See (Rumi 1926, VI:4222–26).
53 See (Chittick 1983, p. 238).
54 See (Rumi 1379).

to thee.
The chickpea said, 'since it is so, O lady, I will gladly boil: give me help in verity!
In this boiling thou art, as it were, my architect: smite me with the skimming-spoon, for
thou smites very delightfully.'[55]

Recapitulating Rūmī's thought as presented in the final verse of the chickpea story, when man journeys in the mystic path and is able to attain the state of inner contentment (*riżā*) during times of suffering, he has truly submitted to the will of God—has become a *Muslim*. Consequently, in patiently enduring suffering, as well as trusting in God and the overall goodness of His creation, man will be able to overcome the anguish and move up the spiritual ladder to reach nearness with God. It should also be mentioned that in Rūmī's mystical path, love of God plays a significant role in the process of man's spiritual growth. As man is reminded of his separation from his Source (*aṣl*), the love of the Beloved is the means by which he will be able to endure the most difficult times, knowing that through God's love he has the potential to reach the elevated state of *riżā*—what the Qur'an refers to as the highest state of tranquility ('*nafs muṭma'inna*')—where man is pleased with his Lord.[56]

7. Conclusions

The notion of evil and human suffering is not portrayed in the Islamic revelation as a "problem" to be resolved but rather as part of the human experience. Therefore, since the Qur'an does not engage its readers in abstract ideas and theological discussions about evil, the formulation of a classical theodicy is not presented. Most of the Qur'anic verses on adversity and suffering suggest that human beings, including prophets, will be tested by difficult times. The ontological nature of evil is referred to as nonexistence and privation of good by Muslim philosophers, while the theologians attribute evil to man's conduct. The Muslim mystical literature as presented in the teachings of Rūmī demonstrates that trials in adversities are necessary to remove man from the state of negligence in order for him to realize his divine source and to choose to set forth on a spiritual journey. In this mystic path, exercising patience, trusting God, as well as loving God, are essential in assisting man reach the state of tranquility. Along the path, man, as the fruit of the creation, will be able to actualize the potentialities of his inner nature and purify his soul to become a perfect mirror in manifesting God's names and attributes.

Conflicts of Interest: The authors declare no conflict of interest.

References

Averroes, Ibn Rushd. 1921. *The Philosophy and Theology of Averroes*. Translated by Mohammad Jamil Rehman. Lexington: ForgottenBooks.

Abdel Haleem, Muhammad A. S. 2004. *The Qur'an, English Translation*. New York: Oxford University Press, US.

Al-Ghazālī, Abū Ḥāmid. 1992. *The Ninety-Nine Beautiful Names of God, al-Maqṣad al-Asnā fī Sharḥ Ma'ānī asmā' Allāh al-Ḥusnā*. Translated by David B. Burrell. Cambridge: The Islamic Text Society.

Al-Ghazālī, Abū Ḥāmid. 2001. *Kitāb al-Tawḥīd wa' l-Tawakkul, Faith in Divine Unity & Trust in Divine Providence*. Translated by David Burrell. Louisville: Fons Vitae.

Al-Ghazālī, Abū Ḥāmid. 2006. *Al-Munqidh min al-Dalal, Deliverance from Error*. Translated by R. J. Mccarthy. Louisville: Fons Vitae.

Bowker, John. 1978. *The Religious Imagination and the Sense of God*. Oxford: Oxford University Press.

Chittick, William C. 1983. *The Sufi Path of Love: The Spiritual Teachings of Rumi*. Albany: State University of New York Press.

Ghaly, Mohammed. 2010. *Islam and Disability: Perspectives in Theology and Jurisprudence*. London: Routledge.

Griffel, Frank. 2009. *Al-Ghazālī's Philosophical Theology*. New York: Oxford University Press.

---

[55] See (Rumi 1926, III:4160–64; 78; 97–98).
[56] For more on the notion of love in Rumi's mysticism, see (Zarrinkub 1388). Also, see (Schimmel 1993).

Heemskerk, Margaretha T. 2000. *Suffering in The Muʿtazilite Theology: 'Abd al-Jabbar's Teachings on Pain and Divine Justice*. London: Brill.

Hick, John. 2004. *An Interpretation of Religion*. New Haven and London: Yale University Press.

Hick, John. 2007. *Evil and the God of Love*. New York: Palgrave Macmillan.

Huxley, Aldous. 2009. *The Perennial Philosophy*. New York: HarperCollins.

Ibn Khaldūn, Abdol Rahman. 1375. *Muqaddimah of Ibn Khaldūn*. Translated by Mohammad P. Ghonabadi. 2 vols. Tehran: Sherkat Elmi Farhangi.

Inati, Shams C. 2000. *The Problem of Evil: Ibn Sina's Theodicy*. Albany: State University of New York Press.

Izutsu, Toshibiko. 2002. *Ethico—Religious Concepts in the Qur'an*. Montreal: McGill-Queen's University Press.

Johns, Anthony H. 2003. 'Job'. In *Encyclopedia of the Qur'an*. Edited by Jane Dammen McAuliffe. 3 vols. Washington: Brill, pp. 50–51.

Johns, A. H. 2008. 'A Comparative Glance at Ayyub in the Qur'an'. In *Deconstructing Theodicy*. Edited by David Burrell. Michigan: Brazos Press, Baker Publishing.

Kermani, Navid. 2011. *The Terror of God (Original Work in German)*. Translated by Wieland Hoban. Cambridge: Polity Press.

Mutahhari, Morteza. 1385. *'Adl-e elahi*. Tehran: Sadra.

Marmura, Michael E. 2005. 'Al-Ghazālī'. In *The Cambridge Companion to Arabic Philosophy*. Edited by Peter Adamson and Richard Taylor. Cambridge: Cambridge University Press.

Nasr, Seyyed Hossein. 2006. *Islamic Philosophy from Its Origin to the Present*. Albany: State University of New York Press.

Seyyed Hossein Nasr, ed. 1987. *Islamic Spirituality—Foundations*. 2 vols; World Spirituality, 1.; New York: Crossroad.

Ormsby, Eric L. 1984. *Theodicy in Islamic Thought: Dispute over Al-Ghazali's "Best of All Possible Worlds"*. Princeton: Princeton University Press.

Ozkan, Tunbar Yesilhark. 2015. *A Muslim Response to Evil. Said Nursi on Theodicy*. London: Ashgate.

Peterson, Michael L. 2011. *The Problem of Evil, Selected Readings*. Notre Dame: University of Notre Dame.

Plantinga, Alvin. 1974. *God, Freedom, and Evil*. Cambridge: WM. B. Berdmans.

Rahman, Fazlur. 1975. *The Philosophy of Mulla Sadra*. Albany: State University of NY Press.

Renard, John. 1994. *All the King's Falcons, Rumi on Prophets and Revelation*. Albany: State University of New York Press.

Rizvi, Sajjad. 2009. 'Mulla Sadra', Stanford Encyclopedia of Philosophy. Available online: http://plato.stanford.edu/entries/mulla-sadra/ (accessed on 13 January 2013).

Robinson, Neal. 2003. *Discovering the Qur'an: A Contemporary Approach to a Veiled Text*. Washington: Georgetown University Press.

Rouzati, Nasrin. 2015. *Trial and Tribulation in the Qur'an: A Mystical Theodicy*. Berlin, Germany: Gerlach.

Rumi, Jalal al-Din. 1379. *Diwan Shams Tabrizi*. Tehran: Peyman.

Rumi, Jalal al-Din. 1926. *The Mathnawi of Jalaluddin Rumi*. Translated by Reynold A. Nicholson. Cambridge: E.J.W. Gibb Memorial.

Rumi, Jalal al-Din. 2004. *Fihi ma fihi (Discourses of Rumi)*. Translated by Arthur John Arberry. London and New York: Routledge.

Schimmel, Annemarie. 1975. *Mystical Dimentions of Islam*. Chapel Hill: The University of North Carolina Press.

Schimmel, Annemarie. 1993. *The Triumphal Sun: A Study of the Works of Jalalodin Rumi*. Albany: State University of New York Press.

Shafiei Kadkani, Muhammad Reza. 1388. *Mowlana Rumi's Ghazaliat Shams Tabrizi*. Tehran: Sokhan.

Surabadi, Abubakr 'tigh Neishabur. 1381. *Tafsir Surabadi*. Edited by Sa'idi Sirjani. 3 vols; Tehran: Farhamg Nashr-Nu.

Soroush, Abdolkarim. 1379. *Ghomar-E 'Asheghaneh: Rumi and Shams*. Tehran: Serat.

Tabarsi, Abu 'Ali al-Fadl ibn al-Hassan. 1350. *Majma' al-Bayan fi Tafsir al-Qur'an*. Translated by Ahmad Beheshti. Tehran: Farahani.

Watt, W. Mongomery. 2007. *The Faith and Practice of al-Ghazali*. Oxford: Oneworld.

Wheeler, Brannon M. 2002. *Prophets in the Qur'an, An Introduction to the Qur'an and Muslim Exegesis*. New York: Continuum.

Wolfson, Harry Austryn. 1976. *The Philosopy of Kalam*. Cambridge: Harvard University Press.

Zamani, Karim. 1384. *Minagar-E Eshgh: A Thematical Commentary of the Mathnawi Ma'nawi*. Tehran: Nashr-e Nay.
Zarrinkub, Abd al-Husayn. 1388. *Sirr Nay: A Critical Analysis and Commentary of Masnavi*. Tehran: Ettellat.
Zarrinkub, Abdolhusin. 1387. *Farar az Madrasah—Life and Teachings of al-Ghazali*. Tehran: Amir Kabir.

Article

Theodicy, Useless Suffering, and Compassionate Asymmetry: Primo Levi, Emmanuel Levinas, and Anti-Theodicy

Jennifer L. Geddes

Department of Religious Studies, University of Virginia, Charlottesville, VA 22903, USA; jlg2u@virginia.edu

Received: 31 January 2018; Accepted: 29 March 2018; Published: 5 April 2018

Abstract: Emmanuel Levinas declares that we have reached the end of theodicy, but we have not reached the end of discussions and books and special issues on theodicy, and people continue to ask, and answer, the questions "Why?" and "Why me?" about their suffering. In this essay, I would like to explore this persistence of theodicy as a topic of scholarly discussion and as an ongoing human activity, despite powerful and convincing critiques of theodicy. How might we take seriously what Levinas calls "the temptation of theodicy" and, at the same time, take seriously the ways that engaging in theodicy might be a vital part of how someone navigates her own suffering? I suggest that we look to Levinas's asymmetrical configuration of the uselessness of suffering—that is, while the other's suffering must remain useless to me, my suffering in response to the other's suffering can be useful—for a parallel asymmetry concerning Levinas's declared end of theodicy: while theodicy that justifies the other's suffering is forbidden to me, I cannot forbid the sufferer's theodicy in response to her own suffering. Further, I suggest that even in Levi's harsh rejection of his fellow inmate's implicit theodicy, Levi still seems to refrain from condemnation of his fellow sufferer, through his use of interrogative and conditional rhetorical structures. Thus, while we might agree with Levinas's argument that we have reached the end of theodicy on a collective or historical or interpersonal or, even, personal scale, we are forbidden from declaring the end of theodicy for the other. The sufferer always has the prerogative to narrate her own suffering in the manner in which she chooses, and the imposition of meaninglessness onto her suffering, through a prohibition of all theodicy, may be a violent imposition, that mimics, in part, the violence of the imposition of meaning onto her suffering.

Keywords: theodicy; anti-theodicy; Emmanuel Levinas; Primo Levi; suffering

---

> Perhaps the most revolutionary fact of our twentieth-century consciousness ... is that of the destruction of all balance between Western thought's explicit and implicit theodicy and the forms that suffering and its evil are taking on in the very unfolding of this century.
>
> —Emmanuel Levinas, "Useless Suffering"

> If I were God, I would spit Kuhn's prayer out upon the ground.
>
> —Primo Levi, *If This Is a Man*

1. Introduction

Emmanuel Levinas declares that we have reached the end of theodicy—that the horrors we have witnessed over the last century outweigh and overwhelm any of the theodicies by which we try explicitly or implicitly to explain them. And yet, we have not reached the end of discussions and books and special issues on theodicy, and people continue to ask, and answer, the questions "Why?" and

"Why me?" about their suffering. In this essay I would like to explore this persistence of theodicy as a topic of scholarly discussion and as an ongoing human activity, despite powerful and convincing critiques of theodicy. How might we take seriously what Levinas calls "the temptation of theodicy" and, at the same time, take seriously the ways that engaging in theodicy might be a vital part of how someone navigates her own suffering?

To think about this question, I begin with a passage from Primo Levi's Holocaust testimony *If This Is a Man*, in which Levi depicts a Holocaust inmate engaging in a kind of theodicy and then offers a powerful indictment of that theodicy. The selection from Levi's work puts us right in the middle of the tension between theodicy's immoral movement towards justifying the suffering of the other and the palliative function to alleviate some of the non-physical pain of suffering that a sufferer might find in it. I then turn to Levinas's anti-theodicy and his prohibition against justifying another's suffering in his essay "Useless Suffering." Finally, I ask: if the proper response to the extreme suffering of others is compassion, a suffering in response to others' suffering, as well as the offering of aid to alleviate that suffering, what are we to do when the sufferer herself is engaged in theodicy, asking the perennial question "Why?" about her suffering? When theodicy is part of her own effort to alleviate or endure her suffering? In this situation, might not the declaration of the end of theodicy function as a violent imposition of *meaninglessness* onto her suffering—an imposition that resembles the prohibited imposition of *meaning* onto it? While Levinas powerfully redraws the territory of the purview of theodicy, extending it beyond the theological effort to justify the goodness and omnipotence of God in the face of evil to any effort to justify the other's suffering, he also leaves us with a moral conundrum about how to respond to the sufferer's own theodicy and what the declaration of the end of theodicy means for her.

I suggest that we look to Levinas's asymmetrical configuration of the uselessness of suffering—that is, the other's suffering must remain useless to me, but my suffering in response to the other's suffering can be useful—for a parallel asymmetry concerning Levinas's declared end of theodicy: while theodicy that justifies the other's suffering is forbidden to me, I cannot forbid the sufferer's theodicy in response to her own suffering. While I must not engage in theodicy that justifies the other's suffering, that is, while I must follow a ban on theodicy in relation to others' suffering, I must not ban the sufferer's theodicy in response to her own suffering. I cannot refuse the possibility that her suffering may have meaning *for her*, may be seen *by her* as useful *to her*. Further, I suggest that even in Levi's harsh rejection of his fellow inmate's implicit theodicy, Levi still seems to refrain from condemnation of his fellow sufferer, through his use of interrogative and conditional rhetorical structures. Thus, while we might agree with Levinas's argument that we have reached the end of theodicy on a collective or historical or interpersonal or, even, personal scale, we are forbidden from declaring the end of theodicy for the other. The sufferer always has the prerogative to narrate her own suffering in the manner in which she chooses, and the imposition of meaninglessness onto her suffering, through a prohibition of all theodicy, may be a violent imposition, that mimics, in part, the violence of the imposition of meaning onto her suffering. The difficulty, of course, is when that narrative has implications for the meaning of the suffering of others, when it implies a theodicy about the other's suffering, as the following scene from Levi reveals.

2. Primo Levi and Blasphemous Theodicy

In his testimony, *If This Is a Man*, Primo Levi describes a scene in the concentration camp barracks: a selection has just taken place; some inmates have been chosen for the gas chambers and others have been passed over to live. Kuhn thanks God for not being selected; Beppo lies in silence, knowing that he is one of those selected for death. Levi writes:

> ... from my bunk, on the top level, I see and hear old Kuhn praying aloud, with his cap on his head, his torso swaying violently. Kuhn is thanking God that he was not chosen.
>
> Kuhn is out of his mind. Does he not see, in the bunk next to him, Beppo the Greek, who is twenty years old and is going to the gas chamber the day after tomorrow, and knows it, and

lies there staring at the light without saying anything and without even thinking anymore? Does Kuhn not know that next time it will be his turn? Does Kuhn not understand that what happened today is an abomination, which no propitiatory prayer, no pardon, no expiation by the guilty—nothing at all in the power of man to do—can ever heal?

If I were God, I would spit Kuhn's prayer out upon the ground. (Levi 2015, pp. 123–24)

From Beppo's defeated and enervated silence in the face of his impending murder to Kuhn's expression of gratitude in response to narrowly escaping a death sentence, "the intensity of this passage is striking" as Nancy Harrowitz notes (Harrowitz 2016, p. 27). In particular, Levi's concluding commentary on the scene—"If I were God, I would spit Kuhn's prayer out upon the ground"—startles and draws our attention. Judith Kelly suggests that "this is one of the rare moments of *If This Is a Man* in which Primo Levi's anger at the situation rises to the surface" (Kelly 2000, p. 35). Why, of all the horrors, injustices, and cruelties that Levi recounts in his testimony, is the occasion of Kuhn's prayer one of the few times during which his anger emerges into view?

Levi is, I would argue, outraged at the theodical logic implicit in Kuhn's prayer, and he exposes this logic by commenting on several aspects of Kuhn's response. First, Kuhn's focus on the results of this particular selection reveal an extremely limited view of the situation—as Levi notes, it is only a matter of time before Kuhn is selected. His gratitude for avoiding death today will likely be replaced by his facing selection in the near future. Kuhn sees the tree of his momentary safety rather than the forest of destruction within which it has taken place.

Further, Kuhn seems unaware of the implications of his loud prayer for Beppo who lies within earshot. Not only does his prayer highlight the insane logic by which a twenty-year-old is chosen to be killed—by thanking God for not being chosen, Kuhn implicitly suggests that God did not save Beppo, that God is responsible for Beppo being selected for the gas chambers. As Jonathan Druker notes, "Kuhn's personal theodicy wrongs his fellow victims yet again" (Druker 2009, p. 33).

Levi wonders about what is going on inside Kuhn that he can be so oblivious to Beppo's suffering and the realities of the situation: "Does he not see ... Beppo the Greek ... ? Does Kuhn not know that next time it will be his turn? Does Kuhn not understand ... ?" All three questions ask about, and express Levi's exasperation with, Kuhn's apparent blindness and incomprehension. They also register Levi's acknowledgement that Kuhn's actions are not an intentional offense against Beppo. Kuhn is not thinking about Beppo in this moment—the answer to Levi's questions are implicit in the tone in which they are asked: Kuhn does not see Beppo; he does not know, he is not thinking about, the fact that next time it will be his turn; Kuhn does not understand.

These failures are certainly understandable in the context of Auschwitz, where thinking alone was difficult—let alone clear, rational, perceptive thinking. Given the terrors of the situation, Kuhn's obliviousness to Beppo is understandable—how could we expect someone who is continually facing the terror of selection and random murder, the effects of near-starvation and brutal physical conditions, and the reduction of all markers of identity to a number, to have any energy left for anything but an immediate reaction to the fact of not being chosen to die? Levi seems to recognize this when he states that "Kuhn is out of his mind." When Levi asks, "Does Kuhn not understand that what happened today is an abomination, which no propitiatory prayer, no pardon, no expiation by the guilty—nothing at all in the power of man to do—can ever heal?," he knows the answer: Kuhn does not have the mental energy left to see the situation from anywhere but up close. Thus, Levi's condemnation attaches not so much to Kuhn himself, as to Kuhn's prayer and the theodicy it suggests. It is Kuhn's prayer that Levi would spit out were he God. Why?

By ascribing responsibility to God for not being selected, Kuhn's prayer of thanks implicitly ascribes responsibility to God not only for Beppo's selection, but by extension, for the whole genocidal system of which it is but one moment. If God is to be thanked for Kuhn's salvation from the selection, this implies that God has ultimate power over not only who is chosen for the selection, but also over the whole system itself. The agency and culpability of the Nazi officials in charge of the selection thus become invisible in this rendering of responsibility. Kuhn's gratitude in the moment shutters out the circles of horror in which the selection took place, extending out to the whole camp, to the system of concentration camps, to the coordinated effort of the Nazis to exterminate all the Jews of Europe (and then perhaps the world). By thanking God for the goodness of not being selected, by ascribing agency to God as the author of his temporary salvation, Kuhn's prayer implicitly ignores the human responsibility for the whole system of abominations in which the selection took place and the culpability of the thousands upon thousands who were participating in it, benefitting from it, leading it, and designing it.

The last line of this passage suggests that not only is Kuhn's prayer an affront against Beppo, it is also an affront against God, a kind of blasphemy. Kuhn's prayer obscures the human origin and culpability for the horrors of the selection and ascribes the abomination to God. It is not simply that the goodness of God is called into question in the process, but that the authorship of evil is ascribed to God. Why would Levi spit out Kuhn's prayer, if he were God? Perhaps because of its insensitivity to Beppo, perhaps because of its failure to hold accountable the Nazis who run the camp and conduct the selection, but perhaps most likely because of the outrage of suggesting that it is God who is responsible for the violent and cruel events of the camps. What kind of god, Levi might ask, would be in charge of such a place as Auschwitz?

Levi would spit out Kuhn's prayer if he were God because he would be offended, perhaps even disgusted, by what such a prayer implies about him as God. A theological view of the world that suggests that all that happens within it is ascribable to God should be, in Levi's view, offensive to God. As he notes later on in his testimony, "Today I think that if only because an Auschwitz existed no one in our age should speak of Providence" (Levi 2015, p. 150). Levi argues against the idea of providence and a theodicy that justifies the evils in the world by claiming that they are in some way part of a divine plan, as many theodicies do. Levi's critique strikes to the heart of theodicy itself, not by proving that God does not exist or that God is not all-powerful or all-good, but by arguing that in the context of the Holocaust, the very engagement in such account-making itself is morally repugnant and deserving to be spat out, even, or perhaps especially, by God.

3. Emmanuel Levinas, Useless Suffering, and the End of Theodicy

Levi's critique of Kuhn's implicit theodicy—as offensive to those who suffered during the Holocaust and blasphemous by its implicit ascription to God of authorship of the evils of the Holocaust—finds a parallel in Levinas's critique of theodicy. This parallel includes their common sense of moral outrage: Druker notes this connection when he describes Levi's "uncharacteristic anger toward Kuhn, [as] akin to the outrage that Levinas claims is provoked in us by unethical justifications of the other's suffering" (Druker 2009, p. 33). Levinas suggests that the kinds of suffering inflicted and endured during the course of the twentieth century have broken any possible balance between those sufferings and the theodicies that try to explain them and justify God's goodness and omnipotence in the process. Levinas argues that "the disproportion between suffering and every theodicy was shown at Auschwitz with a glaring, obvious clarity. Its possibility puts into question the multimillennial traditional faith" (Levinas 1998, p. 97). Like Levinas, Levi finds the scales weighted overwhelmingly on the side of evil and suffering, such that theodicy can never right the scales. Levi declares that the events that comprise the selection, all the decisions made and lives and deaths determined, are "an abomination, which no propitiatory prayer, no pardon, no expiation by the guilty—nothing at all in the power of man to do—can ever heal" (Levi 2015, p. 124).

Levi and Levinas are proposing that too many people have suffered in forms too outrageous, too grotesque, for anyone to claim that there is a divine purpose for that suffering. Such a claim seems to depict a sadistic god—one whose omnipotence is purchased at the price of divine goodness. Levinas writes:

> Perhaps the most revolutionary fact of our twentieth-century consciousness—but it is also an event in Sacred History—is that of the destruction of all balance between Western

thought's explicit and implicit theodicy and the forms that suffering and its evil are taking on in the very unfolding of this century. (Levinas 1998, p. 97)

The very logic, or movement, of theodicy, in which I look at suffering and try to come up with reasons for why an all-good and all-powerful God would allow or cause such suffering is, according to Levinas, the beginning of wrongdoing, injustice, and immorality because it amounts to justifying someone else's suffering: "the justification of the neighbor's pain is certainly the source of all immorality" (Levinas 1998, p. 99). For Levinas, even asking the question "Why?" in relation to suffering that is not one's own becomes a potentially culpable question, because it suggests the effort to justify others' suffering.

Levinas extends the definition of theodicy beyond those efforts that seek to justify God in the face of evil, beyond the effort to solve the conundrum that David Hume so succinctly framed with the questions: "Is he willing to prevent evil, but not able? Then he is impotent. Is he able, but not willing? Then he is malevolent. Is he both able and willing? Whence then is evil?" (Hume 2007, p. 74). Theodicy, Levinas argues, is at its core the effort to justify human suffering. Whether in the traditional religious form in which human suffering is rendered useful or necessary for God's ultimate purposes—a part of God's plan—or in a secular form in which the suffering of others is necessary for the achievement of some greater good, both kinds of theodicy are, according to Levinas, immoral.

The very logic or movement of theodicy can be found at the heart of the worst evils of which humans are capable. These evils begin with the idea that the other must suffer because ... , that it is right/acceptable/required that this person or these people suffer because ... Levinas's expansion of what constitutes a theodicy is also a distillation of theodicy down to a core movement of justifying an other's suffering. An example of a secular theodicy would be the way that the suffering inflicted in punishment and in the prison system is declared necessary and useful for the good of the prisoner, the safety of society, etc. Levinas's extension of the bounds of theodicy asks us to be attentive to any situation in which someone's pain or suffering is justified, or the infliction of pain or suffering on another is justified. For Levinas doubts both the efficacy and the intention of theodicy. He writes:

> Certainly one may inquire into whether theodicy, in the broad and narrow senses of the term, effectively succeeds in making God innocent or in saving morality in the name of faith or in making suffering bearable, or into the true intent of the thought that has recourse to theodicy. It is impossible, in any case, to underestimate the temptation of theodicy, and to fail to recognize the profundity of the empire it exerts over humankind ... (Levinas 1998, p. 96).

Instead of giving in to the temptation of theodicy, Levinas argues, we must respond to the suffering of others with aid, help, medication, efforts to alleviate that suffering, and with compassion, love, and our own suffering in response to their suffering. This response of aid, compassion, and suffering is the basis for the interhuman order in which I respond to the other's asymmetrical call for help, outside of the logic of commerce, reciprocality, and expectations of return. The other's call for help requires my assistance without thought of reciprocation. Levinas describes this as "the suffering of suffering, the suffering for the useless suffering of the other, the just suffering in me for the unjustifiable suffering of the other," and it is this kind of suffering, this compassion, that "opens suffering to the ethical perspective of the inter-human" (Levinas 1998, p. 94).

4. Asymmetry, Conditionality, and the Ban on Theodicy

In both Levi's and Levinas's works, we encounter a critique of theodicy based on its implicit justification of the other's suffering. In the context of the horrific suffering endured during the Holocaust, this justification is seen as not only insensitive, but also morally outrageous. But there is a tension between these powerful arguments against theodicy and the human need to ask why in the face of suffering—and not only to ask the question but to find answers to it. The strongest arguments against theodicy have to do with the way it is used to justify the evil that inflicts suffering either in preparation for it or after the fact—Levinas's prohibition against theodicy is an effort to prevent the justification and infliction of suffering. But what about when theodicy is part of the means by which sufferers are trying to navigate the suffering they are enduring?

What should we say about Kuhn on his bed, "violently" thanking God for his life saved? Surely none of us who were not there can say anything about the appropriateness or inappropriateness of Kuhn's efforts to navigate the irrational hell into which he has been thrust by the Nazis. It may have been the case that the belief that God was orchestrating those events was the only thought that enabled him to survive another day. It seems to me that we are not authorized to make any judgment about any theodicy that Kuhn used to endure his own suffering.

And yet, there is Beppo lying in the next bunk. Do we not have a responsibility to say his selection for death can never be justified, must never be construed as an act of God, cannot even implicitly be deemed "authorized by God"? How can we affirm Kuhn's need to pray, out of his senses, offering God thanks, while also refusing any suggestion that Beppo's selection was part of any plan other than the Nazis' genocidal effort to destroy the Jews of Europe? Isn't it too much to ask (or compassionless to ask) Kuhn to accept his not being chosen as sheer chance, as the Nazis' random overlooking of him this time?

I think Levinas' insistence on an asymmetry in relation to the usefulness of suffering—that is, the other's suffering can never be useful to me, but my suffering in response to her suffering can become useful—may be helpful here. Perhaps we can think about the ban on theodicy as itself being asymmetrical. While I must not ascribe meaning to the neighbor's suffering, I also must not ascribe meaninglessness to the neighbor's suffering against her own theodicy for it. In other words, I cannot declare the end of theodicy for the other. The sufferer may find meaning in her own suffering, engage in theodical thinking that suggests a reason for her own suffering or a narrative within which it makes sense to her. For the imposition of non-meaning or uselessness on another's suffering would follow a similar logic to the imposition of meaning on it, that is, it would make the other's suffering mine to narrate and interpret as useless. It would be co-opting what little the sufferer has left at her disposal in the aftermath, or the present enduring, of extreme suffering.

What I am suggesting is that Levinas's argument implies that prohibiting the other from finding meaning in her own suffering might also be a beginning of immorality because it draws on a similar imperial logic as the justification of the other's suffering. In observing and respecting the other's suffering as hermeneutically off-limits to me, I can neither justify it, nor reject the other's claims about its meaning or justification. Levinas's declaration of the end of theodicy could function as a kind of imposition of uselessness onto the suffering of the other if it precluded the right of the sufferer to find whatever meaning she may find in her own suffering. Might we have to chasten our declarations of the end of theodicy to say that there must be an end of theodicy in me about the suffering of the other, while allowing there might be a continuation of theodicy by the sufferer herself about her own suffering?

In addition to thinking about an asymmetrical ban on theodicy, borrowed from Levinas's asymmetrical understanding of the usefulness of suffering, might we also find some resources in Levi's short passage? While Levi's bitterness towards Kuhn's prayer is viscerally present in his claim that if he were God, he would spit out Kuhn's prayer, it is interesting to note that Levi's treatment of Kuhn himself is somewhat less accusatory. Levi tells us that Kuhn is out of his mind, suggesting a reason for his failure to think about how his prayer must sound to Beppo. Levi asks a series of questions that wonder how Kuhn cannot see or know certain things—questions that Levi could easily have written in the form of accusations or judgments with even more vehemence. He raises questions about the motivations, the realizations, and the meanings of Kuhn's prayer, rather than issuing a straight-out denunciation of them. The use of the repeated interrogative suggests a sense of incomprehension and exasperation, rather than mere accusation.

Further, Levi's closing comment is made in the peculiar rhetorical formation of the conditional. It is, of course, a counter-factual statement that makes no claim to possibility: Levi is not God, of course, and knows it. Why, then, phrase the sentence in such a way? Why not say something along the lines of "God should spit out Kuhn's prayer," or leave God out of the picture altogether and state something along the lines that Kuhn's prayer is offensive. Levi's use of the conditional, the hypothetical "if I were God," suggests a space of distance. Levi is not God, so he is not in a position to spit out Kuhn's prayer, but if he were, he would. Levi comes close to accusation and judgment, but keeps one step away, acknowledging the state that Kuhn is in, even while he registers the implied affront to Beppo. The space created by the conditional, by the hypothetical "if," leaves room for other possible outcomes to Kuhn's prayer. This space, though perhaps smaller and less absolute in Levi, may be akin to the space created by Levinas's asymmetrical configuration of the possibility of useful or meaningful suffering.

What do we do when the sufferer asks us "How could God let this happen?" or simply "Why?" What response shows true compassion in that moment when the sufferer asks us to engage in theodicy? Might it be an unwillingness to suffer with the other that motivates our response to the anguished "Why?" with a well-formulated answer? Might it be a refusal of care and compassion to declare that we have reached the end of theodicy? Like Levi, we are not God: Kuhn's prayer is not addressed to us. We cannot spit out Kuhn's attempt to narrate his suffering within the framework of divine providence. But we also cannot simply be silent when we see its proximity and implication for Beppo the Greek. This is the tension within which we have to move as we seek to respond to the suffering of others.

5. Conclusions

In thinking about Levi's and Levinas's critiques of theodicy, we realize the temptation that theodicy can be both as a means of justifying evils and others' suffering and as a means of foregoing the responsibility to come to the aid of the other who is suffering. But while there may be reasons to declare the end of theodicy, there are also reasons why we cannot make such a ban on theodicy absolute. Only the sufferer herself has jurisdiction over the meaning of her own suffering. As Sarah Pinnock notes, "For individual agents, personal suffering may be voluntarily given religious meaning, as it happens or in retrospect, but it is a moral scandal to impose meaning (including theodicy reasons) on the suffering of others. To do so is illicitly to exercise the privilege and responsibility of the actual victims" (Pinnock 2002, p. 137). There is an asymmetry of theodicy authorship in which I can never impose meaning on the other's suffering, but I also cannot deny the other's possibility to ascribe meaning, or no meaning, to her own suffering.

It may be helpful to be clear about the aim and scope of any engagement in theodicy. While the theodicy that seeks to justify the goodness and omnipotence of God despite the presence of evil in the world often takes place on an abstract, theoretical, theological level—and often does so not so much to respond to suffering but to protect the possibility of continued religious belief—the theodicy that takes place at an individual level in the face of present suffering is often of a quite different kind: rather than seeking a final answer or complete explanation, the sufferer often seeks possible answers, fragments of explanations, moments of faith.

We can think about theodicy less as a complete explanation or final justification, but rather as a space of inquiry in which we raise questions, explore possible responses, register protest and outrage at our sense that things are not the way they should be, and engage the conditional and the hypothetical—forms that keep open the space of conversation, the possibility of error and of dissent, ongoing thought, engagement and unknowing, imagination, and even role playing. Theodicy as inquiry, rather than justification.

Contemporary work on theodicy has extended it as a genre beyond the theological to include secular forms as well as theological ones. Susan Neiman and Larry Bouchard propose extensions of theodicy, beyond a justification of God, beyond a justification of the other's suffering, to a defense of the worthiness of the world or of humanity. Bouchard suggests that we think of theodicy as "any endeavor, theological or otherwise, to bring coherence to the problem of evil and thereby justify humanity to itself" (Bouchard 1989, pp. 1–2). Further he argues that we would do better to think of theodicies as "manifestations and not explanations of the tragic dimensions of human experience and ultimate reality" (Bouchard 1989, p. 2). In *Evil in Modern Thought*, Neiman describes theodicy as a necessary effort to continue to believe in the world. The problem of evil, according to Neiman, is "fundamentally a problem about the intelligibility of the world as a whole" (Neiman 2002, pp. 7–8). Whenever we think, "that ought not to have happened," we are, she argues, engaged in theodicy. This secular theodicy entails a belief that the world should be a certain way and that when it is not that way, something is wrong in a way that demands a response. In this version of theodicy, the effort is less about explaining the existence of evil than in protesting its occurrence and seeking to change it, so that the world more resembles the way we think it should be. Might we even say, then, that Levi and Levinas are themselves engaged in this reconfigured space of theodicy in their very inquiries into suffering; their critiques of the injustices, blasphemies, and outrages of theodicy; and their prescriptions for responding to suffering?

Acknowledgments: Thanks to the anonymous reviewers for their thoughtful comments.

Conflicts of Interest: The authors declare no conflict of interest.

References

Bouchard, Larry D. 1989. *Tragic Method and Tragic Theology: Evil in Contemporary Drama and Religious Thought*. University Park: Pennsylvania State University Press.

Druker, Jonathan. 2009. *Primo Levi and Humanism after Auschwitz: Posthumanist Reflections*. Basingstoke: Palgrave MacMillan.

Harrowitz, Nancy. 2016. *Primo Levi and the Identity of a Survivor*. Toronto: University of Toronto Press.

Hume, David. 2007. *Dialogues Concerning Natural Religion and Other Writings*. Edited by Dorothy Coleman. Cambridge: Cambridge University Press.

Kelly, Judith. 2000. *Primo Levi: Recording and Reconstruction in the Testimonial Literature*. Leicester: Troubador Publishing.

Levi, Primo. 2015. If This Is a Man. In *The Complete Works of Primo Levi*. Edited by Ann Goldstein. Translated by Stuart Woolf. New York: Liveright Publishing Co., vol. 1.

Levinas, Emmanuel. 1998. Useless Suffering. In *Entre Nous: Thinking-of-the-Other*. Translated by Michael B. Smith, and Barbara Harshav. New York City: Columbia University Press, pp. 91–101.

Neiman, Susan. 2002. *Evil in Modern Thought: An Alternative History of Philosophy*. Princeton: Princeton University Press.

Pinnock, Sarah K. 2002. *Beyond Theodicy: Jewish and Christian Continental Thinkers Respond to the Holocaust*. Albany: State University of New York Press.

Article

Horrendous-Difference Disabilities, Resurrected Saints, and the Beatific Vision: A Theodicy

Scott M. Williams

Department of Philosophy, University of North Carolina, Asheville, NC 28804, USA; swillia8@unca.edu

Received: 9 January 2018; Accepted: 2 February 2018; Published: 9 February 2018

Abstract: Marilyn Adams rightly pointed out that there are many kinds of evil, some of which are horrendous. I claim that one species of horrendous evil is what I call horrendous-difference disabilities. I distinguish two subspecies of horrendous-difference disabilities based in part on the temporal relation between one's rational moral wishing for a certain human function *F* and its being thwarted by intrinsic and extrinsic conditions. Next, I offer a theodicy for each subspecies of horrendous-difference disability. Although I appeal to some claims made by Marilyn Adams for this theodicy, I reject one particular claim. I deny that one must be aware that one participates in a horrendous evil when the horrific event occurs. To develop this point and its relevance for a theodicy for horrendous-difference disabilities, I engage with Andrew Chignell's work on infant suffering. In doing so, I show that what partly motivates the claim is a time-bias, i.e., near-bias. By rejecting this time-bias, I show how it is possible, given *post-mortem* life, for persons with profound cognitive disabilities to participate in horrendous evils and how these might be defeated by God.

Keywords: theodicy; problem of evil; horrendous evil; disability; rational moral wish satisfaction; Marilyn McCord Adams

---

1. Defining the Categories: Disability and Horrendous-Evil

In this paper I offer a theodicy for humans who suffer profoundly from certain sorts of disability. The word 'disability' is used in many different ways in the philosophy of disability literature. I give a theodicy for a certain class of individuals who suffer from what I will call 'horrendous-difference disabilities'. I do not discuss all types of disability, but rather limit myself to a subset within the general class of those with a disability, namely those with a horrendous-difference disability. In what follows I give a working description for the sorts of disability I have in mind, for horrendous-evil, and for horrendous-difference disability.

There is much contention whether disability can be defined (Barnes 2016, pp. 9–54). There are many cases of disabilities that do not seem to have any overlap at all. It is challenging to identify necessary conditions that are jointly sufficient for the definition of disability. Fortunately, I do not need to define disability as such; instead, I need to mark out a class of individuals who identify as (or are identified by caregivers as) disabled, that is, I need to identify what this particular subclass has in common. I take Richard Cross's modified social theory of disability as a point of departure for identifying this subclass (cf. Cross 2016). Cross draws attention to the World Health Organization's extensive list of human functions.[1] He calls this list the maximal set of human functions. No individual human can have every kind of human function. So, all individuals have only a subset within the maximal set of human functions. Consequently, an individual's lacking some human function is common to all humans—all humans lack some kinds of human function. Cross suggests that the

---

[1] Cf. http://apps.who.int/classifications/icfbrowser.

badness of one's lacking a human function depends on one's own wishes. If an individual wishes to have some human function F and one lacks F because of one's own intrinsic impediment to F, then one has an *impairment* relative to F. Furthermore, if one has an impairment relative to F and one "lacks the extrinsic conditions necessary for the desired human functioning," (cf. Cross 2016, p. 708) then one has a *disability* relative to F. This account of disability excludes general social disadvantage on the basis of poverty or discrimination because disability relative to F requires impairment relative to F. The impairment is an intrinsic matter, not a matter of social discriminatory practices.

Sometimes the human function that we wish for matters a lot to us, so much so that lacking this human function can seem to devastate one. If the devastation seems insurmountable to one, then one would have reason to doubt that one's life can be a great good to one on the whole. Marilyn Adams calls the worst sorts of evils or suffering, 'horrendous evils'. Horrendous evils are moral evils when the evil is caused by an intentional agent who can be held morally responsible for perpetuating the evil on the victim. Horrendous evils are natural evils when there is no intentional agent that is responsible for the evil that the victim suffers. It can be that an individual suffers from an evil and there is no intentional agent who caused the evil; nonetheless, the victim's suffering is all too real and devastating. Adams defines horrendous evil and gives some examples, saying:

> Evils the participation in which (that is, the doing or suffering of which) constitutes prima facie reason to doubt whether the participant's life could (given their inclusion in it) be a great good to him/her on the whole. The class of paradigm horrors includes both individual and collective suffering [...]. Further examples include the rape of a woman and axing off of her arms, psycho-physical torture whose ultimate goal is the disintegration of personality, betrayal of one's deepest loyalties, child abuse of the sort described by Ivan Karamazov, child pornography, parental incest, slow death by starvation, the explosion of nuclear bombs over populated areas. (cf. Adams 1999, p. 26)

Given the above characterization of a subclass of disability and Adams's definition of horrendous evil, we can define one subclass of horrendous-difference disabilities. This definition is based on rational moral wish satisfaction (RMWS). One has a horrendous-difference disability$_{RMWS}$ if and only if:

(i)   one has a rational wish for some human function F,
(ii) what is wished for is morally permissible,
(iii) what is wished for is impeded from occurring because one has an intrinsic impediment to human function F,
(iv) there are no extrinsic aids that are practically accessible to the individual that would enable the individual to be or have human function F (or approximately F) (cf. Cross 2016, p. 706), and
(v)   on the basis of (i)–(iv) one has prima facie reason to doubt that one's life can be a great good for one on the whole.

Those who suffer a horrendous-difference disability$_{RMWS}$ find their lives devastated because there is a morally permissible way of functioning (being or doing) that they rationally wish for but do not have because of an intrinsic impediment and extrinsic impediment(s) to this functioning.

For example, Sally has begun manifesting bipolar disorder at the age of 19, and it is not successfully managed. Sally has a rational, moral, wish for the intimacy of friendship with another person, Madison, with whom she has been friends during adolescence. Madison wishes to continue being friends with Sally, but Madison finds herself unable to cope with the symptoms of Sally's bipolar disorder and breaks off the friendship because Sally is excessively needy, angry, irritated, mostly talks about her medical condition, has a non-typical sleeping schedule, and calls Madison at all hours of the night. Madison judges that she cannot participate in the intimacy of friendship with Sally anymore because opening herself up that way brings significant and likely harm to herself.[2] Suppose further that Sally is alienated from her family and all others because of these symptoms of her bipolar disorder and that this holds true for the remainder of Sally's life. In effect, bipolar has ruined Sally's life. Sally has a rational moral wish for a certain human function F (in this case, being friends with Madison), but her wish is impeded by an intrinsic property (bipolar disorder) and it is impeded by extrinsic circumstances (e.g., no practical access to medicine and ways to manage the bipolar disorder). Sally lives in a society with few social safety nets and so has no extrinsic aids—e.g., the relevant medicine, doctors, care-givers, or counselors—that might be conducive for maintaining friendship with Madison. Given this overall state of affairs, Sally has prima facie reason (based on (i)–(iv)) to doubt that her life can be a great good for her on the whole. (If Sally's contingent historical circumstances were different in the relevant ways, then Sally would not have prima facie reason to doubt that her life could be a great good for her on the whole.) Given Adams's definition of a horrendous evil, Sally participates in a horrendous evil. Moreover, given that Sally's *prima facie* reason for doubt is (i)–(iv), she has suffered a horrendous-difference disability$_{RMWS}$.

It is important to note that an individual's *impairment* intersects with many other of the individual's intrinsic and extrinsic factors. Individuals with the same type of impairment can have different overall experiences of it depending on other factors including the individual's moral virtues (especially stoic virtues) (Adams 1999, pp. 157–58), wealth, physical resources, health care, and a supportive family or community (cf. Cobb and Timpe 2017, pp. 113–14). Two individuals with the same kind of impairment relative to human function F might experience it differently if one has the external resources to assist in bringing about the desired human function F (or something approximate to it) and the other does not. Moreover, if an individual with the impairment has sufficient external resources, then he or she might not experience the kind of suffering that the other individual experiences. This is why I am focusing on horrendous-difference *disabilities*.

2. The Defeat of Horrendous-Difference Disability$_{RMWS}$

A horrendous-difference disability$_{RMWS}$ is one kind of suffering that raises the problem of evil because horrendous-difference disability$_{RMWS}$ seems incompatible with God's goodness, omniscience, and omnipotence. In what follows I piggyback on much of what Marilyn Adams says in her own theodicy of defeat. It seems to me that a theodicy for horrendous-difference disability$_{RMWS}$ would at least say that God would defeat this suffering for the resurrected saints. About defeating a horrendous evil, Adams says,

> My notion is that reason to doubt can be outweighed, if the evil e can be defeated. The evil e can be defeated if it can be included in some good-enough whole to which it bears a relation of organic (rather than merely additive) unity; e is defeated within the context of the individual's life if the individual's life is a good whole to which e bears the relevant organic unity. If the evil e is defeated within the context of an individual x's life, the judgement 'the life of x cannot be worthwhile given that it includes e' would be defeated, but the judgement 'e is horrendous' would stand; this is because e's inclusion in a good enough whole (even where the whole is x's complete life span) to which it is related by organic unity does not prevent it by itself from counting as prima facie reason for doubting the positive value of x's life. (Adams 1999, pp. 28–29)

Adams goes on to posit several Christian valuables that may defeat a horrendous evil. One of these is the beatific vision.[3] Here Adams focuses on God as "a being greater than any other conceivable being, as supreme or infinite goodness. [...] [I]f Divine Goodness is infinite, if intimate relation to It is

---

[2] For discussion of cases like this, see (Fast and Preston 2006).
[3] Ibid., pp. 80–85.

thus incommensurately good for created persons, then we have identified a good big enough to defeat horrors in every case."[4] I take it that "in every case" includes horrendous-difference disability$_{RMWS}$. Adams has much else to say with regard to Christology and the defeat of horrendous evils, but I want to focus on what Thomas Aquinas says about the beatific vision. Aquinas suggests that a resurrected saint can 'see' more things in God the more perfectly the saint 'sees' God.[5] Given that God is responsible for causing a resurrected saint's beatific vision, it is up to God what other things besides God that God will 'show' the saint. God does not cause the saint to acquire new concepts in order for the saint to cognize more things in God, rather, God just causes the resurrected saint to behold more or less in God.[6] Aquinas's idea is that a saint can behold more or less of God's power. Assuming that God has the power for causing a saint to lose a disability, I infer that a saint with a horrendous-difference disability$_{RMWS}$ not only intellectually beholds God's power for removing the relevant disability but also experiences God's being an extrinsic prosthesis on which the saint depends for the relevant kind of human function *F*. In short, this saint not only intellectual beholds such divine power, but also experiences it efficaciously in herself.

How might God defeat e.g., Sally's horrendous-difference disability$_{RMWS}$? First, as with all resurrected saints who participant in horrendous evil, following Adams, Sally's prima facie reason for doubting whether her life can be a great good to her on the whole is defeated by God who is an incommensurate, infinite, good. Sally would still understand her horrendous-difference disability$_{RMWS}$ to be an objective horrendous evil but its relation of integral unity with the infinite good brings her to understand that her life is a great good for her on the whole. Sally is a meaning-maker such that she comes to make positive meaning out of her whole life and so not only is her participation in horrendous evil objectively defeated but it seems that way to her too.

What I add to Adams's theodicy is this: God may give Sally a rational choice whether to be rid of the extrinsic impediment to human function *F* or to be rid of the extrinsic and intrinsic impediments to human function *F*. If Sally chooses to be rid of the extrinsic impediments, then God would be an extrinsic aid or prosthesis on which Sally depends for her rationally morally desired human function *F*. If the desired function is e.g., friendship with another resurrected saint (e.g., Madison), then God would become an external prosthesis for Sally so that she functions in ways conducive to friendship with Madison. (God would be, very roughly, like medicine that Sally depends on for functioning in ways conducive to friendship with Madison.) If Sally were to make this decision, then she would retain her intrinsic impediment. One reason for this choice might be that retaining this intrinsic impediment would be roughly analogous to what Augustine says of the martyred saints. Augustine claims that saints who had been martyred and lost a limb would receive a new limb and would acquire new scars on their body as signs of their love for God. These bodily marks would not be deformities, but rather signs of love for God.[7] I suggest that we extend Augustine's claim about martyred saints to saints who suffered horrendous-difference disabilities$_{RMWS}$ and nevertheless persevered in their love for and devotion to God. The marks or wounds of such saints can be in the glorified mind or body, and presented to and thereby known by others, in any number of ways depending on the particular kind of horrendous-difference disability$_{RMWS}$. What I want to say about someone like Sally is this. She might choose to retain her intrinsic impediment to *F* as a mark, a sign, of her own suffering that plays an integral narrative role in God's defeating her own horrendous-difference disability$_{RMWS}$. Like the martyrs, this sign plays a narrative part in Sally's own understanding of her life as a good for her on the whole.

Nonetheless, I think it possible that God can offer someone like Sally another choice. Not only could she choose to depend on God as an external prosthesis for functioning in ways conducive

---

4   Ibid., pp. 82–83.
5   Cf. Aquinas (n.d.), *ST* 1a.12.8 ad 3, in http://www.corpusthomisticum.org/sth1003.html#28745.
6   Cf. Thomas Aquinas, *ST* 1a.12.8 corp. and ad 3, in: http://www.corpusthomisticum.org/sth1003.html#28745.
7   (Augustine 1984, book 22, sect. 19, p. 1062). For discussion of this passage, see (Upson-Saia 2011, pp. 104–9).

to her desired human function *F*, but God could offer her the choice to have God remove the intrinsic impediment(s). What might motivate this second choice is that Sally wishes to use the integrity of her own bodily (and mental) configuration for her desired human function *F*. For Sally in particular, this might be a part of how God defeats her horrendous-difference disability$_{RMWS}$. Each choice is consistent with the beatific vision and with the defeat of horrendous-difference disability$_{RMWS}$. The possibility of different resurrected saints who make different choices in this regard is consistent with God's desire for human diversity; some saints have scarred and wounded bodies in the resurrection (as Augustine contends) and some have intrinsic impediments to a rationally and morally desired human function *F* that is nevertheless defeated for the individual and from the individual's point of view.

It is not clear to me which choice someone like Sally might make. Since I accept Adams's stipulation that the defeat of a horrendous-evil depends on the individual participant's point of view, it follows that I am not in a position to say which choice someone like Sally would make. It depends on her, that is, it depends on what it is like to Sally to depend on God as an external prosthesis for the desired function *F* versus what it is like to Sally to depend on the integrity of her own bodily (and mental) configuration for the desired function *F*.

One worry for proposing these two choices is that Sally might not be in a position to decide rationally. An objector might claim that Sally does not know what it is like for her to undergo a change according to which God is an external prosthesis for her functioning in a way conducive to being friends again with e.g., Madison. Though, she could remember what it was like to be friends with Madison (before her manifesting bipolar disorder), back when she used her own bodily (and mental) configuration for being in a friendship with her. But how could she know whether it is better to go with the first option or second option?[8] I do not believe deciding in this sort of situation is akin to deciding whether to undergo a transformative experience that would change your own personal preferences and how you evaluate your own experience. In this situation, if Sally goes with the first option, what would change are not her rational moral wishes but rather she would gain a means by which she could satisfy her rational moral wish. Furthermore, God could, given divine omnipotence, cause Sally to depend on God for her functions conducive to friendship with Madison and that this be a trial-run, so to speak. Having had this experience, Sally would know what it is like. She could then rationally compare the two experiences and decide on that basis. In either case, her participation in horrendous-difference disability$_{RMWS}$ is defeated by her beatific vision of God, her acquisition of the long (rationally and morally) wished for human function *F*, and her making positive meaning out of her life because of these.

3. Horrendous-Difference Disability and Profound Cognitive Disability

There is another subclass of individuals with a cognitive disability who can suffer a horrendous-difference disability. Members of this subclass differ from members of RMWS because they do not in fact have, in this life, any rational moral wishes for some human function *F*, nor do they have, in this life, any wishes. (At least, the type of case I am focused on here is one in which there is no evidence that such members have rational moral wishes. It might be that there are in fact no individuals in this subclass; however, it seems likely there is a small percentage of humans in this subclass.) Members of this subclass have a profound or severe cognitive disability. They do not have sophisticated cognitive capacities nor can they acquire them through typical human developmental stages. Like infants, they do not have a self-conception. What blocks the acquisition of these cognitive abilities are certain intrinsic cognitive impairments (despite any extrinsic supportive and caring social context). These intrinsic impairments might be the result of brain trauma that e.g., leaves the individual in a persistent vegetative state; they might be the result of microcephaly, in which an individual has

---

[8] For this sort of objection, see (Paul 2014, pp. 5–51).

a smaller than a typical size human brain. Given the intrinsic cognitive impairments and so the absence of sophisticated cognitive capacities, the individual has no *de facto* rational moral wishes.[9] For my purposes, I restrict this subclass to individual humans who have not had any rational moral wishes in this life. Further, given the severity of the cognitive impairment, we would be tempted to believe that such individuals do not have remote or proximate potential for the sophisticated cognitive capacities. There are some exceptions in which an individual has e.g., microcephaly and has rational moral wishes. But what I am focused on here are cases in which one in fact has no rational moral wishes, and hasn't had any rational moral wishes, precisely because of an intrinsic cognitive impairment.

For Adams, recognizing one's own participation in a horrendous-evil is required for one's in fact being a participant in a horrendous-evil. Given this criterion, Adams claims that a "severely brain deficient" individual is not a potential meaning-maker, unlike typical functioning children who are potential meaning-makers because typical functioning children develop into mature adults that have a self-concept and rational moral wishes (cf. Adams 1999, p. 28). Although Adams concedes that severely brain deficient individuals may suffer evils, she denies that they can participate in horrendous evils. They lack the requisite cognitive capacities for meaning-making and lack the potential for the requisite cognitive capacities for meaning-making. Given that actual or potential meaning-making cognitive capacities are required for participation in horrendous evil, it follows that the "severely brain deficient" cannot be participants in horrendous evil.

(It seems fairly evident that individuals with a disability$_{RMWS}$ can participate in horrendous evils because of (i)–(iv). They can recognize that their rational moral wish for a human function F is thwarted, intrinsically and extrinsically, and so can they recognize on the basis of (i)–(iv) that they have prima facie reason to doubt whether their lives can be a great good to them on the whole.)

Andrew Chignell considers Adams's criterion that one must recognize one's own participation in a horrendous-evil for one to be a participant in a horrendous evil, and extends it to the case of "brutal infanticide that Ivan Karamazov describes in Dostoevsky's classic novel." (Chignell 1998, p. 206) Chignell summarizes Adams's theodicy saying,

> A theodicy is only successful, says Adams, if for any person *p* it can offer a logically possible and theologically-sound scenario in which 'God ensures that *p*'s life is a great good to *p* on the whole, and any horrendous evils *p* participates in are made meaningful by being defeated, not merely within the context of the world as a whole, but within the scope of *p*'s individual life. This last move involves a change in perspective. It is not sufficient for theodicy that *God* deem *p*'s life meaningful. Rather, *p* must attribute positive value to her life from an 'internal point of view', where such an attribution involves *p* herself recognizing 'some patterns organizing some chunks of her experiences around goals, ideals, relationships that she stabilizes in valuing'.[10]

Chignell reports that Adams claims that God can defeat an individual's participation in a horrendous evil only if the individual is somehow aware of God while participating in the horrendous evil. The suffering experience itself provides the victim with a vision of the inner life of God. Moreover, the suffering experience itself may provide the victim with a way to identify with the suffering Christ, who was (believed to be) God incarnate. Chignell says, "either way, this *visio dei* is supposed to be of enough (incommensurate) aesthetic value to defeat its correlated horror."[11] After discussing whether the victim has a *de re* or *de dicto* awareness of God during a victim's suffering, Chignell observes that the needed sort of awareness must be *de dicto* awareness because "the victim of a horror must judge or recognize that Something which transcends the suffering is being presented to them *while they are in*

---

9   For discussion, cf. (Reinders 2008, pp. 19–24).
10 Ibid. "The Problem of Infant Suffering," pp. 206–7.
11 Ibid. "The Problem of Infant Suffering," p. 209.

the midst of the suffering."[12] He then makes the case for the conclusion that infants who die a brutal and gratuitous death, as described by Ivan Karamazov, do not participate in a horrendous evil because:

> Infants are generally considered to lack significant moral freedom or agency; they have no second-order desires; they cannot posit ideals for themselves; they have no important values; and they do not preface their actions with moral deliberation. Infants lack the capacity for significant aesthetic appreciation; they cannot feel significantly degraded; they are not aware of the symbolic value that their experiences might have or lack. Infants are not competent language users—they cannot tell themselves or others a narrative about their lives. Children under the age of six months seems to have few concepts and very little sense of self-individuation.[13]

Given infants' lack of such cognitive capacities, Chignell infers that infants who suffer brutal and gratuitous deaths cannot participate in a horrendous evil, as defined by Adams, because they lack the relevant capacities for recognizing their own participation in the suffering.

There is a parallel between infants and their lack of the relevant cognitive capacities for participation in horrendous evil and individuals with profound cognitive disabilities who lack the same relevant cognitive capacities. Like infants, the subclass of individuals with profound cognitive disabilities that I am considering, lack the relevant cognitive capacities for recognizing their own suffering or misfortune. Where the two cases diverge is in developmental psychology. Most infants come to have the relevant cognitive capacities through the course of their life. But for those with profound cognitive disabilities, they do not develop the relevant cognitive capacities through the course of their life. (Again, I am only considering cases in which one in fact does not develop these cognitive capacities.)

Chignell contends that infants who suffer brutal and gratuitous death do not participate in a horrendous evil, given their lack of the relevant cognitive capacities, and so do not require that God defeat their horrendous suffering. Quoting Adams, Chignell suggests that such infant suffering is not horrendous, but rather "a small or medium-scale evil" that "'might simply be over-balanced in a good life'. It is not difficult to imagine that the relatively short-lived physical pain that the infants experience will be balanced out (engulfed!) by the value of *post-mortem* intimacy with God."[14] Chignell goes on to say that

> An adult who is in a permanent coma, for instance, would not be susceptible to horrendous suffering (though the events that brought him to that state may constitute a horrendous evil). So we needn't theorize as to how God might be able to defeat his current sufferings or any other that he may undergo after slipping into the coma; we can simply be confident that God will balance them out.[15]

I think that Adams and Chignell are wrong about the stipulated criterion for participation in horrendous evil according to which one must have the requisite meaning-making cognitive capacities during one's suffering or loss of significant meaningful goods in order for that suffering to be horrendous. If I am right about this, then not only must we theorize about how God might defeat infants' brutal and gratuitous suffering that would count as participation in horrendous evil, but so too about how God might defeat the horrendous evils in which those with a profound cognitive disability participate.

My argument for the conclusion that Adams and Chignell are wrong about the stipulated criterion for participation in horrendous evil has two stages. First, we must assume the existence of a God

---

12 Ibid. "The Problem of Infant Suffering," pp. 209–10.
13 Ibid. "The Problem of Infant Suffering," p. 215.
14 Ibid. "The Problem of Infant Suffering," p. 216.
15 Ibid. "The Problem of Infant Suffering," pp. 216–17.

who is omniscient, omnipotent, perfectly good, and who defeats (at least) the resurrected saints' participation in horrendous-evils. Given this assumption, we can infer that God would cause the individual, *post-mortem*, to acquire the requisite cognitive abilities for meaning-making. Furthermore, I assume that God would not lie to the individual about their past life, but the individual would be aware of what one has done and what one has undergone in one's past life. If the individual has meaning-making capacities *post-mortem* and is aware of his or her own past participation in significant suffering, *then* (I take it that) the individual has a prima facie reason to doubt that his or her life can be a great good for him or her on the whole even though the reason is defeated by God (in the ways indicated above).[16]

The second stage of my argument supports this conditional statement. Chignell would object against this conditional statement by claiming that one must have meaning-making capacities "while [one is] in the midst of the suffering."[17] This seems somewhat intuitive. While one participates in a horrendous evil one loses significant meaningful goods. One's awareness of this significant loss can cause one to experience profound emotions such as pain, lamentation, or despair. Typically, one's participation in the loss of significant meaningful goods is accompanied by one's awareness of this loss and profound emotions (somehow) directed at this loss. But notice that there can be significant temporal gaps between one's losing significant meaningful goods, one's awareness of this loss, and one's profound emotions (somehow) directed at this loss. Adams concedes that an infant can participate in a horrendous evil because she is a potential meaning-maker. That is, an infant can undergo loss of a significant good and later in adolescence come to be aware of the loss of the significant good and experience profound emotions (somehow) directed at the significant loss. The losing of the significant good does not temporally overlap with the individual's awareness of this significant good, but the individual can (much) later become aware of the significant loss and experience profound emotions (somehow) directed at the lost good. More specifically, for Adams, the adolescent may come to recognize her own past vague awareness of God's presence during her past suffering. She can find meaning in her recognizing God's presence with her while she was suffering. So, an infant even without the requisite cognitive capacities while suffering nonetheless has a vague awareness of God's presence with her during her suffering. Chignell reports Adams's concession about infants who are potential meaning-makers, but denies that it is relevant to the case of infants who are murdered. First, Chignell questions whether an infant can have a *de dicto* but vague awareness of God's presence during her suffering; this seems to require sophisticated cognitive capacities, capacities that she lacks at that moment in her life. Second, such infants do not exist later in this life and so do not become aware of their past suffering in this life.

Adams and Chignell proposed that if God is going to defeat an individual's participation in horrendous evil, then one must be at least vaguely aware of God's presence with one while one is suffering. Whereas Adams contends that an infant has vague awareness of God while the infant suffers, Chignell denies that the infant can have a vague awareness of God. Against Adams and Chignell, I do not think that one must be aware of God while one participates in a horrendous evil if God is going to defeat it. Of course, if one is aware of God's presence while one is participating in a horrendous evil, then that is one way God might defeat it for the individual. I do not think this is necessary for defeat because defeat can happen in other ways.

Suppose an individual loses a significant good in her infancy, but is unaware of her loss at that time. She is not aware, even vaguely aware, of God's presence with her when she loses the significant good. If the infant continues to exist through childhood and develops typical cognitive capacities, then

---

[16] I assume without argument here, that personal identity through time does not depend on continuity of consciousness, but on something else, e.g., being numerically the same individual substance—that is not assumed by any divine person—through time. For discussion of personhood and why reference to a divine person is relevant, cf. (Williams). For discussion of the denial of continuity of consciousness for personal identity through time, see (Sullivan 2018, pp. 343–63).

[17] Ibid. "The Problem of Infant Suffering," p. 210.

she might become aware of her significant past loss and experience profound emotions (somehow) directed at her loss. Suppose further that she has learned about God through her church family, and believes in God. At this point, while she cannot recognize her own past awareness of God when she was suffering because she was not aware of God at that time, nevertheless, she can recognize (believe) that God was with her then. She can, after the fact, have a true belief that God was with her, and this present recognition of God's past (and current) presence to her can defeat her prima facie reason for doubting that her life can be a great good for her on the whole. The sort of experience in which one comes to realize that God had been present with one but one was unaware of God's presence, is somewhat a common claim among Christian theologians. For Thomas Aquinas, God causes in some the grace ("infusion of grace") for "partaking of the divine nature" without the individual playing an active causal role in this. This can be without the individual's awareness. For example, when an infant is baptized he or she receives certain theological dispositions from God—even though he or she is currently unaware of God's active presence and has no volitions with regard to God at that time.[18] Likewise, John Calvin speaks of the "secret energy of the Spirit, by which we come to enjoy Christ and all his benefits." (cf. Calvin 1960, p. 537).

Chignell, however, contends that if an infant is subject to brutal and gratuitous murder in his infancy, then he cannot later come to recognize God's presence with him when he suffered. Chignell says, [...] From a *post-mortem* point of view the beatified saint could very well continue to find

> her experience of horrors in this world meaningless, even if she found out that the horror had provided an *opportunity* (which she didn't take) for her to gain insight into the divine nature. Now if the victim was [...] a functional adult when the experience occurred, perhaps she *should* have had an intimate awareness of the Divine, and since it was her fault for missing the opportunity, she should not continue to see the horror as meaningless. My main point is that [...] infants [...] are incapable of having an 'excruciating awareness' or an 'intimate encounter' with either the vague transcendent or God during their victimization. Certain advanced cognitive abilities are required to judge or recognize that one is experiencing *tremendum* or envisioning God; and these are abilities which infants lack. So the beatified infants might well look back on the episode and still find it meaningless. (Chignell 1998, p. 211)

I think Chignell is wrong that a beatified infant cannot look back on her past suffering and find God present with them then. Chignell worries that if one is not aware of God while suffering, then it is a lost opportunity through which one has an "intimate encounter" with God. It is a lost, wasted, or meaningless experience. However, even if the infant had not used the experience of suffering as an opportunity for a meaningful union with God while it was happening, there is no reason the beatified infant cannot use the past suffering as an opportunity now (i.e., in the beatified, *post-mortem* life) to have a more intense union with God in the beatific vision. Given Aquinas's claim that saints can 'see' more or less of God's power (in addition to 'seeing' God), we can say that a beatified infant's awareness of her own past suffering is a *post-mortem* opportunity for a more intense beatific experience; it is an opportunity that is in fact taken. Consequently, we can say that the infant participates in a horrendous evil (that is, her past brutal and gratuitous murder) when she becomes aware of it *post-mortem* and that this horrendous evil is defeated by her all the more intense beatific experience. Contra Chignell, an infant who suffers in this way can be a participant in horrendous evil if God resurrects her from the dead and she becomes aware of her past experience; moreover, God can defeat her participation in horrendous evil by the individual's beatific experience. The individual can, *post-mortem*, be a meaning-maker who believes her life to be overall meaningful given her all-the-more-beatific experience.

---

[18] Cf. Aquinas (n.d.), *Summa Theologiae* 3, q. 112, a. 1; and, *Summa Theologiae* 3, q. 69, a. 6.

Having described the case of an infant who has no rational moral wishes or awareness when she suffers brutal and gratuitous murder, it seems to me that the same can be said for an individual with a profound cognitive disability. Again, I have in mind individuals who in fact have no rational moral wishes precisely because of a profound cognitive disability. If Chignell were right about infants that are brutally murdered, namely that they cannot participate in horrendous-evils because the lack the requisite cognitive capacities when they suffer, then the same would be said for individuals with a profound cognitive disability. But, given the two-stage argument against Chignell, we have reason to think that not only might such infants participate in horrendous-evils but so too individuals with a profound cognitive disability. Whereas such infants live a short life, here below (so to speak), individuals with a profound cognitive disability might live a much longer life given appropriate social support and caregiving. Individuals with a profound cognitive disability [=disability$_{PCD}$], like the rest of humanity, can participate in horrendous evils in many different ways. For my purposes, I limit myself to a parallel between individuals with a disability$_{RMWS}$ and individuals with a disability$_{PCD}$.

Suppose Manuel has a disability$_{PCD}$, has been baptized, and is counted by God among the resurrected saints. Would Manuel have anything to complain about, not having had any rational moral wishes in life before he died? I believe he might. Supposes Manuel, *post-mortem*, rationally wishes that his life had gone differently, that he might have been luckier so as to have had conscious interpersonal relationships with his parents and any caregivers he had. Suppose during Manuel's life there was a certain caregiver, Pedro, who cared deeply for Manuel. But in this life Manuel was unaware of what Pedro did or that Pedro cared for him. Surely, *post-mortem*, Manuel wishes that he had a conscious interpersonal relationship with Pedro. If that is possible, as I think it is, then Manuel (*post-mortem*) is analogous to Sally who has disability$_{RMWS}$. Each of them (i) has a rational wish for a human function *F*; (ii) what each wishes for is morally permissible; (iii) each has an intrinsic impediment that prevents them from being or doing *F*; (iv) each has extrinsic impediments that prevents them from being or doing *F*; and (v) on the basis of (i)–(iv) each has prima facie reason to doubt that his or her own life can be a great good for him or her on the whole. Where they differ is the temporal relation between the act of wishing for a human function *F* and when it is thwarted. For Sally, her wishing for *F* is simultaneous or temporally near to the wish's being thwarted by intrinsic and extrinsic impediments. For Manuel, his wishing for *F* is later than when the wish is thwarted by intrinsic and extrinsic impediments. Manuel would believe, "I wish things had been different. I wish that I had a conscious interpersonal relationship with Pedro." Believing this, Manuel would likely be susceptible to profound emotion (somehow) directed at this state of affairs. Given this experience, Manuel would have a reason to doubt that his life can be a great good for him on the whole. In short, Manuel's being aware of his past, in his *post-mortem* life, is a basis on which he participates in a horrendous evil.

But like Sally, Manuel's participation in horrendous evil can defeated. Unlike Sally whose cognitive impairment is not so severe that she lacks rational moral wishes in this life, Manuel's cognitive impairment is so severe that he lacks rational moral wishes in this life. Consequently, if God wishes humans to be social creatures, then God would wish Manuel to be social. For this to be made true, God would cause Manuel (*post-mortem*) to lose his severe cognitive impairment and acquire cognitive capacities so that he becomes aware of himself and forms rational moral wishes. According to Christian belief, God is no liar. So, if God is not a liar, then God would allow Manuel to learn of his past—including the fact that he used to be profoundly cognitively disabled. While this would lead to Manuel's participation in horrendous evil (he would have prima facie reason to doubt whether his life can be a great good to him on the whole), his participation in a horrendous evil would be immediately defeated by God because Manuel would experience the beatific vision that organically integrates into Manuel's own understanding of the overall goodness of his own life. But even more, supposing that Pedro, too, is a resurrected saint, then Manuel and Pedro could develop friendship partly based on the past and partly based on present interactions. Individuals who did not share past experiences of events together when the events occurred, nevertheless can bond over remembering those past events together. Just as a beatified infant can come to believe that God was present with her when she was suffering a horrendous-evil and on the basis of this awareness of God's past presence have a more intense beatific experience, so too could e.g., Manuel have a more intense beatific experience of God, *post-mortem*, based on a belief in God's past presence with him and on a belief in Pedro's past presence with him.

Andrew Chignell tells a different sort of story in order to draw a different conclusion, namely, one must be aware of one's beloved when one suffers, otherwise the presence of the beloved in one's suffering does not make a difference to its being defeated for that individual. I think Chignell misses a crucial point that can be drawn from the story. First, here is the story:

> Retrospectively, Roger takes a job in a strange city, and finds the transition very difficult. He misses his old friends, he isn't sure that he likes his job, and the people who live in the apartment above him are extremely noisy. On top of all this, he one day finds himself in a fast-food restaurant that is being held up by vicious gunmen. Roger and a number of other patrons are herded into the walk-in freezer in the back room where they endure several hours in frigid agony and fear before the police rescue them. Roger is traumatized by this event and spends months in counseling. Things start to turn around for him, however, when he meets Susan at an office party. The two of them hit it off, and are soon married.

> Retrospectively, Roger looks at the various 'minuses' he encountered upon arriving in the new city as made meaningful by the fact that being in that city was a necessary condition for the big 'plus' of meeting Susan. The episode in the fast-food restaurant, however, sticks out in his mind as a particularly pointless and irresolvable evil. One year into his marriage, he tells Susan about it—even though his therapist had instructed him to repress it (the therapist was paid by the fast-food chain). To Roger's amazement, he finds out that Susan had also been in the restaurant that day, and that she had been in the freezer with him!

> Now it seems that even from a post-marital point of view, Roger could continue to find this participation in the fast-food evil pointless and irresolvable, despite the fact that the person he now loves and enjoys more than anything in the world was, without his knowledge, present with him throughout that experience. Roger would not, even upon this later recognition, find that suffering ultimately meaningful. After all, he was not (self-consciously) *aware* of Susan's presence in the freezer (even though he may have touched her!), and the episode was not the occasion for their meeting each other.[19]

I think that a point Chignell fails to draw from this story is this. Roger, having had this experience of robbery, and Susan, having been present with Roger during this experience of robbery, can now (after the fact) remember the robbery together. This would, I believe, make the union between Roger and Susan even stronger than if they did not remember the robbery together. While they did not share the experience together in a meaningful way when it occurred in the past, they can now share in remembering the experience together in a meaningful way. What redeems or defeats that past participation in suffering is the remembering together of that past suffering. Given that Susan was there, Roger experiences the remembering of that event with her in a more intimate way than if he simply reported a past experience to her and she was sympathetic toward him. It is unnecessary that they had been aware of each other's presence during the robbery in order that they later form an intimate union in part by means of each of their experience of the robbery. What matters is that *de facto* each was present at the time, and later they form a yet more intimate union in remembering that past event together.

---

[19] Ibid. "The Problem of Infant Suffering," pp. 210–11.

Likewise, for those with a profound cognitive disability in this life, they can later (*post-mortem*) form more intimate friendships with other resurrected saints on the basis of their collectively being aware of past events that were *de facto* shared. Even though e.g., Manuel had been unaware of Pedro (or anything?), he can later (*post-mortem*) form a deeper friendship with Pedro because they can be aware of past events that each had participated in. Manuel can later (*post-mortem*) be aware of Pedro's having been a great caregiver who had extended the hand of friendship even though Manuel had been impeded from being aware of this. On the basis of this (*post-mortem*) awareness, Manuel and Pedro can become even better friends. Likewise, just as Manuel was unaware of Pedro's presence with him, so too was Manuel unaware of God's presence with him. Nevertheless, in Manuel's coming to learn of God's past presence with him, this is a basis on which Manuel forms an even more intense beatific experience of God because he may 'see' more of God than if his earthly life had gone differently.

I suspect that Chignell's analysis goes wrong in an assumption that bears on the interpretation of the story about Roger. What seems to matter to Chignell is when, exactly, the horrendous event occurs and when one is aware of the beloved's presence to one in that horrendous event. If Roger were aware of Susan's presence when the horrific event occurred, then Chignell indicates that the event might be made meaningful for Roger. However, it seems to me that what underlies this analysis is a time-bias, specifically, a near-bias. If one has a near-bias then one prefers goods in the present or near to the present and prefers bad things or pains either in the past or in the distant future. If we hypothesize that Chignell assumes a near-bias that (partly) determines his analysis, then this predicts that Chignell would infer from the story that Roger simply prefer to be aware of Susan's presence while he suffers (Susan's presence being a good for Roger) rather than at a later time. This is Chignell's interpretation. But suppose our analysis is not time-biased, but assumes temporal-neutrality. If one is temporally-neutral, then one prefers goods in one's life and the temporal location of the goods, as such, does not determine why one prefers to have the goods at the time one has them. Rather, reasons other than mere temporal location would be the basis on which one prefers to have the goods when one has them. While it is outside the scope of this paper to argue for time-neutrality, I am persuaded by arguments for it by Meghan Sullivan and others (cf. Greene and Sullivan 2015; Sullivan 2017, 2018; Finocchiaro and Sullivan 2016). With temporal-neutrality as an assumption in our analysis of the story of Roger, we would not stipulate that Roger must be aware of Susan's presence with him while he is suffering in order for Roger's suffering to be defeated. Rather, we would say that what is required is that Roger at some time in his life be aware of Susan's presence with him when he was suffering and that their remembering together this past experience is a basis on which they form a more intimate and meaningful union that defeats each of their participation in the horrific event.

If we assume time-neutrality in our analysis of how God might defeat horrendous-difference disabilities$_{RMWS}$ and horrendous-difference disabilities$_{PCD}$, then we do not need to posit (as Adams and Chignell do) that one *must* be aware of God's presence with one while one is participating in a horrendous evil. Rather, what is required is that at some time in one's life, whether in this life or *post-mortem*, that one be aware of God's presence when one participated in a horrendous evil.

Conflicts of Interest: The author declares no conflict of interest.

References

Adams, Marilyn McCord. 1999. *Horrendous Evils and the Goodness of God*. Ithaca: Cornell University Press.
Aquinas, Thomas. n.d. *Summa Theologiae*. Navarra: University of Navarra. Available online: http://www. corpusthomisticum.org/ (accessed on 5 December 2017).
Augustine. 1984. *City of God*. Translated by Henry Bettenson. New York: Penguin.
Barnes, Elizabeth. 2016. *The Minority Body: A Theory of Disability*. Oxford: Oxford University Press.
Calvin, John. 1960. *Institutes of the Christian Religion*. Edited and Translated by John T. McNeil. Louisville: Westminster John Knox Press, p. 537.
Chignell, Andrew. 1998. The Problem of Infant Suffering. *Religious Studies* 34: 205–17. [CrossRef]

Cobb, Aaron D., and Kevin Timpe. 2017. Disability and the Theodicy of Defeat. *Journal of Analytic Theology* 5: 100–20.

Cross, Richard. 2016. Impairment, Normalcy, and a Social Theory of Disability. *Res Philosophica* 93: 693–714. [CrossRef]

Fast, Julie A., and John Preston. 2006. *Take Charge of Bipolar Disorder: A 4-Step Plan for You and Your Loved Ones to Manage the Illness and Create Lasting Stability*. New York: Warner Wellness.

Finocchiaro, Peter, and Meghan Sullivan. 2016. Yet Another 'Epicurean' Argument'. *Philosophical Perspectives* 30: 135–59. [CrossRef]

Greene, Preston, and Meghan Sullivan. 2015. Against Time Bias. *Ethics* 125: 947–70. [CrossRef]

Paul, L. A. 2014. *Transformative Experience*. Oxford: Oxford University Press.

Reinders, Hans S. 2008. *Receiving the Gift of Friendship: Profound Disability, Theological Anthropology, and Ethics*. Grand Rapids: Eerdmans.

Sullivan, Meghan. 2017. Personal Volatility. *Philosophical Issues* 27: 343–63. [CrossRef]

Sullivan, Meghan. 2018. *Time Biases: A Theory of Rational Planning and Personal Persistence*. Oxford: Oxford University Press. Available online: https://meghansullivan.org/time-bias-book// (accessed on 5 December 2017).

Upson-Saia, Kristi. 2011. Resurrecting Deformity: Augustine on Wounded and Scarred Bodies in the Heavenly Realm. In *Disability in Judaism, Christianity, and Islam: Sacred Texts, Historical Traditions, and Social Analysis*. Edited by Schumm, Darla and Michael Stoltzfus. New York: Palgrave-MacMillan.

Williams, Scott M. Forthcoming. 'Person' in Patristic and Medieval Christian Theology. Edited by Antonia Lolordo. Oxford: Oxford University Press.

Article

Therapeutic Theodicy? Suffering, Struggle, and the Shift from the God's-Eye View

Amber L. Griffioen

Department of Philosophy, University of Konstanz, 78457 Konstanz, Germany; amber.griffioen@uni-konstanz.de

Received: 26 February 2018; Accepted: 24 March 2018; Published: 27 March 2018

Abstract: From a theoretical standpoint, the problem of human suffering can be understood as one formulation of the classical problem of evil, which calls into question the compatibility of the existence of a perfect God with the extent to which human beings suffer. Philosophical responses to this problem have traditionally been posed in the form of *theodicies*, or justifications of the divine. In this article, I argue that the theodical approach in analytic philosophy of religion exhibits both morally and epistemically harmful tendencies and that philosophers would do better to shift their perspective from the hypothetical "God's-eye view" to the standpoint of those who actually suffer. By focusing less on defending the epistemic *rationality* of religious belief and more on the *therapeutic* effectiveness of particular imaginings of God with respect to suffering, we can recover, (re)construct, and/or (re)appropriate more virtuous approaches to the individual and collective struggle with the life of faith in the face of suffering.

Keywords: anti-theodicy; theodicy; suffering; epistemic injustice; problem of evil

---

Then he said, "You shall no longer be called Jacob, but Israel, for you have striven with God and with humans, and have prevailed".—Genesis 32:28

The problem of human suffering can, from a purely theoretical standpoint, be understood as one formulation of the classical problem of evil, which calls into question the compatibility of the existence of a perfectly good (all-knowing, all-powerful) God with the extent to which human beings encounter and undergo positive suffering.[1] In the context of analytic philosophy of religion, the fact of (what appears to be significant and gratuitous) human suffering has been presented either as *logically inconsistent* with the existence of the God of classical theism or as an *evidential consideration* counting heavily against the probability of that Being's existence or perfection. With respect to the role that suffering plays in these arguments, there are various formulations of both problems, ranging from why human beings suffer at all to why there is not less suffering than there is to why some individuals should suffer horrendous evils or undergo destructive suffering of the kind that leads them

---

1. I use the formulation 'positive suffering' here—not to indicate that there is anything "positively valenced" about the experience itself, nor that there is anything about it that is "good" for the agent who undergoes it—but rather to distinguish the term from the somewhat antiquated, more neutral use of 'suffer', meaning simply to passively undergo, tolerate, or otherwise allow something, as in the case of Christ's injunction to "suffer the little children to come unto me and forbid them not" (Luke 18:16). In what follows, then, the instances of *positive* suffering to which I refer should be understood as generally *negatively*-valenced in some relevant way (even if they should turn out to be instrumentally necessary or "good" for the subject in some other way). Still, although I focus primarily on subjective, experiential suffering in this paper, I leave it open as to whether one could suffer positively without being able to reflectively call on some particular subjective experience or set of experiences, perhaps because one is not aware that one's experience constitutes an instance of suffering or because one does not have the hermeneutical tools to understand—and hence "appropriately" experience—one's own suffering *as* suffering (cf., e.g., the discussion of hermeneutical injustice in Fricker 2007; cf. also fn. 10 below).

to question the very value of their lives as a whole.[2] Yet (although one might not think it from much of the philosophical literature) the problem of suffering neither begins nor ends on the theoretical level. Insofar as suffering—especially in its more horrific and traumatic manifestations—is something that strongly affects the meaning we attach to both our individual lives and our collective identities, the problem is deeply, and perhaps most fundamentally, an *existential* one. Further, in those traditions in which God is presented as some*one* to whom creation is supposed to be essentially bound via a relation of care and with whom creatures are potentially joined in a relationship of love, the problem becomes both *personal* and *intersubjective*.[3]

For this reason, some critics have proposed that analytic approaches which treat the problem of suffering solely as another speculative puzzle about the nature of a purportedly perfect being fail in some relevant way to take the concrete suffering and oppression of particular human beings seriously.[4] Such methodological "anti-theodicists" often claim that the theodical strategy itself displays a kind of detached moral insensitivity or "blindness" to genuine human suffering, insofar as it attempts to abstractly transform that suffering into a necessary evil that serves some "greater" purpose or good—be it the realization of the best of all possible worlds, the creation of opportunities for virtuous "soul-making" or "intimacy" with the divine, the punishment of bad acts of human free will, or the result of some divine reason we cannot fathom given our limited cognitive capacities.[5] Such justifications of God, the anti-theodicist claims, might even *add* to the amount of harm in the world as opposed to alleviating it, insofar as they get God "off the hook" at the cost of failing to recognize suffering as inherently bad or condemnable. As Toby Betenson (channeling Nick Trakakis) puts it: "[I]n responding to the problem of evil by constructing a justification of God's permission of terrible evil, theodicies think the morally unthinkable, they sanction the unsanctionable, they justify the unjustifiable; theodicies render 'ok' what should not be rendered 'ok'. In short, '*Theodicies mediate a praxis that sanctions evil*'" (Betenson 2016, pp. 63–64).[6]

* * *

I share the concerns of many anti-theodicy scholars and activists and have for some time been dissatisfied with way in which genuine human suffering is treated in theodical discourse. More recently, I have come to suspect that many (though certainly not all) of the theodicies in mainstream analytic philosophy of religion stem from a place of relative privilege, in which the dominant voices represent those philosophers who are cognitively and emotionally in a position to be able to distance themselves from particular evils and traumata in a way sufficient to allow them to consider suffering more abstractly and to ask how it might be necessary for (or at least as conducive to) promoting some further divine end. And while the ability[7] to academically "dissociate" oneself in such a way—e.g., in the interest of objectivity—can be beneficial in scholarly discourse, I worry that, in the case of theodicy, the persistent attempt to take up a "God's-eye view" of suffering in the service of justification of the divine may do more harm than good, both to the character of the academic theodicist herself and to those who are undergoing or have undergone existentially significant suffering.[8] It may be

---

[2]   The late Marilyn Adams defines *horrendous evils* as "evils the participation in (the doing or suffering of) which gives one reason prima facie to doubt whether one's life could (given their inclusion in it) be a great good to one on the whole" (Adams 1989, p. 299). In a related (though importantly separate) vein, Michael Stoeber understands *destructive suffering* as "suffering which is and always remains non-redemptive for the person. It has no [positive] spiritually transformative impetus or context for the victim in question" (Stoeber 2005, p. 61).

[3]   Cp. Eleonore Stump's claim that "the problem of suffering is, in a sense, a question about *interpersonal relations*, insofar as the problem has to do with possible morally sufficient reasons for God, an omnipotent, omniscient, perfectly good *person*, to allow human persons to suffer as they do" (Stump 2010, p. 61, my emphasis).

[4]   Cf., for example, Betenson (2016), Trakakis (2008), Phillips (2004), Surin (1986), et al. See also Graper Hernandez (2016) and Bar On (2003) for worries concerning certain forms of philosophical abstraction with respect to discussing concrete suffering.

[5]   This, of course, represents only a few of the many theodical approaches found in the philosophical literature.

[6]   Betenson takes the final quote from Trakakis (2008), pp. 28–29.

[7]   One might even call it a "luxury".

[8]   These categories may and do overlap, of course.

morally harmful, insofar as it contributes to the vicious tendency many of us already have to ignore the suffering of others and promotes the kind of moral insensitivity and blindness mentioned above, the effects of which may have a negative or even re-traumatizing effect on those who actually suffer. It may be *epistemically* harmful, insofar as it ignores or downplays credible sources of testimony in favor of explanations aimed at defending and protecting divine perfection at all costs, which may lead to the development of distorted beliefs and narratives about what it is and what it means to suffer.[9] Bringing these two threads together, philosophical theodicy may serve to propagate a form of *epistemic injustice* that both fails to take seriously the testimony of certain agents as credible sources of knowledge concerning human suffering and constructs an insular theological framework from which many such agents are no longer able to recognize their own lived experience and suffering.[10]

Especially in the context of 20th-century analytic religious epistemology, which overwhelmingly concerned itself with defending the rational permissibility of religious belief in the face of secular and atheist challenges to the contrary, theodicies have tended to be evaluated on the basis of their effectiveness in countering the challenges posed by contemporary forms of the problem of evil and preserving the rationality (or non-irrationality) of religious belief. Indeed, although sometimes mistakenly referred to as "justifications" or "defenses" of *God*, the function of theodicy in these contexts is ultimately aimed at justifying or defending theistic *belief*.[11] Yet if the limited doxastic profits of the theodical strategy (the output of which is always *hypothetical*) are outweighed or undermined by the harms, both epistemic and moral, it may cause to *actual* victims of horrendous suffering and those desiring to act to counter it, what function, if any, is left for theodicy of this kind to serve?

While my proposal in what follows will do little to satisfy the classical theist who is hell-bent on defending the rationality of religious belief against its polemical detractors, I think the discipline of analytic philosophy of religion might do well to shift its attention somewhat from the theoretical God's-eye view to that of the existential and religious situations of those who really suffer—and from the epistemic status of religious belief to the practical situatedness of lived experience. For although suffering is a universal problem, it can only be responded to in the particular. The fact of suffering is shared, but its manifestations are irreducibly specific (even where they are collective). Thus, we might do better to think less about the *rhetorical* gains achieved by particular theodicies and more about their *therapeutic* effectiveness for those persons struggling with faith in the face of suffering. This suggestion does not by any means represent a new approach,[12] but it is something that deserves renewed and more extensive attention. It is intended merely to provide a reminder—if not a balance or corrective—to the dominant approach taken by analytic philosophy of religion.

A modest version of the therapeutic approach suggests only a *shift in perspective*—the question becoming less about how well a generalized characterization of suffering can "square" the divine attributes of classical theism with the extent of human suffering and more about how practically valuable our theologically- and scripturally-grounded imaginings of God and God's relation to creation might be with respect to reconciling the life of faith with the very real effects of particular suffering.

---

[9] For a further perspective on the moral and epistemic harmfulness of the attempt at a God's-eye perspective in philosophy of religion, cf. Anderson (2005, 2012).

[10] Miranda Fricker (2007) refers to these two forms of epistemic injustice as *testimonial* and *hermeneutic* injustice, respectively.

[11] While a distinction is sometimes made in the literature between defenses and theodicies proper, I am not sure the distinction is as relevant in the context of the anti-theodical charge. Perhaps those providing defenses are somewhat "humbler" in their epistemic claims, but they strike me as still likely to promote harms of the type pointed to by the anti-theodicist, even if such accounts are merely pointing to logical possibilities or stories that are, as Peter Van Inwagen (2006) puts it, true "for all we know". Indeed, insofar as such defenses might be asking us to imagine possible worlds that are (for all we know) quite distant from our own, they may end up doing *more* harm than straightforward theodicies by removing the subject imagining such worlds even further from the very real suffering in the actual world.

[12] Indeed, this should not be viewed as a universal condemnation of all analytic treatments of the problem of suffering. I think some analytic approaches to the problem of suffering, e.g., those by philosophers like Marilyn Adams and Eleonore Stump, do try to take the concrete suffering of individuals seriously and grapple with the problem in ways that demonstrate both humility in the face of the problem and a sensitivity to the need for a therapeutically effective response. Whether both approaches actually constitute such a response I leave open here.

A slightly more radical understanding of what I am suggesting proposes a genuine *reappropriation* of the term 'theodicy' to signify, not the various presumptive, quasi-objective *answers* to the problem of suffering from the God's-eye perspective, but rather the of the dynamic, diachronic, and irreducibly diverse *struggle* by which human beings wrestle with the problem of lived faith, the experience of suffering, and the witnessing to evil. From a philosophical standpoint, what is needed is a deep and meaningful analysis of the Jacob-esque process by which we grapple with the divine and with each other in the face of human suffering and the ways in which we may thereby be transformed, for better or, in some cases perhaps, for worse.

* * *

The perspectival shift I am suggesting, in which theodicy is evaluated therapeutically rather than (merely) epistemically, calls for innovative ways of thinking about the problem of suffering. It asks us to relinquish our attempts to generate justificatory reasons from the perspective of the abstracted divine (or, minimally, to refrain from thinking that if we occupied the God's-eye view, we would be in possession of such reasons) in favor of imaginatively taking up the standpoint of *Job* in his concrete suffering. Of course, innovation is sometimes less a matter of coming up with something entirely novel and more about finding creative ways to apply historically relevant and culturally meaningful ideas that already speak to us and may provide fruitful avenues for continued thought in the present day. Such an approach is exactly what Nehama Verbin adopts in a recent article on the problem of suffering, in which she discusses three ways of engaging with the figure of Job—namely, those proposed by Maimonides, Kierkegaard, and Verbin herself ("inspired by the great Hasidic rabbis", Verbin 2017, p. 388)—and the ways in which these approaches understand the situation of Job (who spoke "correctly" of God[13]), his suffering, and how it is (or may be) defeated.

Invoking a term from Kierkegaard, Verbin characterizes her three philosophical re-figurings of Job as different "knights of faith". Maimonides' Job, she claims, appears as a *knight of wisdom*, whose suffering represents a deep form of ignorance—and who transcends his pain via a non-propositional acquisition of mystical wisdom through contemplation of the divine (cf. pp. 384–85). Kierkegaard himself, in contrast, presents Job as a *knight of loving trust*, who recognizes the "central role" that suffering plays in the life of faith (p. 385). This Job, Verbin claims, recognizes that the life of faith may actually increase one's suffering, insofar as faith in the face of suffering entails a paradoxical and dissonant struggle in which the individual both "breaks with the world, and, at the same time, remains within it" (p. 386). He thus does not cease to suffer but nevertheless *transforms* his suffering: he "over[comes] his loss by hanging onto God" (p. 388). Finally, Verbin herself construes Job as a *knight of protest*—a figure of resilience, who "defeats the suffering of an injustice [...] by naming the injustice an injustice, by resisting it, by protesting against it, and by refusing to be reconciled with it" (p. 390). This third Job may forgive God, but he remains unwilling or unable to be reconciled with the divine.

Ultimately, Verbin argues that despite their differences and seeming incommensurability, "all three Jobs [...] may be embraced, both from a philosophically descriptive perspective as well as from a religiously committed one" (Verbin 2017, p. 382). They can be embraced from the standpoint of philosophical analysis, she argues, insofar as each gives voice to various manifestations of faith-based responses to suffering that themselves "render perspicuous the 'grammar' of 'faith'" (p. 391) and reveal it as fundamentally multifaceted. They can also be embraced, she claims, from a religiously committed standpoint—not in the sense of cognitively assenting to each of the propositions these approaches endorse, but rather in the sense of "embracing, or at least seriously considering, the *values* that each of them embodies" (p. 383). Such values may not necessarily be pursuable simultaneously,

---

[13] The reference here is to Job 42:7–8.

but they serve to complement rather than to contradict one another, and their diversity "serves to unmask the different shadows that lurk behind each of our paradigms of perfection" (p. 391–92).

Still, from a therapeutic standpoint, the approach of each of these "knights" brings with it serious potential pitfalls and dangers. For example, characterizing someone's suffering as merely a matter of some "ignorance" that needs to be corrected threatens to fail to take the standpoint of the suffering individual seriously and has the potential to contribute to the testimonial injustice society often inflicts on victims. Likewise, suggesting that those who suffer horrendous evils remain in (but not of) the world by "hanging onto" an unfathomable God might sound like asking a victim of abuse to return to her abuser.[14] Finally, encouraging unwavering protest or moral hatred of God's very self (as opposed, for example, to God's actions) may close oneself off to the possibility of forgiveness, reconciliation, or divine intimacy in ways that merely serve to add to one's suffering, as opposed to overcoming it.[15] Nevertheless, I think that Verbin's pluralistic approach to Job's process of overcoming also demonstrates three ways in which theodicy re-construed as a *dynamic grappling with the problem of suffering* may be therapeutically valuable—at least if these three historical approaches are adapted and appropriated in certain meaningful ways. Indeed, each of her three knights presents those who suffer with a way of being *reoriented* with respect to their suffering—whether it be cognitively, affectively, or volitionally.

For example, although it may be extremely damaging to construe someone who has undergone destructive suffering as merely "lacking" in some relevant knowledge or wisdom, the possession of which would miraculously "fix" her, there is a sense in which, from a purely descriptive standpoint, traumatic suffering itself is characterized by a lack of comprehension (and/or comprehensibility). Insofar as traumatic events often cause a radical break in an individual's self-understanding—an interruption in her self-narrative resulting in an inability to be able to make sense of herself and the world around her—the epistemic consequence of such traumata may be a form of suffering that has a lack of *understanding* at its very core.[16] In this sense, certain forms of therapeutic re-orientation may be helpful, in which, e.g., the repeated *reliving* of a traumatic event (and the re-traumatizing effect it may have on the individual) is verbally articulated and cognitively transformed into a coherent *remembering* with a narrative structure that the agent can incorporate into a more intelligible autobiographical story (cf., e.g., Schauer et al. 2011, p. 3). In this sense, one's reflections on the divine nature and the role one assigns it in the story of one's suffering can bring *meaning* to one's cognitive, affective, and volitional chaos. It may also assist in promoting a kind of *acceptance*—not, perhaps, of the trauma or suffering one has undergone, but of the fact that one will always in some sense occupy a space that others lacking such a narrative will not. One may come to accept that one will, like Kierkegaard's Job, always have one foot in the world and one foot outside it. In other words, like the knight of loving trust, one may have to give oneself over to a narrative that affirms a break with the world, precisely in order to remain within it.

Yet neither of these approaches requires that the role God plays in such a narrative be one that *absolves* the divine of its role in one's suffering. The narrative contemplation of the divine by the knight seeking wisdom may, as with Verbin's Job, lead her to the conclusion that she has "suffered an unjust divine assault against [her], a divine abuse" (Verbin 2017, p. 389). Likewise, although such a narrative

---

14 For more on the question of intimacy and abuse with respect to the divine, cf. Michelle Panchuk (2017) response to Michael Harris' divine intimacy theodicy.

15 Importantly, however, as I discuss presently, I think there may be cases in which such moral hatred is both unavoidable and warranted, and where reconciliation is impossible. Verbin takes this (rightly, I think) to be the case with Job and other "victims of bad intimacy", whose silence reflects the irreparable distance from God and "reveals courage, inner strength, and an uncompromising commitment to justice" (p. 390). Verbin's Job supereragatorily overcomes his resentment by forgiving God and "conduct[ing] a dialogue with the humiliating message that is conveyed by his assault and reject[ing] it" (p. 389), but he does not thereby seek to reconcile himself to the unrepentant divine being.

16 For a discussion of the ways in which "events that threaten, violate, or destroy" a subject's "core assumptive explanatory worldviews", cf. Everly and Lating (2004), pp. 36ff. For a further philosophical discussion of the cognitive and affective repercussions of her own traumatic experiences, cf. Brison (2003).

may (in some cases) serve to transform suffering, making it more manageable to bear, the trust required of such a knight might not be that of placing loving trust in *God*, but rather that of coming to trust *herself* by trusting her own narrative—by "hanging onto" (but by no means justifying or absolving) a God who is a perpetrator. In this way, then, there is always room for the knight of protest, who—in the burdensome wisdom unfairly inflicted upon her through her experience of suffering, and with renewed trust in herself—asserts her theodical narrative precisely by refusing to be reconciled with the kind of God who hurts the objects of its "love".

* * *

Importantly, each of the three approaches Verbin discusses can also be adopted by those in positions of privilege in the service of combatting and alleviating such suffering and standing in solidarity with those who experience such evils. Yet here we must be careful. The sometimes unbridgeable gap in the standpoint of these two parties may also demand a difference in the ways knightly wisdom, loving trust, and protest are virtuously and/or therapeutically exemplified. The struggles of those who suffer from, e.g., poverty, disease, or violence, are not the same as the difficulties encountered by those who witness (to) them from the outside, and thus what counts as wisdom, trust, or protest in these cases may crucially depend on factors of proximity and perspective. The immediateness and reality of evil to those who suffer first-hand is one that is not easily conveyed to second-hand parties. Moreover, characteristic of many individuals and groups in positions of power and privilege is a sense of *apathy* with respect to the genuine suffering of others—a socially-promoted "inability to suffer", as German theologian Dorothee Sölle puts it, in which "the avoidance of suffering as a goal so dominates people that the avoidance of all relationship and contact [with suffering] itself becomes the goal. [. . .] They experience suffering, but they are 'content with it': it doesn't touch them. They have no language and no gestures to deal with suffering. It changes nothing. They learn nothing from it" (Sölle 1973, p. 50).[17] What is lacking in such persons, Sölle thinks, is both the ability to *recognize* or *identify* suffering (both in others and in oneself) and the possession of a *sensibility* or *sensitivity* for that suffering, especially the suffering of others. This "lack of consciousness" and "numbness" (pp. 52–53) with respect to suffering reflects a cognitive and affective deficiency that produces a kind of inability to perceive things as they really are and an associated motivational paralysis. Thus, the apathy of the privileged is both epistemic and moral: a selective blindness to the severity of suffering and a weary unwillingness to fight oppression where it occurs.

Here, again, we might recognize the harms that may be perpetrated by overly abstracted, God's-eye-view theodical reasoning. Yet Verbin's approach also provides us with the tools to combat these ills. While apathy with respect to suffering is ultimately a problem of the *will*, the volitional issue cannot be addressed without a commitment to taking the suffering of others seriously, and this can only be achieved by addressing the cognitive and affective deficiencies that ground such apathy. This will involve an attempt at *understanding* the depth of others' suffering, even if one cannot oneself experience it. Yet such comprehension is not possible without taking seriously the testimony of suffering persons—that is, without lending them the kind of *sympathetic trust* and credibility that we would extend to those with whom we stand in closer emotional proximity. And when we begin to take such testimony as a credible source of knowledge—when we trustingly listen rather than presumptively speaking—we may be moved to *resist* such evil and to stand together with and for those who suffer. Here, the knights of wisdom, loving trust, and protest are transformed into a *knight of compassion*—a knight who, although perhaps unable to feel "with" or "into" those who suffer, feels *alongside* them in a way ("com-passio") that demonstrates understanding, solidarity, and a commitment to resistance.

---

[17] All quotes and phrases from Sölle are my translation.

* * *

One may wonder here where God has gone on such an approach. Can a therapeutic theodicy grapple with faith in the face of suffering without thereby sacrificing the divine—without making God disappear? Certainly there is much more to be said on this point. For now, I can only leave the reader with the following reflections:

First, a shift to the perspective of Job necessarily "disappears God" by taking divine withdrawal, hiddenness, and absence seriously. Indeed, this kind of theodical grappling will always have a God-who-withdraws at its center. Where Job is met with divine silence in the face of his suffering, he may feel a withdrawal of God's very presence. Where he experiences God's overwhelmingly immanent power (think here of the "gird up your loins" speech from the whirlwind[18]), he might feel a withdrawal of or alienation from the presence of divine love. These experiences of absence, withdrawal, and alienation are important aspects of the dynamic theodical experience—they "touch" the individual where it hurts and "carve" her at her metaphysical and spiritual joints in ways that forever change her Self and her relation to the world around her. However, in this sense, God is also always present in the discourse of theodical struggle, even where that presence is marked by a form of felt absence—for perceiving something as absent is not identical to its simply failing to be perceived as present.[19]

Second, the God in therapeutic theodicy is also "absent" insofar as it is a God who awaits imaginative and narrative re(dis)covery. While, from a theological standpoint, the transcendence and inexplicability of the divine idea may put God out of the reach of human understanding, the dynamic struggle of theodicy must wrestle with the way we imaginatively represent God in the life of faith on the ground and what these representations mean for how we react and respond to suffering in the world. What do our imaginings of God convey about the way we understand the world and our relationships to each other? How do certain religious concepts and narratives serve to reinforce oppressive structures and practices? How are those persons whom religion should afford comfort and protection affected by these imaginings? And how might we adapt or complicate our concepts of and narratives involving God to appropriately address those who suffer? Modern philosophical theodicy sacrificed Job on the altar of classical theism. Postmodern philosophical theology slew the God of classical theism on the battlefield of anti-metaphysical transcendence. Perhaps one central task of an analytic philosophy of religion for the 21st century is to turn its careful enquiry to the utter immanence of real human suffering, to recover the perspective of a Job and the tenacity of a Jacob, in order to locate theologically fruitful imaginings of a metaphysical God before whom we can sing and dance[20] but with whom we also can wrestle face to face—a God with whom we can earnestly struggle and against whom we can, perhaps, even loudly protest.[21]

Conflicts of Interest: The author declares no conflict of interest.

---

[18] Cf. Job 38.

[19] For more on experiences of absence, cf. Farennikova (2013).

[20] For competing takes on classical theist imaginings of the divine, cp. Martin Heidegger's complaint that, before the metaphysical "god of philosophy [...] the *causa sui*, "man can neither fall to his knees in awe nor can he play music and dance before this god" (Heidegger 1969, p. 72) and Marilyn Adams' retort that the idea "that we cannot sing and dance before the first cause fails to take seriously Who the first cause really is" (Adams 2014, p. 12).

[21] Many thanks to Jill Graper Hernandez for encouraging me to write the essay that became this article and for her great patience throughout the various stages of its conception. Thanks also to my seminar students from "Klassischer Theismus und die religiöse Imagination": Many of the ideas that find their expression here were cooked up in the context of our discussions together. Finally, thank you to two anonymous reviewers for their thoughtful and constructive feedback.

References

Adams, Marilyn McCord. 1989. Horrendous Evils and the Goodness of God. *Aristotelian Society Supplementary Volume* 63: 297–310. [CrossRef]

Adams, Marilyn. 2014. What's Wrong with the Ontotheological Error? *Journal of Analytic Theology* 2: 1–12.

Anderson, Pamela Sue. 2005. What's Wrong with the God's Eye Point of View. A Constructive Feminist Critique of the Ideal Observer Theory. In *Faith and Philosophical Analysis. The Impact of Analytical Philosophy on the Philosophy of Religion*. Edited by Harriet A. Harris and Christopher J. Insole. Burlington: Ashgate, pp. 85–99.

Anderson, Pamela Sue. 2012. *Re-Visioning Gender in Philosophy of Religion. Reason, Love and Epistemic Locatedness*. Burlington: Ashgate.

Bar On, Bat-Ami. 2003. Terrorism, Evil, and Everyday Depravity. *Hypatia* 18: 157–63. [CrossRef]

Betenson, Toby. 2016. Anti-Theodicy. *Philosophy Compass* 11: 56–65. [CrossRef]

Brison, Susan J. 2003. *Aftermath. Violence and the Remaking of a Self*. Princeton: Princeton University Press.

Everly, George S., and Jeffrey M. Lating. 2004. *Personality-Guided Therapy for Posttraumatic Stress Disorder*. Washington: American Psychological Association.

Farennikova, Anna. 2013. Seeing Absence. *Philosophical Studies* 166: 429–54. [CrossRef]

Fricker, Miranda. 2007. *Epistemic Injustice. Power and the Ethics of Knowing*. Oxford: Oxford University Press.

Graper Hernandez, Jill. 2016. *Early Modern Women and the Problem of Evil. Atrocity & Theodicy*. London: Routledge.

Heidegger, Martin. 1969. *Identity and Difference*. Translated by Joan Stambaugh. New York: Harper & Row.

Panchuk, Michelle. 2017. Does Violence Foster (the Right Kind of) Intimacy? Response to Michael Harris' "'But Now My Eye Has Seen You': Yissurin Shel Ahavah as Divine Intimacy Theodicy". Edited by Association for the Philosophy of Judaism (Symposium). Available online: http://www.theapj.com/event/symposium-on-michael-harriss-but-now-my-eye-has-seen-you-yissurin-shel-ahavah-as-divine-intimacy-theodicy-the-torah-u-madda-journal-172015/ (accessed on 15 February 2018).

Phillips, Dewi Zephaniah. 2004. *The Problem of Evil and the Problem of God*. London: SCM Press.

Schauer, Maggie, Neuner Frank, and Elbert Thomas. 2011. *Narrative Exposure Therapy. A Short-Term Treatment for Traumatic Stress Disorders*, 2nd ed. Göttingen: Hogrefe & Huber.

Sölle, Dorothee. 1973. *Leiden*. Stuttgart: Kreuz Verlag.

Stoeber, Michael. 2005. *Reclaiming Theodicy. Reflections on Suffering, Compassion and Spiritual Transformation*. New York: Palgrave Macmillan.

Stump, Eleonore. 2010. *Wandering in Darkness. Narrative and the Problem of Suffering*. Oxford: Oxford University Press.

Surin, Kenneth. 1986. *Theology and the Problem of Evil*. Oxford: Basil Blackwell.

Trakakis, Nick. 2008. *The End of Philosophy of Religion*. New York: Continuum.

Van Inwagen, Peter. 2006. *The Problem of Evil*. Oxford: Clarendon Press.

Verbin, Nehama. 2017. Three Knights of Faith on Job's Suffering and its Defeat. *International Journal of Philosophy and Theology* 78: 382–95. [CrossRef]

MDPI

St. Alban-Anlage 66

4052 Basel

Switzerland

Tel. +41 61 683 77 34

Fax +41 61 302 89 18

www.mdpi.com

Religions Editorial Office

E-mail: religions@mdpi.com

www.mdpi.com/journal/religions

www.ingramcontent.com/pod-product-compliance
Lightning Source LLC
Chambersburg PA
CBHW041138120626

46547CB00020B/3036